STUDIES IN WELSH HISTORY

Editors

RALPH A. GRIFFITHS   CHRIS WILLIAMS
GLANMOR WILLIAMS

16

IMMIGRATION AND INTEGRATION

THE IRISH IN WALES, 1798–1922

IMMIGRATION AND INTEGRATION

THE IRISH IN WALES, 1798–1922

by

PAUL O'LEARY

*Published on behalf of the
History and Law Committee
of the Board of Celtic Studies*

CARDIFF
UNIVERSITY OF WALES PRESS
2000

British Library Cataloguing-in-Publication Data
A catalogue record for this book is available from the British Library.

ISBN 0-7083-1584-4

Jacket design by Chris Neale
Typeset at the University of Wales Press
Printed in Great Britain by Dinefwr Press, Llandybïe, Dyfed

EDITORS' FOREWORD

Since the Second World War, Welsh history has attracted considerable scholarly attention and enjoyed a vigorous popularity. Not only have the approaches, both traditional and new, to the study of history in general been successfully applied to Wales's past, but the number of scholars engaged in this enterprise has multiplied during these years. These advances have been especially marked in the University of Wales.

In order to make more widely available the conclusions of recent research, much of it of limited accessibility in postgraduate dissertations and theses, in 1977 the History and Law Committee of the Board of Celtic Studies inaugurated a new series of monographs, *Studies in Welsh History*. It was anticipated that many of the volumes would originate in research conducted in the University of Wales or under the auspices of the Board of Celtic Studies. But the series does not exclude significant contributions made by researchers in other universities and elsewhere. Its primary aim is to serve historical scholarship and to encourage the study of Welsh history. Each volume so far published has fulfilled that aim in ample measure, and it is a pleasure to welcome the most recent addition to the list.

CONTENTS

LIST OF TABLES AND MAPS

Tables

Maps

PREFACE

This study of Irish immigrants and their descendants in Wales from the late eighteenth century to the mid-1920s aims to recover the culture of an ethnic minority which has often been neglected or marginalized by historians. It sets out to examine the circumstances in which the immigrants arrived and the means by which they adapted to the receiving society and developed a *modus vivendi* with it. One of the central themes explored here concerns the variety of experiences to be found among the Irish abroad, in terms of their social status, cultural life, religion and politics. Only by integrating the diverse aspects of immigrant life can we begin to form an overall impression of the extent of Irish integration in Welsh society. The participation of all migrants in Irish cultural life once they had left Ireland could not be simply taken for granted. Of course, some points of contact with events in Ireland were maintained, whether through family links, religion or politics, throughout the period under consideration; but this book argues that the cultivation of an ethnic identity in urban Wales was much more than a transplantation of the beliefs and practices of Irish peasant society to a different context. Instead, it entailed the creation of new ways of thinking and behaving which entailed a re-evaluation of what it meant to be Irish.

My own family, members of which arrived in Wales at different stages of the migrations analysed in this book, originally hailed from Co. Cork. Oral tradition in the family alerted me at a young age to the particularity of their experience and the richness of their cultural life. It would be pleasing to say that my formal education helped place that tradition in context; on the whole, it did not. Perhaps the silences about the Irish in Wales in the written histories I encountered at that time lie at the root of my determination to know something more systematic about an ethnic group which has often been cringingly stereotyped in novels and television dramas of industrial Wales. The pernicious

influence of such clichéd representations of the Irish should not
be underestimated, for although they have been in headlong
retreat for many decades they still occasionally resonate in our
culture. Even so, in its conclusions this is fundamentally an
optimistic study.

In recent years, some of the issues addressed in this book have
entered a more general public debate as a result of the
discussions provoked by the sesquicentennial commemorations
of the Great Famine. I have been encouraged and deeply moved
by the commemorative events and day schools organized by the
Wales Famine Forum, whose members have laboured valiantly
to raise an awareness among the public of the impact of the
Famine on Welsh society; their crusade against ignorance of the
consequences of this disastrous event is commendable. One of
the tangible results of the Forum's work is the erection of a
memorial in Cathays Cemetery, Cardiff, as a permanent
reminder of the human cost of the Famine among those who
migrated.

This book is a substantially revised version of a thesis
submitted to the University of Wales for the degree of Ph.D., and
the research on which it is based was funded by the Economic
and Social Research Council. I am grateful to the examiners of
the thesis, Professor Michael Drake and Professor John Davies,
for their incisive comments. In preparing the manuscript for
publication I have benefited enormously from the close scrutiny
of the text and valuable suggestions for improvements made by
the editors of 'Studies in Welsh History', Emeritus Professor Sir
Glanmor Williams, Professor Ralph Griffiths and Dr Chris
Williams. Most of all, I am indebted to Emeritus Professor Ieuan
Gwynedd Jones, who supervised the thesis and who first
introduced me to the fascinating complexities of Victorian
Wales. His finely crafted studies of mid-nineteenth-century
Wales have been a constant source of inspiration to me and
remain the essential starting-point for any student of the period.

During this study's long gestation I have incurred many debts
from colleagues and friends. Some provided valuable advice at
early stages, while others directed me to sources I might not
otherwise have consulted. Particular thanks go to David Bullock,
Martin Davies, Neil Evans, Deian Hopkin, the Revd D. A.

Levistone Cooney, Geraint H. Jenkins, Gwyn Jenkins, Kevin Littlewood, Ursula Masson, Louise Miskell, Teresa Moriarty, Peter Murray, Frank Neal, Jon Parry, Michael Roberts, Michelle Ryan, Barry Tobin and John Wilson. Members of the Lipman Seminar on Ireland provided encouragement and a congenial atmosphere for discussion during a period when I was away from academia. Sean Cleary generously provided me with sight of his research notes from the Derry's Wood Archives of the Institute of Charity. Dr C. Roy Lewis was uncommonly generous in letting me reproduce his maps of Irish settlement in Newport and Cardiff. The staff of the University of Wales Press, especially Ceinwen Jones, guided the book through the press with professionalism and thoroughness.

During the research for this book I have been assisted by the staff of numerous archives and libraries. I am indebted to the staffs of the National Library of Ireland, Dublin; the British Library Newspaper Collection, Colindale; the Public Record Office, Kew; Cardiff Central Library; Glamorgan Record Office; Gwent Record Office; the South Wales Miners' Library, Swansea; and the libraries of the University of Wales Aberystwyth and the University of Wales Swansea. I owe a particular debt to my former colleagues at the National Library of Wales, Aberystwyth, for their assistance over the years. Parts of this book would have been very different without access to the archives of the Archdiocese of Cardiff, and I am grateful to the Archdiocesan Administrator for making room for an academic 'migrant' to work through this extremely valuable collection of papers. The greater part of the collection has since been deposited at the National Library of Wales.

My deepest debts are non-academic. Firstly, to Jennifer Lane, who has suffered the intrusion of nineteenth-century migrants in the late twentieth century with more tolerance of their presence than reasonably could be expected. And, secondly, to my parents, Alfred and Kathleen O'Leary, both children of Irish immigrants who happened to find their way to Wales. For their sacrifice, love and constant support, I dedicate this book to them.

LIST OF ABBREVIATIONS

AAC	Archives of the Archdiocese of Cardiff
Glam. RO	Glamorgan Record Office
Gw. RO	Gwent Record Office
ILP	Independent Labour Party
ISDL	Irish Self-Determination League
NALU	National Amalgamated Labourers' Union of Great Britain and Ireland
NLW	National Library of Wales
PP	Parliamentary Papers
PRO	Public Record Office

INTRODUCTION

By any reckoning, it was the biggest funeral Wales has ever seen. On 3 February 1925, an estimated 100,000 people lined the streets of Cardiff in respectful silence as the cortège slowly wound its way from St Paul's Catholic church in the Newtown district of the city to Cathays cemetery. Following the obsequies, which had been carried out by Monsignor Irvine, Canon Hannon and Fr Grieshaber, the solemn funeral procession moved on to North Road where the coffin, draped in the Union Jack, was transferred from the bearers' shoulders to a gun carriage. The band of the 2nd Battalion of the Welch Regiment moved to the head of the procession – now over a mile long – playing the funeral march, while soldiers of the regiment carried their rifles reversed in honour of a dead comrade. Children from Nazareth House, the city's Catholic orphanage run by the Sisters of Charity, carried striking floral wreaths in honour of their staunchest supporter and patron, while a number of former Welsh boxing champions and representatives of local government and the military were also in attendance. At the conclusion of a brief graveside service in the gathering dusk, the Last Post was sounded: 'Peerless' Jim Driscoll, championship boxer and winner of a coveted Lonsdale Belt, philanthropist and people's champion, fêted son of Cardiff's 'Little Ireland', was dead.[1]

As a member of the pre-1914 generation of Welsh boxing champions, Driscoll had won a devoted following in Wales and garnered uncharacteristic praise across the Atlantic from the otherwise keenly partisan American boxing press. Indeed, it was in the United States that he earned the nickname 'Peerless', and he was dubbed 'the Prince of Wales' on his return.[2] As the latter epithet suggests, Driscoll was an emblematic figure who

---

[1] This paragraph is based on accounts in *South Wales Echo*, 3 February 1925; *South Wales Daily News*, 4 February 1925; and *Western Mail*, 4 February 1925.

[2] Dai Smith, 'Focal heroes', in *idem*, *Aneurin Bevan and the World of South Wales* (Cardiff, 1993), pp.326–32, 334–5.

succeeded in transcending his ethnic origins, without ever fully leaving them behind. He was the son of Irish parents and the product of a distinctive working-class culture in which many of the Welsh-born offspring of Irish immigrants considered themselves to be Irish. Driscoll was a staunch supporter of his community's institutions, especially the church, and he possessed a particular affection for Nazareth House orphanage. Yet, press reports of Driscoll's funeral strongly evoke the suppressed grief of an entire city, not only its Irish inhabitants. With the participation of the military, a procession through the main thoroughfares of the city – where businesses stopped trading temporarily as a mark of respect – and the involvement of representative figures from Welsh public and sporting life, the events of that day closely resemble the ritual of a state funeral. As well as demonstrating the depth of public esteem for a highly-respected sportsman, the response to Driscoll's death illuminates the degree of Irish integration at both civic and national levels of Welsh life.

It was not always so. For centuries the mere mention of 'the Irish' evoked images of wildness, danger and an inability to assimilate to the norms of Welsh society. They were renowned for their drunkenness, vagrancy and 'papism', while their native land was most familiar to outsiders as the site of bloody rebellion. When the Irish intruded into Wales it was believed that they exerted a baneful influence on the native people. A graphic illustration of attitudes in the host society is that, between 1826 and 1882, there were twenty anti-Irish riots in Wales, most of which occurred in the industrial south-east but with some erupting in parts of the north where railway construction provided employment for Irish navvies. As John Davies has commented – in a judgement pregnant with understatement – 'ambiguity has characterised the relationship between Wales and Ireland from the earliest times.'[3]

The stereotype of the indigent, drink-sodden Irish navvy is well known and, like all caricatures, it does not stand up to close scrutiny. An accurate version of the historical experience must acknowledge the existence of a more heterogeneous immigrant community than the stock images would suggest. This entails recognizing the plurality of Irish identities, rather than relying on

[3] John Davies, 'Wales, Ireland and Lloyd George', *Planet*, 67 (1988), p.21.

depictions of the incomers as a homogeneous outcast group. While the majority of the Irish unquestionably belonged to the working class, an understanding of the dynamics of change within immigrant communities must also take account of the presence of doctors and businessmen as well as navvies, of respectable Irish friendly societies as well as the semi-legal drinking dens, of those indifferent to organized religion as well as the Catholic faithful, and of those who left Ireland in search of greater opportunities for advancement as well as those unfortunates exiled by famine. Perhaps most fundamentally, it must recognize that a large minority of Irish immigrants were women.

While some movement from the countryside to the towns had always occurred, it is the sustained nature of the migration from rural society which is one of the central facts of modern history. Its consequences, in particular the concentration of ever larger numbers of people of disparate cultures and beliefs in close proximity to one another, have done much to shape our perceptions of the world. In the Irish case this fundamental transition acquired a distinctive complexion in so far as for the vast majority of Irish men and women an encounter with the urban world entailed leaving their own country behind. Emigration from nineteenth-century Ireland has long been the subject of scholarly attention, as has the impact of the Irish diaspora in Britain, North America and Australia. In Britain, the emphasis to date has been overwhelmingly on the cities and large towns of England and Scotland, where the immigrants were far more numerous than in Wales and comprised a larger proportion of the population than elsewhere. In recent years, however, there has been a growing recognition that a substantial proportion of Irish immigrants did not settle in the bigger urban centres of Liverpool, London, Manchester and Glasgow, but rather found employment in the smaller towns and industrial villages.[4] In this context, the Welsh case is particularly relevant.

[4] There is a valuable overview of the historical literature in Roger Swift, 'The historiography of the Irish in nineteenth-century Britain', in Patrick O'Sullivan (ed.), *The Irish in the New Communities: The Irish World Wide*, vol.2 (Leicester and London, 1992). Graham Davis has synthesized current research in his admirable *The Irish in Britain, 1815–1914* (Dublin, 1991). Of seminal importance are the collections of essays edited by Roger Swift and Sheridan Gilley, *The Irish in the Victorian City* (London, 1985), and *The Irish in Britain, 1815–1939* (London, 1989). A third volume of essays, *The Irish in Britain: The Local Dimension*, is to appear in 1999.

Throughout the century a slim majority of Irish immigrants to Wales settled in four urban centres: the small to medium-sized ports of Cardiff, Newport and Swansea, and the iron-manufacturing town of Merthyr Tydfil inland; the remainder were distributed among the industrial villages of south Wales, while smaller numbers were to be found in the north, especially in the town of Wrexham. The chronology and patterns of immigration reflect the wider Irish experience in Britain in so far as the trickle of the pre-Famine years swelled into a flood in the late 1840s and early 1850s before subsiding gradually thereafter. However, there are some salient differences in the Welsh case. After a decline in immigration in the immediate post-Famine period, the numbers of Irish-born people enumerated in Wales remained remarkably constant for some thirty years between 1871 and 1901, a fact which indicates that immigration was continuing at a steady rate sufficient to offset the natural depletion in numbers caused by death. This late nineteenth-century immigration is more difficult to analyse historically precisely because it was on a smaller scale than during the crisis decades of mid-century, but there can be little doubt that it was related to the swift growth of the south Wales coal industry in the later decades and the resultant growth of ports like Cardiff and Barry, the latter superseding the former as the world's biggest exporter of coal in 1913.

Other factors combined to create a situation where the position of the Irish in Wales was subtly different from that of their fellow-immigrants elsewhere in Britain. Unlike in Scotland and England, the Irish were never the largest immigrant group in Wales, a position which belonged to the English who were always present in far greater numbers. The linguistic context is also germane to a consideration of how the Irish related to the society around them. During the nineteenth century a majority of the people in both industrial and agricultural areas continued to speak the Welsh language, and consequently a significant (if unquantifiable) number of Irish immigrants was compelled by circumstances to acquire a functional knowledge of Welsh. This was particularly the case in Merthyr Tydfil and the smaller industrial settlements, whereas in the coastal towns of south Wales the English language had already made substantial incursions by the middle of the century. In addition, the religious context in Wales differed perceptibly from that in English towns and cities. While the English working class was progressively turning its back on organized religion, in Wales Protestant Nonconformity established an impressive presence among working people in both town and country. In this context, it can be seen that the Irish were one of a series of competing ethnic groups in urban Wales, including that of the majority population.

In the upsurge of interest in the history of Irish immigration to Britain in recent decades, comparatively little has been published about the Irish in Wales; the research which has been carried out has remained mostly in the form of unpublished theses.[5] This contrasts with the determination of writers in the 1920s to disseminate the fruits of their research into the history of Irish migration to Wales to a wider audience. The first publication of significance was Cecile O'Rahilly's wide-ranging study, *Ireland and Wales: Their Historical and Literary Relations* (London, 1924), followed by Fr James Cronin's short pamphlet, *Ireland and Wales: Bonds of Kinship* (Cardiff, 1925).[6] Cronin's carefully researched articles on the history of Catholicism in Wales, which were published in local Catholic magazines, helped to establish a historical awareness that located the Irish firmly in the development of Welsh society. When, in 1935, Donald Attwater published his history of Catholicism in modern Wales,[7] it was clear that he had drawn heavily on the archival research of the two earlier writers. From this point onwards, it was the role of the immigrants in rejuvenating the Catholic church which took centre stage in historical interpretations, a perspective which glossed over the often uneasy relationship between popular beliefs and organized religion and ignored those aspects of social life which appeared to be of little importance to the development of Catholicism.[8]

Another salient factor is the difficulty in easily obtaining statistics about the Irish in Wales. This stems largely from the nineteenth-century census-takers' use of the category 'England and Wales' for many of their tables, whereas Scotland was

[5] See the Bibliography.
[6] See also Cecile O'Rahilly, 'The antipathy of Irish and Welsh', *Welsh Outlook*, VII (September 1920), and miscellaneous articles by Fr J. M. Cronin in *St Peter's Magazine* and *Newport Catholic Magazine*.
[7] Donald Attwater, *The Catholic Church in Modern Wales* (London, 1935).
[8] For one of the better examples, see Gerald Spencer, *Catholic Life in Swansea, 1874–1947* (Swansea, 1947).

viewed as a distinct entity for statistical purposes. Thus, a great
deal of effort must be expended in disaggregating the data on
Wales. The census contains an additional stumbling block to vex
the unwary: it was decided to categorize Monmouthshire as an
English county in the census, thereby removing the second-
largest Welsh county for Irish immigration from the total for
'Wales'. This decision means that not only are the totals for
'Wales' incorrect where they do occur in the published census,
but that the tables for 'England' contain an error also (see
Appendix I for corrected statistics).

The specific case of Irish immigration raises more general
questions about the processes by which minorities integrated into
Welsh urban society and – by extension – about the integration
of all migrant groups. The approach of this study is to analyse
the Irish in terms of ethnicity and by exploring the boundaries
where immigrant and host society met.

There has sometimes been confusion in the ranks of Welsh
historians about how to describe immigrant groups like the Irish.
In his general history of modern Wales, which served as the
standard text for several decades after its publication in 1950,
David Williams described English and Irish immigration to
industrial Wales as creating 'racial divisions' which gave rise to
social problems unknown in England at that time.[9] This idiom
would have been familiar to our Victorian forebears who
frequently used the language of evolutionary social theory to
describe the alleged 'racial' characteristics differentiating one
cultural group from another. While David Williams cannot be
accused of sharing such views, the terminology is, nevertheless,
redolent of a world which was all-too-ready to seek explanations
for cultural differences in terms of physical characteristics and,
consequently, it has no place as a tool of analysis in the vocabulary of modern scholarship.[10] Other writers have referred to the
separate nationality of the immigrants. While this terminology is
inoffensive to modern sensibilities, it, too, is fraught with difficulties. It is clear that many of the Welsh-born sons and daughters of
immigrants perceived themselves as being Irish in a way which
the language of nationality cannot easily accommodate. As Stuart

    [9] David Williams, *A History of Modern Wales* (London, 1950), p.229.
    [10] Of course, rejecting 'racial difference' as a category of analysis is not to deny the
existence of racism as an ideology.

Hall has written about migrants in a different context, 'they are . . . obliged to inhabit at least two identities, to speak at least two cultural languages, to negotiate and 'translate' between them.'[11] If we are to appreciate fully this duality of identification and the strategies employed by individuals in negotiating between one identity and another, an alternative way of conceptualizing the immigrants' relationships with the host society must be found.

Any attempt to write the history of ethnic groups in nineteenth-century Wales, as well as the remainder of Britain, has to confront a historiography organized primarily around the concepts of nationality and/or social class. Within the terms of both these historiographical traditions, minorities are perceived as existing outside the mainstream of society with relatively little to tell us about the experience of the majority.[12] Recent scholarship has begun to question the overarching applicability of these explanatory frameworks. On one flank, students of women's history have posed searching questions about historical generalizations based on the experience of men alone, while on the other, historians of immigrant groups have added another dimension to the debate by exploring the distinctive experiences of minority groups and their treatment by the wider society.[13] There is a danger, however, that studies of individual immigrant groups will proliferate without engaging with the dominant historiographical traditions and thereby suffer marginalization. The central question facing historians of ethnic minorities in Wales, therefore, is how to map these identities onto existing traditions of historical writing.

Since the 1970s, historians of nineteenth- and twentieth-century America have deployed the concept of ethnicity as a

---

[11] Stuart Hall, 'Our mongrel selves', *New Statesman and Society*, 19 June 1992, p.8.

[12] Writing on Scotland, Bernard Aspinwall points out that 'The Irish were allegedly peripheral to the Scottish experience. In fact they were *essential* to the nineteenth-century 'Scottish' experience'. See his 'A long journey: the Irish in Scotland', in Patrick O'Sullivan (ed.), *Religion and Identity: the Irish World Wide*, vol.5 (Leicester/New York, 1996), p.149. On the Irish in Scotland, see also T. M. Devine (ed.), *Irish Immigrants and Scottish Society in the Nineteenth and Twentieth Centuries* (Edinburgh, 1991), and the older, but still useful, James E. Handley, *The Irish in Scotland* (Glasgow, 1964).

[13] On women's history in Wales, see Angela V. John (ed.), *Our Mothers' Land: Chapters in Welsh Women's History, 1830–1939* (Cardiff, 1991). On other immigrant groups, see Neil Evans, 'Immigrants and minorities in Wales, 1840–1990: A Comparative Perspective', *Llafur* 5, 4 (1991); Colin Hughes, *Lemon, Lime and Sarsaparilla: The Italian Community in South Wales, 1880–1945* (Bridgend, 1991); and Ursula Henriques (ed.), *The Jews of South Wales: Historical Studies* (Cardiff, 1993).

means of understanding the way in which immigrant groups have maintained distinctive identities while at the same time relating to the wider society. In recent years some British historians have begun to follow their example, albeit more tentatively.[14] But what is meant by ethnicity? An ethnic group exists only when its members actively identify themselves as belonging to it; that is, it requires active commitment to (not passive acceptance of) a particular way of identifying with people from a similar background. Thus, according to Panikos Panayi in his recent survey of immigrant and ethnic groups in British society, ethnicity is 'the way in which members of a national, racial, or religious grouping maintain an identity with people of the same background in a variety of official and unofficial ways'.[15] Panayi advocates that we should speak of ethnicities in the plural rather than ethnicity in the singular, emphasizing that there are different ways of identifying with the group and that those forms of identification can take different shapes. He also distinguishes between ethnicities from above (embodied in institutions developed by a minority of prominent country men and women) and ethnicities from below (based on phenomena such as residence and marriage).[16] Moreover, Panayi emphasizes that ethnicity is not a static category but one defined in terms of interaction with the society around it and thus has the power to create new forms and institutions. Writers who use this concept as the organizing principle of their work insist that ethnicity does not represent, as is sometimes supposed, the stirrings of primordial feelings and attachments. Rather than being a survival of old and outdated relationships, ethnic institutions can provide a bridge between the minority group and the remainder of society, thereby providing a means of coming to terms with modernity.

[14] One of the more sophisticated studies to do so was conducted by an American historian: Lynn H. Lees, *Exiles of Erin: Irish Migrants in Victorian London* (Manchester, 1979). See also Steven Fielding, *Class and Ethnicity: Irish Catholics in England, 1880–1939* (Buckingham, 1993). In a comparison of the Irish in Britain, the United States and Australia, John Belchem has argued that 'ethnic awareness was at least as important as class affiliation'. John Belchem, 'The Irish in Britain, the United States and Australia: some comparative reflections on labour history', in Patrick Buckland and John Belchem, *The Irish in British Labour History* (Liverpool, 1992), p.19.

[15] Panikos Panayi, *Immigration, Ethnicity and Racism* (Manchester, 1994), p.5.

[16] For an exploration of the difficulties involved in this distinction, see the 'Introduction' in Abner Cohen (ed.), *Urban Ethnicity* (London, 1974), pp. xvii–xviii; and Panayi, *Immigration*.

Ethnic identities are constantly shifting, being contested and redefined over time in response to changing needs and circumstances. It is this characteristic which has led one writer to describe ethnicity as a 'constructed' identity, adding that ethnic groups are not 'natural, real, eternal, stable and static units'.[17] This approach puts a premium on examining the strategies used by members of a group for constructing cultural boundaries at the points of contact between them and the wider society, opening the way for a more nuanced understanding of social interaction. An emphasis on the negotiated cultural boundaries of ethnic groups has particular relevance for recent debates on the Irish in nineteenth-century Britain, leading to a questioning of the extent to which the Irish comprised a segregated out-group in mid-Victorian society. Until quite recently the segregation of the Irish, both culturally and residentially, was a commonplace of the historical literature, but now it has come under attack as a crude generalization which has created only a partial picture of the Irish as a group.[18] A view of the Irish inhabiting ghettos ('Little Irelands') has been condemned as accepting unquestioningly the ideologies underpinning mid-nineteenth-century social commentary.

However, emphasizing ethnicity as a tool of analysis need not lead to the total rejection of social class. Several authors have pointed out that ethnic groups reflect elements of the class system rather than remain outside it.[19] In particular, Steven Fielding, in his study of the Irish in the north of England, has highlighted the variety of ways of identifying with the group, insisting that neither class nor ethnicity ever held exclusive sway. 'There was no linear progression from a 'lower' ethnic feeling to a 'higher' class consciousness', he writes; 'they were, in actual lived experience, organically linked.'[20] Certainly, depictions of the Irish as a homogeneous out-group in Welsh society do not allow for the existence of class differences among the incomers, and yet the

[17] Werner Sollors, 'The invention of ethnicity', in *idem* (ed.), *The Invention of Ethnicity* (Oxford, 1989), pp.ix–xx.
[18] See, especially, Graham Davis, *The Irish in Britain*, and C. G. Pooley, 'Segregation or Integration? The residential experience of the Irish in mid-Victorian Britain', in Roger Swift and Sheridan Gilley, *The Irish in Britain, 1815–1939* (London, 1989).
[19] Cohen, *Urban Ethnicity*, p xxii; Panayi, *Immigration*, pp.60–73.
[20] Fielding, *Class and Ethnicity*, pp.xii–xiii.

dynamic this created was central to the process of defining and redefining what it meant to be Irish in the immigrant context.

If we see the mobilization of an ethnic Irish identity as one means by which the immigrants and their descendants made sense of their new world and began to come to terms with it, then it provides a key to the processes of integration. An evaluation of integration must be based on an analysis of two crucial factors: the nature of cultural difference between the minority group and the wider society, and the ways by which social contact between the two groups was negotiated. To date, most historians of Welsh society have been concerned almost exclusively with cultural difference and residential segregation, depicting the incomers as an alien and unchanging group defined largely by their 'otherness'. Consequently, the Irish have been relegated to the margins of developments in Welsh society, as opposed to being considered as a group whose history can provide valuable insights into more general themes, such as the formation of an industrial labour force, relationships of authority and discipline at the workplace, the adaptation of rural immigrants to urban society, changes in patterns of religious belief and practice, and the mobilization of political support among new mass electorates. Analysing the Irish in terms of these (and other) themes serves as a reminder that integration occurred in different domains of social life at different speeds, and requiring caution when making broad-brush generalizations.

Our ability to address these questions is conditioned in part by the nature of the sources at our disposal. The greatest problem lies in the paucity of personal testimony about how individuals identified with the wider group. Few immigrants to Wales committed their thoughts to paper, and those who did were male and usually upwardly mobile or professionals.[21] While these people constituted as important an element of the migration as the ragged labourer and mendacious vagrant, they are not representative of the experience of the vast majority of migrants. As a result, an adequate explanation of population movements must, of necessity, rely on inference and extrapolation from wider social trends.

[21] See James Mullin, *The Story of a Toilers' Life* (London/Dublin, 1921), and Mark Ryan, *Fenian Memories* (Dublin, 1946).

Testimony by the second-generation Irish is equally, if not more, sparse. Joseph Keating's eloquent autobiography charting his early life in the coal-mining village of Mountain Ash at the beginning of its growth in the 1870s, and his subsequent progression from coal miner to journalist and novelist, is the notable exception.[22] His glowing picture of the moral integrity of humble origins is a valuable counterpoint to the negative images of the Irish found in mid-nineteenth-century investigative journalism. Yet, in one sense, it paints an equally incomplete picture. Keating's family was active in politics and unusually socially mobile: from the same origins, his brother was eventually elected Irish Nationalist MP for South Kilkenny and his sister played an active part in the women's suffrage movement in Cardiff. His autobiography vividly evokes a world he has left behind and suffers from all the problems of idealizing poor origins which often characterize autobiographical accounts by the socially mobile.

The majority of sources mined to reveal information about the Irish in Wales were at best grudgingly accepting of their presence, at worst openly hostile to them. The Irish did not produce their own newspaper or periodical until the end of the century, some four decades after the main immigration had taken place. *St. Peter's Chair*, a monthly Catholic magazine produced in the parish of St Peter's, Cardiff, began publication in 1895, and it was superseded by the more widely distributed broadsheet weekly, *Welsh Catholic Herald*, in 1898. To a large extent, then, our view of the Irish in the preceding decades is inevitably refracted through the prism of observations made by people who, on the whole, distrusted or despised them, or, as in the case of the Catholic clergy, by individuals who often sought to reform their behaviour.

While this problem of evidence is not unique, it must be acknowledged. There is no source available to the historian of the Irish in Wales to compare with the rich body of letters sent home by migrants to the United States, a source which provides an instructive insight into the reasons why they crossed the Atlantic, their responses to the process of migration and their reactions to American society upon arrival. By contrast, the fragmentary evidence on the Irish in Wales is elusive and partial, suggesting avenues of enquiry but rarely enlightening fully.

[22] Joseph Keating, *My Struggle for Life* (London, 1916).

When John Grannin appeared before the Poor Law Guardians of Newport prior to being removed to Ireland in 1839, his deposition plaintively ended with the statement, 'I cannot tell my all.'[23] Silences of this kind have been interpreted to mean that the Irish were victims of forces over which they had no control, but even where the historical record demonstrates that immigrants were able to make choices, their motivation often remains obscure. For example, when questioned by government commissioners in 1871 as to why he did not move from Rhymney to Dowlais, a journey of a few miles which would have extricated him from the clutches of the oppressive truck system of wage payment, Patrick Flanelly replied cryptically: 'I never took any fancy to go to work there, and there are a great many other places that I never took any fancy to.'[24] The sentiments are unequivocal, but the reasons why this Irishman was so resolute in his determination to remain in that particular Welsh industrial town are left unexplored and unexplained.

In the face of such silences, it is a difficult, but necessary, task to extricate ourselves from a mentality which sees the Irish solely as historical victims or, alternatively, as a social problem requiring a 'solution' by assimilation to the receiving society's values. Concern about the potential impact of Irish immigrants on the behaviour and moral condition of the working class ('the contagion of Irish manners', as Lynn H. Lees pithily put it)[25] emerged early in the nineteenth century. It frequently surfaced in government reports and in the press, fuelling the debate on the 'Condition of England' question. It was the anxiety that immigrants from a Catholic peasant society would undermine the morals of English, Scottish and Welsh working men and women, that lay behind the establishment of the government's Report on the Irish Poor in Great Britain of 1836.[26] Uneasiness surfaced at regular intervals thereafter, and especially in the wake of the influx following the Great Famine of the late 1840s. When giving evidence to the Select Committee on Poor

---

[23] Gwent RO, Q/O.R. 71–0005. For a trenchant study of the Irish in America which makes extensive use of migrants' correspondence, see Kerby A. Miller, *Emigrants and Exiles: Ireland and the Irish Exodus to North America* (Oxford, 1985).

[24] PP 1871 XXXVI, Report of the Commissioners Appointed to Inquire into the Truck System, vol. II, Minutes of Evidence, p.508.

[25] Lees, *Exiles of Erin*, p.16.

[26] PP 1836 XXXIV, Report on the Irish Poor in Great Britain.

Removal in 1854, Evan David of Cardiff was asked whether the immigration of Irish labourers raised the moral character of their counterparts in Britain. He responded:

> I believe not; it has a tendency the other way to enhance the character of the Irish labourer; that is my impression . . . after a residence of some years, and mixing with our labourers at home, they adopt their habits, and they live more comfortably; they are better clothed and better fed than we find they are when they first arrive.[27]

The response allayed the worst fears of the questioner, yet, as J. A. Jackson pointed out in his pioneering study of the Irish in Britain, the processes of settlement in, and adaptation to, the host society cannot be explained solely in terms of a model which sees the immigrant as the only variable in the equation; doing so reduces complex relationships to a one-way traffic compelling the immigrant either to assimilate unconditionally to the host society or remain entirely isolated from it.[28]

During the nineteenth century, the receiving society was itself experiencing fundamental change, with many areas undergoing swift industrialization and urbanization. At the interface between immigrant and native groups, both were required to adapt. The reality of life for Irish immigrants in Wales was more complex, in terms both of language and of identity, than the standard histories of nineteenth-century Welsh society or the general surveys of Irish immigration allow. In this context, we must beware of mistaking assimilation (defined as the extent to which the Irish come to resemble members of the host society) with integration. Seeing the relationship in terms of integration or accommodation allows for the possibility of the creation of Irish institutions with a distinct and coherent ethnic identity which functioned as agencies of integration in urban society.

It is unlikely that we shall ever discover documentation rich enough to achieve a fuller understanding of the motivations of these individuals, yet recalcitrant historical sources can yield a great deal of valuable information about the general nature of migration and the character of ethnic institutions. The present

---

[27] PP. 1854 XVII, Report of the Select Committee on Poor Removal, p.486.
[28] J. A. Jackson, *The Irish in Britain* (London, 1963), pp162–3.

study examines the patterns of Irish immigration to Wales and the degree of integration the Irish experienced over the period 1798–1922. Due attention is given to the pre-Famine period in an attempt to underline the existence of immigration before the cataclysm of the Great Famine of the late 1840s propelled many thousands of refugees in the direction of Welsh shores. Given the enormous increase proportionally in the number of Irish immigrants in Wales from this period onwards, the remainder of the book is primarily concerned with the institutions created by these refugees and the processes by which they integrated into Welsh society.

I

VARIETIES OF IRISH IMMIGRATION, 1798–1845

Over the centuries, periodic contact between the people of
Ireland and Wales has arisen from the geographical proximity of
the two countries and the role of the Irish Sea as a highway for
maritime trade. For many generations of Irish migrants, arrival
on Welsh soil was their first experience of life outside Ireland and
provided their initial encounter with the island of Britain. In the
pre-industrial period the causes of migration to Wales were
diverse: political upheavals, economic problems and subsistence
crises have each, in their turn, prompted migration across the
Irish Sea. For example, it was claimed in 1628 and 1629 that an
influx of destitute Irish to Pembrokeshire was the result of 'last
year's death of cattle and dearth of corn' in Ireland.[1] In the
following century, the terrible Irish famine of 1741 gave rise to a
similar movement of people. At Holyhead in that year a House
of Correction was built to accommodate the 'Irish vagabonds
who come in swarms from England being driven thence by law
etc.', and five years later, the Irish presence in Glamòrgan was of
sufficient magnitude for the Quarter Sessions to order constables
to convey convicted vagrants to the nearest port and pay 5s. for
their return passage to Ireland.[2] One small party arriving in 1764
gave rise to rumours of a small army of naked savages who
'devoured sheep etc. and sucked their blood and ate them raw,
and had killed two children near Bridgend, and that they
haunted the woods about Penlline etc. and that they were swifter
of foot than any dogs'.[3]

[1] C. J. Ribton-Turner, *A History of Vagrants and Vagrancy and Beggars and Begging*
(London, 1887), pp.148–50.
[2] E. A. Williams, *Hanes Môn yn y Bedwaredd Ganrif ar Bymtheg* (Anglesey, 1927), p.14;
Hugh Owen, *The History of the Anglesey Constabulary* (Llangefni, 1952), p.11; A. H. John, *The
Industrial Development of South Wales, 1750–1850* (Cardiff, 1950), pp.20–1. For further
information on the pre-industrial connections between Ireland and Wales, see Cecile
O'Rahilly, *Ireland and Wales: Their Historical and Literary Relations* (London, 1924).
[3] Philip Jenkins, 'Connections between the landed communities of Munster and south
Wales, c.1660–1780', *Journal of the Cork Historical and Archaeological Society*, LXXXIV, 240
(1979), 96.

At the end of the eighteenth century political upheavals in Ireland produced a distinctive influx to Wales which serves as a useful corrective to the belief that migration was exclusively the preserve of the poor. The rising of the revolutionary society of United Irishmen in 1798 struck terror into the hearts of well-to-do Irish men and women, already skittish because of the violence associated with disturbances in the countryside, and many fled in fear of their lives. Significant numbers were involved in this movement: one diarist estimated that 2,000 landed in Pembrokeshire alone, and a government official was dispatched specifically to cater for their needs.[4] Possibly the proximity of south-west Wales to Wexford, the centre of the rising, explains the alacrity with which they decamped, especially as those who escaped to Anglesey at the same time were fewer in number and were not dependent on the public purse. Some of the latter contributed to the administration of county matters and their presence helped to diversify the somewhat mundane social life of the provincial gentry.[5] Fear of the United Irishmen was not restricted to well-to-do people. When Mathew Doyle, a captain of the United Irishmen in County Wicklow, entered the town of Wexford on 29 May 1798, he 'formed a corps out of those sailors from Arklow who had not fled to Wales'.[6]

On the whole, the newcomers were greeted with suspicion and distrust, irrespective of their social status. This was particularly the case in those areas which in the normal course of events would see few, if any, immigrants. At Dolgellau, amid the fastnesses of Merioneth, the Revd J. Evans of Oxford and his companions were mistaken for Irish refugees and were nearly

---

[4] Diary of John Davies, Ystrad, 15 June 1798, NLW MS 12350A. In 1822, Francis Fortune of Lombard St., London, circulated a printed appeal for the exportation of food to Ireland, recalling:

> When the troubles of Ireland in 1798, forced great numbers of respectable Persons of property, and others, to Milford and Haverfordwest, who from fear of the horrors of rebellion, had not provided means for any subsistence, I was the humble cause of supplying their exigencies, through the medium of an immediate subscription, and an application to Government, who sent forthwith BROOK WATSON, Esq., the then Commissary General to the spot, with ample relief to every one of them.

A copy can be found in Public Record Office, HO 40/19 (1).
[5] Williams, *Hanes Môn*, p.11.
[6] Ruan O'Donnell, 'The rebellion of 1798 in County Wicklow', in Ken Hannigan and William Nolan (eds.), *Wicklow History and Society: Interdisciplinary Essays on the History of an Irish County* (Dublin, 1994), p.355.

denied hospitality at local inns. A fear that those who had fled from the rebels in haste would be unable to pay their debts was undoubtedly a factor in this distrust, but it was not sufficient to account for what Evans described as 'the violent opposition, (not to say persecution), experienced by these unfortunate people at the hands of the Welsh'. He found that 'a powerful and rancorous enmity possesses the bosoms of the Welsh against the Irish', adding, 'Among the lower classes it rises from rudeness to insult . . . the least encouragement from their superiors would have brought thousands from the mountains, with intentions of massacre, and weapons of destruction'.[7]

This melodramatic description can be attributed in part to Evans's injured pride at being denied the respect commensurate with his social status. Nonetheless, the underlying picture of hostility to outsiders is consistent with prevailing attitudes at that time, especially following the French invasion at Fishguard in 1797 when hostility to foreigners became overt and more pronounced than previously. In this context, Iolo Morganwg's proverb about the characteristics of the Irish, recorded (or possibly invented) in 1799, acquires a sharper topical relevance: 'An Irishman's loves are three: Violence, Deception and Poetry.'[8]

The rebellion of 1798 was swiftly defeated and the vast majority of well-to-do refugees returned to the comfort and security of their former existence. In their place came those fleeing from retribution for their actions during the rebellion; they sought the safety of obscurity far from the prying gaze of the forces of law and order in Ireland. As they were fewer in number, these men and women are more difficult to locate and identify in the historical record. Some were unfortunate enough to be detained by the authorities immediately upon landing in Wales, such as the two rebels arrested at Haverfordwest.[9] Others settled into untroubled obscurity, as in the case of a man by the name of O'Reilly who made good his escape and put down roots

---

[7] Revd J. Evans, *Letters Written during a Tour through North Wales in the Year 1798, and at Other Times* (3rd edn, London, 1804), pp.83–5.

[8] NLW MS Llanover Collection, quoted in *Geiriadur Prifysgol Cymru*, Part XXVIII (Cardiff, 1976), p.1754, *sub* 'Gwyddel'.

[9] Roland Thorne and Robert Howell, 'Pembrokeshire in wartime, 1793–1815', in Brian Howells (ed.), *Pembrokeshire County History*, vol.III, *Early Modern Pembrokeshire, 1536–1815* (Haverfordwest, 1987), p.372.

in Aberafan in Glamorgan. Merthyr Tydfil, already a flourishing centre of the iron industry, attracted two representative refugees from the vicissitudes of these years, one from the rebellion and the other from the reaction. On the one hand, a Miss Rankin who had fled in terror of the rebellion married in 1817 Sir Josiah John Guest, the owner of the Dowlais Ironworks; while on the other, Lawrence Hughes, 'an Irish rebel flying from the vengeance of the law', found that he was the only Roman Catholic in the town.[10] Political upheaval and the fear of legal retribution were potent factors in the decision to emigrate in 1798, and despite the social gulf between Miss Rankin and Lawrence Hughes, their separate decisions to migrate to Wales derive from related events.

Although the terrible bloodshed of 1798 might well have been the final straw for those who had already toyed with the idea of emigrating to North America,[11] the migration to Wales in that year can be characterized as a temporary expedient thrust upon an anxious section of the population who returned to their previous lifestyle at the earliest opportunity. By the dawn of the nineteenth century there was no settled Irish presence in Wales comparable to that which existed in some of the cities and larger towns in England. In 1799, for example, a Catholic priest at Swansea – then the largest Welsh town – observed that 'a few Irish compose the whole congregation'. The town's popularity as a bathing resort and the development of its hinterland as a thriving centre of the non-ferrous metallurgical industry was responsible for this presence. Another priest observed in 1805 that the town was 'much frequented by the Irish', and an appeal issued about 1811 stated that mariners from Ireland were 'usually more or less numerous, accordingly as the winds waft them into Port, or detain them on shore'.[12] Occasional movements of small numbers of sailors and others arose out of the increasing trade between the two countries and paved the way

[10] James O'Brien, *Old Afan and Margam* (Aberavon, 1926), p.158; Charles Wilkins, *The History of the Iron, Steel, Tinplate and Other Trades of Wales* (Merthyr Tydfil, 1903), p.101; Ursula Masson, 'The development of the Irish and Roman Catholic communities of Merthyr Tydfil and Dowlais in the nineteenth century', unpublished University of Keele MA thesis (1975), 22.

[11] Kerby A. Miller, *Emigrants and Exiles: Ireland and the Irish Exodus to North America* (Oxford, 1985), pp.184–9.

[12] Quoted in T. G. Holt, 'The Glamorgan mission after the Oates plot', *Journal of Welsh Ecclesiastical History*, I (1984), 18, 21.

for later migrants who arrived in larger numbers to take advantage of the opportunities for employment in the burgeoning industrial economy of the region; yet all the available evidence indicates that in the early years of the nineteenth century the Irish in Wales were few in number and had a negligible impact upon the country.

Migrants are a self-selecting group whose decision to move is shaped by a combination of factors. These include the conditions in their own society predisposing them to leave and an awareness of opportunities at their destination. The relative importance of these 'push' and 'pull' factors changes over time, and an individual's decision to move frequently consists of a mixture of both, rather than being exclusively the result of one or other.[13] At times it is possible to identify a particular set of circumstances as being overwhelmingly responsible for migration – such as in 1798, when severe political upheaval was the predominant influence on the migration to Wales, or the late 1840s when famine was an expulsive force – but an understanding of the precise configuration of influences which prompted an individual's decision to move is hampered by the inadequacy of the historical record. In cases such as these, it is only possible to sketch the social and economic context in which migration occurred. Moreover, the migrants' destination was selected on the basis of the quality of information available to them and the availability of transport communications to convey them from one place to the other – two 'enabling' factors which also must be taken into account.

According to David Fitzpatrick, 'push' factors predominated in the decades immediately preceding the Famine, largely due to population pressure. Nevertheless, migration was more than a mechanical response to impoverished conditions. Whereas population growth in the decades preceding the 1840s tended to be greatest in the west, the crucial variation in the incidence of migration was from north to south. After a lull during the Napoleonic wars emigration revived, especially in the province of Ulster and adjacent counties as a result of the contraction of linen manufacture in the region.[14] However, although the

---

[13] David Fitzpatrick, *Irish Emigration, 1801–1921* (Dundalgan, 1984), pp.26-7; Panikos Panayi, *Immigration, Ethnicity and Racism in Britain, 1815–1945* (Manchester, 1994), ch.2.
[14] S. H. Cousens, 'The regional variation in emigration from Ireland between 1821 and 1841', *Transactions of the Institute of British Geographers*, 37 (1965), 15–30.

incidence of migration was heavier in some parts of Ireland than in others, it was a feature of life in all parts of the island before the Great Famine.

In the sixty years after 1780, Irish society underwent fundamental change as population growth accelerated at a remarkable pace. By 1801 the population had already reached five million and growth showed no signs of slackening, while the censuses of 1821 and 1841 revealed further startling increases to 6.8 and 8.1 million respectively. Even so, these figures underestimate the actual size of the increase because the large numbers who emigrated must be added to the totals recorded in the census. As K. H. Connell observed, the excess of births over deaths in Ireland in the sixty years before the Great Famine 'added not only four million to the population of Ireland, but one and three-quarter million to the population of Britain and North America'.[15] What is remarkable about this increase is that it was primarily a rural rather than an urban phenomenon, a development facilitated by the adoption of the potato as the staple food. The commercialization of agriculture and the increasing conversion of arable land to pasture led to the peasant's growing dependence on the potato for subsistence. Moreover, pressure on agricultural resources caused by the existence of more mouths to feed was compounded by the subdivision of land. As more productive strains of the plant came into widespread use, sufficient potatoes for subsistence could be cultivated on smaller and smaller parcels of land and poor, marginal land was colonized for potato planting.

By the mid-1840s, as many as three million Irish people – about a third of the population – were dependent upon the potato for their subsistence. Recent research has tended to emphasize the variety of economic activity in Ireland between the Union and the Famine, pointing out that Ulster had a developed textile industry and that smaller industrial enterprises existed elsewhere. Yet the country suffered from a paucity of natural energy resources to sustain industrialization on a wider scale, while geographical proximity to Britain, with its stronger

---

[15] K. H. Connell, *The Population of Ireland, 1750–1845* (Oxford, 1950), p.239; Cormac Ó Gráda, 'Poverty, population and agriculture, 1801–45', in W. E. Vaughan (ed.), *A New History of Ireland*, vol.V (Oxford, 1989), p.120.

industrial base, made open competition more difficult. Consequently, Ireland remained an overwhelmingly agrarian country in which ever-increasing numbers of people were dependent on the potato for their subsistence. In a context where acute pressure was brought to bear on land by overpopulation and poverty, emigration was a rational course of action for many people.

By contrast, south Wales was at the forefront of industrial development in Britain because of its abundance of natural resources – especially iron and coal – which entrepreneurs could profitably exploit. Population growth was substantial, although with an increase of approximately 144 per cent in the century after 1750 it occurred at a slower rate than in Ireland, and it was primarily an urban phenomenon. The pace of industrialization meant that this sector of the economy was largely able to absorb the substantial population growth of the late eighteenth and the early nineteenth centuries. English capital was essential for the creation of the larger industrial concerns and English industrialists increasingly dominated large-scale enterprises such as Cyfarthfa Iron Works in Merthyr Tydfil and the Dowlais Iron Works, where large numbers of workers were employed and huge profits were made. Although small in size in comparison with the larger towns and cities of England and Scotland, the settlements which sprang into life around these works surpassed in size and complexity any Welsh urban settlement which had previously existed. The most dramatic changes were seen in the iron industry, but this should not obscure developments in the area around Swansea, which became the world's principal centre for the production of non-ferrous metals.[16]

Industrialization in the region created new types of trade between Wales and Ireland and established new lines of communication. In the absence of developed passenger communications, migrants tended to follow trade routes. No passenger ships regularly plied their trade between the two countries and so commercial links were of far greater importance in establishing routes. A lively trade in agricultural produce and industrial commodities was already well established by the end of the

---

[16] For a succinct discussion of the relationship between population growth and industrialization, see John Davies, *A History of Wales* (London, 1993), ch.7.

eighteenth century.[17] The Welsh copper industry, centred on the town of Swansea, depended heavily upon the importation of copper ore from Ireland in the early nineteenth century. Copper reserves were exploited in three main areas, in counties Wicklow, Waterford and the southern portions of Cork and Kerry, each of which was within easy reach of the coast for transport to Wales. At its height this trade accounted for more than 23,000 tons of ore per annum. It remained substantial until the end of the 1840s and included other minor ores, such as iron pyrites for the production of sulphur; thereafter it declined.[18]

A network of canals connecting ports with the upland interior of Glamorgan and Monmouthshire was substantially completed in the last decade of the eighteenth century and facilitated the export of bulky commodities. Located along the northern rim of the south Wales coalfield, the iron industry depended heavily on such links to facilitate its expansion. Of the new iron companies, the Guests were aware of a potential market in Ireland as early as the 1780s, when William Taitt toured the country soliciting orders on their behalf.[19] They were not the only iron manufacturers to recognize the value of this market, and by the end of the Napoleonic wars there was stiff competition between Welsh companies, with Dublin, Belfast and Youghal the principal import centres for a vigorous trade in bar iron. During the postwar depression which began in 1815, the Guests had cause to rejoice that their competitors had won a larger share of the Irish market and consequently had greater losses to absorb.[20] Business lost at this time could be difficult to recoup. In 1823 William Wood, a representative of the Dowlais Iron Company, embarked on a business trip the length of Ireland, from Belfast in the north-

[17] For example, exports of tinplate to Ireland increased in value more than ninefold between 1796 and 1805: A. H. John, *The Industrial Development of South Wales*, p.106. See also Jenkins, 'Connections between the Landed Communities of Munster and South Wales', 95–6.

[18] John, *The Industrial Development of South Wales*; Robert Kane, *The Industrial Resources of Ireland* (Dublin, 1844), pp.172ff. Wicklow ore sold at Swansea declined from 11,813 tons (worth £55,818 12s. 0d.) in 1836 to 3,227 tons (worth £12,917 19s. 0d.) in 1843. According to D. Trevor Williams, the total amount of Irish ores sold at Swansea between 1840 and 1849 was 161,182 tons, or 28 per cent of the total ores sold there. See his *The Economic Development of Swansea and of the Swansea District to 1921* (Swansea, 1940), p.71.

[19] Elizabeth Havill, 'William Taitt, 1748–1815', *Transactions of the Honourable Society of Cymmrodorion* (1983), 101–2.

[20] John, *Industrial Development*, p.102; T. R. Guest to Mr Taitt, 28 March 1815, Dowlais Iron Co. Letterbooks, 1815 (1), folio 316, Glam. RO, D/DG.

east to Skibbereen in the south-west, to recover lost orders and solicit new ones. His report of a meeting with Charles Jennings of Newry provides an instructive insight into the keen competition between Welsh companies:

> He buys Iron from many people in Wales – some from Clydach – some from Nantyglo. Bailey Brothers have, he says, refused to sell him under £7 per ton . . . Mr Jennings afterwards came to me at the Inn and said that something might be done between the Dowlais [Iron] Co. and himself by way of Barter – he would send Corn to Cardiff and take Iron back . . . [21]

Of an Irish merchant at Youghal, Wood intimated: '. . . it is strongly suspected that he sells on commission from the Tredegar Co. from whom he receives Cargo after Cargo and gets rid of 500 tons a year.'[22] Other Welsh iron companies were also active in the Waterford area. The trade in iron remained buoyant throughout the century, especially after the construction of Irish railways from the 1830s.

As far as patterns of migration are concerned, the export of coal was far more important than the trade in either iron or copper. Ireland possessed some mines of its own, but reserves were meagre and the collieries at work between 1801 and 1845 met only a fraction of the country's energy demands – probably no more than 5 or 10 per cent. Given the geographical proximity of Wales and its abundant coal reserves, a trade in coal emerged at an early stage. Some requirements were highly specialized. For example, at the beginning of the nineteenth century a large proportion of the trade in small coal with Ireland was purchased for distilling whiskey. In 1806 the production of small coal in the hinterland of Newport came to a halt when distillation in Ireland was temporarily checked. Similarly, a part of the increased shipment of semi-anthracite coals from Swansea and Llanelli can be accounted for by the burning of lime for agriculture. There was keen competition between Welsh ports for the Irish market, forcing companies to provide extremely generous measures in order to maintain their market position. At the western extremity of the coalfield, trade with Ireland picked up markedly in 1809,

---

[21] William Wood to J. J. Guest, 30 September 1823, Dowlais Iron Co. Letterbooks, 1823 (5), folio 433, Glam. RO.
[22] Wood to Guest, 12 October 1823, ibid., folios 443–6.

accounting for approximately a quarter of the vessels out of Llanelli – and probably a greater proportion of the tonnage – between 1811 and 1819; thereafter, local coalmasters switched their attention to the trade exchanging coal and copper ore with the west of England.[23] An impression of the dimensions of the coal trade with Ireland may be gauged from the fact that 550 ships carried cargoes from Newport alone in 1820, compared with only sixteen laden with iron. From 1819 the annual export of coal from Welsh ports in general fluctuated considerably.[24]

Companies could experience difficulties in finding reliable merchants to handle their product. In 1838 the Marquis of Bute encountered problems when a highly recommended Cork agent entrusted with selling coal from the Rhigos colliery went bankrupt. This setback was compounded by difficulties in finding a market for the particular coals sold by the Bute estate. Bute's forays into the coal trade were a distraction from other pressing matters, and by 1840 he had tired of the experiment. Other entrepreneurs were more successful. By 1830 Walter Coffin of the Rhondda sold most of his sale-coal at Waterford and Cork, and in the 1840s there was stiff competition from the collieries of George Insole for this lucrative market.[25]

Irish migrants to Britain were not registered in the ports, so before the Census of Population for 1841 (which enumerated the birth place of residents for the first time) it is difficult to obtain a clear picture of the dimensions of the immigration to Wales between 1815 and 1841. One way of circumventing this problem is to piece together the imperfect evidence provided by government reports, newspapers and private correspondence in order to glean information about the types of migration which occurred and their impact on Welsh society. As has been seen,

---

[23] Cormac Ó Gráda, 'Industry and communications, 1801–45', in W. E. Vaughan (ed.), *A New History of Ireland*, p.42; *Monmouthsire Merlin*, 30 March 1867; report of a paper by Mr A. Bassett, CE, 'The port of Newport and its coalfields', to the South Wales Institute of Engineers. However, A. H. John claims that Scottish coals were used for distilling whiskey: John, *Industrial Development*, p.115. M. V. Symons, *Coal Mining in the Llanelli Area*, vol.I, *The Sixteenth Century to 1829* (Llanelli,1979), pp.260–2, 329. Increased exports from Llanelli might be one contributory factor in the falling off of exports from Newport in 1809: John, *Industrial Development*, p.118.

[24] John, *Industrial Development*, p.119; PP 1830 VIII, Select Committee on the State of the Coal Trade in the United Kingdom, Appendix I.

[25] NLW, Bute Letters, L81/9, 14, 28, 37, 58, 135, 140, 145; L85/71; John Davies, *Cardiff and the Marquesses of Bute* (Cardiff, 1981), pp.218–9; E. D. Lewis, *The Rhondda Valleys* (Cardiff, 1959), pp.45–7, 133n.

migration was not an undifferentiated and indiscriminate phenomenon, and it is possible to identify three broad strands of Irish immigration to Wales in the period from 1815 to 1845 which have usually been conflated into a single stream. A long-standing movement of vagrants between the two countries, which had fallen into abeyance during the Napoleonic wars, resumed and intensified during the post-war depression which afflicted Irish agriculture after 1815. But expulsive forces were only one side of the coin and attempts were also made to recruit labour for both agricultural and industrial work, especially the latter. From the 1820s seasonal harvest labourers were seen in some parts of the Welsh countryside, and a larger number sought work in industry and the towns.

Vagrancy

Irish vagrants followed the same routes as the droves of Irish cattle which poured into England through Bristol, Liverpool and the Welsh ports in 1815. In the early nineteenth century, Irish vagrants travelled along two main routes: via the ports of Holyhead and Liverpool on the one hand, and those of south Wales and Bristol on the other. Both streams reached their confluence in the south of England, with London as the principal destination. Parishes en route between the ports and London were faced with the cost of either relieving or removing the vagrants. The parishes burdened with this responsibility complained bitterly at having to meet the heavy costs and frequently demanded government action to stem the influx. Social distress in Britain (also caused by the post-war depression) prompted parishes to redouble their efforts to return the unwanted Irish to their native land. Between 1816 and 1820, no distinction was made between those moving about in search of work and those who depended on alms – all were treated as vagrants and removed from county to county until they reached the coast. The financial burden of removal lay heavily on coastal counties such as Lancashire, which alone was responsible for shipping 20,000 Irish vagrants between 1823 and 1827.[26]

---

[26] Ribton-Turner, *A History of Vagrants and Vagrancy*.

There are no statistics for the numbers of Irish vagrants moving through Wales in these years, but at times when vagrancy intensified, attempts were made to collect information on the cost of removal to the counties most seriously affected. Returns for selected Welsh counties for the years 1817–22 indicate the dimensions of the problem. In Pembrokeshire, for example, the cost of passing vagrants to Ireland accounted for more than one fifth of the county's total expenditure on poor law removals in 1817, rising to a peak of nearly half the expenditure in 1821. Similarly, in north Wales, the cost of removing Irish vagrants made substantial inroads into local budgets. Approximately half the expenditure on removals from the counties of Anglesey and Caernarfon in the years 1820–2 was absorbed in conveying vagrants to Ireland, while in the counties further east the burden on the public purse was noticeably less. Surprisingly, perhaps, Carmarthenshire figured prominently in the removal of vagrants to Ireland. The county lay outside the principal routes used by vagrants and yet it paid out large sums of money for the removal of the Irish. Payments under this head accounted for 40 to 46 per cent of the county's total expenditure on removals in the years 1818–22. Probably this was owing to the town of Carmarthen being a minor port of communication with Ireland, and so being in no position to shift the cost to an adjacent county.[27] The case of Carmarthen indicates that although vagrants tended to follow familiar routes, they were not confined to the well-beaten tracks. In fact, as they occasionally fanned out from the ports into the Welsh countryside, it is likely that vagrants were the only Irish people encountered by a majority of the Welsh.

With successive regional subsistence crises in Irish agriculture after 1821, vagrants returned to Wales in increasing numbers, to the great discomfort of the native population. The vagrant was feared and despised as the quintessential outsider who, by his or her footloose lifestyle, was considered a potential threat to the established social order. By contrast, attitudes to alms-giving and the poor in nineteenth-century Ireland were radically different.

---

[27] PP 1824 XIX, An Account of the Sums Paid by the Several Treasurers of Counties in England and Wales for the Apprehension and Conveyance of Irish and Scotch Vagrants Removed by Pass to Ireland and Scotland during the Year 1823, 16–17.

There, the absence of a poor law until 1838, and the active encouragement of alms-giving by the Catholic church, created a context within which the mendicant was an accepted part of everyday life and an essential figure in Gaelic folk-culture. In Wales, the vagrant was considered above all an insidious criminal who thought nothing of selfishly defrauding the public purse. 'We understand', the *Cambrian* newspaper of Swansea informed its readers in 1817, that

> a fair number of Hibernians, professing themselves to be the wives of soldiers, and recently to have arrived from the army in France, and landed on the Welsh coast, have imposed upon several parish officers with forged printed passes; they are easily detected as the genuine ones are well engraved on copper plates and have a very different appearance to the letter press. An imposition of this kind was practised a few years ago and several parishes defrauded to a serious amount.[28]

Underpinning widespread anxiety about the unrestricted movement of large numbers of people was this belief in the innate propensity of the footloose individual to indulge in criminal activity. In such a context, vagrants were perceived as being particularly responsible for crimes of fraud. Such cases undeniably occurred, although it is doubtful that they can be attributed exclusively (or even particularly) to vagrants. At Swansea in December 1818 tradesmen complained of the increasing circulation of Irish pennies and halfpennies, a development which was attributed to 'one or more designing individuals' seeking to make a profit, while at Carmarthen Great Sessions in 1820 Cornelius Leary and Daniel McCarthy were sentenced to one year's imprisonment for 'uttering counterfeit money'.[29] Counterfeiting required the possession of specialist equipment and a degree of expertise which few vagrants could have possessed. However, the prevailing view was summed up by a poor law commissioner who maintained that vagrants in Wales provided a bad example and demoralized the people they met. For good measure, he added: 'the annoyance to which individuals are exposed from the importunity, insolence and petty thefts of vagrants is also a great inconvenience.'[30]

---

[28] *Cambrian*, 14 June 1817.
[29] *Cambrian*, 12 December 1818, 2 September 1820.
[30] PP 1834 XXIX, Report from Her Majesty's Commissioners for Inquiring into the Administration and Practical Operation of Poor Laws, Part II, Appendix A, p.189.

Harvest Labourers

The long-standing movement of vagrants from Ireland followed particular routes along the north and south Wales coasts. From mid-century, the alignment of the first branches of the new railway network reinforced the significance of these routes, with the Chester and Holyhead Railway following the north Wales coast to Anglesey, and the South Wales Railway linking the ports of south Wales. From 1821 the use of steamships to carry the Royal Mail between Holyhead and Dublin was an important step towards ensuring that a regular and comparatively speedy link was maintained between the government in London and its administration in Dublin.[31]

Other migrants were in a position to be more discriminating in their choice of destination. Harvest labourers seeking seasonal work in England and Wales followed the same routes as vagrants, but their annual migrations operated to a distinctive pattern and rhythm. For the Irish cottier, spring was a busy time spent planting the potato crop and cutting a year's supply of turf. In June, many would cross to Britain to harvest the grain crop, returning to Ireland with sufficient money to pay the rent in time to raise the potato crop.[32] There was a long tradition of Irish harvest labourers finding temporary employment in Wales, but their presence attracted particular attention in the late 1820s. At first, their impact was felt indirectly. In June 1828, Mr R. A. Slaney intervened in the House of Commons to protest that Irish labour was displacing the Welsh harvest workers who migrated annually from Merioneth and Montgomeryshire in north Wales across the border to Shropshire. 'They were driven out of the fields of Shropshire', he maintained, 'by the immense crowds of Irishmen, who annually came over and reaped the harvest at a much lower rate than the Welsh could afford to do.' This was not an isolated incident, as is shown by the disturbance involving migrant labour in Cheshire in the 1830s when the conflicting

---

[31] Williams, *Hanes Môn*, p.74.

[32] On seasonal migration, see J. H. Johnson, 'Harvest migration from nineteenth century Ireland', *Transactions of the Institute of British Geographers*, 41 (1967), 98–9; B. M. Kerr, 'Irish seasonal migration to Great Britain, 1800–1838', *Irish Historical Studies*, III (1942–3); and David Fitzpatrick, ' "A peculiar tramping people": the Irish in Britain, 1801–70', in Vaughan, *A New History of Ireland*, pp.630–3.

claims of the Irish, on the one hand, and labourers from Wales, Cheshire and Lancashire, on the other, proved irreconcilable.[33]

Despite the odious reputation the Irish soon acquired as intruders who unceremoniously snatched the labourer's bread from his mouth by undercutting wages and stealing jobs which were the rightful preserve of locals, in many areas they played an essential role in gathering the harvest. Only two months after Slaney denounced the incursion of Irish harvesters into Shropshire in 1828, the complaint in the Vale of Glamorgan was of a lack of reapers to gather the harvest. 'When reaping commenced', it was reported,

> labourers were scarce, as it came on earlier than expected, with much hay also abroad; advanced wages were required and in some cases obtained, which could be ill-afforded by the farmer; but at present there are sufficient, a great number of Irish reapers and others having arrived, and scattering about the country were soon engaged.[34]

The initial scarcity of hands in the Vale of Glamorgan in 1828 led to calls for better and more efficiently disseminated information to enable harvesters to proceed to the areas where the need was greatest.[35] Harvesting was a precarious occupation at best, depending as it did upon a combination of good weather and the availability of a far larger number of labourers than could be employed during the remainder of the year. Against this background, it has been argued that Irish harvest labourers had a positive effect on rural employment outside the harvest season: as farmers only sowed crops they knew they could harvest, the availability of outside labour at harvest time meant that a larger crop could be cultivated and thus a higher level of employment sustained during the other ten months of the year.[36]

In the absence of regular passenger traffic between south Wales and Ireland, the empty coal ships, or 'colliers', returning

[33] *Hansard's Parliamentary Debates*, second series, XIX, cols.1513–14; PP 1836 XXXIV, Report on the State of the Irish Poor in Great Britain, p.471.
[34] *Cambrian*, 16 August 1828.
[35] A novel published in 1841 describes Irish harvest labourers being hired at a hiring fair at Denbigh in north Wales. The description, in Digby Beste, *Poverty and the Baronet's Family* (London, 1841), is quoted in Ruth-Ann M. Harris, *The Nearest Place That Wasn't Ireland: Early Nineteenth-Century Irish Labor Migration* (Ames, Iowa, 1994), p.32.
[36] Graham Davis, *The Irish in Britain, 1815–1914* (Dublin, 1991), pp.102–3.

to Wales were used by migrants as a cheap method of travel. This arrangement suited sea-captains, who otherwise would have used soil or rocks to stabilize their vessels, as well as the penniless migrants with no alternative means of travel. As there was frequently no suitable return trade from Ireland which could be stowed in the coal-dirty holds, the captains were more than happy to obtain a little extra money for what otherwise would have been an unremunerative trip in ballast. This practice came to light in 1836 when R. M. Muggeridge, migration agent to the poor law commissioners, turned his attention to the western ports of Britain. Initially, Muggeridge was faced with a conundrum: how to explain why the number of passengers leaving Bristol for Ireland exceeded the number travelling in the opposite direction, when all other evidence pointed to large numbers of Irish men and women migrating to Britain. The reason, he discovered, was that many Irish seasonal workers entered Britain cheaply via small ports on the Welsh coast in colliers returning in ballast from Ireland. After gathering the harvest in England, they had more money at their disposal and hence were able to return via Bristol on the more comfortable – and costly – packets.[37] Such practices, designed to reduce the cost of seasonal migration, increased the migrants' familiarity with the industrial developments taking place in south Wales. In this respect, they acted as conduits of information about job opportunities for those who remained at home.

For employers of agricultural labour, labour costs were a sore point. In 1836, Evan David of Radyr Court, a substantial farmer of 730 acres in the Vale of Glamorgan, stressed the unfair advantage enjoyed by Irish agriculture because of the low cost of labour in Ireland and the absence of poor law dues there. He calculated that his labour costs were treble those of Irish farmers. Furthermore, he bitterly observed that the coal trade with Ireland enabled the Irish farmer to send his corn to the growing iron-producing town of Merthyr Tydfil nearly as cheaply as half the farms of Glamorgan could. Due to the comparative scarcity of labour in the Vale at that time, Evan David paid his Irish labourers more than the 6d. a day considered the minimum

---

[37] PP 1836 XXIX, Poor Law Commissioners Report, Part I, Appendix B, p.419.

acceptable wage, although he probably paid them less than he did the locals.[38]

During the 1840s, labourers from the south-west of England and Ireland were used increasingly in the Vale of Glamorgan to replace the locals who had migrated to adjacent mining areas where they could obtain higher wages. This meant that employment was available in the winter months as well as during the summer harvest season. The incomers were employed at the most laborious tasks, such as drawing, cleaning and trimming turnips for consumption, for which they were paid less than were the locals; they lived in out-houses and sheds, and subsisted on a meagre diet of potatoes, turnips and bread. Seasonal labour was essential to ensure the successful harvesting of the crops, as shown by the hiring of a hundred Irish labourers during the season in the village of Llancarfan. In other villages the numbers tended to be more modest. Despite this fact, Irish labourers in the Vale played a disproportionately large role in replenishing the depleted ranks of the local labour force: for example, the five Irish labourers enumerated at the village of Cowbridge in 1851 accounted for more than an eighth of the total labouring workforce in agriculture.[39] From mid-century, the importance of Irish labour to agriculture in Wales declined, although at the rim of the south Wales coalfield there continued to be some occasional movement between industrial and agricultural occupations.

Harvest labour in agriculture furnishes a clear example of how the availability of waged work in Britain acted as a magnet to peasants who needed the cash to pay the rent on their small parcels of land. For them, seasonal migration was a stratagem designed to ameliorate domestic conditions. In fact, Irish society contained an agricultural labour force with extensive links with labour markets in Britain, a fact which promoted movement

[38] PP 1836 VIII, Select Committee on the State of Agriculture, Part I, pp.198–212. Poor communications inland between the countryside and the towns meant that in the mid-1840s three-quarters of the flour consumed in Merthyr Tydfil came from Ireland, Bristol and Devon. See David Howell, 'Farming in south-east Wales c.1840–80', in Colin Baber and L. J.Williams (eds.), *Modern South Wales: Essays in Economic History* (Cardiff, 1986), pp.83–4.

[39] D. T. Alexander, *Glamorgan Reminiscences* (Carmarthen, 1915); Rosemary A. Jones, 'A study of the 1852 general election in the Cardiff Boroughs', unpublished University of Wales MA thesis (1982), 47, 71; Elfyn Scourfield, 'Rural society in the Vale of Glamorgan', in Prys Morgan (ed.), *Glamorgan County History*, vol.VI, *Glamorgan Society, 1780–1980* (Cardiff, 1988), pp.226–7.

between the two countries. From the 1820s, however, the over-whelming majority of Irish immigrants to Wales gravitated towards industry and the towns. A discussion of this strand of immigration requires a broader consideration of the character of crafts and skill, and the meaning of work in the early industrial revolution.

Irish Labour and Industry

When the Irish first appeared in the labour force of industrial south Wales in the 1820s, they were often employed in low-status manual occupations, like navvying, which the Welsh were not predisposed to accept. From an early date, discussion of the social effects of Irish immigration focused on an alleged tendency to reduce the wages and standard of living of the host society. As early as the 1820s, Malthus and other writers asserted that immigration from Ireland depressed wages by increasing the labour supply; subsequently, the press and other commentators axiomatically made this connection and historians have tended to follow their lead.[40] Wage differentials between Britain and Ireland provide *prima facie* evidence in support of this view. Between 1790 and 1850 the money wages of labourers in Ireland underwent a relative decline of 7 per cent, compared with an increase of 40 per cent in the wages of their counterparts in Britain.[41] By crossing the Irish Sea, migrants moved from a low-wage economy to a high-wage one.

However, the received view of Irish labour performing only the undesirable tasks while at the same time undercutting wages contains one major unresolved contradiction; that is, if the Irish occupied such an unenvied niche in the labour market, with whom did they compete to undercut wages? Nor is this the only

---

[40] Arthur Redford, *Labour Migration in England, 1800–1850* (Manchester, 1976 edn), pp.159–62; John Davies, *A History of Wales* (London, 1993), p.385; Trevor Boyns and Colin Baber, 'The supply of labour, 1750–1914', in Arthur H. John and Glanmor Williams (eds.), *Glamorgan County History*, vol.V, *Industrial Glamorgan* (Cardiff, 1980), pp.320–1. The last-named is based on the assumption that workers were attracted to industry by high wages, but that the Irish were not because they were expelled from Ireland. This is to conflate pre- and post-Famine migration and to underestimate the severity of depression in many parts of rural Wales in the period 1815–50.

[41] 'Editor's Introduction' in Arthur J. Taylor (ed.), *The Standard of Living in Britain in the Industrial Revolution* (London, 1975), p.xix.

factor to be considered. As David Fitzpatrick has pointed out, the claim that the Irish undercut wages rests upon the answers to three questions: whether home supply was sufficient to meet the growing demands of industry for labour; whether Welsh and Irish workers competed for employment in the same sectors; and whether immigrant workers undermined 'combinations' seeking to safeguard working-class conditions?[42] The last of these can be dismissed immediately, as there is no evidence to suggest that the Irish impeded attempts to organize the working class in Wales. The extent to which home supply was sufficient to meet the needs of industry, and the degree of competition between the Irish and Welsh for jobs, require more detailed consideration, for both questions relate to the kind of migration which took place.

Industrial development in south Wales in the century after 1750 occurred predominantly around the port of Swansea and in the sparsely populated upland interior where agriculture was poor, and employers faced acute problems in assembling a labour force at industrial concerns. Consequently, immigrants from the Welsh countryside contributed the greater part of the labour force upon which the iron foundries, copperworks and coal mines depended. Industry produced a ripple effect in the areas adjacent to the works, from which agricultural labourers from the nearest parishes were the first to migrate, closely followed by workers from slightly further away. Thus, agricultural labourers from the Vale of Glamorgan and the neighbouring counties of Breconshire, Pembrokeshire and Cardiganshire formed the core of the industrial workforce in Glamorgan and Monmouthshire. Attracted by the prospect of high wages, these labourers made the short-step migration to the works and, at times of economic down turn, back again. Some were already well used to seasonal migration, having harvested the crops in the English Midlands for many years; for them, winter work in the iron industry either supplemented their summer migration or even came to supersede it completely.[43] Workers from further afield, such as England and Ireland, formed a much smaller proportion of the industrial workforce, although the English presence was much stronger on the eastern flank of the coalfield where labourers from the border counties of Herefordshire and Gloucestershire found employment.

High wages were the magnet which drew agricultural workers inexorably to the centres of iron production. Unimpeded by the administration of laws of settlement and poor relief in the region, labourers were in a position to maximize their earnings by migration. By contrast, employers experienced greater difficulty in recruiting skilled labour. The vast majority of rural workers who migrated to the iron-producing and coal mining districts of south Wales possessed neither the specific technical knowledge required to secure the better jobs, nor the more general experience of working in industry which might provide a basis for acquiring new skills. Employers in the iron industry frequently recruited experienced industrial workers from established centres in England, such as Staffordshire and Shropshire, to form a nucleus of skilled workers who would then train others on the job.[44]

How do the Irish fit into this picture? There has been a tendency to see the Irish as an exception to the general pattern of migration to south Wales, being perceived as a group expelled from Ireland by distress rather than as one attracted by higher wages. This conclusion has depended upon an erroneous belief that Irish immigration was either negligible or non-existent before the 1840s. While the absolute numbers of Irish immigrants were relatively small, employers occasionally recruited Irish workers for specific tasks in preference to native labour. For example, employers seeking workers to excavate major projects such as the new dock at Porthcawl in the early 1820s,[45] and the excavation of the Bute Ironworks in the Rhymney Valley in 1825, procured labour direct from Ireland. Once these projects were completed, the labourers moved elsewhere to find similar work on other projects. Thus, a view of Irish labour as particularly suited to the heaviest work and constituting the most disposable element of the workforce was reinforced. Whether Welsh or English workers would have undertaken this work in the absence of the Irish is open to question, but persistent claims that the Irish undertook tasks rejected by others suggest that they

[44] Boyns and Baber, 'The supply of labour, 1750–1914', pp.323–8.
[45] St Peter's Magazine, V (1925), 206.

would not. To this extent, the workforce of the receiving society was inadequate to the needs of industry; the role played by the small numbers of Irish immigrants was an important one.

According to A. H. John, they performed 'the heaviest manual labour, and so did not compete with the colliers and the skilled and semi-skilled workers'.[46] However, not all Irish immigrants to industrial Wales conformed to this description, as was demonstrated by the census returns of 1841. This source indicates that while the majority of the Irish found employment in labouring jobs, by no means all of them did so, a significant minority working in skilled or semi-skilled jobs.[47] In the absence of accurate information about occupations before this date, one rough indicator of the extent of competition during the 1820s–1840s is the character and extent of ethnic conflict at the workplace. Taken together with a consideration of the ways in which skill was defined in the early industrial economy, it is possible to arrive at a modification of received views about the character of Irish immigration to the region.

The 'modernity' of work in the early industrial economy can be overemphasized. To be sure, some industrial processes, such as puddling in the ironworks, demanded highly specific skills which could be acquired only by persevering at that occupation over an extended period of time, usually from a young age. Thus, agricultural workers with no experience of the craft would not be employed in that capacity. But there existed a wide range of transferable skills developed in a rural economy which could be applied to various facets of the production processes of early industrial enterprises or utilized in services demanded by life in the towns. Carpenters, smiths, masons, and so on, were in a position to adapt the skills of their crafts to the more specialized needs of the metalworks and coal mines. Other skilled trades, such as shoemaking or tailoring, were in demand from consumers in an urbanizing society. A prior knowledge of the demands of an industrial economy was not necessarily more

---

[46] According to A. H. John, the wages of indigenous labourers were unaffected by the Irish until the 1840s, when a serious economic depression led to anti-Irish disturbances, particularly in the eastern part of the south Wales coalfield. In reality, ethnic conflict at the workplace occurred much earlier and suggests that competition for some jobs existed from the outset. John, *The Industrial Development of South Wales*, p.68.; Boyns and Baber, 'The supply of labour, 1750–1914', p.320.

[47] See ch.II for a more detailed analysis.

widespread among immigrants from rural Wales, and yet the Irish have been singled out as particularly lacking in the skills which could have secured higher-status jobs and a better standard of living. To what extent was this the case?

An individual's ability to perform a particular task competently was not the only criterion for apportioning jobs; employers might also consider a worker's age, gender and ethnic background to be salient factors. This often meant that where immigrants from rural Ireland competed for jobs – semi-skilled jobs in particular – they were frequently overlooked in favour of Welsh workers. In short, 'skill' was a cultural as much as a narrowly technical category. Irish immigrants were expected to conform to the stereotype of the heavy manual worker. Where the Irish competed directly for skilled or semi-skilled jobs, they also encountered a determination among the workforce to control entry into coal mining and ironworking. Strenuous efforts were made to restrict the acquisition of knowledge about work processes and prevent newcomers from being trained in the requisite skills, thereby contributing to the tight maintenance of skill differentials. In this context, a 'stranger' achieving a skilled position could be interpreted as a threat to the workers' received codes of social justice. Such codes of behaviour depended on a status system in which esteem was earned on the basis of ethnic origin as well as occupation or financial distinctions. Wage rates were not the only, or necessarily in every case the central, issue of concern to workers confronted with an influx of outsiders.

The compound of issues underpinning tensions at the workplace is revealed in the first recorded disturbance between Irish and Welsh workers which occurred in 1826. The incident took place at the village of Rhymney on the border between Glamorgan and Monmouthshire a year after Irish labour had been imported, specifically to build three blast furnaces on the Marquis of Bute's land near the village. By early 1826 the prospect of a depression in trade precipitated a hostile reaction to the 'strangers'. Matters came to a head on 1 March, St David's Day, when an attempt was made to drive the Irish away from the works and eject them from their houses. A crowd of several hundred assembled in the village to eject the group of sixty or seventy Irish who lived there. William Forman, an ironmaster from Merthyr Tydfil, was present at the time, and initially it appeared as though his prompt action in reading the Riot Act would lead to the crowd dispersing. Hopes that this might lead to a peaceful resolution of events were dashed when a marching gang arrived from Tredegar and began to unsettle the crowd. In the confusion, Forman struck a miner with his stick, prompting the very response he had tried to avoid by reading the Riot Act. Both Forman and the Irish were showered with stones by the incensed crowd and were compelled to seek refuge together in a house nearby. There they remained under siege for some time. Some of the Irish escaped to Merthyr Tydfil and refused to return until accompanied by a detachment of troops three days later.[48]

It has been asserted that wages were the overriding bone of contention at the Bute Ironworks in 1826,[49] but it was not until the summer of that year that wage reductions were generally enforced in the area, and it seems unlikely that this is sufficient to explain the vigorous response of the crowd. William Forman was closer to the mark when he reported that the Welsh were 'dissatisfied that any people but their own Countrymen should be employed'.[50] It was less a concern about wages than a determination to control the labour supply in a falling market which lay behind the action of the crowd. For the workers, a depression meant underemployment, unemployment and a more rigorous enforcement of the despised truck system, in addition to lower wages. Any action which delayed, or even resulted in avoiding, such contingencies was a means of exerting control over events at the workplace at a time when any vestige of control was passing relentlessly away from the worker and into the hands of employers. This method of collective action was also deployed in other parts of south Wales. The copper industry in and around Swansea was a flashpoint of ethnic violence in the late 1820s when determined efforts were made to eject the Irish working there. In July 1827 Welsh coppermen attempted to exclude the

[48] See 'The Catholic registers of Abergavenny, Mon., 1740–1838', in *Publications of the Catholic Record Society*, XXVII, *Miscellanea* (London, 1927); and Masson, 'The Development of the Irish and Roman Catholic Communities of Merthyr Tydfil and Dowlais in the Nineteenth Century'. The last-named reports fifty-two Irish men at the Rhymney and Bute Ironworks in 1827 (34).

[49] E. W. Evans, *The Miners of South Wales* (Cardiff, 1961), pp.21–2; Masson, 'The development of the Irish and Roman Catholic communities of Merthyr Tydfil and Dowlais in the nineteenth century', 28.

[50] William Forman to Robert Peel, 7 March 1826, PRO, HO 40/19(1).

Irish from the Rose copperworks, while in May of the following year the local magistrate found it necessary to alert the cavalry after clashes between the two groups.[51] As a recognizably distinct group of outsiders, the Irish were the first and most visible target of Welsh discontent, the butt of what E. J. Hobsbawm has termed 'collective bargaining by riot'. To be properly understood, these incidents must be seen as part of a wider shift in the consciousness of the industrial working class in south Wales. During the 1820s there was a perceptible change in the purpose of collective action in the region as the emphasis shifted from the defensive protest of earlier decades to a determination to exert control over the productive process itself.[52]

That Irish workers enjoyed a precarious position in the labour force was clearly demonstrated in the early 1830s. When the economy went through a period of cyclical downturn, the Irish were affected disproportionately by unemployment as they tended to occupy the lower-paid jobs and were invariably the first to be discharged by employers intent on trimming their wages bill. Commenting on the incidence of unemployment in south Wales in 1833, Alexander Murray found that 'a great many Irish labourers who were employed at the ironworks are dismissed now owing to the want of demand and the low price of iron'.[53] As the events at Rhymney in 1826 demonstrated, the employers' policies were reinforced, albeit unconsciously, by the hostile attitudes and behaviour of the workforce. Hostilities resumed in May 1834 when an attempt was made to drive the Irish away from Varteg Ironworks near Pontypool on the pretext that they had undercut wages; dissatisfaction over the same issue led to violent clashes at the coal pits of Walter Coffin and Messrs. Powell near Cardiff in September of the same year.[54] The accusation that the Irish were willing to undercut wages, or work 'under price', provided a powerful impetus to the Welsh to assert their own sense of popular justice by attempting to expel those

[51] NLW, Calendar of the Diary of Lewis Weston Dillwyn, vol.II, 19 July 1827 and 22 May 1828.

[52] E. J. Hobsbawm, *Labouring Men: Studies in the History of Labour* (London, 1968 edn), p.7; Gwyn A. Williams, 'Locating a Welsh working class: the frontier years', in David Smith (ed.), *A People and A Proletariat: Essays in the Social History of Wales* (London, 1980), pp.28–9, 36–7.

[53] PP 1833 V, Report from the Select Committee on Agriculture, p.14.

[54] *Monmouthshire Merlin*, 10 May 1834; *Cardiff and Merthyr Guardian*, 13 September 1834.

who they believed had transgressed the community's unwritten codes of behaviour.

A belief that the newcomers had violated accepted codes of behaviour is reinforced by the actions of the 'Scotch Cattle' during 1834. The Scotch Cattle were a secret society of Welsh workers which enforced communal justice against strike-breakers, immigrants, bailiffs and grasping shopkeepers – indeed against any person believed to be an enemy of the people of the industrial settlements of western Monmouthshire and eastern Glamorgan. Their ritualized mode of operation was adapted from the 'ceffyl pren', or mock-trial, of the Welsh countryside, and they were likened by the irate press to the Irish Terryalts. Visiting their victims at night, members of the 'herd' blackened their faces and disguised their clothes, indulging in the kind of behaviour associated with 'rough music': blowing horns, the noisy lowing of the 'Cattle', followed by the ritual humiliation of the object of their visit.[55] Anonymous threatening letters an-nouncing the Cattle's visit, depicting in lurid and blood-curdling terms the projected fate of their intended victim, were an important part of the society's armoury. There is a record of one such letter being sent in the summer of 1834 to frighten an employer into sacking the Irish workers in his employ. On 19 June Lady Charlotte Guest, wife of Josiah John Guest of the Dowlais Ironworks, confided to her diary that a letter had arrived threatening to 'Scotch Cattle' Dowlais House on or about 2 July, unless all the Irish were discharged from the works.[56] It is difficult to imagine the Scotch Cattle exposing themselves to the real dangers of being recognized or caught by undertaking such an audacious attack on the home of a major employer, but the homes of lesser employers were occasionally attacked and the incident does suggest that such letters were perceived by their senders as a potentially effective deterrent in themselves. While striking terror into the hearts of their victims and opponents, the anonymous 'Scotch Bull' described himself in these letters as 'gelyn pob dychryndod' (the enemy of all fear).

[55] D. J. V. Jones, *Before Rebecca: Popular Protest in Wales, 1793–1834* (London, 1973). See also R. A. N. Jones, 'Women, community and collective action: the *Ceffyl Pren* tradition', in Angela V. John (ed.), *Our Mothers' Land: Chapters in Welsh Women's History, 1830–1939* (Cardiff, 1991).

[56] Earl of Bessborough (ed.), *Lady Charlotte Guest: Extracts from Her Journal, 1833–52* (London, 1950), p.30.

The Cattle challenged Irish workers in Monmouthshire in a more direct way in September 1834, when they visited the house of John Corbet at Blaen Rhymney. This incident occurred after two Irishmen living locally had been brought to court for stabbing a Welshman in a pub brawl, and it was revealed that there had been conflict between Welsh and Irish in the area for some time previously. John Corbet was an Irish mason employed at the Bute Ironworks and there is no evidence that he was directly involved in these disturbances. Regular employment and a wage of 18*s.* a week put Corbet in a different category from his neighbours. In addition, his wages were augmented by the rent from half his converted farmhouse which he let to another Irishman. Corbet's status was tellingly revealed by a neighbour who observed, 'Corbet was better off than I, we had no money or watch.' Possession of a watch was more than a sign of conspicuous consumption; in a society increasingly dominated by the discipline of the clock rather than the rhythms of pre-industrial society, it also conferred prestige on its owner.[57] This attack was by no means untypical of the Cattle's activity, deploying as it did the full panoply of disguise and intimidation used by them elsewhere. Yet the incident stands out because of one notable feature: whereas previously violence against the Irish had been directed at unskilled, low-paid workers, the object of attack was now a craftsman of better means. In this instance, there is no evidence to suggest that the Irish as a group threatened to displace members of the host society, and it is difficult to resist the conclusion that resentment was directed at this Irishman's comparative prosperity, deriving from his position as a skilled worker.

To some degree, therefore, attempts to exclude the Irish can be seen as periodic skirmishes in the long-drawn-out battle over control of the workplace. In this context, wage rates were not the only, or necessarily the central, issues of concern. Wages were not mentioned in all cases where clashes took place and were merely one bone of contention in the protracted struggle over workplace control. Moreover, there appears to be no direct link between the volume of immigration and the degree of hostility

---

[57] *Cambrian*, 7 March 1835; Jones, *Before Rebecca*, p.106. A visiting friend on the night of the attack was James Heggarty, a tailor from Varteg.

encountered. In fact, many disturbances occurred where the Irish were in a tiny minority, such as the industrial villages along the heads of the south Wales valleys, where unrest erupted into violence in 1843.[58]

A depression in the iron industry in the area provided the context for anti-Irish disturbances in the villages of Nantyglo and Blaina. A period of simmering discontent and sporadic violence came to a head when the Irish were turned out of their homes, and the houses of those who sheltered them were attacked. Prompted by the severity of these actions, the ironmaster Crawshay Bailey posted notices around the works warning his employees that if they participated the cost of damage to property would be deducted from their wages. Fears that the rioting would spread to other areas led the magistrates to call on the services of police reinforcements from Newport, while the 73rd Regiment of Foot at Pontypool was put on stand-by.[59] Whatever the causes of these events, a widely publicized address to Crawshay Bailey, signed by forty Irishmen, did little to ease tensions in the aftermath of the riots. The language and form of the benediction in the final paragraph suggests that it was drafted by a Catholic priest:

> Respected Sir, – We the undersigned Irishmen employed at Nantyglo, Beaufort, and the Works adjacent, beg leave respectfully to offer you our heartfelt thanks for the prompt, kind and energetic manner in which, on the 26th ult., and on the subsequent days, you protected us, our wives and little ones from the daring threats and outrages of the Blaina rioters.
>
> And, as in duty bound, our gratitude shall be shown by the sobriety and honesty of our conduct, and by the increased diligence with which we shall attend to the various occupations in which you may employ us.
>
> May the Almighty, in His goodness, prosper the works over which you preside with so much ability, and may He bestow upon you his choicest blessings in this life, and eternal happiness in the life to come.[60]

The publication of this document reinforced a view of the Irish as a group of detested interlopers, imported by hard-faced masters specifically to undercut wages.

[58] A contemporary study of Blaenavon, for example, found that the eighty-six Irish immigrants living there comprised no more than 1 per cent of the village's population, compared with nearly 2,000 English, or 38 per cent. See G. S. Kenrick, 'On the parish of Trevethin', *Journal of the Statistical Society of London*, IX (1841), 367, 373.

[59] *Monmouthshire Merlin*, 13 May 1843; *Cardiff and Merthyr Guardian*, 13 May 1843.

[60] *Monmouthshire Merlin*, 13 May 1843. The address is dated Nantyglo, 8 May 1843.

Occurrences of ethnic conflict provide invaluable insights into the distribution of the pre-Famine Irish in south Wales. They also shed a revealing light on relationships at the workplace, a site of struggle and negotiation which is otherwise 'opaque' to the gaze of the historian.[61] The cultural boundaries between different groups were drawn and redrawn according to volatile economic circumstances as well as events outside the workplace. However, not all immigrants were the butt of riotous or violent behaviour, and the geography of conflict did not coincide exactly with those areas which experienced the highest levels of Irish settlement. Workplace conflict was always more common in the iron industry than elsewhere in south Wales, although it was never entirely absent from other industries. Some workplace conflict went unreported in the press. For example, in 1844 work on the new dock at Cardiff was interrupted by disturbances between Welsh and Irish labourers. The only record of the fracas occurs in a private letter by the overseer of the project who averred, 'Whether their Quarrels arose from Repeal Agitation, or their dislike of each other, I cannot say.'[62] In this case, there is no mention of a dispute over wages, but the Welsh did have a long-standing grievance as the Irish were originally imported in order to break a strike by the navvies employed on the project.[63] But these were exceptional circumstances.

By reducing workplace conflicts to a battle over wage rates to the exclusion of other factors, historians have underestimated the significance of wider changes in the patterns of authority and discipline at the point of production. In these early years of industrialization the meaning of work underwent a change whereby it came to denote paid employment only. This change entailed a partial shift in the meaning of work from an exclusive concern with the productive effort itself to the predominant social relationship.[64] Similarly, skill was defined not simply in terms of the technical ability to perform a particular set of tasks, but included assumptions about the cultural attributes of those

---

[61] Clive Behagg, 'Secrecy, ritual and folk violence: the opacity of the workplace in the first half of the nineteenth century', in R. D. Storch (ed.), *Popular Culture and Custom in Nineteenth Century England* (London, 1982).

[62] NLW, Bute Letters, L89/41, J. Evans to Mr Collingdon, 5 February 1844.

[63] John Howells, 'Reminiscences of Cardiff, 1838–40', *The Red Dragon*, V (1884), 232.

[64] Raymond Williams, *Keywords* (2nd edn, London, 1984), *sub* 'work'.

who could be considered skilled workers. 'Outsiders' who achieved positions as skilled workers could be deemed to have transgressed received codes of social justice and thus were perceived to have made themselves open to exclusion, if necessary by force. One of the consequences of this readiness to exclude the Irish has been the construction of an image of them as a footloose lumpenproletariat. Furthermore, by focusing on wages to the exclusion of all else there has been a tendency to obscure the true nature of the immigration, with distinctions between pre-Famine and post-Famine migrations becoming blurred. Evidence for conflicts over wage rates is more convincing for the years during and after the Great Famine of the late 1840s than it is for the preceding period. While distress in the Irish countryside existed before the Famine, migration was not at its heaviest in the poorest areas.[65] Consequently, it can be inferred that in the main the attractive qualities of the expanding economy of south Wales were equally, if not more, important in determining the destination of those who chose to leave Ireland than expulsive forces in that country.

It would be misleading to see pre-Famine Irish migration in terms of a once-and-for-all translation of individuals from their place of origin to a single destination overseas. For harvest labourers migration was a circular movement entailing temporary sojourns at different farms in order to accumulate the optimum amount of cash before returning home. Other groups of mobile workers, such as navvies employed in excavating the docks, canals and railways, shared some of the same characteristics, notably the regular movement from one contract to another. Even those employed at the docks, ironworks and other industrial concerns might move elsewhere in search of new employment or better conditions, as occurred during the depression in the iron trade in 1842. Yet some migrants did settle in south Wales on a permanent basis or for substantial portions of their lives, whether it had been their original intention to do so or not, and it was these who created networks of ethnic institutions which enabled successive waves of migrants to adapt to urban society on their own terms.

---

[65] Cousens, 'The regional variation in emigration from Ireland between 1821 and 1841', 15–30.

II

PRE-FAMINE SETTLEMENT,
SOCIAL LIFE AND POLITICS

In the first half of the nineteenth century, industrial south Wales was an immigrant society *par excellence*. By 1841 a quarter of the population of Glamorgan and a third of that of Monmouthshire had been born outside those counties' boundaries. The nature of the immigrant experience was determined to a large extent by the relationship between two factors: the numbers migrating and the degree to which they settled and clustered together in the new society. A small, tightly knit group practising endogamy might succeed in maintaining a distinctive identity, but the creation and maintenance of a broader spread of ethnic institutions required larger numbers. Moreover, for endogamy to become the norm, something approaching a balance between the sexes among the Irish was imperative. By clustering together in the same tenements, streets and neighbourhoods, immigrants increased the likelihood of encountering one another in their everyday lives and thus made the creation of ethnic networks and of their own distinctive institutions a more viable enterprise. The extent to which this occurred in Wales before the Great Famine can be gauged by an examination of the settlement patterns, institutional life and politics of the immigrant community.

When the census of 1841 – the first to record the birth-place of the people – was published, it revealed a pattern of Irish settlement in Wales that was to continue in broad outline throughout the century. In that year, 8,201 Irish-born people were enumerated in the thirteen Welsh counties, accounting for a mere 0.8 per cent of the population of Wales as a whole.[1] This figure represented only those born in Ireland and did not include their children if born elsewhere. Even so, the number was small

---

[1] The figures used here include the county of Monmouth. Confusingly, tables in the published census failed to include the statistics for Monmouthshire under 'Wales', including them instead under 'England'. This means that where the census refers to either 'England' or 'Wales' separately, both figures are incorrect. The correct statistics are unravelled in Appendix I below.

when compared with the statistics for the Irish-born in Scotland and England. In 1841, 126,321 Irish-born people were enumerated as living in Scotland, while England was home to 281,203 Irish-born residents. Even when considered in percentage terms, the immigration to those countries was heavier, accounting for 4.8 per cent and 1.9 per cent of the Scottish and English populations respectively. However, the impact of the Irish presence was possibly more localized in Wales than elsewhere in Britain, with ten of the thirteen Welsh counties containing an Irish-born population of less than 0.4 per cent. (The rural border county of Radnorshire, for example, had only thirty-three Irish-born inhabitants in 1841.) Monmouthshire and Glamorgan accounted for three-quarters of all Irish immigrants to Wales. Even within these counties the Irish population was clearly localized. At Cardiff the 965 Irish-born represented 10.7 per cent of the borough's total population and nearly a third of Glamorgan's Irish population. Other significant concentrations of Irish immigrants in the county were to be found in the towns of Merthyr Tydfil and Swansea, while the remainder were distributed among the smaller industrial villages. In Monmouthshire, 87 per cent of the Irish-born were to be found in two enumeration districts, those containing and surrounding the town of Newport.

Given the nature of industrial development in Wales, it is hardly surprising that greater numbers of Irish men than women were attracted to Wales. Before 1841 statistical evidence concerning the sex ratio among Irish immigrants is scarce and fragmentary, but a record made by a Catholic priest who visited Rhymney to celebrate Mass in the wake of the riot of 1826 demonstrates that women were part of the migration from the outset: of the ninety-nine Irish names he recorded, fourteen were female.[2] When the census of 1841 was published, it revealed that female immigration was more substantial, accounting for a little more than two-fifths of the total. When determining his 'laws of migration' later in the century, E. G. Ravenstein would claim that 'Woman is a greater migrant than man'; that women accounted for a relatively low proportion of the Irish in Britain

---

[2] 'The Catholic registers of Abergavenny, Mon., 1740–1838' in *Publications of the Catholic Record Society*, XXVII, *Miscellanea* (London, 1927), pp.208–9.

should not, he believed, obscure the scale of female emigration.[3]
The discrepancy between the sexes was most pronounced in the
15–35 age range, a group from which industry derived the vast
majority of its male labourers. In fact, general labourers
accounted for nearly half the occupied Irish-born males at
Swansea in 1841, and more than half of those at Newport.
Nevertheless, the Irish were not an undifferentiated mass. Those
engaged in skilled occupations – including shoemakers, tailors,
masons, coppermen, blacksmiths and carpenters – made up a
significant proportion of the remainder. As the census enumerators were not required to list the occupations of women who
lived in a household with a male head, the evidence on female
employment is more fragmentary. Some worked as domestic
servants and dressmakers, and there was the occasional female
schoolteacher, but the majority of women engaged in waged
work probably earned a living as hawkers, dealers or labourers.
The decisive preponderance of Irish males over females inevitably determined the shape of immigrant social and cultural life.

Some occupational groups stand out. Most notable in this
respect is the military. Between 1830 and 1870 Ireland
contributed a disproportionate number of men to the ranks of
the British army, usually accounting for some 50,000 'other
ranks'. At Newport the military accounted for a significant
proportion of occupied Irish males in 1841: some seventy-five
Irish men, or 14.34 per cent of Irish men whose occupations are
listed in the census, were employed in some capacity by the
army. To a large extent, Newport was an exceptional case, as the
memory of the armed Chartist rising of 1839 was still very much
alive and the continuing presence of a garrison can be seen as an
insurance against the re-emergence of armed struggle in the
town's hinterland; but there were also smaller numbers of Irish
soldiers at Swansea in 1841 and a contingent at Pembroke Dock
in 1842.[4] A soldier's destination and duration of residence in a

[3] E. G. Ravenstein, 'The laws of migration', *Journal of the Statistical Society*, XLVIII
(1885), 196.
[4] David Fitzpatrick, ' "A peculiar tramping people": The Irish in Britain, 1801–70',
in W. E. Vaughan (ed.), *A New History of Ireland*, vol.V (Oxford, 1989), p.641; census
enumerators' books; Thomas Sisk to Bishop Brown, 21 April 1842, AAC, box 119. The
eleven Irish soldiers at Swansea comprised 5.36 per cent of the town's occupied adult
Irish males in 1841.

particular town were determined by military requirements and militated against putting down roots outside Ireland.

By 1841 a small but influential Irish middle class was already in existence in Newport, a group for whom marriage to non-Irish women appears to have been the norm. The local press was owned by an Irishman, Edward Dowling, who employed an Irish reporter, and there were several Irish merchants, shopkeepers, an excise officer, a land surveyor, a coalshipper and a surgeon. Well integrated into the public life of the town, these people were probably Protestant in religion, and it is questionable whether they identified themselves with the majority of lower-status Irish men and women living around them. One of the few recorded examples of these well-to-do immigrants jumping to the aid of the working-class Irish was seen in the wake of the Chartist rising at Newport in November 1839 when Dowling's newspaper staunchly defended them as loyal and law-abiding citizens whose heads had not been turned by talk of sedition.[5] On a day-to-day basis, however, it is unlikely that there was much contact between the well-to-do Irish and the remainder of their poorer compatriots. Their position in society was determined by class rather than an identification with the lower-class Irish.

To migrants from a peasant society, migration entailed risks as well as new opportunities for employment and higher wages. In rural Ireland, potato plots had provided an indispensable source of nutritious food for the peasantry. Under the conacre system, a labourer offered the farmer labour in exchange for use of a small plot of land. Without recourse to this non-financial resource, Irish migrants were forced to rely on monetary contributions from each member of the family. Evidence gathered by a government commission inquiring into the condition of women and children in the mines in 1842 underlines the precariousness of life of some immigrants and the poor standard of living which they were often compelled to endure. Timothy McCarthy, a 'filler' whose work entailed shovelling lime, coke and minestone into the furnaces at the Blaenavon Ironworks in Monmouthshire,

---

[5] *Monmouthshire Merlin*, 23 November 1839. The accuracy of this claim is discussed below. Newspaper editors and journalists are difficult to place in class terms as pay tended to be low, as was their social status until the 1850s. See Aled Gruffydd Jones, *Press, Politics and Society: A History of Journalism in Wales* (Cardiff, 1993), pp.55–60.

described the harsh reality of interdependence between parents and children among a family to produce a living wage:

> I have a large family, six here and one in Ireland; I have two boys working with me here – Thomas, 10 years old, and Timothy, 14 years old; they help in pushing the barrows called 'dandies' back and forward to the top of the furnace. Tom is rather young to come to work, but I don't put him to do much, and I have a large family, and am obliged to put them to do something as soon as they are able; he has not been to work long, not a year; if I had not had him I should be obliged to employ a boy, which I could not afford.[6]

Young children found a niche in industry at an early age and soon became inured to the hard work demanded of them. Patrick Phlin, who was 'near 11 years old', was employed as a refiner's assistant at the British Iron Company's works at Abersychan. 'The work is hot sometimes', he said, 'but it is not hard; I like it very well. I have tended masons, it is no harder than that.'[7] That a child of his age could refer so casually to a varied work experience is indicative of the extent to which families were pressed to rely on children to augment their earnings.

Nor should the importance of strategies for reducing the proportion of earnings spent on rent – such as sharing accommodation with other families and accepting lodgers – be underestimated. In industrial Wales the comparatively low wages of many Irish labourers and the decreasing availability of waged work for women meant that the family economy was a fragile construct. Should accident or death befall the principal wage-earner, the rest of the family might have to resort to vagrancy or fall on the mercy of often unsympathetic poor law authorities. A significant proportion of Irish vagrants appear to have been workers and their families who had been pauperized by illness, bereavement, desertion, or changes in the job market brought about by cyclical depression in industry. In addition, the Irish were adversely affected by periodic attacks on the system of outdoor relief for paupers.

[6] PP 1842 XV, First Report from the Commission of Inquiry into the Employment and Condition of Children in the Mines and Manufactures, p.616.
[7] Ibid., p.604.

The significance of the actions of local guardians was seen in the concerted attempt to remove the Irish who were chargeable to the borough of Newport in 1839. In these cases a long period of residence in Wales was no defence against summary removal. The case of John Grannin provides a good illustration. He had left Ireland eighteen years previously, spending twelve of them in Newport where he had married, yet in January 1839 he was removed to Ireland because he was unable to obtain employment 'on account of distress'.[8] In this context it is hardly surprising that more recent arrivals received short shrift. In April 1839 William Cleary, who had left County Tipperary three years previously, found himself unemployed with a pregnant wife and two children; they, too, were removed to Ireland.[9] Before a removal could be authorized, vagrants had to be examined formally about their circumstances and the information thus collected formed the basis on which a warrant was issued. These brief depositions sometimes provide a tantalizing insight into the unsettled life of the poor migrant. In January 1839, Bridget Horgan, a single woman, told of how she had left Ireland two months previously and travelled to Bristol to find employment in service:

> I staid [sic] at Bristol about a week and then came to this town [Newport] where I have been about seven weeks. I sold my clothes to find me the means of subsistence. The cloak I have now on my back is not my own. I borrowed it to come here . . . I have never been in service in this town. I have no means of subsistence.[10]

The removal of these Irish men and women and many others from Newport during 1839 was the outcome of months of correspondence between the local Poor Law Guardians and Whitehall as well as the consideration of reports outlining the practices followed at Bristol and Liverpool. In the end it was concluded that Monmouthshire could learn little of value from Liverpool because that port had a daily steamer trade with Ireland whereas Newport did not. Sir Digby Mackworth's report to the Quarter Sessions recommended that magistrates should

---

[8] Gw. RO, Q/O.R. 71–0005.
[9] Gw. RO, Q/O.R. 71–0036.
[10] Gw. RO, Q/O.R. 71–0006.

'look carefully into the cases of the Individual paupers presented to them for removal, and to remove none but such as have become legally chargeable on a parish for their maintenance; and not merely the casual vagrant Poor'.[11] It is difficult to tell whether the evidence of removals from Newport in 1839 is representative of the type of cases found elsewhere, but if they are, then widowhood, desertion and pregnancy were among the principal life crises compelling women to seek assistance from the poor law authorities. In January 1839 Ellen Sullivan was removed from Newport to Ireland after trying in vain to find her husband:

> I came into this town about four weeks ago, I slept here one night. I went from here to Tredegar Iron Works. I remained there four nights and four days. I then came back here and went to Bristol. I returned from Bristol to this Town and remained here three days and three nights. I again went up to Tredegar Iron Works. I have been all the time in search of my husband. I came here today the last time. I have no means of subsistence.[12]

Similarly, Ellen Long, who had been deserted by her husband, was removed in September 1839, by which time she was 'far advanced in a state of pregnancy and in a destitute state', while Bridget Collins was left destitute by her husband with two sick infants to care for.[13] Widows were removed irrespective of the duration of their sojourn in Britain. Mary McCarthy and her four children were removed to Ireland in February 1839 following the death of her husband, despite having lived in Wales for fifteen years.[14]

However, it would be a mistake to see the Irish solely as victims battered and buffeted by conditions outside their control. Some at least took measures to ameliorate their condition and improve their prospects. Friendly societies were a popular means of guarding against the financial burdens which befell working people at times of hardship, such as when accidents occurred at work or a family member died. Regular contributions were

---

[11] Gw. RO, Q/O.R. 66–0019, 5 October 1838. For the documentation on Liverpool, see files Q/O.R. 66–0016/7/8 and Q/O.R. 66–0025/6/7.

[12] Gw. RO, Q/O.R. 71–0007.

[13] Gw. RO, Q/O.R. 71–0036 and Q/O.R. 71–0012.

[14] Gw. RO, Q/O.R. 71–0002.

added to a fund for providing assistance when unpredictable misfortunes prevented a member from working. In addition to their economic *raison d'être*, membership of these societies entailed the acceptance of particular values and behavioural norms – sobriety, self-help, thrift, loyalty to the constitution, and an Irish patriotism based on 'brotherly affection' between nations. Club rooms were located in the more respectable public houses, not the seedier beerhouses which were noted for their disorderly conduct. Formal celebrations and parades were held on festivals, especially St Patrick's Day, when members wore their best clothes and attended Mass at the local Catholic church before repairing to their club room for refreshments. Onlookers repeatedly expressed their surprise at the respectable demeanour of the participants.

Irish friendly societies were akin in spirit to those of the host society and adapted their rituals to the needs and preoccupations of the immigrants. As early as 16 October 1830, Dennis McCarthy of Newport deposited with the clerk of the peace a copy of the rules of the Hibernian Liberal Benefit Society which met at the Ship on Launch public house. These rules were described as being 'in all *material* respects a copy of the Rules of a Brotherly Society called "the ancient Briton Society" '.[15] A report in 1837 suggests that St Patrick's Day was an established festival in the town,

> being celebrated with more than usual display . . . Irishmen assembled at an early hour in the morning at their club room, wearing sashes of green and displaying in rich profusion, the shamrock . . . Shortly after 11 o'clock they went in procession, headed by a green banner . . . and proceeded to the Catholic Chapel where Divine Service was celebrated. Afterwards an excellent band playing national airs, accompanied them on march through the town . . . They then returned to Bush Inn Commercial Street to an excellent dinner, taken with hilarity and humour which characterises the fellowship of natives of the Green Isle over the flowing bowl. Full justice was done to the memory of St Patrick, while the claims of living benefactors to Ireland were not forgotten.[16]

---

[15] Gw. RO, Q.S./F.S.R. 17.3. In January 1831 this society met at the Ship and Pilot Boat Inn. See J. T. Pratt, *A List of the Friendly Societies in the County of Monmouth* (London, 1856), p.21.

[16] Quoted in *St Peter's Magazine*, April 1924, 112.

The following year, a St Patrick's Club in the town celebrated its patron saint's day 'with their accustomed fervour', with a procession led by a band, attendance at the Catholic chapel and a dinner at the club room in the Bush Inn.[17] The festival was celebrated in a similar manner the following year when participants were dressed in their 'holiday suits' and presented 'a very respectable appearance', while some carried banners on which were displayed 'appropriate mottoes and devices'.[18] These characteristics represent the template adhered to by this and similar societies for the remainder of the century. In 1840 a public dinner in honour of St Patrick's Day was inaugurated at Newport, supported by the newspaper proprietor Edward Dowling. It brought together Irish and local 'gentlemen', and the initiative was praised as a token of 'the progressive spirit of fraternal regard evinced by the gentlemen of Monmouthshire towards their Irish fellow-citizens'.[19]

By 1839 the Newport Irish boasted two friendly societies. A Hibernian Independent Benefit Society, which met at the Daniel O'Connell Inn, was enrolled in May of that year, and a Hibernian Friendly Society was enrolled two months later.[20] Newport was not the only town in Wales where such societies were established, although it provides the earliest examples. A Hibernian Benefit Society met at the British Lion Inn, Abersychan, near Pontypool, from December 1839 and went from strength to strength over the following twenty years.[21] At Cardiff there is no evidence of a permanent organization until 1845, when the Hibernia Liberal Benefit Society of Tradesmen and Others was established;[22] although it would appear that Irish workers brought over to excavate the Bute Dock in the late 1830s had established a system whereby each man would pay 3d. weekly into a general fund for relieving the sick and burying the dead. 'In cases of sickness or accident', it was observed, 'they always succoured each other, with a generous promptitude that

---

[17] *Monmouthshire Merlin*, 24 March 1838.
[18] *Monmouthshire Merlin*, 23 March 1839.
[19] Quoted in *St. Peter's Magazine*, April 1924, 112.
[20] Pratt, *Friendly Societies*, p.22; P.P. 1842 XXXVI, A Return Relating to Friendly Societies Enrolled in the Several Counties of England and Wales, p.27.
[21] Pratt, *Friendly Societies*, p.3; *Monmouthshire Merlin*, 23 August 1856.
[22] P.P 1883 LXVII, Reports of the Chief Registrar of Friendly Societies, Appendix I, p.1042.

would have done honour to any class.'[23] Informal arrangements of this kind could well have established the habit of thrift over several years preceding the legal enrolment of a society, and in a large number of cases societies did not bother to enrol at all.[24]

Annual festivities included exhortations by the parish priest to moderate behaviour and adopt a respectable mien. In 1842, for example, Fr Metcalfe of Newport preached on the subject of 'enforcing the principles of sobriety, brotherly affection, obedience to the laws and loyalty'. It would appear that his audience took this counsel to heart, as on that occasion the evening festivities were spent 'cheerfully and temperately together . . . hilarity was so well blended with moderation, even by the lowest classes of Milesians in the town, that the improvement is a subject of very general remark'.[25] Similar sentiments were expressed when eighty-eight members of the town's True Hibernian Sisters Liberal Benefit Society met to celebrate their anniversary at the Wexford and Kinsale Arms in August 1844. This society, as well as the Daughters of Erin Liberal Benefit Society which was enrolled at Newport in 1844,[26] provided an opportunity for Irish women to socialize outside the home among women from a similar background as well as supplying a mutual-benefit scheme. To this extent the society's existence is evidence of a degree of financial and social independence from the men's societies and a logical extension of the ideology of self-help and personal 'independence' expounded enthusiastically by the friendly society movement and its supporters. This was not how everyone viewed the actions of the women's societies and in this case the family was considered to take precedence. 'This sisterhood', commented the *Monmouthshire Merlin* in patronizing tone, 'cherish their husbands and families, love their neighbours, respect the laws of moral society, and mind their own business.'[27]

[23] *Monmouthshire Merlin*, 13 February 1847. The navvies arrived without their families but soon saved enough from their wages to send for them. See John Howells, 'Reminiscences of Cardiff, 1838–40', *The Red Dragon*, V (1884), 232.

[24] See Dot Jones, 'Did friendly societies matter? A study of friendly societies in Glamorgan, 1794–1910', *Welsh History Review*, 12, No. 3 (1985), 324–49.

[25] *Monmouthshire Merlin*, 19 March 1842.

[26] Pratt, *Friendly Society*, p.23. The Daughters of Erin Liberal Benefit Society met at the Odd Fellows' Arms Inn.

[27] *Monmouthshire Merlin*, 17 August 1844. On the women's movement in general, see Dot Jones, 'Self-help in nineteenth century Wales: the rise and fall of the female friendly society', *Llafur*, 6, 1 (1984), 14–26.

The models of behavioural rectitude embodied in the aims and mores of friendly societies provided ideals to which many aspired but few succeeded in fully realizing on all occasions. Sobriety was an important theme in the discourse of those who sought to 'improve' the working class. Drunkenness was equated with a lack of self-discipline at a time when an industrial economy demanded of its workers regular behaviour and reliable time-keeping. The attempt to make the workforce a calculable factor of production depended on the eradication of pre-industrial attitudes to drink and sociability which often led to an extension of the 'weekend' into Monday. And yet friendly societies invariably met and conducted their business in public houses and were to some extent dependent on them. It is this which explains in part the emphasis on moderate drinking rather than total abstinence in the associational life of these societies.

At a time when few other venues for secular recreational activities existed, public houses assumed a central role in social life. However, a clear distinction was drawn between the status accorded the more organized and disciplined social life focused on the public house and that which revolved around the beer-houses which proliferated in industrial Wales in the wake of the Beer Act of 1830. Many working-class families took advantage of this new legislation – which was designed to make beer both accessible and cheap – and moved into the new trade. While many beerhouse keepers were beyond reproach, their houses were frequently seen as the breeding-ground of political sedition and the resort of criminals and other undesirables.[28]

It was customary to ascribe Irish criminal activity to an inherent weakness of character combined with an alleged in-ability to cope with strong drink. Consequently, their beerhouses in Welsh towns became the objects of police supervision. The *Monmouthshire Merlin* was representative of contemporary opinion when it stated confidently in 1840 that 'many of the crimes of the Irishman proceed from the use of ardent spirits'.[29] The opening hours of beerhouses were more strictly circumscribed than those of public houses, and the authorities used this as a pretext for

---

[28] W. R. Lambert, *Drink and Sobriety in Victorian Wales, c.1820–1895* (Cardiff, 1983), pp.18–19.
[29] *Monmouthshire Merlin*, 28 March 1840; see also 'Illicit distillation', in K. H. Connell, *Irish Peasant Society* (Oxford, 1968), pp.17–18, 21–2, 46.

keeping a watchful eye on Irish beerhouses in particular. At Cardiff in July 1841, for example, the police entered the Shamrock beer house on one occasion at 12.30 a.m. when they found twelve people drinking and smoking, while in November 1845 the mayor had cause to admonish the owners of the Waterford and Wexford Arms beerhouse in Whitmore Lane and the Hibernia beerhouse in Trinity Street for similar offences.[30]

Conformity to the ideals of temperance and respectability was encouraged by middle-class opinion, but such ideals also provided immigrants with the materials to construct their own ethnic identity rather than simply accepting unquestioningly the negative images prevalent in the host society. Parades on festival days and municipal occasions supplied the opportunities for the Irish to make public displays of their adherence to the values of self-reliance and good order. This point was driven home by the presence of 150 members of the Hibernian Society in the parade through Newport to celebrate the opening of the new dock in October 1842. Those 'Hibernians' parading were the equivalent of some 16 per cent of the entire Irish-born male population of the town, although some may have been second-generation Irish. Members were bedecked in green scarves and carried banners, one of which proclaimed: 'May justice to Ireland cement love between the Sister Isles', and it was observed that they were second only to the Oddfellows in number and respectability.[31] Such public demonstrations are evidence of the presence of some immigrants with a more settled mentality, demonstrating a willingness to invest both financially and culturally in a future in south Wales.

The priest's role in the celebrations of friendly societies is a reminder that the Catholic church was the immigrant institution most readily associated with the Irish. In fact, adherence to that religion has usually been accepted as the quintessential badge of the immigrants' ethnicity. Although it remained the religion of a tiny minority in Wales, Catholicism experienced a startling rate of growth in the early nineteenth century. Between 1773 and 1839 the number of practising Catholics in Wales increased by 735 per cent, compared with an increase of 212 per cent in England over the same period. From the 1820s the increase was

---

[30] Glam. RO, D/Dx Ha (5/8). Notes from Cardiff Police Journal, 17 July 1841 and 16, 22 November 1845.
[31] *Monmouthshire Merlin*, 22 October 1842.

almost completely attributable to the influx of Irish workers, who outnumbered native Catholics by then. The emergence of an Irish Catholicism in a country whose popular religious culture was expressed predominantly through Welsh-speaking Protestant Nonconformity served to define denominational constituencies on ethnic lines. Consequently, it was possible to be 'Catholic' by association as well as by practice in nineteenth-century Wales. Under these circumstances, the church should have been well-placed to set about the onerous task of building churches, establishing parish networks and asserting its structures of discipline and authority among the migrants. Only by achieving this could it ensure that Catholic values were transmitted from generation to generation.

Catholic chapels or churches were concrete symbols of a rooted Irish presence and the priest frequently took it upon himself to act as the immigrants' spokesman in both secular and religious matters. This was particularly the case as native Catholics were few in number and largely restricted to rural areas along the English border, where they clustered in congregations connected with long-established landed families such as the Herberts of Llanarth and the Mostyns of Talacre. With the church's resources and personnel concentrated in these places, the provision of services for the Irish who worked at industrial concerns was no mean task. The first problem faced by the church in ministering to the Irish was that of locating them. Outside the large towns Catholicism enjoyed a precarious existence and its fortunes fluctuated according to changes in the demand for labour. In 1819 Fr James Fleetwood wrote to his bishop: 'with respect to the mission in the neighbourhood of Pyle, there are not above twenty Irishmen since the completion of the railway.' This itinerant priest attended to the spiritual needs of the navv:es employed in the 1820s on the excavation of Porthcawl Dock where he said Mass in a joiner's shop, but by 1825 the work had ceased and the men had dispersed.[32] It was not until the riot broke out at Gelligaer in 1826 that the nearest clergy became aware of an Irish presence there and despatched a priest to celebrate Mass on St Patrick's Day.[33]

---

[32] J. B. Dockery, *Collingridge: A Franciscan Contribution to Catholic Emancipation* (Newport, 1934), p.138; *St Peter's Magazine*, V (1925), 206.

[33] 'The Catholic Registers of Abergavenny, Mon., 1740–1838', in *Publications of the Catholic Record Society*, XXVII, *Miscellanea* (London, 1927).

Economic fluctuations could affect religion in the larger settlements also. At Merthyr Tydfil in the 1820s repeated attempts were made to establish a permanent congregation. Few priests were willing to shoulder this awesome responsibility in such an uncongenial and uncertain environment. At least one priest refused to serve the area and there was opposition from the Irish of neighbouring Varteg when it was rumoured that their own priest, an Irish-speaker, would be moved to the town. One of the problems facing a priest at Merthyr was the vast area under his care. The parish covered iron and coal mining country of difficult terrain some twenty-six miles in length, and the congregation could not provide resources for buying and maintaining a horse. In 1827 it was reported that there were approximately 300 Irish men and women at Merthyr, including the outposts of Tredegar and Sirhywi, of whom only 188 contributed to the upkeep of the mission.[34]

When Fr Patrick Portal from Waterford became Merthyr's resident priest in 1827, he found the mission 'severe and disagreeable'. Members of the congregation were either incapable or unwilling to contribute to the establishment of a place of worship and few could understand why he should make personal sacrifices on their behalf. Although he found that all the respectable shopkeepers were 'more than ordinarily civil' to him, the condition and lack of prospects of this mission progressively undermined his spirits. 'Nothing here', he lamented, 'but hardship when out and solitude at home!'[35] Following the departure of many of the Irish during the upheaval created by the Merthyr rising of 1831, Portal left for Newport. These problems were highlighted by the experience of Fr J. M. Carroll at Merthyr Tydfil. Arriving from Dublin in 1835, he experienced similar difficulties to those of his predecessor. By all accounts, Carroll was an enterprising individual who eked out his living by selling salt fish and retailing vegetables grown in his own garden, but he was no more optimistic about his flock's attitude to the church than Portal had been. 'If they contribute anything to the intended new Chapel', he reported dejectedly in 1841, 'it is

[34] Dockery, *Collingridge*, p.146; Donald Attwater, *The Catholic Church in Modern Wales* (London, 1935), p.66; *St Peter's Magazine*, VII (1927), 3.
[35] Attwater, *Catholic Church*, pp.70–1.

deducted from what a few were in the habit of contributing monthly for the support of the Priest, the newcomers mostly declaring that they do not care whether Mass is said here or not, whilst others refuse to subscribe.'[36]

Attempts to establish a Catholic mission at Cardiff in the 1820s met with similar problems. In 1825 the dozen Irish Catholics in the town requested the occasional services of a priest from Merthyr, some twenty-five miles distant. This arrangement persisted until the end of the 1830s when Cardiff experienced a large influx of Irish workers and their families to excavate the new Bute Dock. As Mass was celebrated in private houses or a public house because of the poverty of the mission, the extra numbers made a dedicated place of worship a necessity if the clergy were to persuade them to attend.[37] Bishop Baines supported an appeal in the Catholic press for funds for the Cardiff mission in 1838, emphasizing that it was intended 'to erect an edifice of the most economical kind, with no other pretensions than to provide for the spiritual necessities of the poor congregation'. However, the appeal appears not to have been successful because in 1839, when the first resident priest was sent to Cardiff, Bishop Brown made a second appeal 'to save the missioner at Cardiff from being forced to sell, before it was a fact, the pig on which he had to reckon for rent of his humble residence'.[38] In 1841 there were only 114 Easter communicants – Easter Communion being the minimum duty required of a practising Catholic – in a notional Catholic population of 1,200.[39]

The Catholic church's experience at both Merthyr and Cardiff underlines the importance of a core of practising lay people for the maintenance of a mission during these years. Where a group of this kind was absent, it was difficult to maintain a resident priest, while the vagaries of the trade cycle or political upheaval could result in the church's temporarily

---

[36]   Fr J. M. Carroll to Bishop Brown, 7 September 1841, AAC. Reproduced in J. S. Williams, 'The origins and subsequent development of Roman Catholic education in the "Heads of the Valleys" region', unpublished University of Wales M.Ed. thesis (1974), 79.

[37]   See Fr Signini's reminiscences in *St Peter's Magazine* (1924), 265–7.

[38]   G. J. J. Lynch, 'The revival of Roman Catholicism in south Wales in the late eighteenth and early nineteenth centuries', unpublished University of Wales MA thesis (1941), 202–3.

[39]   Fr Signini's reminiscences in *St Peter's Magazine* (1924).

withdrawing a priest from a particular town, requiring it to found the mission afresh when conditions improved. At Newport, on the other hand, the mission had become established more securely and there is some evidence of a more successful attempt to evangelize the Irish in the town. Since 1809 it had been seen as a base from which Catholic activity in south Wales could be launched, being a port attracting Irish immigrants in close proximity to the rural centres of Welsh Catholicism. A proper place of worship was built at an early date and Catholic poor-schools were set up. Part of the church's success in the locality in the early years can be attributed to the co-operation between the Irish and the town's few Welsh Catholics. Newport's growth and success as a centre of Catholicism in the region were such that in 1850 Bishop Brown made it the seat of the new diocese of Newport and Menevia.[40]

Not all priests reported a lukewarm response. In 1824, a Welsh Franciscan, Fr Edward Richards, found the Irish at both Maesteg and Bridgend in Glamorgan to be 'eminent propagandists of the Faith'.[41] But this was a minority view. In some cases, the picture of an indifferent laity derived from the intense frustration and self-sacrifice of a clergy fired by missionary zeal at discovering that the objects of their enthusiasm had not lived up to expectations. Priests invariably wrote in withering tones of the lack of co-operation on the part of the Irish and the latter's 'insolent' response to requests for financial help. The overwhelming body of evidence suggests that the majority of Irish immigrants were indifferent to organized religion in this period. Fr Portal reported in 1827 that many of the Irish at Merthyr had neglected their religious duties for between three and ten years, 'so that I have much to do with them'.[42] At Swansea in 1835, a newly ordained English priest discovered that the Irish resident in the town 'have not confessed for 2, 3, or 4 years, and yet they have nothing to tell you'. His questioning revealed that 'they don't say their prayers or come to chapel'.[43] At the same town in 1842, Fr Kavanagh maintained that 'no one will come to Mass

[40] Dockery, *Collingridge*, p.134; Lynch, 'The revival of Roman Catholicism', 152–60a.
[41] Attwater, *The Catholic Church*, p.70.
[42] Lynch, 'The revival of Roman Catholicism', 192.
[43] Quoted in Gerard Connolly, 'Irish and Catholic: myth or reality?', in Roger Swift and Sheridan Gilley (eds.), *The Irish in the Victorian City* (London, 1985), pp.227–8.

on Sundays who is not absolutely obliged to do so', and backed his statement with figures showing that of the 400–600 Catholics in the area, only 120 took Easter Communion.[44] In the same year, the Irish employed at Pembroke Dock were tellingly described as 'concealed Catholics'.[45]

The unresponsiveness of the majority of Irish immigrants to organized religion was not the product of cultural disorientation arising from emigration. While many of the Irish were baptized Catholics, they had been to a large degree 'unchurched' before leaving home. The Catholic Counter-Reformation in Ireland had been singularly ineffective in its attempts to enforce a code of religious observance based on regular attendance at mass and participation in the sacraments. This failure, combined with the restrictive context created by penal legislation discriminating against Catholics resulted in a situation where the proportion of priests to lay Catholics in Ireland by 1800 was 1:2,100. This ratio had, if anything, worsened by the 1840s under the pressure of the great increase in population. Pre-Famine church attendance was possibly as low as a third of the Catholic population, although there were significant regional variations. Either there were not enough churches, or not enough places in those which did exist, to accommodate all. This picture did not change until after the Great Famine.[46]

Despite this background, the Catholic Church in Britain regarded the Irish as potential saviours of an ailing cause. In spite of the poor condition of the missions, the apparent indifference of the Irish and the inadequacy of places of worship, there was increasing optimism among senior clergy that a sea-change in the fortunes of Catholicism was imminent. To this end, Bishop T. J. Brown was appointed vicar apostolic of the newly created Welsh District in 1840, a diocese carved out of the unmanageable Western District of England and Wales which had included the

---

[44] Fr Kavanagh to Bishop Brown, 11 August 1842, AAC, unnumbered box.
[45] Thomas Sisk to Bishop Brown, 21 April 1842, AAC, box 119.
[46] John Bossy, 'The Counter-Reformation and the people of Catholic Ireland, 1596–1641', in T. D. Williams (ed.), *Historical Studies* VIII (Dublin, 1971), pp.155–69; Emmet Larkin, 'The devotional revolution in Ireland, 1850–75', *American Historical Review*, 77 (1972), 626, 636; David W. Millar, 'Irish Catholicism and the Great Famine', *Journal of Social History*, IX (1975). For an approach which suggests change over a longer time span, see Thomas McGrath, 'The Tridentine evolution of modern Irish Catholicism, 1563–1962: a re-examination of the "devotional revolution" thesis', *Recusant History*, 20, 4 (1991).

counties of south-west England as well as the whole of Wales.
(The 'Welsh District' included the English county of Herefordshire.) Brown set about his task with an enthusiasm disciplined by
a realistic appraisal of the problems he faced. In 1839 there were
6,269 practising Catholics in Wales, more than half of whom
lived in Monmouthshire, while three-quarters of the remainder
were to be found in Glamorgan.[47] At the same, time the church
was rediscovering an evangelical stance towards the Irish poor in
the towns. Detailed reports on the condition of the Welsh
Vicariate appeared in the pages of the *Catholic Directory and Annual
Register*. From 1843 this publication was used as a vehicle for
soliciting financial aid from Catholics in the rest of Britain and
beyond. The Society of St David, established in June 1842, was
the formal basis of this appeal and boasted patrons among the old
English landed families. Appealing to the pocket by way of the
heart, readers of the *Register* were reminded that in the counties of
Anglesey, Merioneth, Montgomery, Cardigan, Radnor, Pembroke and Carmarthen, 'Forming a territory a hundred and thirty
miles from north to south and a hundred miles from east to west;
even the meanest covering cannot be found under which a priest
of God may break the bread of life to famishing multitudes.'[48] It
was a successful strategy. By November 1843 the appeal had
realized £1,423 15s. and was augmented by smaller sums in
subsequent years. The application of these funds presented no
problem to the bishop. 'We are advised by venerable authority',
he wrote, 'to look first to the head, and afterwards we shall be
able to throw new life and energy into the body.'[49]

The prudence of concentrating financial resources at a central
repository made sense in the context of an organization with a
clerical hierarchy and congregations acutely vulnerable to the
vicissitudes of the trade cycle. This fact was underlined by the
impact of the trade depression of 1843 in south Wales. Catholic
congregations at Cardiff, Merthyr and Rhymney, Pontypool and
Nantyglo were severely depleted when iron production stagnated
and large numbers of the Irish sought work elsewhere. Individual
missions were financed by the voluntary contributions of those
attending Mass, and had it not been for the bishop's assistance

---

[47] See Appendix I.
[48] *Catholic Directory and Annual Register* (London, 1843), p.102.
[49] *Catholic Directory and Annual Register* (London, 1844), pp.130–1.

from the funds of the Society of St David, a number of missions would have closed.[50] Voluntary contributions from members of the congregations were rarely large enough or sufficiently regular, even at the best of times. Where adequate funds existed small chapels were erected. More frequently, Mass was celebrated in the room of a private house, as at Cardiff, or at an inn, as at Abersychan, Tredegar and Rhymney. This flexible response was not without its own difficulties. Fr Woolett reported in 1844 that the mission at Nantyglo, served from Pontypool, was jeopardized when the owner of the house where Mass was celebrated moved away.[51] Against this background of uncertainty thirteen new places of worship were built and put into service during the 1840s.

Bishop Brown was deeply aware of the fact that the perpetuation of Catholicism among the Irish depended primarily on the transmission of a body of teaching and a moral code. In nineteenth-century Wales, where there existed a plurality of denominations, the maintenance of religious continuity was best achieved through a combination of parental example and Catholic schools. Yet when Brown looked back on the first year of his episcopate, he recalled that in south Wales 'there was not a single school-room fit for its purpose'.[52] In the absence of state provision, religious bodies and private individuals assumed responsibility for elementary education. As the employment of teachers was beyond the meagre resources of most parishes, the resident priest frequently assumed the mantle of teacher. As early as 1842, Fr Carroll alternated between Merthyr Tydfil and Tredegar, teaching a total of sixty children. 'Education makes but little advances', he reported glumly,

> I keep up two day schools, assisted in the expenses by two charitable friends . . . The children of both sexes are employed so early picking or piling minerals or coals. They are removed about seven years of age, which early removal generally deprives them of all taste for instruction.[53]

[50] Ibid., p.71.

[51] *Catholic Directory and Annual Register* (London, 1840), pp.32–3; Thomas Jones, *Rhymney Memories* (Newtown, 1938), p.17; Fr Woolett to Bishop Brown, 31 January 1844, AAC, unnumbered box. As an Irish JP in Wales recalled, 'However strongly we may object to the drink evil, it cannot be denied that our Catholic forebears were glad to use the tavern club-room to assist at Mass when other places were denied them.' James O'Brien, *Old Afan and Margam* (Aberavon, 1926), p.126.

[52] Attwater, *Catholic Church*, p.95.

[53] P.P. 1842 XV, First Report from the Commission of Inquiry into the Employment and Condition of Children in Mines and Manufactories, p.506.

He went on to suggest that schools with a more technical and scientific curriculum would 'tend greatly to elevate the social condition and character of the working classes'. In making this suggestion, Carroll was mindful of the potentially subversive Chartist presence in the area and the increasing importance of Irish issues for British radicals. Denominational schooling was underpinned by the unshakeable belief that the inculcation of literacy could be positively harmful unless firmly located within a sound religious framework.

By 1843 there were four Catholic poor-schools in Wales. Three of these were maintained 'with great difficulty' by the priests at Merthyr, Wrexham and Cardiff; the fourth was probably at Newport where, in 1846, the school boasted an annual income of £46 16s., besides £18 in school pence.[54] Here, again, these enterprises received financial assistance from a diocesan education fund which provided £19 annually.[55] The impact of these fledgling schools on their mainly Irish pupils can be evaluated even less precisely than the sketchy evidence on their funding. An impression of the type of education offered and the proportion of Irish children reached by it can be gleaned from the evidence for Cardiff submitted to the Education Commissioners in their report of 1847. According to Fr Millea, the Italian parish priest, the congregation was composed, with few exceptions, of the poorest of the labouring classes; only eighty or ninety of the 220 children in need of instruction actually attended school. The highest charge levied on a pupil was 4d. per week, but many parents felt that even this sum was beyond their means. There was a common belief among members of the congregation that the most basic ability to read was adequate education in itself, and consequently few would strive for additional instruction. The school used the class books of the National Schools of Ireland and the curriculum included arithmetic, geography and English grammar, as well as some elementary practical skills. Until that time, the school had been held in 'some back place fit for cattle', whereas during 1847 a new and larger school was being constructed.[56]

[54]   *Catholic Directory and Annual Register* (London, 1843), p.43.
[55]   *Catholic Directory and Annual Register* (London, 1846), p.68.
[56]   PP 1847 XXVII, Report of the Commissioners of Inquiry into the State of Education in Wales (Part I), pp.371–2.

In its partial success in attracting Irish children to classes, Cardiff's Catholic school was unexceptional. Infrequent attendance – in some cases any attendance at all – was the single most important factor militating against the schools becoming the bulwark of orthodox Catholicism at this time. As a group, Irish migrants were characterized by high geographical mobility, a factor hardly conducive to a settled education, and Catholic schools could hope to develop only basic literacy and numeracy and inculcate no more than elementary tenets of the Faith. An awareness of these deficiencies strengthened the clergy's commitment to the expansion of educational facilities. Towards the end of the decade, funds were channelled to Wales to construct and support schools through the Catholic Poor School Committee of England and Wales, with Dowlais receiving £20, Wrexham £15, Bangor £15, Abermarlais £10 and Chepstow £20. Capital allowances of £100 and £90 had been made to Pontypool and Swansea respectively. However, as Fr Millea percipiently observed in 1847, an effective education system would need to be free, compulsory and devoid of religious prejudice.[57] It was only under these conditions that Catholic schools could adequately perform their stated function, and those conditions would not obtain until after the passage of the Education Act of 1870.

Thus, despite the comparatively small number of Irish immigrants in Wales, and partly because the majority of them were concentrated in a few towns, a number of institutions closely identified with them or specifically designed to meet their needs came into existence. The variety within Irish social and associational life at this time underlines a plurality of experience which belies the images cultivated by contemporary writers who perceived the Irish as an undifferentiated alien group. By the 1840s Irish immigrants in the major towns of south Wales, and in a smattering of the lesser industrial settlements, had access to a varied, if small, network of ethnic institutions. These included the highly visible presence of the Catholic church and numerous friendly societies and clubs, together with the more shadowy beer-shops which peppered the back-streets and secluded courts

[57]   Ibid.

of the towns. The existence of Irish institutions in Wales is usually taken as evidence of the immigrants' alienation from the host society, a view amply supported by the frequency of anti-Irish disturbances from the 1820s and the growth of Roman Catholicism. Yet, the growth of Irish friendly societies – particularly in Newport – would suggest that some of the Irish shared the same basic values of respectability and self-improvement as Welsh members of friendly societies; for these immigrants, 'alienation' is not an adequate description of their relationship with the host society.

One further arena of contact between the Irish and Welsh society remains to be examined, that of politics. Between 1798 and the rise of Chartism in the 1830s, Irish immigrants were too mobile, too isolated and congregated in groups too small to have any discernible effect on political life in Wales. It has been suggested that during the Reform crisis the Irish supported the Merthyr rising of 1831, when the town was held for several days against troops dispatched to suppress it. However, the single piece of evidence adduced to support this is ambiguous and far too slender a basis from which to extrapolate a wider Irish participation in the town's radical politics.[58] In Ireland during these years the most popular political campaign was that which pressed for Catholic emancipation, culminating in legislation in 1829. Agitation for this measure under the adroit leadership of Daniel O'Connell was primarily an Irish affair, and although the issue was debated keenly in the Welsh press, there is no evidence to suggest that immigrants played a part in either the debate or the campaign.

The attitude of Irish immigrants to political developments in Britain in the first half of the nineteenth century is best measured by their relationship with the Chartist movement.[59] As a mass

[58] J. B. Bruce to Home Secretary, 5 June 1831, PRO, HO 52/16; D. J. V. Jones, *Before Rebecca: Popular Protest in Wales, 1793–1834* (London, 1973), ch. 4; Gwyn A. Williams, *The Merthyr Rising* (London, 1978), pp.150, 160n. It is likely that the Irish moved out of Merthyr *en masse* after the rising, as the town was left without a Catholic priest for two years, 1832–3. Papers of Fr J. M. Cronin, Glam. RO, D/Dxha (4/1).

[59] There is an extensive debate about the contribution of Irish immigrants to Chartism. For a succinct summary, see Graham Davis, *The Irish in Britain, 1815–1914* (Dublin, 1991), ch.5; R. O'Higgins, 'The Irish influence on the Chartist movement', *Past and Present*, 20 (1961); J. H. Treble, 'O'Connor, O'Connell and the attitudes of Irish immigrants towards Chartism in the north of England, 1838–48', in J. Butt and I. F. Clarke (eds.), *The Victorians and Social Protest* (Newton Abbot, 1973); Dorothy Thompson, 'Ireland and the Irish in English radicalism before 1850', in J. Epstein and D. Thompson (eds.), *The Chartist Experience: Studies in Working Class Radicalism and Culture, 1830–1860* (London, 1982).

movement which set out its aims in the form of a charter of democratic rights for all classes in society, and one of the few British movements to lend its support to repeal of the Union between Britain and Ireland, its potential appeal to Irish immigrants is evident. Despite this, Daniel O'Connell, the charismatic leader of the campaigns for Catholic emancipation and repeal of the Union, was hostile to Chartism, and his views carried considerable weight. In this context, therefore, Irish participation in Chartist activities could not be taken for granted.

In Wales, the connection between the Irish and Chartism has focused on events surrounding the abortive Chartist rising in south Wales in November 1839. For many years it was the received wisdom that the Irish had been either blithely indifferent to the movement's activities or, in some cases, actively opposed to them. The belief that ethnic ties were stronger than class consciousness, and that the Irish were predisposed to side with the authorities, largely derived from a report in the *Monmouthshire Merlin* claiming that one hundred Irishmen had enlisted as special constables at Cardiff to defend the town. The loyalty of the Irish was trumpeted by the newspaper, whose editor was an Irishman. In addition, Daniel O'Connell's forthright public condemnation of the rising, stressing the part played by the largely Irish contingent of the 45th Regiment which defended Newport against the Chartist attack, has been interpreted as confirming the general picture. (In private he wrote triumphantly to a friend: 'It was *we* beat the Chartists at Newport. Twenty-eight poor raw Irish lads beat five thousand rebels.')[60] This evidence, together with the fact that only one Irishman was indicted after the rising, has been taken as evidence that the Irish were notable for their absence from movements for social reform. Viewed against the backdrop of ethnic conflict at the workplace mentioned earlier, this conclusion should not be surprising; however, there is evidence to suggest that the immigrants' allegiance was not as clear-cut as was once believed.

The staunchly Protestant second marquis of Bute, who had done everything in his power to prevent the sale of land for a

---

[60] Daniel O'Connell to Richard More O'Ferrall, 29 November 1839, in Maurice R. O'Connell (ed.), *The Correspondence of Daniel O'Connell*, vol.VI, *1837–40* (Dublin, 1982), pp.286–8; *Monmouthshire Merlin*, 23 November 1839; David Williams, *John Frost: A Study in Chartism* (Cardiff, 1939), p.240.

Catholic chapel in Cardiff where he was the principal land-owner, was dismayed to read in the press that a body of Catholic Irishmen had been made special constables and were entrusted with the defence of Cardiff. Placing Catholics in such a position of responsibility clearly offended his religious sensibilities, and he demanded an explanation for the act from the mayor of Cardiff. The latter replied that the 118 special constables sworn in comprised 'the most respectable inhabitants and tradesmen of the Town . . . and a few mechanics who were known to some of the Gentlemen present'. He appended a list of names of those who had been sworn in as evidence of the inaccuracy of reports in the press. In his eagerness to mollify the marquis, he claimed that the list did not include a single Irishman, thereby overlooking 'Chas. McCarthy – Druggist'.[61] Despite this incontrovertible evidence that the Irish had not rushed to defend the town against the Chartists, it would appear that no public attempt was made to correct the misapprehension created by the *Monmouthshire Merlin*, and belief in Irish opposition to Chartism was assiduously cultivated.

The first full narrative of events at Newport appeared in the *Dublin Review* in 1840, in which it was claimed that only two or three Irish people were implicated in the rising and that Irish attitudes could be gauged by the fact that of the sixty persons indicted for treason for their part in the events only one was Irish. The Catholic Church also stressed that the immigrants had stayed at arm's length from Chartism. In March 1840 the vicar apostolic of the Catholic Western District of England and Wales issued a pastoral letter praising the Irish for their industry, devotion to family duties and their stoicism in the face of revolt. More than sixty years later, a Catholic guidebook to Newport would describe melodramatically how the Catholic chapel, under construction in 1839, was saved from the Chartists by divine providence.[62] Yet much of this, too, was based on the misleading impressions conveyed by inaccurate newspaper stories.

---

[61]   Charles C. Williams to the marquis of Bute, 18 December 1839, Cardiff Central Library, Bute Papers, box XX, No.137. Some Cardiff Catholics travelled to London to ask Daniel O'Connell to put their case about land for a chapel to Bute, but he was intransigent. *Monmouthshire Merlin*, 21 December 1839.

[62]   Anon., 'The history of the rise and fall of Chartism in Monmouthshire', *Dublin Review*, VIII (1840), p.285; *Monmouthshire Merlin*, 7 March 1840; *The Official Guidebook of the 16th Annual Conference of the Catholic Truth Society* (Newport, 1902), p.81.

One of the problems in trying to assess whether there was an Irish presence among the thousands who marched on Newport in 1839 is our inability to identify the faces in the crowd. Given the fact that the precise number of those killed during the disturbances is uncertain because relatives of some dead men were seen taking the bodies away for secret burial, it is unlikely that Irish participants would have boasted of their presence in the aftermath of the event. Nevertheless, one observer hinted strongly that some of the Irish working at Tredegar had marched with the Chartists. On hearing news of the events at Newport on the morning following the rising, Lady Charlotte Guest of Dowlais travelled across the heads of the Valleys to Tredegar where she witnessed the undisguised grief of Irish women lamenting the possible fate of their absent husbands.[63] Moreover, there had been Irish Chartists at Newport from the outset. A Working Men's Association was formed in the town in the summer of 1838, and by January 1839 it boasted 340 card-carrying Chartist members. Among the early officers of the Association was Richard Rorke, a veteran of the Irish Rebellion of 1798 who was believed by *The Times* to have been 'mixed up very considerably with Whiteboyism'. When questioned about his activities, Rorke staunchly maintained that he was 'always for supporting morality' and had always spoken out against the use of physical force to attain the aims of the Charter.[64] Nevertheless, it is clear that he was the author of a document describing the structure of the Chartist movement in south Wales, a document considered sufficiently incriminating by other Chartists for them to destroy it in case they were arrested with it in their possession. At his trial at the Monmouthshire Quarter Sessions in April 1840, Rorke was acquitted, largely due to his advanced age, but his son was found guilty of conspiracy and riot, and sentenced to six months with hard labour. In addition to this father and son, a section of Irish men from the Pillgwenlly area of Newport mobilized in support of the rising under the leadership of Patrick Hickey.[65]

---

[63] Earl of Bessborough (ed.), *Lady Charlotte Guest: Extracts from Her Journal, 1833–52* (London, 1950), pp.100–1.

[64] *The Times*, 30 November 1839; Gw. RO, Q.S.D. 32.0015, evidence of Richard Rorke, 27 January 1840.

[65] Gw. RO, Q.S.D. 32.0016, evidence of Samuel Etheridge. See also D. J. V. Jones, *The Last Rising: The Newport Insurrection of 1839* (Oxford, 1985), p.216; Ivor G. Wilks, *South Wales and the Rising of 1839* (London, 1984), pp.139–40; Brian Davies, 'Empire and identity: The "case" of Dr William Price', in David Smith (ed.), *A People and a Proletariat: Essays in the History of Wales, 1780–1980* (London, 1980), pp.75–6.

In summary, it would seem that the evidence for Irish participation in the rising is more compelling than many contemporary commentators were willing to concede. Anti-Chartist Irish journalists such as John O'Dwyer – a reporter and leader writer for the *Monmouthshire Merlin* who served as a special constable during the rising[66] – have imposed their own perspectives on the historical record at the expense of alternative viewpoints. Whether or not the Irish who worked in the iron-works to the north of Newport actually took part in the insurrection is open to question, but a section of the Irish population at Newport undoubtedly did, and were integrated into the radical culture of the town. On the other hand, the only conclusive proof of Irish opposition to Chartism consists of the presence of an army garrison largely composed of Irish soldiers, and the activities of one Irish police constable.

With the failure of the rising and the imprisonment of many of its leaders Chartism in Wales suffered a serious setback. Paradoxically, this reverse also contained the seeds of renewal. John Frost, credited with being the prime conspirator, achieved the status of a martyr and the prisoners' defence was relentlessly pursued by Feargus O'Connor through the columns of the *Northern Star* and in public meetings held throughout Britain. By 1842, the movement's fortunes had revived considerably. In that year the Chartist petition to Parliament received 48,000 signatures in Wales, the high point of its growth.[67] An attempt was made on at least one occasion during the intense agitation of that year to make common cause between Chartists and those campaigning for repeal of the Union with Ireland. At a Chartist meeting at Merthyr Tydfil in May 1842, local speakers were joined by an Irishman who spoke in favour of repeal and the rights of labour in Britain, arguing that the Irish should lend their assistance to the campaign for the Charter. In his view, the Irish suffered from an oppressive Parliament which denied them their freedom, while British workers suffered misery because of bad and corrupt legislation passed by those who did not have their best interests at heart.[68] In the previous year, the Catholic

---

[66] Jones, *Press, Politics and Society*, p.159.

[67] Jones, *The Last Rising*, pp.215–16; Angela V. John, 'The Chartist endurance: industrial south Wales, 1840–1868', *Morgannwg*, XV (1971), 25.

[68] *Cardiff and Merthyr Guardian*, 14 May 1842; Heather Jordan, *The 1842 General Strike in South Wales* (London, n.d.), p.9.

priest at Merthyr Tydfil had complained to his bishop about the behaviour of four independently minded teetotallers in his congregation who had been in contact with Chartism and were threatening to take over his schoolroom. Chartism was a perennial cause of anxiety to him: 'We had flattered ourselves that Chartism had sunk here to rise no more', he lamented in August 1842, 'but the midland counties has [sic] revived it, the nightly meetings have recommenced.'[69]

After the intense activity of 1842, Chartist activity dwindled and the movement fragmented. Demoralization set in after the petition was rejected by Parliament for the second time, and land reform became an increasingly important preoccupation. Irish radicals found plans to expand peasant proprietorship as a means to alleviate the problem of surplus labour particularly attractive. Land reform was an integral part of Feargus O'Connor's thinking, and activists such as Richard Rorke at Newport were prominent supporters of the Land Company venture. From 1845 Merthyr Tydfil had three flourishing Land Plan branches, one of which was named Emmet's Brigade after Robert Emmet, who had been executed for leading an unsuccessful rising in Ireland in 1803.[70] However, it was news of events in France which would breathe new life into the movement and cement the link between Irish and Welsh radicals. After a long period of demoralization in the 1840s, both Chartism and the Young Ireland movement were energized by the news of revolution in Paris in February 1848. However, the Young Irelanders' ill-prepared attempt to establish a republic by force ended in ignominious failure and the transportation of its leaders, while the Repeal Association was marginalized after the death of O'Connell in 1847.

At Merthyr Tydfil an attempt was made to unite the cause of the Charter with that of repeal. Writing to the Home Secretary from Carmarthen, Colonel Love reported the display of a poster announcing a public meeting in the Market Square, Merthyr Tydfil, on 10 April 1848. The poster proclaimed:

---

[69] Fr J. Carroll to Bishop Brown, 11 May 1841 and 15 August 1842, AAC. Both reproduced in J. S. Williams, 'Roman Catholic education', 78–80.

[70] John, 'The Chartist endurance', p.32; Ryland Wallace, *'Organise! Organise! Organise!' A Study of Reform Agitations in Wales, 1840–1886* (Cardiff, 1991), pp.51–3. On Irish nationalists' connections with Wales, see *Monmouthshire Merlin*, 16 June 1843 and PRO, HO45/453, fol.23.

THE
REPEAL FOR IRELAND
THE
CHARTER FOR ENGLAND!
SONS OF LIBERTY
RALLY AROUND YOUR OWN STANDARD!
LOOK AT THE STATE OF EUROPE! SHALL WE ALONE
BE SLAVES?

The meeting had been convened 'for the purposes of adopting a Petition to Parliament for an Immediate Repeal of the Legislative Union between Great Britain and Ireland'. Colonel Love confidently predicted that many Irish would attend. In the event, the meeting was postponed until 12 April, when there were 'not above 2,000 present'. The Catholic priest made public his opposition to the meeting and it passed off without incident.[71] Although an anti-climax, this meeting was not the end of co-operation between the Irish and Chartists at Merthyr. In June 1848 a local newspaper commented on the incongruity of Irish men leading Merthyr's Chartists. 'Have not the Welshmen of Cyfarthfa sufficient talent among themselves?', it queried acidly.[72] When reassuring the Home Office two months later, Colonel Love referred to Chartism and the Irish in the same breath. 'The Irish labourers and Chartists', he averred, 'appear to meet with little or no sympathy from the great mass of the people, and therefore there is no reason to apprehend (what was at one time feared) any manifestation in favor of the disaffected in Ireland.'[73] Such co-operation is difficult to square with the frequent conflicts between Irish and Welsh workers referred to in chapter I. It is difficult to account for the occurrence of anti-Irish riots at the same time as some immigrants were participating in radical politics. Perhaps part of the explanation lies in an increasing willingness in the early nineteenth century to separate the world of work from that of political activity, treating the Irish differently according to the context.

[71] Colonel Love to Home Secretary, 8 April 1848, 10 April 1848 and 14 April 1848, PRO, HO45/2410 (AK).
[72] *Cardiff and Merthyr Guardian*, 17 June 1848.
[73] Colonel Love to Home Secretary, 2 August 1848, PRO, HO45/2410 (AK).

Events in Merthyr clearly demonstrated that combining two influential ideologies in one movement was insufficient in itself to guarantee success. By the late 1840s any prospect of concerted political action by the Irish in Wales had been undermined by the influx of large numbers of destitute refugees from the Great Famine who swelled the already overcrowded population of urban slums. Participation in political agitation required reserves of energy, both emotional and physical, which few of these immigrants possessed. To some extent, this mirrored the fate of politics in Ireland. After the death of Daniel O'Connell in May 1847, the Repealers were an inchoate grouping without leader or direction. The irrelevance of the Repeal Association in a land which faced the more pressing problem of famine was illustrated by the abortive and somewhat pathetic attempt to begin an uprising in 1849. By the 1860s, when Irish immigrants re-appeared as visibly active participants in political life in Wales, Irish Nationalists had invested emigrants with a new status in the struggle to achieve independence for their homeland. That status derived in no small part from the bitter consequences of the Great Famine.

III

THE DELUGE: THE GREAT FAMINE, 1845–1850

After a period of thirty years during which the Irish had been attracted to Wales by the 'pull' of economic opportunity provided by the quickening of industrialization, an older pattern reasserted itself. In the years between 1845 and 1850 it was the 'push' factor which dominated once again as hundreds of thousands of starving people took flight from their native country to escape the human and ecological disaster of the potato famine. During these years Irish immigration to Britain reached unprecedented levels. Between the censuses of 1841 and 1851 the number of Irish-born in Wales increased by 153 per cent (compared with an increase in the population as a whole during the same decade of only 11 per cent), and the flood continued well into the 1850s. Because of the intensity of the influx in such a short period of time, and the association of a range of social problems with the newcomers, a distorted image of Irish settlement as a product of the Famine years alone soon became indelibly fixed in the minds of the Welsh. Unwanted and unwelcome, the starving refugees were easily cast in the role of social outcasts.

The series of agricultural crises which ravaged Irish society between 1845 and 1850, known collectively as the Great Famine, has achieved such notoriety because it occurred in western Europe at a time when country-wide subsistence crises of that magnitude had ceased to occur.[1] In the decades before the Famine the population of Ireland grew from about five million in 1801 to 8,175,124 in 1841, and continued to increase up to 1845. And yet only six years later – in 1851 – this trend had been reversed and the population plummeted to 6,552,385. It is the

---

[1] There is an extensive and growing literature on the Great Famine. The principal studies are: Christine Kinealy, *This Great Calamity: The Irish Famine, 1845–52* (Dublin, 1994); Patrick O'Sullivan (ed.), *The Meaning of the Famine: The Irish World Wide*, vol.6 (London, 1996); Cormac Ó Gráda, *The Great Irish Famine* (Dublin, 1989); Joel Mokyr, *Why Ireland Starved* (London, 1983); Cecil Woodham-Smith, *The Great Hunger: Ireland, 1845–49* (London, 1962); and R. Dudley Edwards and T. Desmond Williams (eds.), *The Great Famine: Studies in Irish History, 1845–52* (Dublin, 1956).

swiftness of this collapse, the intense human suffering and death it entailed and the enormous emigration it precipitated which have left an enduring mark on Irish popular culture. The exact number of those who perished cannot be known with any certainty, and estimates vary from 800,000 at the most conservative to as many as 1.5 million at the upper end of the scale. Whatever the precise figures, it is clear that within six short and painful years Ireland lost nearly a quarter of its population through a combination of death and emigration.

Although failure of the potato crop on the scale which occurred in the late 1840s could not have been foreseen, there had been signs in preceding decades that subsistence farming was in a precarious condition. Since the end of the Napoleonic wars, partial failure of the crop had been common. In 1821 and 1822 failure was complete in the provinces of Connaught and Munster, while 1830 and 1831 were years of failure in counties Mayo, Donegal and Galway. A number of districts suffered each year between 1832 and 1836, with Ulster suffering acutely in 1835; the crop failed in many districts throughout Ireland in 1836 and 1837, and it came under threat again in 1841 and 1844. An increasing proportion of agricultural land was brought under the potato crop during these years in an attempt to feed the growing population, while at the same time more productive but less reliable types of plant, such as the 'lumper', were widely used. By the 1840s the potato was the sole food of roughly one-third of the Irish people and had become an important element in the diet of a far larger number.[2] In this context, the susceptibility of the lumper to disease took on a grave aspect.

Potato blight (*phytophthora infestans*) first appeared in North America, arriving in Ireland in the autumn of 1845. Botanists were divided as to the causes of this new disease, and no effective antidote was discovered until later in the century. Consequently, the Irish peasantry was fortunate that part of the crop was saved that year and distress was not as acute as it might have been. In the following year the crop succumbed to swift and total failure. The Whig government's response to the tragedy was sluggish and inadequate. In London, reluctance to intervene was the product of a widely held conviction that the Irish habitually

---

[2]   Gearóid Ó Tuathaigh, *Ireland Before the Famine, 1798–1848* (Dublin, 1972), p.203.

exaggerated their plight, and it was compounded by an un-swerving allegiance to the tenets of *laissez-faire* political economy. However, as the death rate rose inexorably during the autumn of 1846, the government finally conceded that a human disaster of enormous proportions was imminent and instituted a pro-gramme of public works consisting almost entirely of road-building. A more effective response to the problem of subsistence was provided in the form of soup for the poor.[3]

Meanwhile, middle-class philanthropists in Britain sought to ameliorate the condition of the starving Irish by providing aid collected by public subscription. South Wales was no exception: in January 1847 a public meeting at Chepstow in Monmouth-shire raised £100 for this cause, and the example prompted a similar meeting at Newport; at Merthyr Tydfil £112 was sub-scribed in one meeting.[4] These donations were indicative of genuine concern and much goodwill, but the comparatively small sums collected in these and similar meetings throughout Britain were unequal to the size of the disaster. Some con-temporaries were fully aware of the inadequacy of these sums; after listening to a sermon at Swansea on behalf of the starving Irish, Lewis Weston Dillwyn recorded in his diary that 'only' £100 had been raised.[5] Although the Swansea press praised the energy of a group of ladies for making up coarse clothing for the starving Irish, it was scathing in its criticism of the remainder of the town's populace for failing to make a greater effort than towns half its size.[6] Residual suspicion of the Irish in some quarters continued to overshadow the little sympathy expressed for their plight. One Welsh periodical insisted that the Irish were well-practised in the art of deception by overdramatizing their problems. They were, it cautioned, 'beggars by nature' who knew how best to elicit alms from the trusting English. Adding insult to injury, it asserted that the money obtained in this way was diverted from its true purpose and used instead for purchasing guns, powder and bullets to undermine British rule.[7]

---

[3] See Kinealy, *This Great Calamity*, ch.4.
[4] *Monmouthshire Merlin*, 16, 23, 30 January 1847.
[5] 'The diary of Lewis Weston Dillwyn', in *South Wales Record Society Publications*, No. 5 (Newport, 1963), p.96.
[6] *Cambrian*, 12 February 1847; R. T. Price, *Little Ireland: Aspects of the Irish and Greenhill, Swansea* (Swansea, 1992), p.46.
[7] *Seren Gomer*, January 1847, 25.

Such claims were entirely unfounded. Soon, however, the true character and magnitude of the problem became clearer as starving refugees inundated the western seaports of Britain and intruded rudely on the lives of those same philanthropists.

Although the vast majority of Famine emigrants arriving in Wales landed on the southern coast, there is evidence that some fled to other parts of Wales in their desperate attempt to avoid starvation, arriving at areas well away from the usual migration routes. For example, a Welsh-American periodical reported in July 1851 that the Irish were 'like a plague on the land' in Merioneth in north Wales, where they temporarily displaced Welsh gypsies. It was claimed that the large Irish influx in the county caused a reduction in labourers' wages, while the women and children 'begged and pilfered' across the countryside. However, the vast majority soon dispersed and the gypsies returned;[8] according to the census of 1851, the county contained only seventy-seven Irish-born residents, a figure which had fallen to sixty-one ten years later. Even though Merioneth was one of the counties with the fewest Irish-born inhabitants in Britain, the same pattern is discernible throughout north Wales, the largest concentration of immigrants in that region being found in Wrexham, where only 711 Irish-born lived in 1851. Curiously, Holyhead, the major port of departure for Ireland in north Wales, failed to attract or retain many emigrants despite success in consolidating its position as the main channel of postal communication between London and Dublin; a Select Committee reporting in 1860 found that there were 'comparatively few' Irish at the port.[9]

Geographical proximity was itself not enough for a port to attract and retain Famine emigrants – the means of transport available to them was a factor of even greater importance. Unlike Liverpool and the west of Scotland, the ports of south Wales lacked a direct steam link with Ireland (a fact which complicated attempts by the poor law authorities to return paupers to that country).[10] Consequently, the chief mode of

[8] *Cyfaill o'r Hen Wlad* (July 1851); Angus M. Fraser, 'George Borrow's *Wild Wales*: fact and fabrication', *Transactions of the Honourable Society of Cymmrodorion* (1980), 170.

[9] PP 1860 XVII, Select Committee on the Irremoveable Poor, pp.86–9.

[10] On the Famine immigration to Liverpool and the west of Scotland, see Frank Neal, *Sectarian Violence: The Liverpool Experience, 1819–1914* (Manchester, 1988); idem, 'Black '47: Liverpool and the Irish Famine', in E. Margaret Crawford (ed.), *The Hungry Stream: Essays on Emigration and Famine* (Belfast, 1997), pp.123–36; James E. Handley, *The Irish in Scotland* (Glasgow, 1964), pp.177–98.

travel for migrants to south Wales was a by-product of trade between the region and southern Ireland. Colliers – ships exporting coal to Ireland – frequently returned empty as there was no comparable trade in the other direction and so a small income could be accrued by carrying passengers as human ballast. This practice had existed before the Famine, but now it intensified and became more widespread.

Municipal authorities in Welsh towns were faced with a daunting problem which they did not understand: an influx of destitute people they could not halt or regulate and which showed no signs of abating. The institutions of local government were poorly equipped to meet the demands now made on them. For as long as they misunderstood the nature of the problem facing Irish society, the local authorities in Wales directed their energies towards deflecting the newcomers or compelling them to return home. This was a reaction which resurfaced regularly during subsequent years. As late as 15 June 1850, the *Cardiff and Merthyr Guardian* opined, 'It is a pity that the landowners of Ireland cannot be compelled to take the consequences of the grievous manner in which their estates have been mismanaged.' Even at that late stage it appeared as though there was a failure to comprehend the true nature of the calamity which had befallen Ireland.

Among the earliest ships bearing refugees to arrive in south Wales was the *Wanderer* of Baltimore, west Cork. It had left Ireland on 23 December 1846 and spent more than five weeks at sea in inclement weather before arriving at Newport on 1 February 1847, when the ship was described as 'that floating pesthouse'. Captain Casey delivered 113 destitute men, women and children to the town, some twenty-six of whom were dying. 'Human conception can scarcely reach the depth of misery in which a large number of them appeared', commented a local newspaper, and Sir Benjamin Hall was moved to bring the case to the attention of parliament.[11] A fortnight later, an editorial in the same newspaper remarked on the 'alarming and lamentable appearance' of the streets of Newport, crowded as they were with 'many hundreds' of famishing Irish.[12] It was believed that many

---

[11] *Monmouthshire Merlin*, 6 February 1847; *Hansard's Parliamentary Debates*, 3rd series, XCI (1847), cols.269–71.

[12] *Monmouthshire Merlin*, 20 February 1847.

of the men had been lured to the town by promises of work on the railways and in the ironworks at wages of four shillings per day, with women promised washing and domestic work 'in whatever numbers they please' for between two shillings and half a crown per day. It was also claimed that handbills had been distributed to this effect in Ireland and that a bell-ringer had been engaged to spread the message at the markets of County Cork. In reality, the vision of waged work as the escape route from starvation and destitution was no more than a cruel chimera. With this misplaced hope in mind, 'hosts of squalid beings' were 'induced to embark on board filthy hulks, totally unsuited for a living freight, the miseries of whom, densely stowed on damp ballast, suffering from famine and sickness during this tempestuous season, are almost beyond human expression'.[13]

During the first six weeks of 1847, Newport's Refuge for the Destitute provided food and temporary accommodation for 369 men, 360 women and 402 children, quite apart from the aid distributed to 'an enormous extent' by the Poor Law union. It was hoped that it would be possible to take care of 'these miserable strangers' until better times arrived. Great pride was taken in this philanthropy and especially in the local relief fund which exceeded £1,000. Sharp criticisms were aimed in particular at the 'local committees' in Ireland who, it was believed, were paying the cost of paupers' passages to Wales in order to alleviate their own burden.[14] During April and May 1847 the influx intensified. In addition to the one thousand Irish recently relieved by the poor law authorities at Newport, an additional 'several hundred' Irish entered the town during the second week of April. Even before their arrival, the Refuge for the Destitute, a temporary hospital and the old lock-up had been filled by previous arrivals.[15] As the town's limited resources were stretched to breaking point, anxiety turned to anger. When two ships carrying more than two hundred Irish paupers docked at Newport during the following week, the *Monmouthshire Merlin*

[13] Ibid.; *The Times*, 19 February 1847. On the Famine in Cork, see James S. Donnelly, *The Land and the People of Nineteenth-Century Cork: The Rural Economy and the Land Question* (London, 1975), pp.73–131.

[14] *Monmouthshire Merlin*, 20 February 1847.

[15] *Monmouthshire Merlin*, 10 April 1847.

began to suspect 'obdurate landlords' trying to avoid their legal responsibility by shipping the Irish poor to Wales. By this time the municipal authorities were taking a stern attitude to the newcomers and summarily sent one hundred of them back to Ireland. When another five hundred men, women and children arrived during the first week of May they, too, met with a harsh response. After being provided with nothing more than temporary relief, these unfortunates were ordered to leave the town.[16] The sense of deep shock and concern felt by the inhabitants of Newport early in 1847 was a product of the strain placed on the town's institutions and an *ad hoc* response to the desperation and helplessness of the continuously arriving contingents of famished Irish. At the same time, attitudes to Irish beggars inland at Merthyr Tydfil had begun to harden to the extent that some of them, when begging, resorted to acting as if they were dumb in an attempt to disguise their origins.[17]

Newport was not the only port in south Wales to undergo this experience, although probably it suffered more acutely than any of the others. Both Swansea on the coast and Merthyr Tydfil inland also received large numbers of poor Irish. But it was Cardiff which experienced the largest influx in Glamorgan and provides some of the most graphic and chilling accounts of events at this time. Recalling the first ships to arrive, Jeremiah Box Stockdale, the Superintendent of Police, stated that there were:

> at first 13 or 14 in a vessel, then increasing to upwards of 200 in one vessel . . . They were many of them apparently starving, and many in advanced stage of disease. One was found dead in the bottom of the hold, and an inquest was held on the body; many died shortly after landing.[18]

Stockdale maintained that in 'hundreds of instances' he had been told that a specific, though unnamed, landowner near Cork city had paid 2s. 6d. for the passage of each Irish man and woman. On receipt of this report in March 1847, the Marquis of Bute

---

[16] *Monmouthshire Merlin*, 17 April, 8 May 1847.
[17] Ursula Masson, 'The development of the Irish and Roman Catholic communities of Merthyr Tydfil and Dowlais in the nineteenth century', unpublished University of Keele MA thesis (1975), 62.
[18] PP 1847–8 LIII, Reports and Communications on Vagrancy, p.31.

informed the Secretary of State of the matter before instituting his own inquiries as to whether relief funds were the source of passage money. By April he was suggesting that the mayor of Cardiff address an official complaint to the Secretary of State in order to bring the landowners and authorities of south-west Ireland 'to a proper sense of their duty', and that a complaint should be made directly to the Kinsale poor union, in particular about its behaviour in allegedly shipping destitute families to Wales.[19] The claim that the government's Relief Committees were diverting funds to underwrite the cost of sending paupers to Britain was first drawn to the government's attention in February 1847. An investigation at that time revealed only one documented case of this happening, when those in charge of the relief depot at Skibbereen in west Cork sent destitute paupers to Newport. It was generally believed that the practice was more widespread, but Sir Randolph Routh concluded that 'the more usual course is for the landlord to pay these expenses'.[20]

In the absence of official statistics, it is impossible to make an accurate estimate of the number of Irish arrivals from Ireland during these years. Using the number of vessels entering port as a base, Frank Neal has suggested an upper limit of estimated Irish arrivals at Newport of 19,275 for 1847, a figure roughly equal to the town's total population at that time.[21] Even so, the estimate of arrivals by sea does not take account of those who landed at other places along the coast of south Wales and made their way to Newport overland. Estimating the number of arrivals in the region is further hampered by the fact that not all Irish immigrants landed at the major ports of Newport, Cardiff and Swansea. Vessels disgorging starving and diseased passengers along the coast from Milford Haven in the west to Newport in the east often did so away from the larger and busier ports, preferring instead clandestine landings in order to avoid the

---

[19] Bute to James Lewis, 27 March 1847, NLW, Bute Collection, box 70, letterbook dated 1 January 1847–18 March 1848; Bute to Lewis, 23 April 1847. Names of those supplying passage money are given as Mr Stewart and the Revd M. McGrath, Bute to Lewis, 15 April 1847.
[20] See the correspondence between Mr Hughes and Sir Randolph Routh, 12 February 1847; Mr Stephen to Mr Trevelyan, 16 February 1847, and Sir Randolph Routh to Trevelyan, 20 February 1847, all printed in PP 1847 LII, Correspondence Relating to the Measures Adopted for the Relief of Distress in Ireland (Commissariat Series), Second Part, pp.130, 159–60.
[21] Frank Neal, *Black '47: Britain and the Famine Irish* (London, 1998), pp.109–10.

attentions of officialdom and the hostility of the Welsh. This coast, indented with many small, sheltered bays, was conducive to unnoticed landings, but disembarking was a hazardous exercise for the passengers, as shown by the horrific fate of an Irishman who drowned by sinking in a mud flat in the face of an oncoming tide at Penarth in May 1847.[22] Because a significant proportion of famine refugees did not settle locally, the numbers passing through the region are difficult to quantify.

Starvation and illness went hand in hand as lack of food increased the susceptibility of the poor to disease. The winter of 1846–7 in Ireland brought with it an epidemic of 'famine-fever' – in reality, the two diseases of typhus and relapsing fever – rapidly followed by dysentery and scurvy. Confined in large numbers in the small holds of sailing ships, often in close proximity to livestock, emigrants found themselves in an ideal environment for the spread of disease; on landing, many were enfeebled and dying.[23] The manager of the tramp house at Newport estimated that 40 per cent of the Irish in the town in 1847 suffered from fever, while nearby at Chepstow the comparable figure was 20 per cent.[24] Dysentery was common and frequently fatal. Between May and November 1847 Dr Tuthill Massey worked at the temporary fever hospital at Newport, during which time 6,000 Irish men and women were treated. His record of his first day at the hospital, though published in a medical journal, eschewed clinical language in favour of a description evocative of a living hell:

> The thermometer was several degrees above summer heat when I entered the barn, not worthy of the name hospital – a shocking place. The darkness terrified me as I stepped over the beds of those creatures as they lay side by side, moaning and groaning, and those who were able, calling for 'water! water! Oh the thirst!' A candle was required to examine the anxious faces, the flushed cheek and the parched tongue, of those who lay in the angles of the building. According to the report of last week, thirty had died yet the barn was still full; the places of the dead were quickly taken. Those many deaths alarmed me.[25]

[22] *Monmouthshire Merlin*, 1 May 1847.
[23] E. Margaret Crawford, 'Migrant maladies: unseen lethal baggage', in *eadem* (ed.), *The Hungry Stream: Essays on Emigration and Famine* (Belfast, 1997), pp.137–49.
[24] PP 1847–8 LIII, p.37.
[25] Tuthill Massey, 'Letter on fever in South Wales', *Dublin Quarterly Journal of Medical Science*, VIII (1849), 439.

In some cases Massey believed that refugees would have been better off had they remained in Ireland, although it is likely that most contracted typhus before leaving. It has been estimated that there were 1,000 Irish deaths from fever in south Wales during 1847.[26]

During this crisis many members of the medical profession and other officials who came into contact with the diseased Irish succumbed to fever. The total self-sacrifice of many Catholic priests in an attempt to alleviate the plight of the Irish was proverbial. Their spiritual duties included administering the last rites and hearing deathbed confessions. In 1847 three of them died from typhus while serving their congregations: Fr Metcalfe of Newport, Fr Mulcahy of Bangor, and Fr Carroll of Merthyr. After seeing a priest at Newport kneeling beside a dying girl, Dr Massey warned him that he was in danger of infection if he remained so close to her; a few days later, the priest exhibited the painful symptoms of the disease, 'the head greatly engorged, fever running high, with paroxysms of delirium'.[27] Whether the priest concerned was Fr Metcalfe, who died from the disease, or Fr Sentini, who recovered from it, is not clear. Fr Carroll's parish of Merthyr Tydfil consisted of a sprawling area at the Heads of the Valleys and some days before his death he had been seen trudging for miles over the inhospitable mountains in driving rain on a sick call.[28] Other priests narrowly escaped death while continuing with their pastoral duties in similar circumstances.

As fear of contagion gripped the citizens of the ports, a variety of schemes to control the influx were hastily mooted. In February 1847 the mayor of Cardiff told the Poor Law guardians that a part of Longcross barracks could be used for the reception of Irish fever victims. However, in March a local newspaper insisted that all paupers arriving from Ireland should be sent back immediately, arguing that the authorities at Cardiff had 'no right to sit still and let pestilence walk in amongst us'.[29] A month later,

[26] Frank Neal, *Black '47: Britain and the Famine Irish*, p.171.

[27] Tuthill Massey, 'Letter on fever in south Wales', 440.

[28] *Catholic Directory*, 1848, p.91; *Monmouthshire Merlin*, 5 June 1847; *Catholic Opinion*, 25 September 1869. The Catholic clergy were not deterred by these fatalities. During the cholera epidemic of 1848–9, Fr Cavalli of Newport laid out the bodies of a family which had been obliterated by the disease, while the neighbours who helped him were infected and died soon afterwards, *St Peter's Chair*, August 1892, 177.

[29] Frank Neal, *Black '47: Britain and the Famine Irish*, p.166; *Cardiff and Merthyr Guardian*, 12 March 1847.

the marquis of Bute, the most powerful landowner in south Wales, advised the mayor of Cardiff to place all vessels from Ireland under quarantine so that the state of health of the passengers could be ascertained. He drew up a detailed plan to detain all vessels offshore in Penarth Road under the yellow flag, and their passengers were to be deposited at 'a place . . . fitted up out of the Town in the nature of a Lazaretto', which would have meant the use of Flat Holm island as an off-shore quarantine station.[30] Nearly a year later, a Poor Law official stressed the suitability of islands off the Welsh coast as reception points where the Irish could quarry rock for repairing roads, thereby easing the financial burden which had descended unexpectedly on the ports.[31] Whether the impetus derived from a desire to isolate diseased incomers or from concern about the cost of relieving the poor, it was an idea which was not acted on. However, similar plans were put in operation in North America, on Grosse Isle in the St Lawrence River for Quebec, on Deer Island for Boston, and Staten Island for New York.[32]

The depth of anxiety about the threat to public health posed by the Famine immigrants was matched by an equally persistent concern about the cost of relieving the starving and destitute who became chargeable to the receiving parishes. Although the statistics of those being relieved at Houses of Refuge do not differentiate between the Irish and other nationalities, there can be little doubt that the sharp upturn in numbers observed at this time was a result of the Irish influx. The numbers receiving relief at the Newport House of Refuge in January 1847 was four times the figure for the previous January. The numbers peaked in April 1847, but they continued at an exceptionally high level well into 1848. Rural Poor Law unions were particularly fearful of the increase in Irish vagrants and expressed alarm at the prospect of having to provide them with poor relief for an indefinite period. The increase in their financial burden was substantial. Of those

[30] NLW, Bute Collection, box 70, letterbook dated January 1847 to March 1848, 14–15; Bute to James Lewis, 15 April 1847.

[31] PP 1847–8 LIII, p.13.

[32] T. W. Rammell, *Report to the General Board of Health on a Preliminary Inquiry into the Sewerage, Drainage and Supply of Water, and the Sanitary Condition of the Inhabitants of the Town of Cardiff* (London, 1850), p.41. Hilbre Island in the River Dee in north Wales was also suggested as an isolation hospital for Liverpool: Frank Neal, *Sectarian Violence: The Liverpool Experience, 1819–1914* (Manchester, 1988), p.103, n.51.

paupers not belonging to a parish in the Chepstow union, there were more in the first six months of 1847 than in the previous eighteen months taken together, while the numbers relieved in the Brecknock union increased threefold during 1847.[33] This method of relieving the poor was severely tested by the sheer weight of numbers.

Most of the Irish were categorized as 'tramps' or vagrants and were thus usually ineligible to be admitted to the workhouse. The nature of the accommodation made available to them varied widely from one parish to another. At Swansea there existed provision for only thirty vagrants, while at Neath the relieving officer simply provided each applicant with sufficient money for lodging and bread. At Newport, Cardiff and Chepstow, Irish applicants for poor relief were lodged in buildings under the control of officers employed by the guardians but separate from the workhouse. Accommodation at the tramp house at Newport was typical of that provided elsewhere. The lodgings consisted of two large rooms on the ground floor of the old workhouse, both floored with brick, where the occupants slept on rugs on the ground. According to the matron, Mrs Huxtable, straw was not provided because 'if we did, we could not keep the place free from vermin'. Upstairs there was a room containing twelve beds for tramps suffering from minor ailments 'and any other clean persons who may occasionally come'. Even this limited and primitive provision was considered a magnet for paupers by some magistrates, who wished to see the refuge closed on that account.[34] Strenuous attempts were made to deter the able-bodied from applying for poor relief. Mr Bentley, the relieving officer at Neath, threatened with the police those who came more than once a month, a stratagem which was not always successful. 'Some will not be frightened', he complained, '*and will have money*, which I am obliged to give, to get rid of them, and for the sake of peace.'[35] At Cardiff, vagrants applied directly to Superintendent Stockdale, who had been delegated the responsibility of relieving the able-bodied, while the sick were referred to the workhouse. Stockdale's policy for dealing with

---

[33] PP 1847–8 LIII, pp.29–30, 95. The Monmouth union demanded a change in the law to solve the problem, ibid., p.78.

[34] Ibid., pp.26–9.

[35] Ibid., p.46.

Irish vagrants was to send them back to Ireland as soon as possible. A barracks which had been used as a hospital and a night-asylum had both been discontinued during the previous twelve months and the only accommodation available for the destitute at Cardiff was a room with straw for bedding.[36] It would appear that the use of a police officer in the administration of poor relief was a favoured method of deterring able-bodied Irish vagrants from applying for assistance. The authorities at Newport copied the example to great effect.[37]

The poor law authorities took a stern attitude to those individuals applying for relief who were shown to be less than utterly destitute; vagrants who possessed the means to purchase their own food but persisted in demanding alms were prosecuted. The experience of John Collins, 'a forbidding looking Irish vagrant', illustrates this clearly. One Sunday in June 1847 Collins visited the village of Llandaff on the outskirts of Cardiff pleading that he was starving, and he ate some raw cabbage stumps to prove it. However, on being searched, it was found that he had ample amounts of bread, cheese, meat and money in his pockets to maintain himself, and a constable escorted him out of the village, instructing him not to return. Nevertheless, Collins 'lounged about' until Monday morning, when he began begging again. He was arrested and committed to gaol for one month.[38] In 1848 an Irish family applying for assistance at Newport were searched and found to have £3 of their own money; they were sent home at their own expense.[39] Similarly, when an Irish vagrant was searched at Merthyr Tydfil in May 1850 and found to have money on his person, a portion was taken from him and paid to the treasurer of the Board of Guardians.[40]

Even those who were sent away could return within a matter of weeks, as Superintendent Stockdale readily conceded. Some sought work inland at the ironworks while others trekked further afield to English cities. As the local economy was unable to absorb all of the immigrants, the women, children and aged members of many families remained at the port of entry,

---

[36] Ibid., pp.30–1.
[37] PP 1854 XVII, Select Committee on Poor Removal, p.494.
[38] *Cardiff and Merthyr Guardian*, 26 June 1847.
[39] PP 1847–8 LIII, pp.23–4.
[40] Glam. RO, U/M Merthyr Board of Guardians Minute Book, 1849–51, 210; the incident was also mentioned in the *Morning Chronicle*'s report on the town.

maintained by the poor law, while the men travelled in search of work elsewhere. 'Some of the Irish families', opined the master of the Chepstow workhouse, 'appear to be making for no place, and we see them often in their rounds.'[41] The poor law inspector, W. D. Boase, summed up the evidence collected from officials throughout south Wales when he reported in 1848 that 'by far the greatest proportion of Irish vagrants in Wales were women with small children, old men apparently feeble, pregnant women, and girls and boys about 10 years old'.[42] Boase proceeded to contrast the nature of Irish immigration to south Wales with that to Liverpool. Those arriving at Liverpool were predominantly able-bodied young men who had tramped long distances across Ireland from the western counties such as Mayo, Roscommon and Sligo to board ship at Dublin or Drogheda on the east coast. Their ability to make this arduous journey on foot suggested that they were fit enough to earn their own livelihood and support themselves without recourse to charity, a characteristic which Boase believed was not evident in south Wales. There, in his view, the Irish were 'nearly all helpless and burdensome to the community'.[43]

Table III.1 Numbers and cost of relieving Irish paupers, 1848

Place	Individuals	Amount
Cardiff	2,063	£868 14s. 7d.
Newport Union	12,661	£184 15s. 7d.
Merthyr Tydfil Parish	1,346	£212 8s. 0d.

Source: PP 1849 XLVII, Numbers of Irish Poor Relieved during 1848.

It is clear that responses to refugees were conditioned by the cost of providing relief and medical services, responsibilities which strained the resources of small towns and gave rise to a mixture of outrage and anxiety. Table III.1 gives some indication of the size of the problem. These statistics demonstrate that the cost per head of relieving Irish paupers varied from one place to another. The contrast between Cardiff and Newport is

[41] PP 1847–8 LIII, p.17.
[42] Ibid.
[43] Ibid.

particularly striking in this respect. The most important factor determining such expenditure was the length of a pauper's sojourn in a particular locality: the longer the stay, the greater the cost. Both ports were the sites of landfall for significant numbers of immigrants who spent only a short period in the town before moving in search of work elsewhere, but transients were a particular feature of the immigration to Newport. Consequently, the per capita cost of relieving paupers at Newport was proportionately lower than at Cardiff.[44]

Among those relieved in south Wales, W. D. Boase identified a large number of widows with small children who came over 'to get a bit for the children', married women whose husbands had preceded them, young girls and boys in search of parents, brothers and uncles, and numbers of old women. Initially, the latter had attempted to earn a living by street-selling, but had found it unprofitable. Influenced by prevailing ideas about the existence of a hereditary 'dangerous class' of paupers, Boase was inordinately exercised by the fear that should the Irish settle they might produce a new generation of dependants.[45]

Developments of this kind spurred the authorities to explore methods whereby the immigration might be stemmed. They were provided with an example of how they might act in December 1847, when the coal and iron masters at Newport resolved to punish the captains of vessels which had carried Irish refugees to the port by refusing to send freight in their ships, an act which led to a temporary lull in the influx.[46] In the longer term, an unbending enforcement of the law concerning the carriage of passengers at sea was the preferred strategy at Newport, where it was reported in July 1848 that while many captains possessed licences to carry up to ninety passengers, a large number were willing to risk illicit landings of larger numbers on the mud flats below the entrance to the harbour as a means of avoiding legal constraints.[47] In February 1849 the master of a vessel was fined £5 at Newport for exceeding the terms of his passenger licence, and the penalties for infringing

---

[44] For a lucid discussion of these issues, see Frank Neal, *Black '47: Britain and the Famine Irish*, pp.254–5.
[45] PP 1847–8 LIII, p.17.
[46] *Cambrian*, 3 December 1847.
[47] *Monmouthshire Merlin*, 15 July 1848.

such regulations became progressively harsher during the year. After landing destitute Irish immigrants at Cardiff and Newport in March 1849, William Sutton, the master of the *Mary* of Cork, was imprisoned for two months in default of payment of a £50 fine, while in June Robert Travers, captain of the schooner *Two Friends*, was fined £10 with 15s. costs for the illegal carriage of Irish immigrants from Courtmacsherry to Newport. In a vain attempt to deter captains from carrying immigrants, the most trivial contravention of regulations was punished. An example of this occurred in July 1849 when William Shea, the master of the *Purilla*, was charged with failing to display sufficiently clearly on his vessel a copy of the Passenger Act.[48]

Other towns in the region looked on with great interest. In April 1848 the Swansea press commended the zeal with which captains were prosecuted at Newport, suggesting that 'their example ought to be followed by all others'.[49] For those bewildered by the seemingly unstoppable inundation, the prospect of controlling and ultimately stopping the influx of immigrants by enforcing regulations governing the carriage of passengers helped to identify a tangible cause of their confusion and held out the possibility of a panacea for their problems. Writing to the mayor of Newport in June 1849, the Revd G. A. Cockburn, the incumbent of a small parish near Milford Haven in Pembrokeshire, requested precise information about the legislation 'whereby these rascally captains might be laid hold of', adding that 'it would not be permitted to remain inactive by me'.[50] In spite of this public enthusiasm for enforcing the law, few towns prosecuted captains as systematically or as successfully as at Newport and, as has been seen, even there it is questionable whether prosecutions deterred captains or merely encouraged them to seek landfall on more secluded parts of the coast. Admitting the failure to prosecute captains docking at Cardiff, the chairman of the Cardiff Board of Guardians informed the Secretary of State that paupers were deposited clandestinely on the coast near the port while the vessel continued on its journey to Newport; those who landed in this way made their way to Cardiff where relief had to be provided. In July 1849 the

---

[48] *Monmouthshire Merlin*, 3 March, 10 March, 9 June, 21 July 1849.
[49] *Cambrian*, 14 April 1848.
[50] *Monmouthshire Merlin*, 16 June 1849.

Secretary of State acceded to a request that the coast guards along the south Wales coast should be instructed to report to the authorities at Cardiff any infringements of the laws on carrying passengers.[51] After all, as H. J. Paine of Cardiff succinctly pointed out, there was a grim economic rationale of supply and demand which ensured the continuation of this traffic: 'The captains, it appears, find it cheaper to ship and unship this living ballast than one of lime or shingles.'[52]

Having failed to stem the inflow, the local authorities resorted to their last line of defence: the ability to return Irish paupers to their native country should they become chargeable to a parish in Wales. Alterations to regulations and changes in attitudes concerning the law of settlement in the late 1840s resulted from the continuation and extension of the debates on the new Poor Law legislation of the previous decade, and created the cultural and legal matrix within which poor relief was dispensed. Poor Law guardians had no way of knowing when the high rate of immigration would end and so derived some small consolation from the knowledge that they possessed the legal right to remove Irish paupers. Any threat to this right was greeted with great apprehension. Just such a threat occurred on the eve of the Famine, when the rules governing removals were clarified in both Glamorgan and Monmouthshire to comply with new government regulations. The Act of 1846 stipulated that a five-year residence in a parish would now be sufficient qualification to gain a settlement, raising the spectre of the irremoveability of the Irish poor, and there is evidence that some poor law unions adopted a more systematic policy of removal than had been the case hitherto in order to prevent the Irish from obtaining the right of settlement.[53] Within Wales practice varied considerably. Of a total of 216 removals from Caernarfonshire in north Wales in the period 1845–9, twenty-nine (13.4 per cent) were Irish; a

[51] PRO, H.O. 100/257, 34303, Charles Williams to Sir George Grey, 7 June 1849; *The Times*, 2 July 1849. With his letter to Sir George Grey, Charles Williams enclosed a copy of a poster offering a £10 reward for information leading to the conviction of a captain illegally landing Irish passengers between Aberthaw and the River Rumney. As late as 1854 coal ships returning in ballast were landing large numbers of starving Irish on the south Wales coast. See PP 1854 XVII, pp.434–5.

[52] Rammell, *Report to the General Board of Health*, p.41.

[53] Glam. RO, CL Q/S CBO Exh 8; Gw. RO, Q/O.R. 66–0020 to 66–0023; Michael E. Rose, 'Settlement, removal and the new Poor Law', in Derek Fraser (ed.), *The New Poor Law in the Nineteenth-Century* (London, 1976), pp.25–44.

similar pattern is discernible in Swansea, where the thirty-two Irish removals during the same period represented 15.8 per cent of the total. By comparison, the practice at Cardiff was conspicuously different, for the 444 Irish paupers removed represented 99.3 per cent of all removals from the union.[54]

Shipping individuals or families back to Ireland was not a simple task and could itself be costly, at least in the short term. It was necessary formally to question those concerned and issue a warrant for removal based on this examination; a copy was then handed to the master of the vessel carrying the paupers by an official employed specifically to ensure that those being removed remained on the ship until after it set sail. In Monmouthsire, for example, a report to the Quarter Sessions in January 1846 recommended the appointment of William Witheycombe Harris as conductor of the poor charged with the responsibility of conveying Irish paupers from different parts of the county to Newport 'by the Railway or other public conveyance', from where they would be shipped to Ireland. The costs involved were substantial. For making out the warrant and the examination on which it was based, the clerk to the justices of the Newport Union was paid 2s. 6d., plus 1s. for each duplicate warrant and 1s. per copy of the examination. In addition to these expenses, the Quarter Sessions authorized the payment of allowances to Harris of 3s. per day for 'time and trouble' and travelling expenses at a rate of 6d. per mile. For the maintenance and lodging of each person entrusted to him, he was provided with 6d. per day and travelling costs per person of 3d. per mile. On top of these expenses was the cost of passage to Ireland, for which the Quarter Sessions allowed 4s. 2d. for the journey to Cork and Waterford and 10s. for the passage to Dublin and other ports.[55] The substantial costs incurred in removing the Irish poor had to be weighed carefully against the potential cost of maintaining them over an indeterminate period of time.

In June 1848 Superintendent Stockdale informed a government inquiry that almost all of the Irish paupers who had applied for assistance at Cardiff during the previous two years had been sent back to Ireland at a cost of 10s.–20s. per head, adding:

---

[54] PP 1850 L, Orders of Removal, p12.
[55] Gw. RO, Q/O.R. 66–0022, report of the Committee on Poor Removal, 17 January 1846.

I shall send away half-a-dozen tomorrow, or to-day (according to the wind) for 10s. 6d. per head including provisions . . . Within the last three months a Cork vessel landed upwards of 200 at this port, of whom I took between 60 and 70 (who applied for relief immediately upon landing) to Bristol, and shipped them back to Cork in a steamer, so that they would get home in about a fortnight from the time of their coming. Some of those so sent have come back here again within a fortnight, but did not apply for relief.[56]

This manner of dealing with Irish paupers was attractive only in so far as it represented a cheaper option than providing monetary relief. By the early 1850s this had ceased to be the case because of an increase in the cost of returning paupers via Bristol, there being no direct passenger service from Cardiff. Consequently, the number of removals to Ireland dipped sharply.[57]

As these statistics suggest, the absolute numbers of Irish arriving in south Wales cannot compare with the far larger deluge experienced at Liverpool. For example, the number of paupers relieved at Cardiff in the twelve months from September 1846 amounted to 3,555, whereas at Liverpool nearly 24,000 were relieved on one day alone in January 1847.[58] However, when making comparisons of this kind, the particular contexts must be borne in mind. The impact of relatively small numbers of destitute immigrants on a town of little more than 18,000 people could be substantial, and threw into high relief the inadequacies of day-to-day urban administration at a time of rapid population growth. The parish continued to be the basic unit of poor law administration based on an ideal of deferential face-to-face social relationships which was being progressively undermined by rapid demographic change.

In the absence of such deferential attitudes, some parishes faced severe difficulties in using the powers they possessed. The Merthyr Tydfil union, for example, was frustrated in its attempts to remove Irish paupers in February 1848 when the latter simply refused to appear before the justices. The same union was also hampered by difficulties in obtaining information about vessels

[56] PP 1847–8 LIII, p.31.
[57] PP 1854 XVII, p.481.
[58] Woodham-Smith, *The Great Hunger*, p.281. On Liverpool, see Frank Neal, *Sectarian Violence*, ch.3.

willing to carry the Irish and about the times of sailings.[59] As alarm at the scale of Irish immigration increased, it was feared that the system of local administration – the basis of the evolving urban structure itself – would disintegrate under the pressure of unprecedented demands on the Poor Law. As the conditions for granting relief became stricter, some vagrants resorted to petty crime in order to obtain a warm bed and food in a police cell. This had become sufficiently common during the winter months for visiting magistrates to recommend in 1850–1 that offenders 'should be kept upon the lowest scale of prison diet . . . and that means should be taken to make the confinement so distasteful as to operate as a real punishment'.[60]

Against this background, the right to remove Irish paupers was defended with particular vigour. It acquired almost totemic significance, irrespective of the numbers actually removed, as the following exchange between a government commissioner and Mr James Slater, the relieving officer of the Newport Union, demonstrates:

> Q. It appears that the main effect of the law of removal is to prevent persons from asking for legal relief, and to make them seek relief by beggary?
> A. Yes.
> Q. It does not prevent them coming from Ireland?
> A. I do not see that it prevents them coming from Ireland at all.[61]

The heat generated by the animated discussion of the right of removal fuelled speculation about the scale of poverty among the immigrants, a government commissioner asserting somewhat improbably in 1847 that 'there is but little poverty, except among the Irish'.[62] Whatever the precise degree of poverty, there was certainly a discrepancy between the number of Irish who could be removed legally and the number who actually were removed.

---

[59] Glam. RO, U/M Merthyr Board of Guardians Minute Book, 1847–8, especially 12, 19, 26 February 1848, 215, 221, 227; Tydfil Thomas, *Poor Relief in Merthyr Tydfil Union in Victorian Times* (Bridgend, 1992), p.33.

[60] *Cardiff and Merthyr Guardian*, 4 January 1851, quoted in David Jones and Alan Bainbridge, 'The "conquering of China": crime in an industrial commmunity, 1842–64', *Llafur*, 2, 4 (1979), 14.

[61] PP 1854 XVII, p.502.

[62] PP 1847 XXVII, Reports of the Commissioners of Inquiry into the State of Education in Wales, Part 1, p.366.

According to Evan David, chairman of the Cardiff Board of Guardians, some 2,000 of an estimated Irish population in the town of 4,800 in 1854 could not claim a five-year residence and so were liable to be removed should they apply for parish relief. He estimated that almost an equal number were in fact paupers, yet only a tiny proportion were actually removed.[63] In reality, despite the varied attempts to divert the Irish elsewhere or return them home, large numbers of those who arrived in south Wales entered a debilitating cycle of grinding poverty, insanitary accommodation and disease in the overcrowded lodging houses and tenements of urban Wales. Faced with these conditions in Cardiff, one commentator described the Irish in a tragically evocative phrase as bringing with them nothing more than 'pestilence on their backs, famine in their stomachs'.[64] Not all immigrants were mired in abject poverty, but enough found themselves in that condition for this generalization to ring true.

Parochial poor relief was only one of many ways in which Famine refugees came in contact with authority in Wales. As has already been seen, the newcomers were also identified as a public health problem in dire need of attention. The adoption of public health legislation by individual towns at this time created a fledgling local bureaucracy which permitted – indeed, positively encouraged – close surveillance of the inhabitants of the most insanitary districts. Detailed social observation by a network of local functionaries which included Poor Law officials and the police as well as the Officers of Health, supported these accusations. In fact, there were many instances where the responsibilities of these officials overlapped and the distinction between their roles became blurred. This was the case at Cardiff, where Superintendent Stockdale combined his police duties concerning vagrants with delegated powers from the relieving officer, allowing him the discretion to relieve those who applied for assistance late at night. The result was persistent police surveillance of lodging houses, as shown by Stockdale's description of Michael Harrington's lodging house in Stanley Street:

> On visiting today I found 45 inmates, but many more came in to sleep at nights . . . There are no bedsteads, but all lodgers lie on the ground or

[63] PP 1854 XVII, p.480.
[64] Rammell, *Report*.

floor. The children were sleeping on old orange-boxes and on shavings; that is, the younger ones, or they would be liable to be crushed in the night by persons rolling over them. Each party has with them all their stock, consisting of heaps of rags, bones, salt-fish, rotten potatoes, and other things. The stench arising from this crowded house was hardly endurable. There were only two stump bed-steads in the house. The yard at the back was unpaved; there was stagnant water in the yard, and the privy was running, and was covered with filth of the most disgusting description. The stench was sickening.[65]

Understandably, such graphic descriptions caused widespread alarm, and must have played some part in shaping attitudes to the Irish.

Popular reaction to the Famine immigrants varied from the all-too-rare cases of sympathy to the more common response of overt hostility. Irish men and women making landfall at Aberavon were provided with food and temporary shelter by a local farmer, while those striking inland to Pontypridd further east were sheltered in the cottages of working people and at the local Oddfellows Hall.[66] Yet such commendable acts of charity were no more than islands in a sea of pervasive resentment. A more typical response was reported by the government commissioners inquiring into the state of education in Wales in 1847, when they noted that 'the prevailing sentiment' among the people of the mining areas of Monmouthshire was that 'if the Government wanted to mend their condition, it had better "tackle their masters", and stop the Irish coming among them'. This comment arose specifically out of a strike against the employment of Irish labourers who, it was claimed, had caused a reduction in wages. Anticipating a major disturbance, a local magistrate was preparing to read the Riot Act at Pontypool.[67] That this incident was representative of a deeper and more widespread hostility in the region is demonstrated by events in the following year.

Tensions arising from the cumulative impact of heavy immigration, epidemics and the disruption caused by railway

[65] PP 1847–8 LIII, pp.30–1; Rammell, *Report*, p.36.
[66] James O'Brien, *Old Afan and Margam* (Aberavon, 1926), pp.159–60; David James Rees, *Pontypridd South, Past and Present* (Risca, 1983), p.47.
[67] PP 1847 XXVII, Reports of the Commissioners into the State of Education in Wales, Part. II, p.293.

construction precipitated numerous instances of ethnic conflict in the towns along the south Wales coast, culminating in a particularly serious anti-Irish riot at Cardiff in November 1848. In May of that year two Welshmen were murdered at a beer-house near Swansea by a group of Irish navvies working on the South Wales Railway, an event which sent a frisson of horror through the local populace. Anonymous threatening letters were sent to members of Swansea's Irish community and rumours of assaults on the Irish abounded in the press.[68] Later that year, in June, the houses of the well-established Irish community in the village of Llantrisant, near Cardiff, were attacked, 'without any provocation, and in the dead of night', with the aim of driving the Irish away. The cause of the outbreak remains a mystery and there was no attempt to invoke the customary justification of a reduction in wages. Nevertheless, it was reported that colliers in the neighbouring Rhondda Valley had expressed a willingness to complete the work begun by the locals but were frustrated from carrying out their threat by the intervention of the police. Further trouble in the locality was anticipated and magistrates swore in thirty special constables, whose presence in the village for the best part of a week succeeded in preventing more violence.[69] Coverage of these events in the local press occurred at the same time as reports of the arrival of Famine refugees and contributed to a composite picture of the Irish as a diseased and destitute group of lawless individuals whose presence inexorably led to disturbances of the peace. In one sense, therefore, the riot at Cardiff in November 1848 can be seen as both a product of local circumstances and a culmination of the year's hostilities in the region.

In the early hours of Sunday, 12 November 1848, a Welsh-man was stabbed by an Irishman in an altercation in Stanley Street, at the heart of an area with a large Irish population. A police constable was quick to appear on the scene of the crime, but he was too late to prevent John Connors, the murderer, from slipping away into the darkness and eluding arrest. What happened next is crucial to an understanding of the events of the following three days. The police failed to discover Connors's

[68]   *Cambrian*, 12, 19, 26 May 1848.
[69]   *Cardiff and Merthyr Guardian*, 24 June 1848.

whereabouts, even though he remained in the vicinity for the whole of Sunday before escaping. This fact enabled the press to accuse the Irish, as a group, of harbouring a murderer, and thus of being collectively culpable of the crime. 'He knew he was safe enough', thundered the *Cardiff and Merthyr Guardian*, 'and why should he conceal himself? His secret was in good hands. No one knew it but the Irish; and they never betray murderers – never.'[70] As a result, the newspaper felt justified in broadening the scope of its invective to encompass all Irish immigrants who were, in its opinion, 'the worst specimens of Irish barbarism'. Their alleged way of life caused particular offence:

> their habits filthy and degrading, having no more regard to the ordinary decencies of life than the beasts that perish . . . they are content to live in misery and idleness rather than exert themselves; and those of them who have acquired the habit of working, spend their money in thoughtless and beastly dissipation.[71]

This diatribe concluded with a pointed reference to the capacity of the law 'on this side of the channel' to make them 'adopt a mode of life more in accordance with the advanced notions of social advancement'. Such intemperate language did nothing to mollify the Welsh, but it has to be seen as a reflection of popular hostility rather than as contributing to its cause, because by the time these words appeared in print a crowd had attacked the Catholic church and the priest had fled the town.

At the Sunday evening service at St David's Roman Catholic chapel on the corner of Stanley Street, Fr Millea had exhorted anyone in the congregation with knowledge of the murderer's whereabouts to give him up to the police, an appeal which made a favourable impression on a number of the Welsh people present. However, during the afternoon of the following day, Millea observed an ominous scene as three horse-drawn carts deposited their loads of stones in the street opposite the chapel and small groups of bystanders gathered nearby. Shortly after six in the evening, a large crowd, which Millea estimated at 9,000,

---

[70] *Cardiff and Merthyr Guardian*, 18 November 1848.
[71] Ibid. For a journalist's perspective on the incident, see John O'Sullivan, 'The Stanley Street murder', in Stewart Williams (ed.), *The Cardiff Book*, III (Cardiff and Bridgend, 1977), pp.101–6.

but which was more realistically put at 2,000 by another source, gathered outside the chapel.[72] Following an exchange between Millea and a few individuals in the crowd, two police constables and three other men were permitted to search the premises for the murderer. The search was fruitless and there is no evidence to suggest that Connors had been given refuge there at any time, but the crowd smashed a few windows before attacking the houses of Irish immigrants close by, breaking their doors and smashing windows and furniture. Fr Millea seized this opportunity to flee to a safe house outside the town before moving on to the bishop's house at Chepstow. Following his departure, the crowd returned to smash the windows of the chapel and the priest's house, causing considerable damage. Hundreds of Irish people were seen thronging the roads hurrying away from the town.[73]

Although by no means all of the immigrants were practising Catholics, they were, nevertheless, provided with a rallying point for defending themselves as a group. This became apparent on Tuesday, 14 November, when three hundred Irish navvies working on the South Wales Railway entered the town determined to protect the priest and the chapel 'with their lives'. In response, the magistrates posted bills warning against any further violent attacks on people or property. Thereafter, riotous behaviour subsided into an uneasy peace, while the murderer remained at large.[74] That the events at Cardiff reverberated throughout the whole region is demonstrated by the contents of an advertisement placed in the *Cardiff and Merthyr Guardian* by the parish priest of Dowlais and Merthyr Tydfil; it publicized the resolutions of a public meeting of the Irish, which unanimously declared their abhorrence at the murder in Cardiff and their determination that the accused would not find sanctuary in their midst. A resolution deploring the attack on the Catholic chapel and the priest's house was sweetened by a collection of £2 for the dead man's widow. The conduct and resolutions of the meeting

---

[72] *The Tablet*, 18 November 1848. This informative article is signed 'T.J.B. – Nov. 15th, 1848'. It was probably from the pen of Bishop T. J. Brown, as Fr Millea fled Cardiff for the bishop's residence at Chepstow. See *Monmouthshire Merlin*, 18 November 1848.
[73] *The Tablet*, 18 November 1848.
[74] *Monmouthshire Merlin*, 18 November 1848.

were welcomed by the newspaper, which hoped it would have 'a beneficial effect upon the public mind'.[75]

John Connors was finally apprehended ten miles away at the town of Pontypridd on 19 November after the police had kept Irish lodging-houses in the area under surveillance.[76] However, the fact of his capture did not signify the end of ethnic conflict. The Irish lodging-house keeper at Pontypridd, where Connors was arrested, had the windows of his house smashed, despite the fact that he had alerted the police to the murderer's presence, and three Irishmen working in the Rhondda were chased down the valley by a large crowd of colliers. The grim legacy of the event continued until the end of the year. At the end of November 1848, Irish people leaving Sunday Mass at the Catholic chapel in Dowlais, near Merthyr, were attacked 'by a party of idle fellows', forcing them to flee for shelter; the clash was attributed to a combination of factors, including the murder in Cardiff and a reduction of wages in the iron industry which was blamed on the Irish.[77] This incident was closely followed by the attempted murder of an Irish girl at Cardiff and the manslaughter of an Irish hawker at Newport, allegedly simply because he was Irish.[78]

The navvies' action in defence of the church had held out the prospect of an escalation of the conflict and brought into sharp focus the signal failure of the police to intervene to prevent the destruction of property. While it could be argued that the local police were unable to call on sufficient numbers to make a decisive intervention in events, it was also the case that the mayor had refused to authorize the use of a contingent of sixty-five soldiers billeted in the town. Official inaction prompted an anonymous writer in the Catholic press (probably Bishop T. J. Brown) to accuse the civil authorities in Cardiff of criminal misconduct originating in 'disgraceful anti-Irish feeling'. He insisted that there was sufficient evidence of dereliction of duty to warrant a government investigation.[79] As E. J. Hobsbawm has pointed out in his study of the 'city mob', there existed a

---

[75] *Cardiff and Merthyr Guardian*, 25 November 1848.
[76] Ibid.
[77] *Cardiff and Merthyr Guardian*, 8 December 1848.
[78] *Cardiff and Merthyr Guardian*, 15 December 1848; *Monmouthshire Merlin*, 2 December 1848; *The Tablet*, 23 December 1848.
[79] *The Tablet*, 23 December 1848.

potential body of rioters in all important pre-industrial cities where the police and military were slack. Although Cardiff in the late 1840s did not possess all the characteristics of a 'pre-industrial city', it is possible, nevertheless, to discern here some of the key characteristics of the city mob as described by Hobsbawm,[80] especially the complicity of the police in assisting members of the crowd to search the Catholic chapel, and, by their inaction, the tacit acceptance by the mayor and magistrates of the validity of communal justice until the prospect of a counter-disturbance by the navvies materialized.

Far from constituting a casual assembly of people representing a degeneration into wanton 'lawlessness', the crowd comprised a group of people with specific goals which they sought to achieve by direct action. Principal among their objectives was the capture of John Connors who, it was believed, had been concealed in the chapel, a supposition based in part on the images of Catholicism circulated in 'No Popery' literature, which depicted Catholic chapels as places where dark and dreadful deeds occurred. When the search of the chapel proved fruitless, the crowd focused its attentions on what it considered to be the institutional symbol of the Irish presence in the town, thus endowing the conflict with a wider significance. The location of the Catholic chapel on the corner of the street in which the murder took place in an area of concentrated Irish settlement undoubtedly reinforced its symbolic significance as a key and highly visible ethnic institution. The riot was a manifestation of popular anger, representing both a severe warning to the Irish and a stern reproach to the authorities for failing to apprehend the murderer.

The disturbances which occurred along the south Wales coast in 1848 demonstrate the interplay between local grievances and wider regional developments. They took place against a background of large-scale immigration, acute strain on the poor law, severe overcrowding of lodging houses, and an increasing awareness of the dangers to public health posed by insanitary living conditions. Furthermore, the situation was further complicated by the disruption resulting from the construction of the South

---

[80] E. J. Hobsbawm, *Primitive Rebels* (Manchester, 1959), pp.108–25; Gwyn A. Williams has written that the city mob existed in 'close symbiosis' with city government: 'The primitive rebel and the history of the Welsh', in *idem*, *The Welsh in Their History* (London, 1982), p.4.

Wales Railway and the presence of a large body of Irish navvies. Under these circumstances, the Irish became a focus for the tensions generated by a sudden increase in population and rapid urbanization. Neither these conditions nor the Famine immigration came to an end in 1848.[81]

Immigration resumed in the spring of 1849. Reporting on the removal of Irish pauper families from Cardiff in March, the *Cardiff and Merthyr Guardian* despaired that although the Irish were sent away by the score, immigration took place by the thousand.[82] Problems associated with the renewed influx and the resulting overcrowding of lodging houses were exacerbated by the outbreak of a cholera epidemic. The first case to be identified in Wales occurred in Cardiff on 13 May 1849, the outbreak reaching its height early in June. By the 23rd of that month, 138 deaths in the town had been attributed to the disease and many of the inhabitants had fled in terror, leaving their houses vacant, especially, it was noted, the Irish lodging houses. Blame for the outbreak was swiftly placed on the Irish, who were accused of importing the disease 'direct from Skibereen and Clonakilty'. As a result, the dying embers of anti-Irish hostility were fanned once again.[83] That the incidence of cholera was generally higher in working-class districts and lower in the more salubrious neighbourhoods was a fact which either went unnoticed or was subsumed in the belief that the Irish had undermined the condition of the natives.

At Merthyr, where the death toll reached 1,467, it was reported that there had been instances where, after a death in the house, the Irish inhabitants had fled, 'carrying the key to the front door; and it was necessary, in order to save breaking in the door, to get out the corpse for interment through the front window'.[84] Catholic priests ministering to their congregations in

---

[81] In north Wales, where the immigrants were much less numerous, ethnic hostility at this time was more explicitly linked to religious anxieties, the principal stimulus being the so-called 'Papal aggression' crisis of 1850. In December of that year the Irish Roman Catholics of Mold in Flintshire were attacked by a 'No Popery' mob. See *Liverpool Mercury*, 13 December 1850.

[82] *Cardiff and Merthyr Guardian*, 17 March 1849.

[83] G. Penrhyn Jones, 'Cholera in Wales', *National Library of Wales Journal*, X (1957–8), 290–1; *Morning Chronicle*, 8 April 1850, reprinted in J. Ginswick (ed.), *Labour and the Poor in England and Wales, 1849–1851* (London, 1983), p.62; *Cardiff and Merthyr Guardian*, 2, 8, 16 June 1849.

[84] *Morning Chronicle*, reprinted in J. Ginswick, *Labour and the Poor*, p.67.

such circumstances were fortunate to avoid death. At Newport, the neighbours who helped Fr Cavalli to lay out the bodies of a whole family which had been obliterated by the cholera contracted the disease themselves and died, but the priest escaped unscathed.[85] During the winter of 1849–50 a public subscription at Swansea raised fifty sovereigns for Fr Kavanagh – who had established a quarantine area of tents in open fields – in recognition of his 'long unwearied exertions during the late visitation of Cholera in the town and neighbourhood, regardless of personal risk or inconvenience, and impartially exercised towards all in need, independent of creed or opinion . . .' Another priest recalled that when the cholera had abated in Swansea, the indefatigable Fr Kavanagh moved on to assist at Cardiff.[86]

Living conditions in the worst parts of these towns were generally appalling. Rapid immigration, unregulated jerry-building of cramped and inadequate housing, the absence of a protected water supply, poor drainage and rudimentary sanitation constituted ideal conditions for the spread of disease. The areas inhabited by the Irish were singled out as being particularly worthy of condemnation. Weeks before the cholera epidemic reached Swansea, G. T. Clark undertook an inquiry into the sanitary condition of the town on behalf of the Board of Health. He took particular exception to a court known as 'Little Ireland', which, with other areas of Irish settlement, suffered worst from the epidemic on its arrival six weeks later.[87] With these conditions in mind, the populace of towns which had escaped the epidemic expressed considerable foreboding about the unrestricted movement of large groups of people. In June 1849 the rector of Coity, near the market town of Bridgend, chaired a meeting of local inhabitants who were anxious about the prevalence of cholera in the surrounding district. 'Bridgend stands between Cardiff & the Western Seaports', he informed the General Board of Health,

---

[85] *St Peter's Chair*, August 1892, 177.
[86] *Cambrian*, 21 December 1849; Archives of St David's Priory, University of Wales, Swansea, (37) b, f, g, h.
[87] G. T. Clark, *Report to the General Board of Health on a Preliminary Inquiry into . . . the Sanitary Condition of the Town and Borough of Swansea* (London, 1849), p.10; Penrhyn Jones, 'Cholera in Wales', 293.

and vast numbers of destitute Irish are continually passing through the Town – many of them now remain here fearing to go elsewhere lest they may be attacked by the disease. It is computed that as many as 700 of this wretched class slept here a few nights ago, and the Town was previously much crowded by men engaged in the formation of the South Wales Railway.[88]

The impression of an unspeakable horror closing in on an island of undefiled purity is palpable and created a siege mentality among the inhabitants. Sadly, the town did not escape the ravages of cholera, fifty deaths attributable to the disease occurring there by the end of the year.[89]

The cholera epidemic of 1849 prompted local authorities to adopt the Public Health Act of 1848. Once this was done, the new Officers of Health set about the difficult task of identifying the sources of disease before embarking on the business of enforcing reforms. Streets, courts and lodging houses which accommodated a high proportion of Irish immigrants were quickly identified as one of their primary concerns. In their detailed annual reports, the officials charted the course of diseases and passed confident moral judgements on the behaviour of the inhabitants of lodging houses and slums. From these reports, there emerges a picture of the Irish as being guilty of overcrowding and of habits inimical to effective urban sanitation. Consequently, when cholera broke out again in 1854, attention homed in on the Irish. The outbreak of 1854 coincided with an upturn in Irish immigration. Statistics of passengers landing at Newport between 1849 and 1853 show a steady increase during these years (Table III.2). While it is unlikely that the influx reached the same high levels as those in the crisis years of 1847–9, nevertheless ships disgorged as many as 100–200 people at a time, all starving and in a wretched condition. Once again, the captains were accused of landing large numbers at secluded sites on the coast, principally because of the hostility they encountered from poor townspeople congregating at the ports to jeer at them. As in the late 1840s, women and children formed a large proportion of the newcomers, a fact underlined by the disproportionate expenditure of the Poor Law authorities on

[88] J. Harding to the General Board of Health, 4 June 1849, PRO, MH 13, box 31/1 (i) – (iii).

[89] Penrhyn Jones, 'Cholera in Wales', 295.

Table III.2 Irish passengers landed at Newport, 1849–1853

1849	1,702
1850	2,140
1851	3,739
1852	3,052
1853	4,812

Source: PP 1854 LV, The Number of Passengers Landed at this Port from the Coast of Ireland, 1849–53.

Irish midwifery cases. While poor Welsh and English women preferred to be attended by a woman, the poor Irish (particularly at Newport) invariably sent for a doctor whose services were paid for by the relieving officer.[90] The response of the local authorities to the Irish continued in the same vein as in the late 1840s. The use of the police in public health matters during the measles epidemic in Cardiff in 1854, an outbreak which was confidently attributed to the Irish presence, demonstrates that the new-comers were regarded as a problem of social control; on that occasion, it was reported that the Irish were 'being kept in subjection by the intelligent and unwearied Officer of Health, aided by the Superintendent of Police'.[91]

Many of those arriving in 1854 followed in the footsteps of members of the families who had already made the crossing to Wales. While in some cases it was claimed that priests in Ireland paid for the emigrants' passage, in others Post Office orders of 1s. 6d. to 2s. were sent by brothers and sisters in Britain to pay for relatives to join them. This is an excellent example of chain migration, the practice of an individual moving to a destination where relatives or people from the same village have settled who can provide financial assistance with the cost of the journey. This practice enabled family units to be reassembled after a period of separation. But, as one of the few first-hand accounts of this movement demonstrates, enormous risks were involved. Bridget Sullivan, a widow from Bantry in County Cork, was removed from south Wales to Ireland with six of her eight children in 1854. She described how

[90] PP 1854 XVII, pp.474, 492–4.
[91] *Cardiff and Merthyr Guardian,* 28 April 1854.

about a month ago my eldest daughter left Bantry for Wales, and on last Friday week, the 2d instant, I was wishful to go to Wales myself with my children; some men allowed me to ride in a car from Bantry to Ballycolley, and from there I went to Cork; on Tuesday after, I went to Mr Adams, the poor overseer (that was the term she gave), and told him that I wanted bread for my children and myself, and asked him for relief, and I also asked him to send me to Wales by the 'Wave of Cork', Captain John Sutton, and begged him to give me a note to Captain Sutton to take me to Newport. He asked me what I should do there, and I told him that many people said that at Abergavenny my eldest boy and girl would earn 10s. a week, and everything there was so nicely to be got; he said, I think they are too young for that, and I said, if you will only send me over, I am satisfied with the good account. He then went to Captain Sutton and asked him to take me, and the Captain agreed, and I promised Mr Adams to send him back 10s. when I got it in Wales. The captain kept me on biscuits and coffee, and when I came to Newport he gave me 6d., and afterwards 4 1/2d., and potatoes and meat. I declare that but for the good report I had, I should not have come; and if Mr Adams had not spoken to the captain I could not have come.

The mark x of Bridget Sullivan, 14 June 1854.[92]

In this case, the desire to reunite kin came to grief. It was a poignant reminder that broken links in the chain might be difficult to repair.

However, despite the superficial similarities between the influx of the late 1840s and that of 1854, fever was not as close a companion of the destitute as it had been on the earlier occasion. In spite of the claim that the Irish were responsible for an outbreak of measles at Cardiff,[93] there does not appear to have been a direct link between renewed immigration and the outbreak of cholera (although it is likely that the emaciated and undernourished newcomers succumbed more readily once the epidemic began). Measured in terms of mortality, the outbreak of 1854 was much less serious than its predecessor five years earlier: at Merthyr Tydfil, for example, there were 455 fatalities in 1854 compared with 1,467 in 1849.[94] Even so, the death rate was scarcely negligible. Many inhabitants of neighbourhoods where

---

[92] PP 1854 XVII, pp.491–2.
[93] *Cambrian*, 28 April 1854.
[94] Penrhyn Jones, 'Cholera in Wales', 295–6.

the disease took hold fled in fear for their lives. In September 1854 it was reported that a quarter of the Irish had left Merthyr, and that the outflow had not yet abated. Cholera was particularly virulent among the Irish of Caedraw and Merthyr, and it was claimed that by October, twenty-five of every thirty fatalities in these areas were of Irish men, women or children.[95]

The Famine immigration and its after-effects in the 1850s evidently precipitated an urban crisis in the ports of south Wales. Towns such as Newport and Cardiff experienced unprecedented immigration and were faced with social problems over which they had no control. At a time when the state was chary of intervening in social and economic life, the primary responsibility for the health and subsistence needs of the newcomers lay with the comparatively weak institutions of local government, such as the poor law, which had not been designed to cope with sudden large increases in the numbers of ill and destitute people. Especially during the worst years, 1847–9, local functionaries were clearly bewildered by the scale of the influx and frustrated by their inability to stop it at source. Complaints that Irish landlords were shirking their responsibility to relieve the starving poor betrayed an inability to comprehend the scale of the Famine and a misplaced faith in the integrity of social relationships in the Irish countryside. As emigration from Ireland lost its urgency in the 1850s and the number of immigrants to Wales decreased, pressure on the poor law eased considerably: at Newport, for example, the number of Irish applications for poor relief declined by more than two-thirds between 1849 and 1853.[96] It was clear by the mid-1850s that the civic institutions so severely strained by immigration and epidemics had weathered the storm and remained intact.

These years support a view of migration as a disorientating and disorganizing experience, uprooting individuals and families and casting them willy-nilly into an alien society with different

[95] Glam. RO, D/DG, Dowlais Iron Company Letterbooks, 1854 (2), nos. 477, 479 and 493; *Cardiff and Merthyr Guardian*, 13 October 1854. See also Tydfil Thomas, *Poor Relief in Merthyr Tydfil Union*, pp.53–60, 134–9.

[96] PP 1854 XVII, p.496. On the decline in emigration, see David Fitzpatrick, *Irish Emigration, 1801–1921* (Dundalgan, 1984), pp.28–9.

norms and values. And yet out of this apparent confusion grew a vibrant and varied ethnic culture expressed through distinctively Irish institutions. As a result, many observers perceived the Irish as a uniquely clannish minority tenaciously clinging to their own culture and replicating the customs and usages of rural Ireland rather than assimilating to Welsh society. Yet they also developed new ethnic institutions which grew out of their experiences in urban Wales and shaped their interaction with members of the wider society. The success with which they did so depended to some extent on the degree to which they clustered together in the towns and villages, enabling them to interact on a day-to-day basis with those who shared the same cultural background.

IV

'SECTIONAL COLONISTS': PATTERNS OF IRISH SETTLEMENT, 1851–1871

By crossing the Irish Sea, the Famine refugees made the transition from a rural, peasant society to an urban and industrializing one. Some might have encountered town life before – albeit briefly – as seasonal harvesters *en route* to work on British farms, but it is likely that the vast majority were totally unprepared for the new conditions they faced.[1] Urban life presented novel opportunities for immigrants, even though not all were equally well equipped to take advantage of them. In the immediate post-Famine years, it was the constraints of poverty and low-quality accommodation which were prominent as the majority grappled with the problems attendant upon their swift transplantation to a new society. For at least twenty years after the Famine, the consequences of that tragic experience continued to shape the attitudes of the host society towards the Irish. The immigration of those years occurred at a critical juncture in the process of urbanization in Wales, when the acute pressure of population growth and the unprecedented demands for assistance from the poor law placed an almost intolerable weight upon civic institutions. To middle-class observers the Irish epitomized the potentially threatening confusion of a mass society resistant to regulation by authority. More than any other group the Irish were subjected to critical scrutiny by the new agencies of urban reform and control, ranging from the Medical Officers of Health appointed under new public health legislation to the new county police forces created in 1856, as well as investigative journalists and charitable and religious organizations. Consequently they appear in the literature of the time as a 'problem' to which a 'solution' must be found.

---

[1] 'In general the intensity of internal migration and rural–urban movement [in Ireland] was low compared with that in nineteenth-century Britain.' David Fitzpatrick, *Irish Emigration, 1801–1921* (Dundalgan, 1984), p.5.

An ability to regroup and fashion an ethnic identity capable of negotiating contact with other groups in the receiving society was an important theme during these years. The Famine influx led to a substantial increase in the number of the Irish in Wales. Between 1841 and 1861, their numbers increased by 344 per cent to reach a high point of 28,089. Although modest in comparison with the numbers resident in cities like London, Liverpool and Glasgow, this increase was the basis for a proliferation of ethnic societies and institutions, thereby contributing to the development of a more richly textured immigrant experience. If an ethnic identity was to be sustained over time it required the close residence of those from a similar background. The exact extent to which this occurred has been the subject of intense debate in recent years, and has focused on the extent to which the Irish were segregated from the host society.[2]

Broadly speaking, pre-Famine patterns of settlement persisted in Wales after 1850, with a slim majority of the Irish concentrated in the four largest towns. Merthyr Tydfil, Newport, Cardiff, and Swansea accounted for 54 per cent of the Irish-born in Wales in 1851, the vast majority of the remainder being dispersed among the smaller towns and industrial villages of the south Wales coalfield. These smaller settlements also varied in size and structure: at one end of the spectrum was the small iron-producing town of Tredegar in Monmouthshire, which had established the rudiments of urban life by the mid-nineteenth century, whereas at the other end were villages such as Llantrisant in Glamorgan, which retained a semi-rural character but provided accommodation for Irish workers at the local coal mines and their families. With the exception of Wrexham in north-east Wales, very few settled outside these areas. The principal towns of Irish settlement in Wales also varied significantly in size and economic structure, and Famine refugees entered them at very different stages of their development.

---

[2] Graham Davis, *The Irish in Britain, 1815–1914* (Dublin, 1991); M. A. Busteed, R. I. Hodgson and T. F. Kennedy, 'The myth and reality of Irish migrants in mid-nineteenth century Manchester: a preliminary study', in Patrick O'Sullivan (ed.), *The Irish in the New Communities, The Irish World Wide*, vol.II (London, 1992); Colin G. Pooley, 'Segregation or integration? The residential experience of the Irish in mid-Victorian Britain', in Roger Swift and Sheridan Gilley (eds.), *The Irish in Britain, 1815–1939* (London, 1989), pp.60–83; Roger Swift and Sheridan Gilley (eds.), *The Irish in the Victorian City* (Beckenham, 1985).

Merthyr Tydfil was the largest Welsh town in 1851 with a population of 46,378. Its growth and prosperity over the previous seventy years were intimately linked to the fortunes of iron manufacture, which formed the backbone of the local economy and determined the town's occupational structure. Dominated by four great iron companies with resident quasi-feudal capitalists, the town possessed a distinctive character. Lacking a developed and articulate middle class to mediate between the all-powerful ironmasters and the working class, it also lacked effective civic institutions to weld together the disparate urban villages of which it was composed. Merthyr retained the character of a frontier town until the 1860s, when determined efforts in the field of sanitary reform finally tamed the urban environment and provided a focus for civic politics which avoided the bitter class conflict of earlier decades.[3] In 1851 it had an Irish-born population of 3,051, or 6.6 per cent of the whole. Although somewhat smaller in size, the three ports of Swansea, Newport and Cardiff were more heterogeneous in social and economic terms.

By contrast, Swansea had an established civic identity by the mid-nineteenth century. It contained a thriving middle class with literary, philosophical and antiquarian institutions as well as commercial interests. One visitor claimed in 1850 that with its 'wide and airy' streets and handsome public buildings, it had no rival in the principality, although his verdict on the housing of the poor was less complimentary.[4] As late as the 1820s the town was still renowned as a bathing resort, in spite of its prominence as a centre of commerce and the existence of heavy industry in the locality. In fact, its expansion in the early nineteenth century is mainly attributable to the growth of the copper and associated metal industries. As these enterprises were not as labour-intensive as iron or coal production, the pace of population growth was not as swift here as in Merthyr, a factor which made Swansea a more stable urban community during these otherwise

---

[3] Harold Carter and Sandra Wheatley, *Merthyr Tydfil in 1851* (Cardiff, 1982); Gwyn A. Williams, *The Merthyr Rising* (London, 1978). There is a valuable general survey of urban development in Glamorgan in Harold Carter, 'The structure of Glamorgan towns in the nineteenth century', in Prys Morgan (ed.), *Glamorgan County History*, vol.VI (Cardiff, 1988), pp.151–71.

[4] Report from the *Morning Chronicle*, reproduced in J. Ginswick (ed.), *Labour and the Poor in England and Wales, 1849–1851* (London, 1983), pp.175–6.

turbulent decades. With a population of 31,139 in 1851, it was –
in the words of one historian – 'a composite town, a community
of lesser industrial villages aware of their own individuality but
acknowledging the greater reality of the whole'.[5] Its Irish-born
contingent of 1,333 represented 4.2 per cent of the town's
population.

Also on the coast, Newport (with a population of 19,323 in
1851) owed a great deal to the export of iron and coal. Its location was ideal for serving its hinterland of the industrializing
Monmouthshire Valleys, and the port benefited from an
exemption from the duties levied on coal and culm in the coastal
trade. After reform of the municipal corporation in 1835, there
followed a decade of expansion, with the construction of
working-class housing in the Pillgwenlly area and the erection of
public buildings such as banks and a town hall. However,
Newport was superseded by Cardiff as the region's principal coal
exporter by the end of the 1840s, a key contributory factor being
the early construction of the railway between Merthyr and
Cardiff in 1841. Newport lagged behind its neighbour by a
decade in developing railway communications with its industrial
hinterland; it continued to rely on canals and tramroads. Unlike
Merthyr, Newport possessed an articulate middle class.[6] The
Irish-born represented 10.7 per cent of the town's population in
1851, the seventh highest percentage of the largest British
towns.[7]

By comparison, Cardiff, with a population of only 18,351 in
1851, was smaller than the other three and had yet to experience
the spectacular growth which, from the 1870s, would transform
it into the world's premier coal-exporting port. In the 1850s it
had no more than a rudimentary urban structure and, with a
'mottled' settlement pattern, it displayed many of the characteristics of the pre-industrial town. Consequently, the impact of
heavy Irish immigration in the late 1840s was felt more keenly

---

[5] I. G. Jones, 'The city and its villages', in Ralph A. Griffiths (ed.), *The City of Swansea:
Challenges and Change* (Stroud, 1990), p.82.

[6] J. H. Morris and L. J. Williams, *The South Wales Coal Industry, 1841–1875* (Cardiff,
1958); Brynmor P. Jones, *From Elizabeth I to Victoria: the Government of Newport (Mon.),
1555–1850* (Newport, 1957), pp.134–41; David Williams, *John Frost: A Study in Chartism*
(Cardiff, 1939), chs.2–3.

[7] By 1871 it had slipped to twelfth position, although still higher than Merthyr Tydfil
at sixteenth. Pooley, 'Segregation or integration?', pp.66–7. Because Cardiff was a
comparatively small settlement at this time, it does not feature in the list.

there than in other Welsh towns. Before the Famine, the Irish contingent at Cardiff was largely composed of navvies working on the Bute Dock and their families. With the completion of that project in the early 1840s, many of these workers moved elsewhere in search of employment, so it is reasonable to assume that refugees from the Famine formed a higher proportion of the Irish-born here in the mid-nineteenth century than in other towns in south Wales. The comparatively small number of 3,317 Irish-born residents in 1851 comprised 18.1 per cent of the town's population. Cardiff's growth was inextricably linked to the powerful leadership of the Bute estate, whose officials wielded enormous influence on both the expansion of dock capacity and the development of residential areas.[8]

Table IV.1 Irish-born in the principal towns of south Wales in 1851

Town	Popn	Irish-born	Percentage
Merthyr Tydfil	46,378	3,051	6.6
Swansea	31,139	1,333	4.3
Newport	19,323	2,069	10.7
Cardiff	18,351	3,317	18.1

Source: Census of Population, 1851.

The nature of Irish settlement in these towns was determined by the demands of the local job market, as is revealed by variations in the sex ratio among Irish immigrants. At Merthyr, for example, the hegemony of the iron industry meant that there were few opportunities for women to secure paid employment. Consequently, the imbalance between the sexes was more pronounced there than in other Welsh towns, with women comprising 42 per cent of Irish-born residents in 1861. At the opposite extreme, Irish women were in a slight majority at Newport, where they accounted for 51.5 per cent of the borough's Irish-born population in 1861. Specific reasons for this female predominance are difficult to identify, as the town lacked

---

[8] C. Roy Lewis, 'A stage in the development of the industrial town: a case study of Cardiff, 1845–75', *Transactions of the Institute of British Geographers*, 4, 2 (1979); M. J. Daunton, *Coal Metropolis Cardiff, 1870–1914* (Leicester, 1977); John Davies, *Cardiff and the Marquesses of Bute* (Cardiff, 1981), ch.V.

the kind of industries (especially textiles) most readily associated with female employment in other parts of Britain; neither did it have a particularly high demand for female domestic servants. Nevertheless, the town had a more developed service sector than predominantly industrial towns like Merthyr and offered women opportunities for general labouring at the docks. In fact, a report in February 1847 claimed that agents in many rural districts in Ireland were promising that women at Newport would be 'engaged in whatever numbers they please at 2 shillings and 2/6 per day, at washing and other domestic work'.[9] The sex ratio in other towns fell somewhere between these extremes, with women comprising 44.6 per cent of the Irish-born in Wales as a whole.[10]

A factor common to these towns of contrasting size and character was the attempt to regulate the urban environment and create a civic identity to which citizens could give their allegiance. This aspiration was articulated against the background of increasing spatial differentiation. One of the most important changes in the internal structure of nineteenth-century towns was the increasing tendency for social differences to be translated into spatial distance. As the middle classes abandoned the town centres in favour of the outskirts and the new suburbs, central areas became more solidly working class in character. The timing of this development varied from town to town and could take on different forms. Thus, whereas Newport and Cardiff increasingly developed satellite suburbs from mid-century, at Merthyr Tydfil the ironmasters removed themselves as much by the grandeur of their houses and surrounding parkland as they did by physical distance.[11] This is not to say that working-class areas were homogeneous and socially undifferentiated. Significant differences in status demarcated one street from another, and distanced the residents of streets from the adjacent populous and secluded courts, which were reached by alleys off the main thoroughfares.

How do Irish immigrants fit into this picture? Some historians have argued that on the basis of place of residence they were a highly segregated minority in urban Wales. According to Martin

    [9] *The Times*, 19 February 1847.
    [10] For comparisons with other British towns, see Colin G. Pooley, 'Segregation or integration?', pp.66–70.
    [11] Harold Carter and Sandra Wheatley, *Merthyr Tydfil*, p.106.

Daunton, for example, the Irish in Cardiff were almost as segregated in 1871 as the black population of Philadelphia had been in 1860, a comparison which suggests a high degree of segregation indeed. Similarly, in her study of Swansea in mid-century, Joan Rees found that the Irish were the most highly segregated migrant group whose position actually worsened in the twenty years after the Famine, while at Merthyr Tydfil the Irish were not so firmly segregated but were, nevertheless, concentrated in specific areas of the town and remained under-represented in areas where the Welsh working class predominated.[12] However, indices of segregation are only one strand of a bigger story. There were compelling reasons – both cultural and economic – for the Irish to cluster together. A common background and place of origin were of great importance, although this factor may have been overstated by outside observers during the early years of settlement, as, according to Canon Richards, Wexford people originally lived apart from the remainder of their compatriots in Swansea, while those hailing from Waterford, Tipperary and Cork all had their distinctive customs. These disparate elements became 'a united and increasing and lively community' only 'by degrees'.[13] The Irish were also drawn together by the attitudes of outsiders, who perceived them as a homogeneous pariah group constituting a very real threat to the health, employment and values of the host society. Hostility was a powerful solvent of divisions in immigrant ranks and helped to create a context within which a new shared identity could be forged.

Towns are often seen as melting pots in which people of different cultures and backgrounds intermingle and interact, creating new institutions and ways of behaving; they are also sites of profound social divisions and inequalities which frequently assume a territorial aspect. To take but one example, participants in anti-Irish disturbances appear to have acted according to their own mental maps of the towns in which they lived, breaking the doors, smashing the windows and destroying the

---

[12] Daunton, *Coal Metropolis*, pp.134–6; J. C. M. Rees, 'Evolving patterns of residence in a nineteenth century city: Swansea, 1851–1871', unpublished University of Wales Ph.D. thesis (1983), vol.II, 406–8; Harold Carter and Sandra Wheatley, *Merthyr Tydfil*, pp.29–31.

[13] J. W. Richards, *Reminiscences of the Early Days of the Parish and Church of St Joseph's, Greenhill* (Swansea, 1919), p.10.

furniture of the houses considered to lie in Irish territory. This was the case in Cardiff in 1848, when the crowd shifted the focus of its attack from the Catholic church to the streets of Irish settlement nearby. Even in the small town of St Asaph in north Wales, during the so-called 'Papal aggression' crisis of 1850 police officers felt compelled to divert a 'No Popery' crowd bent on vigorously burning effigies of Guy Fawkes and Cardinal Wiseman away from the street where Irish Catholics were concentrated.[14] At Ebbw Vale in 1879, English and Welsh rioters 'commenced the wholesale smash of windows in the two top rows of houses in Newtown, this being the principal quarter of the Irish',[15] while at Tredegar in 1882 the movement of rioters from one part of the town to another revealed the existence of an ethnic geography which allowed them to identify targets to attack.[16] Hostility was a compelling reason for immigrants to cling together.

Another factor of critical importance in explaining Irish clustering in the period immediately after the Famine was the tendency for newcomers to find cheap accommodation in Irish-run lodging houses. This was particularly true of the main ports and other settlements near the coast. Even in the small towns of north Wales, where comparatively few Irish settled, the same phenomenon was observed. At Bangor, the Irish were dispropor-tionately concentrated in squalid lodging houses in a handful of streets. The town's Medical Officer of Health complained in 1849 of the overcrowding prevalent in these houses, claiming that on one night in October of that year there were 111 men, women and children resident in nine houses.[17] Irish lodging-house keepers exploited the distress of their destitute compatriots by sub-letting rooms and turning a blind eye to further sub-letting by tenants. It was these dwellings which featured so prominently in the reports of local Medical Officers of Health. Indeed, in Cardiff in the 1850s intensive surveillance of lodging houses to combat overcrowding resulted in the focus of Irish

[14] *Carnarvon and Denbigh Herald*, 9 November 1850.
[15] *Monmouthshire Merlin*, 2 January 1880.
[16] See Louise Miskell, 'Custom, conflict and community: a study of the Irish in south Wales and Cornwall, 1861–1891', unpublished University of Wales Ph.D. thesis (1996).
[17] G. T. Clark, *Report to General Board of Health, on a Preliminary Inquiry into the Sewerage, Drainage, and Supply of Water, and the Sanitary Condition of the Inhabitants of the Borough of Bangor* (London,1849), pp.7–14.

settlement shifting from the neighbourhoods surrounding Stanley Street in the centre of the town to the adjacent area of Newtown. By 1871, 54.3 per cent of the population of Inner Newtown was Irish-born, while those who identified themselves as 'Irish' but had not been born in Ireland accounted for a sizeable portion of the remainder.[18]

In one sense, this achieved nothing more than shifting an intractable problem from one part of the town to another, as the evils of the lodging-house system reappeared in the Newtown district under a different guise and with greater virulence. By concentrating their efforts on eliminating contagious diseases by the removal of filth, middle-class reformers had left the problem of overcrowded working-class housing unaddressed. Newtown was a district of new housing to the east of the original area of Irish settlement. It consisted of two- and four-roomed cottages thrown up by speculative builders, and it contained few registered lodging houses which could be legally inspected and regulated. Instead, tenants of private houses simply sub-let rooms in the dwelling or, having rented a room, even sub-let bed space to other families. This practice was a result of the high rents of between 5s. 6d. and 6s. per week charged to labourers earning no more than 12s. per week. In his report for 1855, H. J. Paine quoted the example of Bartholomew Sullivan who rented 6 Whitmore Street at a rent of 6s. per week plus 2d. for water. Together with his wife and two children, Sullivan occupied the front room on the ground floor, which also doubled up as a shop for selling dried fish; the back room was let to a married couple and their three children. Upstairs, a room containing no furniture other than a bed was rented to a married couple, while the adjoining room was occupied by three single women. The income from these sub-tenants provided Sullivan with rent for the whole house, with 6d. to spare. It was calculated that Cardiff had 393 such Irish houses containing more than one family.[19]

The lack of sufficient working-class housing at Newport was exposed to a searing attack by Fr Richardson in 1873. In an

---

[18] Allan M. Williams, 'Migration and residential patterns in mid-nineteenth century Cardiff', *Cambria*, IV (1979), 6–8; annual reports of the Medical Officer of Health, H. J Paine; Roger Lee Brown, *Irish Scorn, English Pride and the Welsh Tongue* (Tongwynlais, 1987), pp.33–4.

[19] H. J. Paine, *Third Annual Report of the Officer of Health to the Cardiff Local Board of Health* [for 1855] (Cardiff,1856), pp.12–14,17.

address to the town's Catholic Association for the Suppression of Drunkenness, he identified overcrowding as the principal social evil inimical to provident behaviour and sobriety. His most trenchant criticisms were reserved for the town's capitalists, who had 'forgotten their duty to their own bone and sinew' by failing to provide adequate accommodation for working people:

> Go into the Brick-yard and the courts of Cross-street; into Jones-court, with its reeking cesspools close before their doors, and tell me, are these the habitations you rich merchants of Newport provide for your noble, generous workmen, who are helping you to make your fortunes?[20]

Although he conceded that a start had been made by pulling down slum areas like Friars' Fields and Westlake's Court (the latter having been described in 1850 as 'inhabited by low Irish, low in position, filthy and unhealthy'),[21] this act had not been an unalloyed blessing, as no provision had been made for the many hundreds made homeless as a result. The poor Irish suffered disproportionately from these developments, and so their need for accommodation as lodgers intensified.

An analysis of census data for 1851 shows that a high percentage of the Irish in Cardiff (50.3 per cent) lived as lodgers. This was undoubtedly a product of the acute social problems facing Irish immigrants in the late 1840s, as by 1871 the proportion of Irish lodgers had decreased appreciably (50.3 per cent of the Irish at Cardiff were lodgers in 1851, but only 17.5 per cent in 1871). Similar results have been reported for other towns. At Swansea in 1851, lodgers were three-and-a-half times more likely to have been born in Ireland than elsewhere, while Irish households in the upland mining parishes of south Wales had a higher percentage of lodgers than those of any other group residing there. At Merthyr Tydfil, shared accommodation and the taking in of lodgers was particularly associated with the Irish. A significantly higher proportion of shared households was to be found among the Irish-born in Merthyr than among other

---

[20] *Star of Gwent*, 6 December 1873.
[21] G. T. Clark, *Report to the General Board of Health, on a Preliminary Inquiry into the Sewerage, Drainage, and Supply of Water, and the Sanitary Condition of the Inhabitants of the Borough of Newport* (London, 1850), p.26.

groups, and 87 per cent of Irish lodgers in 1851 resided in other Irish households.[22]

Cultural preferences and economic imperatives cannot easily be disentangled. Whatever the relative significance of these factors, there was undoubtedly an economic rationale for clustering together which reinforced the ethnic dimension. While the majority of newcomers to an area were in need of cheap accommodation, it was also the case that families offering that accommodation were themselves in need of the paltry sums paid by lodgers in order to keep a precarious domestic economy afloat. For those engaged in low-paid employment, and frequently underemployed, the income provided by lodgers could make the difference between utter destitution and a more bearable condition of acute hardship. The margin between the two was wafer-thin. Nevertheless, the prevalence of Irish lodgers and the tendency for them to find accommodation in Irish households or Irish-run lodging houses suggest that ethnic solidarity was a significant factor in determining where some newcomers settled. Lodgers tended to belong to the more mobile section of the population and possibly sought out people of the same ethnic origins as a defence against what has been shown to be a particularly hostile environment. Yet the sharp decline in lodgers as a proportion of the whole by 1871 would suggest that for many migrants lodging with other families was a temporary expedient associated with either the specific conditions surrounding their arrival in the new society or an individual's position in the life cycle, or both.

Family life underwent substantial change in the transition from rural Ireland to urban Wales. In some cases families migrated in their entirety, all at once or in stages; in others – despite the imbalance in the sexes – single migrants found partners among other exiles. E. G. Ravenstein summed this up as follows: 'the elements which make up families will be found to exist amongst Irish emigrants, and this fact, amongst others, explains their slow assimilation with the peoples among whom

---

[22] Allan Williams, 'Migration and residential patterns', 15; Rees, 'Evolving patterns', vol. I, 236; J. Gwyn Davies, 'Industrial society in north-west Monmouthshire, 1750–1851', unpublished University of Wales Ph.D. thesis (1980), 74, 86–8; S. E. Wheatley, 'The social and residential areas of Merthyr Tydfil in the mid-nineteenth century', unpublished University of Wales Ph.D. thesis (1983), 161.

they settle.'[23] Foremost among changes to the way family relationships were structured was the separation of home and workplace. The fact that home and workplace were no longer identical meant that members of the family no longer shared the tasks of production. Thus, migration deprived families of non-financial assets such as domestic gardens. Married women in particular suffered acutely from these changes, especially in south Wales where the prevalence of heavy industry meant that the opportunities for waged work for women were restricted. Because of this fundamental transformation of the family from a unit of production to one of consumption, other strategies had to be found to supplement income. These could take a variety of forms, one of which was the farming-out of orphan children to the Irish, as at Merthyr Tydfil where the absence of a poor house made this an attractive proposition to the Poor Law guardians.[24] However, taking in lodgers was far more common, and it was this practice which created the misleading impression that the Irish had bigger families than had the Welsh.

In 1850 the correspondent of the *Morning Chronicle* confidently equated the size of Irish families with poverty, opining of the unskilled cinder-fillers at Merthyr, who were employed to fill trams with cinders, that 'having large families, their condition is necessarily abject and pitiable'. In support of this belief, he cited the case of one of the cinder-fillers who told him:

> I am a labourer in the works. I earn 10s. a week, on which I have to support a wife and five children, and to pay out of it 2s. a week for rent. During the two years that I have been here I have not used a pound of butter or cheese altogether. I contrive to give my family a little meat on the Sunday – some cow's cheek or that like. I don't know how we shall live after the reduction that is going to take place in the wages.[25]

In reality, there is little evidence to sustain the view that the Irish produced exceptionally big families, and it is possible that the writer was confusing family size with the size of households. In

[23] E. G. Ravenstein, 'The laws of migration', *Journal of the Statistical Society*, XLVIII (1885), 196.
[24] Report on 'Labour and the poor' in the *Morning Chronicle*, reproduced in Ginswick (ed.), *Labour and the Poor in England and Wales, 1849–1851*, pp.86–8.
[25] *Morning Chronicle*, 21 March 1850, reproduced in Ginswick (ed.), *Labour and the Poor in England and Wales*, p.35.

the mining parishes of north-west Monmouthshire in 1851, the mean family size for Irish immigrants was 4.1 persons, a figure hardly distinguishable from that for the native Welsh in the district and slightly smaller than that for some groups of English immigrants. Moreover, with a mean figure of 2.3 children per family, the Irish family structure differed hardly at all from that of the native population. Where the Irish displayed their particularity was in the size of their households. For the various groups which comprised the local population, the mean household size varied from 5.0 to 5.9 persons, whereas the comparable figure for the Irish was 8.3. The difference in size between Irish families and households is explained by the high proportion of lodgers residing with them. Also – in contrast to Welsh and English lodgers – more than half of Irish lodgers were married males and their families. In short, Irish households tended to include more than one family.[26]

A similar, if less exaggerated, picture can be painted for Swansea. There, the mean family size for the town's population was 4.19 persons, compared to a slightly higher figure of 4.65 for the Irish. Once again, Irish households were bigger, the mean size being 5.41 persons as against 4.94 for the town as a whole, the disparity being accounted for by the larger number of lodgers in Irish households.[27] Taken together, then, these figures suggest that whereas family size varied according to socio-economic group in mid-nineteenth-century Wales, household size was a function of ethnicity. Perhaps it was these characteristics which led to the Irish being berated for their alleged self-segregation. After the anti-Irish riots at Tredegar in 1882, the isolation of the Irish was contrasted unfavourably with the readiness of English immigrants to integrate. Following that disturbance, an exasperated letter-writer to the *Western Mail* exploded with indignation: 'Why an Irish quarter in every town rather than a Welsh or English quarter? Why their isolation? Why their violence?'[28]

That there were higher numbers of Irish immigrants in some districts than others is not in question (see maps). More contentious is the interpretation of such data as evidence of the existence of an Irish ghetto, a term with overtones of forced

[26] Davies, 'Industrial society', 86–8, 90–1, 124.
[27] Rees, 'Evolving patterns', vol.I, 245, 247.
[28] *Western Mail*, 9 July 1882.

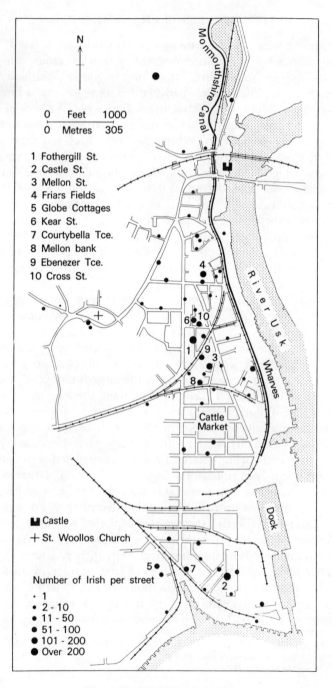

Map 1: The Irish in Newport in 1851

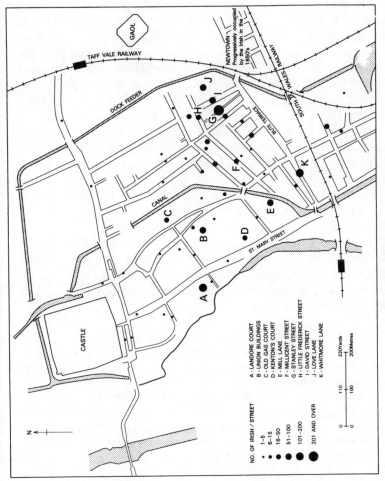

Map 2: The Irish in Cardiff in 1851

GAOL

TAFF VALE RAILWAY

NEWTOWN
Progressively occupied
by the Irish in the
1850's

DOCK FEEDER

SOUTH WALES RAILWAY

BUTE TERRACE

CANAL

CASTLE

ST. MARY STREET

N

NO. OF IRISH / STREET

1-5
6-15
16-50
51-100
101-200
201 AND OVER

A - LANDORE COURT
B - UNION BUILDINGS
C - OLD GAS COURT
D - KENTON'S COURT
E - MILL LANE
F - MILLICENT STREET
G - STANLEY STREET
H - LITTLE FREDERICK STREET
I - DAVID STREET
J - LOVE LANE
K - WHITMORE LANE

0   110   220 yards
0   100   200 Metres

segregation and alienation. Until recently, a 'ghetto' model of Irish settlement emphasizing economic deprivation, cultural separateness and residential segregation was unhesitatingly accepted by historians. The Irish were characterized as Catholic interlopers bunched at the base of the social pyramid, distanced from the host society by a combination of imposed external constraints and a tenacious adherence to a separate culture with its own customs and mores.[29] This view has a long pedigree. An identification of Irish immigrants with urban squalor in the cities of England was entrenched by the 1850s. It derived principally from the literature of social observation in Manchester and can be traced to the writings of Dr J. P. Kay during the cholera epidemic of 1832. The area he chose to vilify was not exclusively inhabited by Irish immigrants, nor was it the only area of the city where they lived, yet Kay's flawed depiction of the area proved to have a remarkably durable influence on generations of commentators. By identifying the Irish with the problems of overcrowded slum conditions, disease and drunkenness, he and successive writers found a convenient scapegoat for denouncing the very nature of industrial capitalism. According to the historian Graham Davis, however, the claim that there existed ghetto-like 'Little Irelands' in British towns and cities was no more than 'a product of creative imagination and contemporary ideology'. He continues:

> Of course what lent credence to the association of the Irish and slum conditions was the undoubted reality that *some* Irish migrants did live in *some* of the most squalid conditions in cities like Liverpool and Manchester, both before the famine migration and for many years afterwards. From that association the image of the 'ghetto-Irish' emerged and with it the package of fears among the host community. Specifically Irish habits – the diet of potatoes, sleeping on straw and allowing the children barefoot in the streets – were identified and deplored as potentially contaminating influences.[30]

[29] Gwyn A. Williams, *When Was Wales?* (Harmondsworth, 1985), p.187; Ness Edwards, *The Industrial Revolution in South Wales* (London, 1924), p.29; D. Gareth Evans, *A History of Wales, 1815–1906* (Cardiff, 1989), p.46.

[30] Graham Davis, *The Irish in Britain, 1815–1914* (Dublin, 1991), p.59; emphasis in the original. See also Busteed, Hodgson and Kennedy, 'Myth and reality'.

Manchester's 'Little Ireland' provided a useful metaphor for the failings of the new social order and the resulting debasement of the human condition.

Because of the relatively small Irish presence in Wales before the Famine, this ideology did not find fertile ground among Welsh commentators until the influx of the late 1840s. When writers sought evidence of the deleterious effects of industrialization in Wales, they visited Merthyr Tydfil, where the startling appearance of the iron foundries captured the literary imagination.[31] The town exhibited all the characteristics of rapid and unregulated development coupled with intense class conflict. The area in the town which epitomized for contemporaries moral degradation under the impact of industrialization in a comparable way to the district of Manchester identified by Kay was Pontystorehouse, known colloquially as 'China', and although Irish people were to be found there, they were too few in number to make the term 'Little Ireland' a remotely credible designation. Criminality in general and prostitution in particular were the targets of middle-class opinion.[32] Three-quarters of a century later, the sociologist J. Ronald Williams would claim that Irish integration in Merthyr had been assisted by 'the fact that they had never lived in distinct colonies'.[33]

It was only during and after the Famine years that a ghetto model was first applied to Irish settlement in Wales. A small district of Swansea was referred to as 'Little Ireland' as early as 1849, and the term became common currency in subsequent descriptions of urban squalor, and was soon being applied to similar areas in other Welsh towns.[34] In some cases, individual streets acquired the opprobrium of being nicknamed 'Irish Row', as in the case of Newport, where 'Irish Row' consisted of twenty-two overcrowded and insanitary houses, occupied by several

[31] For an important essay on the nature of social commentary in nineteenth-century Wales, see I. G. Jones, 'Observers and the observed in mid-Victorian Wales', in *idem*, *Mid-Victorian Wales: the Observers and the Observed* (Cardiff, 1992), pp.1–23.

[32] See David Jones and Alan Bainbridge, 'The "conquering of China": crime in an industrial community, 1842–64', *Llafur*, 2, 4 (1979); Keith Strange, 'In search of the celestial empire: crime in Merthyr, 1830–60', *Llafur*, 3, 1 (1980); and ch.VI below.

[33] J. Ronald Williams, 'The influence of foreign nationalities on the life of the people of Merthyr Tydfil', *Sociological Review*, XVIII (1926), 150.

[34] G. T. Clark, *Report to the General Board of Health on a Preliminary Inquiry into . . . the Sanitary Condition of the Town and Borough of Swansea* (London, 1850), p.10; *Cambrian*, 23 September 1853. The Welsh and English were also highly segregated in their own communities: see I. G. Jones, 'The city and its villages'.

families among whom the practice of sub-letting bed space to lodgers was common.[35] Districts such as Newtown in Cardiff, Friars' Fields in Newport, and Greenhill in Swansea were associated with a large Irish presence and the immigrant community life which grew from it.

The contention that there existed identifiably Irish districts of low status and poor sanitation in all the large towns ran through the social commentary of these years as clearly as the Glamorganshire Canal ran from Cardiff to Merthyr Tydfil, and it had influential currency among social investigators and municipal élites. The theme was summed up by an anonymous correspondent of the *Morning Chronicle*, who painted a stark picture of the contrasting lifestyles of the Irish and Welsh during his visit to Merthyr Tydfil in 1850. He observed that Irish houses were 'unfurnished, foul and stinking' and their children uncared for, 'not from necessity but from natural habits'. 'They are', he asserted,

> compelled to segregate in their dwellings, for the Welsh will not reside among them. They inhabit the lowest and worst quarters of the town. There is in Pen-y-darran, on the high road, an 'Irish colony', in which the passer-by may see, through the open doors and in the street, the striking difference that exists between the same class of labourers in the Irish and the Welsh . . .[36]

His judgement was supported by the testimony of local functionaries, whose professional work brought them in contact with the Irish. Looking back from the vantage point of 1885 on forty years' work as Cardiff's Medical Officer of Health, H. J. Paine identified one of the most intractable problems he had faced over the years as the fact that the Irish had established themselves 'in small sectional colonies in different parts of the town, separate and distinct from the other inhabitants'.[37] For

---

[35] G. T. Clark, *Report to the General Board of Health, on a Preliminary Inquiry into the Sewerage, Drainage, and Supply of Water, and the Sanitary Condition of the Inhabitants of the Borough of Newport* (London, 1850), p.20.

[36] *Morning Chronicle*, in Ginswick (ed.), *Labour and the Poor*, pp.64–7. For some incisive comments on these reports, see I. G. Jones, 'Observers and the observed in mid-Victorian Wales', pp.10–12.

[37] H. J. Paine, *Report on the Sanitary Condition of Cardiff During the Last Forty Years, as also for the Year 1885* (Cardiff, 1886), pp.2–3.

Paine, as for so many other commentators, the Irish were synonymous with the worst social evils and sanitary problems created by urban development.

Government commissioners, journalists and local Officers of Health all emphasized the immigrants' so-called 'clannishness', that is, their propensity to live close to people of the same ethnic origins. In this literature the Irish were inextricably associated with a subculture of poverty rooted in insanitary slum housing. Contemporary writers reached their conclusions about the spatial distribution of the Irish from personal observation of Irish dwellings, and their accounts were garnished with evocative descriptions of the distasteful sights and smells which they encountered. In particular, by penetrating the secluded 'courts', of which the middle class knew little and which they had no cause to visit in the course of their everyday lives, they provided insights into an alien world. Consequently, their writings took on the air of intrepid social exploration of the unknown. This world was composed of distinctively Irish pubs, beerhouses, and Catholic chapels, from which the Irish were believed to sally forth only when necessary.

Observations of Irish living conditions revealed deep anxieties about the impact of the newcomers on Welsh society. Middle-class writers regarded overcrowded and insanitary Irish habitations as an environment conducive to a debased sexual morality. When the correspondent of the *Morning Chronicle* alluded to the practice of farming out children to willing families at Merthyr, he remarked that they were 'boarded and lodged in the worst quarters of the town, often in the filthy houses of the Irish, where the only society is that of thieves, prostitutes and vagrants, so that their training is derived from the example of vice, recklessness, and infamy'.[38] After visiting only three houses, he contrasted the personal appearance, intelligence and good behaviour of pauper children lodged with poor Welsh families with the 'stupidity' of those brought up by the Irish in squalor, rags and filth. Public health reports, with their full panoply of scientific language and statistical tabulations, added their authoritative voice to such contentions. H. J. Paine identified early marriage and illegitimate

[38] *Morning Chronicle*, 22 April 1850, reproduced in Ginswick (ed.), *Labour and the Poor*, pp.89–90.

births among the Irish as the inevitable consequence of the sexes' occupying the same rooms in overcrowded accommodation. 'A marriage of improvidence is with them the *rule*', he averred, 'a marriage of providence the *exception*.'[39] However, references to the prevalence of illegitimacy and early marriage should be treated with caution. The illegitimacy rate in pre-Famine Ireland was generally regarded as uncommonly low, and the Irish were notable for their under-representation in prosecutions for illegitimacy in at least one Welsh town.[40]

Closely related to the picture of the Irish as a sexually debased group was the suggestion that they had not risen far above the level of beasts. Thus, the Irish were described repeatedly as 'swarming' in unventilated and insanitary slums, terminology appropriate to the ant-hill rather than human habitations. The language of the animal world was harnessed to describe an undifferentiated subhuman mass outside the bounds of civilized society. In the charged atmosphere of the riot at Cardiff in 1848, for example, it was asserted that the Irish had 'no more regard for the decencies of life than the beasts that perish', spending their money 'in thoughtless and beastly dissipation'.[41] The Medical Officer of Health at Newport preferred a more specific comparison. In his first annual report on the state of the town's health, he described the Irish as 'huddling like so many sheep in a pen',[42] while another Medical Officer of Health wrote in 1860: '. . . a recent investigation into the mode of living of our Irish population, has brought to light a frequent system of herding together, which can hardly be imagined in a civilized country.'[43] Confronted with the squalid living conditions of the urban poor, observers found the descriptive capacity of the language at their disposal inadequate, and so resorted to a convenient metaphor which was immediately intelligible to their audience. It was a metaphor which denied the immigrants their humanity. The use of bestial metaphors surfaced in descriptions of the native

[39] H. J. Paine, *Annual Report of the Officer of Health to the Cardiff Local Board of Health* (Cardiff, 1854), p.3.
[40] K. H. Connell, *Irish Peasant Society* (Oxford, 1968); H. A. Bruce, *Merthyr Tydfil in 1852* (Merthyr Tydfil, 1852), p.7.
[41] *Cardiff and Merthyr Guardian*, 18 November 1848.
[42] Robert F. Woolett, *First Report of the Officer of Health* (Newport, 1853), p.3.
[43] H. J. Paine, *The Eighth Annual Report on the Sanitary Condition of Cardiff* [for 1860] (Cardiff, 1861), p.16.

working class too, but Irish peasants transplanted to British towns presented middle-class observers with an even stranger subject of inquiry. As Patrick O'Sullivan has commented on what he wryly describes as the 'Engels's pig' school of commentary, the Irish were not only observed as bringing their pigs with them to British towns and perceived as living like pigs, but in the eyes of many commentators they *were* pigs. A bestial image of the Irish was established in the local press well before the simianized figure of 'Paddy' appeared in Tenniel's infamous cartoons in *Punch* magazine.[44] In reality, statements about Irish licentiousness and bestiality reveal more about the cultural framework in which the observers operated than they do of the observed.

It is unlikely that Irish overcrowding and clustering would have received so much anguished attention had it not been for the fever associated with the immigration of 1847 and the outbreak of epidemics of Asiatic cholera in 1849 and 1854. As was seen in chapter III, the blame for introducing the disease was laid squarely at the door of the Irish, and, consequently, they were believed to be umbilically attached to its spread during subsequent epidemics. However, cholera was not the single most serious cause of mortality in urban Wales. In fact, typhus and other zymotic diseases were endemic killers, causing many more deaths than the sporadic epidemics of Asian cholera; but cholera generated panic because of its apparently indiscriminate choice of victims and stimulated others to grapple with the problem of public health.[45] The attitudes of Medical Officers of Health were shaped by the experience of the epidemics and insanitary living conditions they encountered during the late 1840s and early 1850s, conditions which continued to colour their perceptions long after the problems with which they were associated had

---

[44] Patrick O'Sullivan, 'Introduction', in *idem* (ed.), *The Irish in the New Communities, The Irish World Wide*, vol.II (London, 1992), pp.3–4. The reference is to F. Engels, *The Condition of the Working Classes in England* (1845). Racial characterizations of the Irish pervaded intellectual life. A correspondent with a Welsh antiquarian journal in 1859 claimed that the descendants of Irish immigrants in rural Cardiganshire 'from immemorial times' were still described as 'the Gwyddyl' (the Irish) by locals: 'From their marked physical characteristics, they could be picked out at a glance, in a crowd of their Welsh neighbours: black hair, and dark eyes, in which a fierce restlessness of expression reminds one of the look of a wild animal . . .' 'The Gwyddyl in Cardiganshire', *Archaeologia Cambrensis*, V, 3rd series (1859), 306–7.

[45] I. G. Jones, 'The people's health in mid-Victorian Wales', in *idem*, *Mid-Victorian Wales*, p.35; Neil Evans, 'The urbanization of Welsh society', in T. Herbert and G. E. Jones (eds.), *People and Protest: Wales, 1815–1880* (Cardiff, 1988), pp.13–14.

abated. The coincidence at that time of rapid urban growth, virulent epidemics, and the arrival of large numbers of destitute Irish immigrants were the co-ordinates in which they conceived of the problems of public health for the remainder of their careers. To officials like H. J. Paine in Cardiff, Irish over-crowding was an especially repugnant social evil, the eradication of which attracted his unswerving attention and unstinting exertions for over forty years.[46]

However, as Graham Davis has pointed out, that certain districts acquired the sobriquet, 'Little Ireland', should not obscure the fact that not all of their inhabitants were Irish, nor did all of the Irish live in so-called 'Irish quarters' or streets nicknamed 'Irish Row'. To a greater or lesser degree, the Irish and Welsh shared streets and neighbourhoods. This settlement pattern was also evident in the smaller towns and industrial settlements. At the iron- and copper-producing village of Cwmavon, near Port Talbot, 43 per cent of the Irish-born in 1851 lived in Dan-y-Coed Row, a street which was promptly christened 'Bandon Row', after the Cork town of that name; the remainder were dispersed among streets throughout the village. Although there were fewer Irish immigrants in the towns of north Wales, similar settlement patterns can be discerned there. At Wrexham, for example, the small contingent of 564 Irish-born (representing 8.4 per cent of the town's population) was heavily concentrated in a small group of streets but was not confined to them. In fact, there is some evidence that the Irish in Wrexham dispersed more widely throughout the town in the decades after 1841.[47]

A portrayal of the Irish in nineteenth-century Britain as outcasts restricted to general labouring and to particular neigh-bourhoods is a misleading and partial one. In reality, the Irish were a more heterogeneous group than many contemporaries

[46] H. J. Paine, *Report on the Sanitary Condition of Cardiff During the Last Forty Years, as also for the Year 1885*, pp.2–3. If, as Ieuan Gwynedd Jones has suggested, the definition of 'urban' was as much on the basis of the types and intensities of diseases as on what would normally be regarded as 'urban' features, then the Irish were an integral part of what constituted 'urbanism' in mid-nineteenth-century Wales. Ieuan Gwynedd Jones, 'The people's health in mid Victorian Wales', p.33.

[47] Louise Miskell, 'The Irish in mid-nineteenth century Wales: a village perspective', unpublished University of Wales BA dissertation (1992), 34–9; Sandra Irish, 'Spatial patterns in the small town in the nineteenth century: a case study of Wrexham', unpublished University of Wales Ph.D. thesis (1987), 212–24.

conceded and were distributed more widely throughout the urban hierarchy than the emphasis upon clustering in particular districts of towns would allow. An emphasis upon the social and cultural diversity of Irish immigration demonstrates that their experience varied not only in towns but also between towns and cities of different sizes and economic structures. In short, the whole of Irish immigration has been confused with its most visible component. To some extent, the concentration of large numbers of Irish immigrants in particular neighbourhoods in the towns can be accounted for by divisions based on social class. By residing in the same streets and neighbourhoods as the Welsh or English of the same class, they had ample opportunity for interaction on a day-to-day basis. Irish immigration to south Wales was overwhelmingly, though not exclusively, working class in character, and because the Famine Irish accounted for such a large proportion of the whole, the Irish as a group were identified with urban squalor and the public health problems of the middle decades of the century. A class analysis of public health problems was implicit in a table showing variations in the death rate included by H. J. Paine in his report on Cardiff for 1853 (Table IV.2).

The census enumerators' books provide a more exact picture of the occupational distribution of the Irish. At both Swansea and Cardiff the majority of Irish-born workers fell into the unskilled category. In 1851 more than 60 per cent of the Irish at Cardiff fell into this category compared with only 27.4 per cent of the town's population as a whole. By 1871 a little under 40 per cent were to be found in this category.[48] A similar situation obtained at Swansea, where more than 60 per cent of the Irish-born were engaged in unskilled occupations compared with a figure of 17.5 per cent for the town as a whole. However, in the case of Swansea the following twenty years saw negligible change in these proportions, the proportion of unskilled Irish actually increasing somewhat by 1871.[49] This heavy concentration of Irish workers among the unskilled in mid-century meant that the Irish were under-represented in skilled and professional

---

[48] C. Roy Lewis, 'The Irish in Cardiff in the mid-nineteenth century', *Cambria*, VII (1980), 13, table IV; Allan M. Williams, 'Migration and Residential Patterns in mid-nineteenth century Cardiff', *Cambria*, IV (1979), 11–12.

[49] Rees, 'Evolving patterns', vol.II, 387, table 11.9.

Table IV.2 Death rate in selected streets in Cardiff in 1853

Street	No. houses	Popn	Deaths	Rate per '000 deaths	Class of inhabitants
Ellen St.	33	437	24	54.92	Principally Irish
Pendoylan St.	29	319	12	37.62	labourers and
William St.	33	429	21	48.95	mendicants
Thomas St.	28	340	15	44.12	
Total	123	1,525	72	47.21	
Crockherbtown	64	402	11	27.36	Gentry,
Charles St.	35	222	3	13.51	professionals,
High St.	31	176	3	17.05	and others
Angel St.	17	92	2	21.74	
Total	147	892	19	21.30	

Source: H. J. Paine, *Annual Report of the Officer of Health to the Cardiff Local Board of Health* (Cardiff, 1854), p.7.

occupations. Moreover, they stood out in stark contrast with every other immigrant group in the towns, including those from England and rural Wales. On the criterion of birthplace, therefore, Irish immigrants were members of the most disadvantaged group in Welsh society.

Yet, while accepting the fact that the Irish-born were disproportionately and overwhelmingly concentrated in lower-status occupations, it would be a mistake to overlook those who were not. The obverse of the statistics quoted above is that in Cardiff in 1851 some 13.6 per cent of the Irish-born were engaged in skilled employment (as defined by the census enumerator), while in Swansea at the same date, a full 24 per cent were skilled workers.[50] Just as household structures changed over the ensuing decades as greater prosperity in the Irish community led to a decline in the number of Irish lodgers, so too economic

[50] Allan M. Williams, 'Social change and residential differentiation: a case study of nineteenth century Cardiff', unpublished University of London Ph.D. thesis (1976), vol.I, 190; Rees, 'Evolving patterns', p.237. In his study of the Irish in Cardiff in 1851, based on a 50 per cent sample, C. Roy Lewis gives a higher figure of 15.05 per cent for Irish-born skilled workers. Lewis, 'The Irish in Cardiff', p.13.

expansion had an impact on the occupational structure. In towns like Cardiff, which experienced rapid economic growth and where the Irish were well established, the occupational structure of the Irish-born altered dramatically, with a precipitous decline in the unskilled element and a corresponding increase in the proportion classed as skilled workers. It was these people and the small middle class who were responsible for establishing and maintaining the more visible ethnic institutions such as the Catholic church and Irish friendly societies.

As the century progressed, the views of élites in the host society were challenged by those who claimed to speak on behalf of the Irish, including both the Catholic clergy and the emerging Irish middle class. Derogatory perceptions of the Irish as an intransigent social problem requiring careful monitoring were countered by alternative views which stressed the orderliness, religiosity and moral integrity of the immigrant community. In 1890, for example, when a Royal Commission collected evidence on the operation of the Sunday Closing (Wales) Act of 1881, Catholic clergy and prominent Irish lay people were in a position to qualify claims that the Irish were solely responsible for the existence of shebeens at Cardiff. A view of Irish community life emerged from the writings of such spokesmen (women's voices are noticeable by their absence) which emphasized loyalty to neighbours, church and parish priest.[51] Even more significant, given the entrenched association of the Irish with squalor and disease in mid-century, was an incident in 1893 when an official report by the Medical Officer of Health at Cardiff made a connection between an outbreak of typhus and the 'Irish quarter' of the town. During the Council's deliberations on the report, Alderman Carey proposed a resolution that 'all the references to the Irish residents in the above report of the Medical Officer of Health be eliminated'.[52] That the resolution was passed demonstrates how Irish participation in municipal politics enabled them successfully to challenge statements by public officers which cast the Irish in a poor light.

---

[51] PP 1890 XL, Report of the Royal Commission Appointed to Inquire into the Operation of the Sunday Closing (Wales) Act, 1881, pp.64–6.
[52] J. H. Mathews (ed.), *Cardiff Records*, vol.V (Cardiff, 1905), p.178; John Hickey, *Urban Catholics* (London, 1967), p.102.

Images of Irish communities defined in terms of their apartness, alien cultural practices and social disorganization were replaced with alternative constructions of community which stressed the positive aspects of Irish working-class life. The most eloquent description of Irish immigrant life in nineteenth-century Wales is provided by Joseph Keating in his remarkable autobiography, *My Struggle for Life*. Recalling his childhood in the mining village of Mountain Ash in the early 1870s, he wrote:

> We who lived in The Barracks . . . were intensely proud of the place. Its people were hard-working, honest and neighbourly. They gave generously to their church; of course, there was only one church for them – the Catholic Church. They were kind to one another. If illness or poverty happened to be in one house, nearly every other house proffered help.
>
> If one man was killed in the pits, his neighbours helped carry his body from the pit to his home and from there to his last home on the hillside. Everybody's home was open to everybody else, and there was great friendship. There was not a thief in the district. Loafers and swindlers were not able to live there. Matrimony was regarded as a sacrament, and the colony had no need of divorce courts.
>
> There was no bawdy talk in the young men's conversation . . . The girls of the colony were bright-eyed and pure . . . the rate of illegitimacy would work out at, perhaps, two in a million . . .[53]

This description, from within an Irish settlement, shows the reverse of the immorality described by hostile observers. Its emphasis on community solidarity, shared cultural values and moral rectitude is at odds with the prevailing views of contemporary social commentary which had become fixed during the crisis decades in mid-century. A view of the Irish as a clannish minority (a 'colony') set apart from the host society appears here in a different, albeit more benign, guise. Yet, as has been seen, we should be wary of generalizations about the apartness of a homogeneous Irish 'community', whether they derive from the observations of hostile outsiders or from sympathetic insiders. The image of a monolithic community peopled exclusively by the Catholic faithful does not provide an adequate basis for understanding the diversity which existed among immigrants.

In the nineteenth century, it served the purposes of a variety of

---

[53] Joseph Keating, *My Struggle for Life* (London, 1916), pp.13–14.

people to portray the Irish as a homogeneous group, and, until recently, Irish cultural and residential segregation from the host society was a commonplace of historical literature. A view of the Irish inhabiting ghettos ('Little Irelands') is now seen as accepting unquestioningly the contemporary ideologies underpinning social commentary which sought a scapegoat for the unattractive consequences of industrial capitalism and found it in Irish immigrants. And rather than using value-laden terms such as 'segregation' to describe the uneven spread of Irish immigrants in Welsh towns, it is perhaps more accurate to speak in terms of 'clustering', a term which permits a consideration of concentrations of Irish immigrants at the level of the individual houses and courts as well as the larger scale of the neighbourhood. Analyses based on measuring Irish segregation in British towns have tended to assume that spatial difference is the most important feature of their settlement patterns. Of course, some proximity of residence was necessary for the immigrants to develop and maintain a distinctive group identity and to establish their own ethnic institutions, but over-emphasizing their segregation from the wider society results in crude generalizations which create only a partial picture of the historical experience.

V

THE IRISH IN THE LABOUR MARKET, 1850–1900

Social and economic life in Wales underwent far-reaching changes in the middle decades of the nineteenth century as the economy shifted even more decisively away from agriculture and towards industry. During the first phase of industrialization, beginning at the end of the eighteenth century, iron and copper had dominated the industrial economy, whereas from the 1840s these industries were overtaken by coal mining, a development marking the start of what can be described as the second phase of the industrial revolution. Coal mining rapidly established itself as the dominant element of the economy of south Wales and came to exert an enormous influence on social life, either directly in the coalfield itself where new settlements were established around the mines or indirectly in the ports which exported large quantities of coal around the globe. In this development, the late 1840s and early 1850s were a critical period of readjustment, when capital investment in the economy in general was declining and the railways had only just begun to provide a new outlet for investors. The abundance of Irish labour in the job market from the late 1840s augmented the labour force at precisely the time when economic expansion was slowing.

For the majority of the Welsh, the Famine immigration was an unwelcome phenomenon which could only lead to a reduction of wages. In industries where casual labour was a significant component of the workforce, the Irish presence led to bitter competition for jobs. At least initially, many Irish labourers undercut wages in order to obtain work. This was the case at Cardiff in 1849. For discharging or wheeling ballast from ships, employers had customarily paid 2½d. per ton, and 3d. for filling; to avoid starvation, the Irish agreed to perform the same tasks for ½d. and 1d. respectively.[1] A reduction of this magnitude inevitably meant that the Welsh were unable to compete with the newcomers on the same terms. Lacking the workplace

---

[1] *Cardiff and Merthyr Guardian*, 5 May 1849.

organization or solidarity which existed in the metallurgical and coal industries, dock labourers were placed at a severe disadvantage when faced with an influx of labourers willing to work for lower wages. Cheap labour occasionally posed a threat in the iron industry also. At Merthyr Tydfil in December 1848 a reduction of wages was attributed to the Irish influx, although this seems to have been the result of extraordinary conditions; in April 1850 it was noted that the town had been 'literally besieged' by troops of Irishmen for nearly three weeks and that 'They work almost for nothing, but even at that rate few of them are employed'.[2]

Elsewhere, ironworkers mobilized older traditions of collective action to combat the challenge. A belief that the Irish were responsible for lowering wages was at the root of bitter disturbances at the Beaufort Ironworks in Monmouthshire in June 1850, when only the rapid deployment of troops and the swearing in of sixty-five special constables prevented an escalation of unrest. The accusation of undercutting wages was levelled at the Irish in this area again during the summer of 1853, when attempts were made to expel them from Ebbw Vale and Brynmawr.[3] Similarly, at Pontlottyn, near Rhymney, as late as August 1869, it was estimated that over a thousand men, women and children took to the streets against the Irish. On that occasion, the immigrants' houses were attacked and badly damaged, resulting in the death of one Irishman. Although the issue of wage rates was reportedly the principal cause of the disturbance, it is difficult to account for the ferocity of the attack by this alone. Wage levels were only one grievance among a number of factors contributing to friction in the workplace: equally important was the long-standing antipathy between the two groups in the village and a tradition of violent collective action stretching back more than forty years.[4]

---

[2] *Cambrian*, 8 December 1848, 5 April 1850.
[3] PRO, HO 45/3472T, letters of Colonel Love, 2, 8 June 1850, and of G. A. A. Daniels, 6 June 1850; *Y Diwygiwr* (August 1853), 257.
[4] *The Bee-Hive*, 28 August, 4 September 1869. Brenda Collins is wrong to assert that Irish labour in south Wales was 'relatively readily absorbed without friction' because of the expanding iron and coal industries: 'The Irish in Britain, 1780–1921', in B. J. Graham and L. J. Proudfoot (eds.), *An Historical Geography of Ireland* (London, 1993), p.377. See Paul O'Leary, 'Anti-Irish riots in Wales, 1826–1882', *Llafur*, 5, 4 (1991), and Louise Miskell, 'Custom, conflict and community: a study of the Irish in south Wales and Cornwall, 1861–1891', unpublished University of Wales Ph.D. thesis (1996).

As in the pre-Famine period, Irish over-representation in the lower echelons of the hierarchy of work was believed to reflect a lack of appropriate skills. Labourers used to rough agricultural work in a poor peasant economy, it was asserted, did not possess the requisite technical skills or the tradition of disciplined, methodical working for employment in an industrial society. Given the nature of the Famine immigration from the late 1840s, there is an element of truth in this line of reasoning, but it does not account for the fact that this initial disadvantage continued to encumber the Irish for a longer period than it did other rural immigrants. Migrants from rural Wales or rural England did not suffer the same long-term handicaps. The reasons for this are complex and encompass the recruitment policies of employers, the actions of native workers and the widespread portrayal of the Irish in the press as pariahs.

Social reportage at the time of the Famine influx set the tone. The reports on 'Labour and the Poor' in south Wales, which appeared in the *Morning Chronicle* in 1850, are among the most sophisticated examples of this genre in mid-nineteenth-century Wales, and they depict a workplace culture in which the Irish were routinely found at the lower end of a hierarchy of skill. Describing the industrial processes in use at the Dowlais Ironworks, the anonymous reporter commented on the area where the molten iron was refined as follows: 'I should say that the "cinder-fillers", who attend to the loading of trains with slag – a laborious duty exposed to great heat – earn on an average, as they told me, 10s. 6d. a week. These men are mostly Irish.'[5] He discovered that higher-status occupations were largely the preserve of the Welsh, claiming that at Dowlais 'such a wonder as an Irish puddler was never heard of'.[6] He observed similar demarcations along ethnic lines in other places and in different industries. Where there was a clearly demarcated hierarchy of skill, the Irish were most often found in the ranks of those labouring for the skilled workers. At Swansea, for example, the same writer quoted an informant who referred to the 'masons, plasterers, bricklayers, and the Irish labourers who tend upon them'.[7] By this time the writer's image of

    [5] *Morning Chronicle*, 18 March 1850, reprinted in J. Ginswick (ed.), *Labour and the Poor in England and Wales, 1849–51* (London, 1983), p.26.
    [6] *Morning Chronicle*, 21 March 1850, reprinted in Ginswick, *Labour and the Poor*, p.36.
    [7] *Morning Chronicle*, 8 June 1850, reprinted in Ginswick, *Labour and the Poor*, p.176.

the Irish was clearly fixed. Later, at the yards where imported copper ores were stored and work took place in the open air, he found the Irish with ease. 'They told me', he reported,

> that they were all paid alike, men, women and boys. When the weather is bad and they cannot work full-time for rain, they earn, perhaps, 6*d.* a day – at others 1*s.* 6*d.* In the long days of summer they earn 2*s.* 6*d.* Suspecting they were mostly Irish, I asked if that was the case; a man replied 'Yes, it is Irish we are; there is nobody else would work for the price we do it. Last week I earned but 7*s.* 3*d.*; the gentleman who deals in copper be too sharp for us, and the times are bad'.[8]

Social reportage of this kind constructed persuasive images of the Irish as low-wage, unskilled and casual labour. The reporters of the 'Labour and the Poor' series aimed at building up detailed factual reports of working-class life which would convey to their audiences an intimate impression of the social reality they encountered. These reports established exacting standards for the observers who followed in their footsteps. Information on working-class life was drawn from a variety of sources, including public functionaries and interviews with some workers them-selves. Supporting statistics were rarely available to substantiate an individual reporter's observations, and the conversations reported, though illuminating, cannot be regarded as represent-ative in all cases. Nevertheless, even more sympathetic observers such as John Denvir, who visited Monmouthshire in 1882, reported: 'At the iron-works the Irish are at the hardest labour, which neither Englishman nor Welshman can nor will do.'[9]

Part of the explanation for this belief lies in the over-repres-entation of the Irish in unskilled and semi-skilled occupations (although as was shown in the last chapter, not all Irish immigrants were confined to the lower echelons of the labour force). However, part of the explanation also lies in the attitudes of employers who recruited labour for specific tasks and grades according to age, gender and ethnic origin. Employers defended their practice of purchasing labour in the cheapest market, even at the expense of antagonizing the native workforce, because

---

[8] *Morning Chronicle*, 14 June 1850, reprinted in Ginswick, *Labour and the Poor*, p.183.
[9] John Denvir, *The Irish in Britain* (London, 1892), p.303.

they required a large pool of casual labour to allow them to reduce or augment their workforce as the market demanded. This equation was set out by Evan David, an employer of agricultural labour in the vicinity of Cardiff, before the Select Committee on Poor Removal in 1854. He believed that an important factor in attracting the Irish to Wales was the existence of differential wage rates between the two countries, 'common labourers' earning some 6s. to 8s. per week in Ireland compared with 12s. in the Cardiff area. On the whole, he felt that the Irish influx during the previous ten years had tended to depress wage rates, because of the increased competition for jobs. He underlined his point by stating the received wisdom that 'labour like any other commodity, of course, is regulated by the law of supply and demand'.[10] David went on to express the opinion that although Cardiff did not derive any direct benefit from the swollen supply of labour resulting from the Irish immigration, and was in effect subsidizing the coal and iron manufacturing areas to the north of the town by providing poor relief for destitute immigrants on their arrival, 'all the manufacturing interests derive an advantage from the low rate of labour'. In reality, large manufacturers were not the only beneficiaries, as David had employed Irish labourers himself.

The practice of recruitment for specific tasks could lead to an admission that under conditions of labour scarcity the Irish were indispensable. This was particularly the case in the iron industry. During the cholera epidemic of autumn 1854 over a quarter of the Irish deserted the town of Merthyr Tydfil and, consequently, the Dowlais Ironworks was confronted with such a shortage of labour that continuation of production was threatened.[11] None the less, this recognition was tempered by the prevailing belief that they were suited only to tasks of a particular kind. When G. T. Clark, one of the trustees of the company, was asked in 1867 whether the Irish filled the place of emigrating Welshmen. He replied firmly,

No, the place of the Irish emigrant is filled, no doubt, by an Irish immigrant, but the place of the skilled Welshman cannot be filled by an Irishman. The men we get for that purpose are men who have been bred up in the rural districts, they speak Welsh only . . .[12]

[10] PP 1854 XVII, Select Committee on Poor Removal, pp.482–8.
[11] Glam. RO, D/DG, Dowlais Iron Company letterbooks, 1854 (2), nos.477, 479 and 493.
[12] PP 1867–8 XXXIX, Fifth Report of the Royal Commission on Trade Unions, p.92.

At neighbouring Cyfarthfa Ironworks the manager also accorded contrasting traits to different ethnic groups, praising the Irish for their docility. According to his experience, the English were too argumentative and Welsh attendance too irregular, but the Irish 'told to do certain work went and did it'.[13]

The impact of employers' recruitment policies was compounded by the attitudes of their other workers, although all the evidence does not point in one direction. Ethnic tensions existed at Merthyr Tydfil and Dowlais, but at no time did the occasional Saturday night brawling or 'faction fight' escalate to a full-scale riot. On rare occasions, and under certain conditions, Irish and Welsh workers managed to forge an effective solidarity in industrial action. This occurred at Dowlais in 1861 when the Irish withdrew their labour in support of action by their fellow workers, an act of co-operation which astonished the local press on account of its rarity.[14] This was an isolated incident and simply underlines the fact that, elsewhere, riot continued to be the ironworkers' favoured method of excluding the Irish; it might even be the case that the determination of employers in Merthyr Tydfil and Dowlais to allocate jobs on the basis of ethnicity was sufficiently effective and sufficiently well known to obviate the need for the Welsh to act against them. In these circumstances, any possibility of social mobility within the industry was severely curtailed. Evidence from the north of England confirms the view that opportunities for advancement were severely restricted for the Irish working in the south Wales iron industry. In 1861 approximately 61 per cent of skilled ironworkers living in Middlesbrough came from Wales. As in south Wales, Irish labour at the ironworks was heavily concentrated in unskilled occupations, with the singular exception of a significant number of Irishmen who had migrated to the area via south Wales, a move which was associated with career advancement. Had they been able to achieve advancement in south Wales, such a move would have been unnecessary.[15]

---

[13] Charles Wilkins, *The History of the Iron, Steel, Tinplate and Other Trades of Wales* (Merthyr Tydfil, 1903), p.258.

[14] *Cambrian*, 31 May 1861.

[15] On Middlesbrough, see Malcolm Chase, 'The Teesside Irish in the nineteenth century', in Patrick Buckland and John Belchem (eds.), *The Irish in British Labour History*, Conference Proceedings in Irish Studies, No.1 (Liverpool, 1993), pp.48–9.

Unequivocal indications of an employer's recruitment policy of the kind recorded for Dowlais are rare. Employers acted on the basis of unspoken assumptions, resulting in tasks being allocated on the basis of ethnicity, gender and age; these assumptions were articulated publicly only in exceptional circumstances. Thus, when the manager of the Cwm Dyli copper mines in Snowdonia in north Wales was called before the company board in the 1870s to answer charges of mismanagement, one of the misdemeanours listed was the introduction of Irish miners and their families: he should have known, it was claimed, that the Welsh and Irish would not work together.[16] To some extent, therefore, it would appear that in the post-Famine decades employers' attitudes to the Irish continued to structure the workforce on ethnic lines.

Irish women were doubly disadvantaged by the prejudices of employers, suffering because of their sex and their ethnicity. South Wales was dominated by heavy industries which offered few employment opportunities for women, with the exception of activities ancillary to iron manufacture, like brick-making. Many Irish women existed on the margins of a waged economy, earning a precarious living by hawking and dealing or labouring, some resorting to begging. A graphic example of how women were involved from a young age in contributing to a family economy is provided by the following description of 'tip girls' at Swansea:

> Greenhill teemed with children, who mostly went with naked feet, partly by choice, more often by necessity . . . In the early morning before school you could see troops of little Irish girls, their backs laden with sacks of coke, picked from the recent additions to the mountains of refuse from the Vivian Copper Works. It was almost the only firing many of our people knew. These black bundles of small, unpresentable and almost unrecognisable humanity would soon reappear in school as girlhood, clean and sweet, yet pale and prematurely sad.[17]

Such work was unwaged, but no less important to poor families for all that.

---

[16] N. C. Beck, 'A brief account of the copper mines in Cwm Dyli, Snowdonia', *Transactions of the Caernarvonshire Historical Society*, 31 (1970), 51.

[17] J. W. Richards, *Reminiscences of the Early Days of the Parish and Church of St. Joseph's, Greenhill* (Swansea, 1919), p.12.

General labouring at the docks provided the best opportunities of waged employment for women. Despite disapproval from some quarters, women were engaged in the unloading of ships at Newport and Cardiff docks. This work attracted, it was said, 'a very rough class of Irish women and is miserably paid', although one source stressed that 'a large proportion' were Welsh. These women were noted for their militancy. At Newport in March 1872 about one hundred women engaged in unloading potatoes struck for an advance of wages, which was swiftly conceded by their employers.[18] An investigator at Cardiff in 1893 noted that some thirteen years earlier the women working at the docks had struck successfully for a rise in wages and shorter working hours.[19] Conditions similar to those described as resulting from that strike were conceded to the women unloading potato ships in 1890. Cardiff was the third largest importer of potatoes in England and Wales in the 1890s and the women shrewdly chose their employers' most vulnerable time to strike – when there were fourteen vessels waiting to be unloaded. Following success in achieving their demands, some employers were reported to be considering using only dependable male labourers in future![20] Despite a willingness to unite to win better conditions of work, the women remained outside formal union structures. The same was true of sack-sewing, an occupation composed mainly of Irish women who earned slightly more than those unloading ships.[21]

At times, observers' generic statements about the Irish at the workplace included both men and women, but as the latter were progressively excluded from employment in heavy industry, it must be assumed that their comments increasingly related to men only. Once excluded from paid employment, the opportunities for interaction with women from other groups at a workplace must have decreased, resulting in Irish women creating their own neighbourhood networks around domestic work and other activities connected with organized religion. While it may be true to say of Irishmen employed in the iron industry that they 'occupied the worst seats in the best theatres', it was rare for

[18] *Star of Gwent*, 30 March 1872.
[19] PP 1893–4 XXXVII (Part 1), Royal Commission on Labour, the Employment of Women: Reports by Lady Assistant Commissioners, p.241.
[20] *South Wales Daily News*, 5, 6, 8 March 1890.
[21] PP 1893–4 XXXVII (Part 1), Royal Commission on Labour, p.242.

Irish women in south Wales to be admitted to the metaphorical 'theatre' at all.[22]

Despite the modernity of some work processes, such as those involved in the production of iron and copper, the abundance of cheap, casual labour in some sectors of the economy erected a barrier against technological innovation by removing the need to substitute capital investment for hand labour. Paradoxically, in an age when the dominant images of work were so closely identified with the machine and steam power, hand labour remained a remarkably important factor in economic life.[23] Instead of progressively replacing all forms of strenuous manual labour with the machine, new technology created new forms of hand labour requiring even greater numbers of manual labourers. Karl Marx was one of the earliest commentators to recognize this fact, maintaining that a 'disposable industrial reserve army' of labour was a requisite of early capitalist production,[24] and many of the Irish occupied an unenviable position in the rank and file of this highly mobile body of men and women. Three categories of work deserve special attention in this connection: navvy work excavating the railways and other public works; coal mining; and general labouring at the docks.

An easily recognizable and highly mobile worker, the navvy marched from project to project and camped temporarily at each one with his fellow workers and members of their families. Work of an intensely demanding physical nature led to the formation of a group solidarity that spawned its own cultural ethos. Navvies developed their own marriage customs and were recognizable by their boisterousness, their distinctive clothing and unique slang. Continuing the military metaphor quoted above, Marx described the navvies as the 'light infantry of capital, thrown from one point to another according to its present needs'.[25] Navvies were notorious for their riotous behaviour. The most disturbed project involving Irish navvies in Wales was the Chester and Holyhead Railway, a line that was to

---

[22] The phrase belongs to David Fitzpatrick, *Irish Emigration, 1801–1921* (Dundalgan, 1984), p.34.

[23] R. Samuel, 'Workshop of the world: steam power and hand technology in mid-Victorian Britain', *History Workshop Journal*, 3 (1977), 6–72.

[24] Karl Marx, *Capital: A Critique of Political Economy*, vol.1 (Harmondsworth, 1976), especially pp.781–94.

[25] Ibid., p.818.

run along the north Wales coast, crossing the Menai Straits to the island of Anglesey. Violence erupted on several occasions, yet one historian has hailed this project as 'pioneering some of the improvements in industrial relations in Victorian England [*sic*]'. This statement is based on the company's reputation for employing benevolent contractors and the fact that some £300 was contributed towards the employment of Scripture Readers from the Town Missionary Reader and Scripture Society to care for the navvies' spiritual welfare. Six readers worked between Chester and Bangor, while another two worked on Anglesey. One of these men reported that 'the Welsh labourers were very steady, sober men; I had never seen anything like it'. The apparent docility of the Welsh navvies contrasted favourably with the intractable behaviour of navvies in the north-east of England.[26]

This benevolence in religious matters must be placed in the context of the system of contracting labour, a system that existed on all railway lines in Britain. Aspects of the work were leased to subcontractors who took over the responsibility for paying wages to workers on their contract. The practice meant that lines of authority and responsibility at the workplace were often unclear; the resulting confusion over roles could allow the navvies to assert their own codes of behaviour, but it could also permit dishonest subcontractors to decamp with wages, leaving the navvies without an avenue for redress. A case illustrating the hazards of subcontracting for workers was heard at Flint Petty Sessions in February 1846, when Michael May and Martin O'Hara, two Irish navvies, brought an action against a contractor of the Chester and Holyhead Railway for refusing to pay a balance of wages. The nub of the question was whether the Irishmen had been employed by the contractor or the subcontractor; it was judged that the latter had been the employer and so the action for the retrieval of wages was dismissed. The two men who appeared in court represented a larger number of navvies waiting outside, all with substantial amounts of wages outstanding. Abuses of the system of pay and contracting on the

[26] Peter E. Baughan, *The Chester and Holyhead Railway*, vol.1 (Newton Abbot, 1972), pp.58–60; cf. J. H. Treble, 'Irish navvies in the north of England, 1830–50', *Transport History*, VI (1973), 227–47.

railways were roundly condemned by a government Select Committee that same year.[27]

Industrial relations on the Chester and Holyhead line deteriorated rapidly in early 1846. In March, the navvies on the Saltney side of the River Dee struck for a rise of 6*d*. per day, but failed to bring out the workers on the rest of the line. At the end of April, navvies on the Holyhead section struck for a whole week for a wage increase, and a gangsman (supervisor) was fined at Bangor for assaulting an Irishman.[28] In the light of subsequent events, this assault can be seen as indicative of more general ethnic tension. The months of industrial unrest and ethnic friction came to a head on Friday, 22 May 1846, when a large group of Welsh workers marched westwards from Penmaenmawr to Bangor, driving some sixty or seventy Irish navvies before them in an attempt to remove them from the line.[29] The incident originated at the No.8, or Pen Maen Bach, contract and rapidly progressed through the adjacent works. Gathering supporters as they went, the Welsh pursuers numbered about three hundred by the time they reached Bangor. It was at this point that the riot ceased to be 'merely' another navvy disturbance, rapidly becoming transmuted into a symbolic threat to the authority of the ecclesiastical city itself.

By coincidence, the same day had been appointed for the meeting of the Petty Sessions. One of the new magistrates, the Revd Vincent, had witnessed events while travelling to Bangor and managed to arrest a man he believed to be among the ringleaders. When the seizure of this man became known to the assembled crowd at Bangor, they retaliated by attacking two constables and demanded the release of their comrade from the lock-up. The Revd Vincent left the safety of the lock-up to remonstrate with the crowd and received an injury to his face for his trouble. Inside, the other magistrates began swearing in and arming special constables from among the railway contractors and the ten or twelve Irishmen who had found shelter there. An attack on the building was anticipated, but the tension was

[27] *Carnarvon and Denbigh Herald*, 7 February 1846; PP 1846 XIII, Report from the Select Committee on Railway Labourers, pp.iv–ix. An almost identical case to that at Flint occurred at Swansea in January 1847; see *Cambrian*, 15 January 1847.

[28] *Carnarvon and Denbigh Herald*, 21 March, 2 May, 15 May 1846.

[29] The following account is based on reports in the *Manchester Guardian*, 27, 30 May 1846, and *Carnarvon and Denbigh Herald*, 15 January 1847.

reduced by the escape of the prisoner over the back wall of the gaol. The atmosphere changed perceptibly. A witness described what followed:

> The spirit of defence which actuated the rioters may be inferred from the circumstances of their having brought the runaway in triumph back to perform sundry antics, in the humour of a dance, to the magistrates' teeth, daring anyone to retake him. With the small force available, it would have been sheer madness to have attempted a thing of the kind; and having enjoyed their triumph sufficiently, the gallant 'navies' twirled their bodies off in the most grotesque manner conceivable.[30]

These actions constituted a direct challenge to the magistracy and bore all the hallmarks of a symbolic inversion of official authority; moreover, it did not end with the departure of the navvies from gaol on the Friday. Anticipating further trouble on the following pay-day, the magistrates requested the assistance of troops from Chester. A company of the 68th Foot arrived by sea via Liverpool late on Saturday night. The troops remained for a whole week and were roundly criticized for their behaviour over the weekend as well as for the heavy-handed way in which they arrested some of the navvies. Between midnight on the following Tuesday and midday on Wednesday, the soldiers made their way to the navvies' hill-camp with all the trappings of a military campaign to arrest suspected rioters. The soldiers were greeted by 'old women begging with uplifted arms and suppressed laughter', and the arrests were accompanied by 'jeers and laughter' from the other navvies.[31] The action of the women of the camps added sexual overtones to the humiliation of the military, a humiliation already experienced by the civil authorities.

Tensions between Welsh and Irish navvies existed on Anglesey at this time also,[32] but it was not until 1851 that they took on a serious and violent form. Dissatisfaction among the Welsh arose from the continued employment of the Irish at a time when

---

[30] *Carnarvon and Denbigh Herald*, 15 January 1847. Spelling of the word 'navvy' was not yet standardized.
[31] Ibid.
[32] PP 1846 XIII, Report of the Select Committee on Railway Labourers, p.77, evidence of Samuel Morgan Peto.

unemployment in general was rising. Late in December 1850, eighty-five labourers, twenty-five masons and an unspecified number of carpenters were discharged from their work on the new breakwater at Holyhead. Conditions in the port prompted an appeal to the Quarter Sessions in March 1851 for an increase in the police force at the port, while in May a strike by Welsh and English navvies against the continued employment of the Irish between Caernarfon and Bangor was attributed to the stubborn 'unnatural antipathy' between the Welsh and Irish.[33] Later in the same month, one of the Irish navvies murdered a Welshman at Holyhead in a drunken brawl. This incident would have been sufficient in itself to cause an ugly disturbance, but occurring as it did at a time of increasing unemployment and dissatisfaction with the Irish, it precipitated a riot. On this occasion, a number of the Irish were forced by the Welsh to leave the country, placing them securely on the Irish express packet, despite the fact that many had family remaining in Holyhead.[34] The respectable inhabitants of the town reacted to these turbulent events by petitioning the government on 'the unreasonableness of suddenly localising hundreds and thousands of a labouring population in their parish, without making any provision for their efficient legal control or for the maintenance of law and order'. This argument had already been set out by one of their number in an influential Welsh periodical.[35] By this time, Holyhead was not only the port of departure for the Irish mail; it also provided the most important sea link between the government in London and its administration in Dublin. Disruption of the work on improvements to these communications was viewed with such gravity that the Home Office dispatched an inspector of the Metropolitan Police and an Admiralty ship to monitor the situation.[36]

A number of factors contributed to the unrest on the Chester and Holyhead line between 1846 and 1851. The changing needs of contractors led to periodic unemployment and the search for

---

[33] *Carnarvon and Denbigh Herald*, 4 January, 3 May 1851; correspondence in PRO, HO 45/3472T.

[34] *Carnarvon and Denbigh Herald*, 17 May 1851.

[35] *Carnarvon and Denbigh Herald*, 7 June 1851; Richard Jones, 'Caergybi', *Y Traethodydd* (January 1851), 126–7.

[36] PRO, HO 45/3472T, correspondence of Captain Frazer, Inspector W. Cummings and Lieut. G. M. Jackson.

scapegoats. The vagaries of navvy work and the constant movement from one temporary camp to another created unsettled conditions among the workers, while the impact of the railway on the towns of north Wales created a situation of flux and a feeling of uncertainty. All these factors coalesced to create social discord, and the Irish were the most convenient object upon which anger and frustration could be vented.

The presence of temporary labour routinely provoked resentment and hostility, even if animosity did not always escalate to the level of rioting. Evidence of this can be gleaned from the song which greeted Irish workers engaged to construct the woollen mills at Drefach Felindre in west Wales:

> O claddwch y Gwyddelod
> Naw troedfedd yn y baw
> Ac arnynt rhowch yn helaeth
> O ffrwyth y caib a rhaw,
> Ac arnynt rhoddwch feini
> A rheiny o dan sêl
> Rhag ofn i'r diawled godi
> A phoeni'r oes a ddêl.[37]

[Free translation: O bury deep the Irish / Nine feet in the muck / And heap upon them freely / With the mandrel and the pick / And heap upon them rocks and stones / And those sealed hard and good / For fear the devils rise again / To worry those they could.]

Another version of the song current in the south Wales coalfield simply substituted the word 'blackleg' (that is, a strike-breaker) for 'Irish'.[38] Songs were lyrical mnemonics for reinforcing ethnic stereotypes.

Whereas up to the 1840s the main site of conflict had been the iron industry, resistance to the Irish in the post-Famine period was at its most acute in the coal mines where there was a stark demarcation in status and remuneration between those who cut coal at the face and the remainder who undertook labouring jobs above ground. In 1850 it was claimed that the Irish in Wales never understood skilled work at the mines, being confined to rough work above ground. More than twenty years later, this

---

[37] J. Geraint Jenkins, *Dre Fach Felindre and the Woollen Industry* (Llandysul, 1976), p.25.
[38] W. H. Davies, *The Right Place – the Right Time* (Llandybïe, 1972), p.71. The song was sung to the folk tune 'Ffarwel i Blwy Llangywer'.

view was corroborated by Mr T. A. Wales, the Inspector of Mines in south Wales, who outlined a similar situation.[39] In some quarters this state of affairs was interpreted as little more than an Irish preference to avoid work underground,[40] but it is clear that the attitude of Welsh miners was an important consideration in the singular absence of the immigrants from the coalface. Because of the frequency of roof falls and accidents and the resulting high incidence of serious injury and death, dangerous work below ground in confined spaces required an implicit trust in one's fellow worker. Such a bond of trust between Irish and Welsh workers clearly did not exist.

The section of the coalfield most closely associated with the rapid growth of the industry is the Rhondda Valleys. During the first period of steam-coal mining, covering the years 1850–64, a period characterized by small mines and native entrepreneurs, the workforce consisted mainly of labourers formerly employed in agriculture who had made the short-step migration from neighbouring areas. Among these were some Irish workers who had arrived via labouring in agriculture in the Vale of Glamorgan. The absence of deep pits and the lack of any developed technique of colliery management at this time meant that there was relatively little demand for 'skilled' labour – skill being understood here as the possession of some previously acquired experience or training in the requirements of the industry. Consequently, the adaptation to new work practices was relatively painless, even if changes in wider social relationships took longer to occur. In these early decades, the social life of these new coal-mining settlements was reminiscent of that which existed in the countryside, including its deferential class relationships. In addition, practices of community discipline and exclusion were utilized as enthusiastically against 'outsiders' here as they had been in rural society.[41]

---

[39] *Morning Chronicle*, 27 March 1850, reprinted in Ginswick (ed.), *Labour and the Poor*, p.101; PP 1873 X, Report from the Select Committee on the Dearness of Coal, pp.58–9.
[40] Richard Rowe, *How Our Working People Live* (London, ?1868), p.27.
[41] E. D. Lewis, *The Rhondda Valleys* (London, 1959), pp.67, 234; A. H. John, *The Industrial Development of South Wales* (Cardiff, 1950), pp.58ff.; I. G. Jones, 'The south Wales collier in the mid-nineteenth century', in *idem*, *Explorations and Explanations: Essays in the Social History of Victorian Wales* (Llandysul, 1987); R. A. N. Jones, 'Women, community and collectice action: the *Ceffyl Pren* tradition', in Angela V. John (ed.), *Our Mothers' Land: Chapters in Welsh Women's History, 1830–1939* (Cardiff, 1991).

Repeated attempts were made to exclude the Irish from the Rhondda. In November 1848 Irish workers were driven down the valley as far as Pontypridd, where the police intervened to prevent further violence.[42] During the first period of the coal industry's expansion in the hitherto rural valleys, a number of additional disturbances occurred. The extension of the railway into this steeply inclined and confining valley brought Irish navvies to the area and provided the occasion for riots in August 1852 and December 1853, when they were driven out by a combined force of Welsh and English workers.[43] Given this turbulent background, the importation of Irish labourers as strike-breakers at a colliery in 1857 was akin to pouring oil onto a naked flame. The interlopers' houses were stoned by the enraged colliers, who destroyed every door and systematically smashed every pane of glass. Once again, the Irishmen were driven down the valley by several hundred colliers, although the wives and children were left unharmed. The rout was cut short by the appearance of a small body of police. At a later date it was claimed that 'very few Irishmen were to be found in any part of the valley for many years after this event'.[44] Nearly a decade later, Irish workers were once again the objects of unwelcome attention in the Rhondda. At a court case held at Aberdare in the neighbouring valley in June 1866, six Welshmen and a boy, who had been aided by forty or fifty others, were accused of interfering with the employment of the Irish at the Dunraven colliery in the Rhondda. The Welsh complained that the Irish had undercut wages and taken their jobs. It was reported that after stones were thrown at the doors of houses occupied by the Irish, a threatening letter, only part of which was read to the court, was pushed under an Irishman's door:

June 23 1866

Dear Timber's,

We have sent you these few lines to inform you that you are to leave this place (Paddy's Row), in less than one hour; and the lodgers, except the

---

[42] *Cardiff and Merthyr Guardian*, 25 November 1848.
[43] *Cambrian*, 6 August 1852, 16 December 1853.
[44] Ibid., 18 September 1857; NLW MS. 4378E, 'An Essay on the "History of the Development of the Coal Industry of the Rhondda Valleys for the Last 50 Years"', Treorchy Eisteddfod [?1895].

family. So no more at present from the officer of the Black army. The family must go on next Saturday night and you must look sharp about it.

The remainder of the letter was considered to be 'very filthy indeed, and totally unfit for publication', a solicitor commenting cryptically that the Black Army was 'a name not unfamiliar to the people of that district'. Unfortunately, he failed to disclose any more information about this secret society, whose activities resembled those of the Scotch Cattle, active in the mining areas to the east thirty years earlier. It was widely believed that only the presence of the police had prevented a full-scale riot.[45]

The frequency and violence of disturbances in the Rhondda undoubtedly prevented the establishment of more rooted Irish settlements such as those which existed in Merthyr Tydfil and the coastal towns. While the population of the Rhondda grew spectacularly in the late nineteenth century due to the enormous expansion of coal mining, fewer than a thousand Irish-born people were enumerated there in 1911 in a predominantly immigrant population of 152,781.[46] Coal mining began its pell-mell expansion in the 1870s, by which time the high point of Irish immigration had passed. Nevertheless, the inflow had not dried up completely and it is somewhat surprising that greater numbers did not make their way to the principal centre of this labour-intensive industry, where output was directly linked to the number of hewers employed, and which acted as a magnet for immigrants from elsewhere in Wales and from rural England.

Animosity towards the Irish existed in other new coal-mining settlements. At Mountain Ash in the neighbouring Cynon Valley, for example, there was little love lost between the two groups – so much so that the Irish who had migrated to the United States via the Cynon Valley preserved a memory of their harsh treatment in Wales, citing it as supporting evidence of Welsh oppression of the Irish when they encountered the Welsh community at Scranton in the United States.[47] At the time of the vicious anti-Irish riots at Tredegar in 1882, the police at Mountain Ash feared that long-standing tensions and periodic

---

[45]   *Cardiff and Merthyr Guardian*, 29 June 1866.

[46]   Lewis, *The Rhondda Valleys*, pp.229, 238.

[47]   William D. Jones, *Wales in America: Scranton and the Welsh, 1860–1920* (Cardiff, 1993), pp.65–6.

brawls between the Welsh and Irish would escalate into a more serious clash, although in the event this did not happen.[48] An indicator of the tenacity of prejudice is the way in which ethnic stereotypes became embedded in the language of everyday experience. Mrs Ellen Murphy recalled clashes between children of the local board school and those attending the adjacent Catholic school at Mountain Ash in the 1890s, when the Irish children were decried as 'Irish black pats'.[49] This deceptively simple term of abuse is rich in levels of hostile meaning. In a coal-mining township the association of the word 'pat' (the colloquial term for an Irishman) with the colour black conveyed a vivid image of the dust-covered Irish coal miner returning through the streets to bathe at his lodgings. Also, in local usage the term 'black pat' was the name of the beetle carried in the coal dust which impregnated the miner's working clothes. In the days before pit-head baths, these clothes were brought above ground to the miner's home, where the beetles would swarm over the ground floor of the house at night. In the ecology of the pit the black pat was the lowest form of animal life – at least a miner knew when he had stepped on a rat. By association, and used in a particular context, the phrase also carried the suggestion of 'blackleg' (that is, strike-breaking) labour. Yet despite the depth of this animosity there was no ingrained tradition of ethnic violence at Mountain Ash comparable to that which existed in the Rhondda. Thus, despite their many similarities arising from their one-industry structure, mining settlements varied significantly from place to place according to the depth and location of the pits. Social relations within them were influenced by the scale of urban development and the nature of immigration; not all developed traditions of violent collective action and protest. In Mountain Ash, for example, there is no evidence of a concerted attempt to expel the Irish.

General labouring in the docks is the third major sector in which the Irish were employed. This was a peculiarly fluctuating labour force. Irregular employment – resulting from the vagaries of the weather, tide and the trade cycle, together with the capricious hiring practices of employers – was the norm. Here,

[48] *South Wales Daily News*, 1 July 1882. See also the correspondence in PRO, HO 144/100/A18355.
[49] Information provided by the late Mrs Ellen Murphy, Mountain Ash.

the maintenance of a permanent reserve army of labour was comparatively easy. Interestingly, this sector furnishes two rare examples of Irish labourers protesting about their low wages, both of which occurred at Swansea. In July 1848 four Irishmen were prosecuted for assaulting one of their comrades in the town's Greenhill district because he had worked for less than the going rate.[50] Five years later, in August 1853, the Irish were prime movers in strike action at the docks which resulted in a prosecution of those accused of intimidating their fellow workers to down tools. They had been lured to Wales on a promise of wages of 3s. 6d. a day whereas on arrival they received between 1s. 6d. and 2s. Their aim in withdrawing their labour was parity of remuneration rather than the lowering of wages.[51] It was precisely because of conditions like these that dock work was not a propitious area for union recruitment in mid-century, and employers were not faced with the phenomenon of mass unionism on the Welsh waterfront until the 1880s.[52]

Accounts of the 'New Unionism' of the 1880s, which resulted in a more extensive unionization of general labourers than ever before, have tended to stress the influence of the London dockers' strike of August–September 1889 in causing ripples of agitation among the quiet backwaters of unorganized labour in the regions. In recent years this interpretation has been reappraised in the light of regional evidence suggesting a more complex picture.[53] Before the famous conflict of dock labour in London, other events had already begun to stir unskilled and semi-skilled workers outside the metropolis, which meant that the great ferment of industrial activity from 1889 to 1890 did not find a completely unprepared audience. There were notable signs of increased activity on the Welsh waterfront from 1888. In March of that year the Cardiff Coal Trimmers' Association was established (although it was confined to a particular category of dock labour), and in October J. Havelock Wilson succeeded in establishing the first of a number of branches of his National

[50] *Cardiff and Merthyr Guardian*, 7 July 1848.
[51] *Cambrian*, 26 August 1853.
[52] P. J. Leng, *The Welsh Dockers* (Ormskirk, 1981), pp.7–9.
[53] See E. J. Hobsbawm, *Labouring Men: Studies in the History of Labour* (London, 1968 edn), chs.9–11; L. J. Williams, 'The New Unionism in south Wales, 1889–92', *Welsh History Review*, 1 (1960–3); D. Hopkin and L. J. Williams, 'New light on the New Unionism in Wales, 1889–1912', *Llafur*, 4, 3 (1986).

Amalgamated Sailors' and Firemen's Union at Cardiff and Newport.[54] The progress of Wilson's Seamen's Union was closely connected with the establishment of the grandiloquently titled National Amalgamated Labourers' Union of Great Britain and Ireland (NALU) at Newport by Albert Kenny. Kenny had helped to organize the Seamen's Union at Dublin, Cork and Whitehaven, but despite the NALU's auspicious title and Kenny's extensive experience this particular union's activities were restricted to south Wales alone.

The NALU was established at Cardiff in June 1889. By the end of the following year it had capitalized upon the general upsurge in interest in, and support for, the general unions and boasted sixteen branches in south Wales, with 5,531 members and a bank balance of more than £2,500. According to the general secretary of the union, they could 'now command respectful consideration and negotiation with Employers, a fact until recently unknown in the ranks of our toiling, wealth-producing labourers'.[55] When reviewing the 'rise and progress' of the union as early as 1891, T. J. O'Keefe, the district secretary, spoke in millenarian terms of the new dawn of combination, the bright sun of a new day and the fetters falling away from the aching limbs of the unskilled. In fact, this rhetoric belied a prosaic reality in which some branches were better organized than others and the actual size of the membership appears to have been overestimated.[56] The NALU's emphasis on benefits gave it the appearance of a craft union, but it does not fall squarely into either of the two accepted categories of labour organizations of the period, of 'craft organization' or 'new union'; rather, it suggests a hybrid, exhibiting some characteristics common to both types.

Although a breakdown of the union's membership on ethnic lines is not available, the NALU clearly appealed to, and succeeded in organizing, some of the Irish, especially in Newport. A number of Irishmen took a prominent part in the union's affairs and assumed positions of leadership from the outset. The

[54] P. W. Donovan, 'Unskilled labour unions in south Wales, 1889–1914', unpublished University of London M.Phil. thesis (1969), 34–5.
[55] NALU, *Report of Branches and General Statement and Summary of Accounts from Opening of the Union, June 6th, 1889, to Dec. 27th, 1890* (Cardiff, 1891).
[56] T. J. O'Keefe, *Rise and Progress of the National Amalgamated Labourers' Union of Great Britain and Ireland* (Cardiff, 1891), pp.5–6; Hopkin and Williams, 'New Light', 74–5.

position of the Irish in the NALU is comparable to some degree with the position of the Irish on the London waterfront before the dockers' strike of 1889. As John Lovell has pointed out, the conservative sectional loyalties of the Irish enabled them to establish a number of defensive and highly decentralized bodies, the very antithesis of Ben Tillett's centralized and all-embracing Dockers' Union. Kinship was an important factor in organizing grass-roots activity. T. J. O'Keefe of the NALU implicitly recognized this when he stated, 'We must unite, not only to protect our own pecuniary interests, but we must unite to safeguard ourselves and our families.'[57] The same point was made more bluntly thirty years later in the obituary of Councillor Tim Sheehan of Swansea. 'As a dock stevedore', it was reported, 'he provided work for a large number of his countrymen, particularly in the dark days when the work was so confined that "no Irish need apply".'[58] Workplace relationships of this kind were not always superseded by trade-union structures, often being incorporated within them.

Advances made by the NALU were capitalized upon by the new national unions from the end of 1889, resulting in sharp rivalry between the different organizations. However, the progress of Tillett's union was patchy and it managed to dislodge the NALU effectively only in Swansea, where the latter's membership at the end of 1890 was 380, compared with 2,250 at Newport and 1,120 at Cardiff. During the first eighteen months of its existence, the NALU had quickly consolidated its position in the region, but as the economic situation deteriorated from 1891, the employers' counter-attack seriously undermined the strength of the waterside unions. There followed an extended period when economic conditions were inimical to union expansion. After an initial decline in membership, the NALU managed to stabilize and maintained levels at above 3,000; membership fell below this threshold on only three occasions between 1892 and 1910.[59]

---

[57] John Lovell, 'The Irish and the London dockers', *Bulletin of the Society for the Study of Labour History*, 35 (1977), 16–19; O'Keefe, *Rise and Progress*, p.14.

[58] *Welsh Catholic Herald*, 8 January 1921.

[59] Leng, *The Welsh Dockers*, pp.7–9.

The experience of Irish workers in these three categories of hand labour must be viewed against the background of changing patterns of immigration from the 1870s. Irish immigration to Wales increased noticeably between 1871 and 1881, with a net increase of 865 Irish-born during the decade. Although in absolute terms this increase is small, it is all the more remarkable because it masks the depletion caused by death among existing immigrants over the same period and because in the previous decade there had been a reduction of 21.7 per cent in the number of Irish-born in Wales. Thus, the 1870s were a period of renewed immigration, with migrants coming directly from Ireland or via towns and cities elsewhere in Britain. In part, this continued immigration can be ascribed to the need for labour in the older industrial districts, which were increasingly abandoned by workers seeking higher wages in the booming coal industry. This development stimulated a small-scale annual movement from west Cork to the smelting furnaces of south Wales about the year 1880.[60] By this time, ethnic conflict at the ironworks was in decline. Anti-Irish riots continued to occur at Ebbw Vale in 1879 and, more seriously, at Tredegar in 1882. The latter was a response to a heady brew of grievances which included radical structural change in the local economy, religious tensions arising from the evangelizing activities of the Salvation Army in the town and Welsh indignation at the murder of two government officials in Phoenix Park in Dublin. The ferocity of the attacks on the Irish and their homes led to a temporary withdrawal of many of the Irish inhabitants from Tredegar, and the events left a lasting scar on relationships in the town. But from 1882 there was a decisive break with the practice of rioting as a means of excluding Irish workers in Wales.[61]

Brinley Thomas estimated that 3,000 Irish-born people entered Glamorgan during the decade 1881–91 (accounting for only 2.8 per cent of the total immigration) and that this figure

[60] PP 1890 CI, Report on Migratory Agricultural Labourers, p.6.

[61] On Tredegar, see Evan and David Powell, *History of Tredegar* (1884; 2nd edn, Newport, 1902), pp.103–4; Jon Parry, 'The Tredegar anti-Irish riots of 1882', *Llafur*, 3, 4 (1983). The definitive account of the events can be found in Louise Miskell, 'Custom, conflict and community'. An indication of the longer-term impact of the riots locally can be gauged from the fact that Oliver Powell, a native of Tredegar interviewed in 1973, believed that the riot had occurred during his childhood even though he was not born until 3 October 1897, some fifteen years after the events occurred. See transcript of the interview with Powell at the South Wales Miners' Library.

doubled in the following decade to 6,600 (6.9 per cent).[62] In Wales as a whole, the Irish-born experienced a net reduction of only 13.8 per cent in the last thirty years of the century, a figure which supports the view that there was a fairly constant inflow of young migrants to offset losses due to death or movement elsewhere. Some of these migrants were attracted by the possibility of an opening in this rapidly expanding economy, landing at Cardiff or the new port of Barry and finding work at the docks or in other industries inland. Others were recruited for specific tasks. A temporary labour shortage occurred in some Welsh iron companies as a result of enthusiastic Welsh enlistment for the Boer War. Acting on behalf of the Dowlais Iron Company in April 1900, John Crowley publicized in southern Ireland an appeal for labourers, prudently emphasizing, 'No strike, but owing to men going to war'. Several hundred labourers responded and invaded the Cardiff steamer at Waterford, but the company underwrote the passage of only fifty-four of them; another fifty labourers arrived in Wales in May independently of the company and in anticipation of employment.[63] At the end of the same month, the agent of the Blaenavon Steelworks was prompted by 'a great dearth of labourers' to advertise for forty hands at Cork. Once again, the agent was inundated with applications and fifty men embarked for Newport in June.[64] It is likely that other companies sought to make good the loss of workers in the same manner.

By this time the Irish had acquired a secure foothold in the fledgling trade-union movement, although the strength of commitment to organized labour varied from town to town and from industry to industry. On the whole, the 1890s had been a decade of limited union expansion followed by a period of enforced caution. In the south Wales coalfield industrial relations continued to be governed by the sliding-scale agreement. This voluntary regulating mechanism, which tied wages in the coal industry to fluctuations in the price of coal, was a tangible embodiment of the belief that the economic interests of masters

[62] Brinley Thomas, 'The migration of labour into the Glamorganshire coalfield, 1861–1911', in W. E. Minchinton (ed.), *Industrial South Wales 1750–1914: Essays in Welsh Economic History* (London, 1969), pp.51–2.
[63] Glam. RO, D/DG Dowlais Iron Company Collection, Section C, box 5: 'John Crowley's visit to Ireland to obtain labourers, 1900'.
[64] *South Wales Daily News*, 5 June 1900.

and men were indissolubly welded together. When this mechanism failed, as it did in 1898, the social consensus of Liberal
Wales was fractured irreparably by a bitter lock-out.[65] The Irish
in the coalfield were particularly badly affected by the five-
month-long dispute. After the dispute had ended in unmistakable
defeat and the pointed humiliation of the miners, Bishop Hedley
circulated the Catholic clergy requesting information about the
effect of the strike on their congregations. The response showed
that where a congregation was largely composed of the Irish,
great distress had occurred. At Ebbw Vale and Tredegar all but
half a dozen of the congregation were affected, while at
Brynmawr only the manager and a clerk of the Blaina furnaces
and the stationmaster escaped direct hardship. At neighbouring
Pontypool the whole Catholic population of more than 400 was
idle. This pattern was repeated across the coalfield. Of the 600
Catholics at Rhymney, some 550 were affected, while at
Tonypandy all 270 were without work for the duration of the
strike.[66] As the coal industry dominated the regional economy of
south Wales by this date, this picture of Irish hardship should not
be surprising: it merely mirrored the experience of the workforce
as a whole. Equally significantly, there was no hint of a suggestion that the Irish had been anything other than supportive of
the action taken. Given the central importance of exports to the
Welsh coal trade, the strike also had a considerable effect upon
the well-being of transport and dock workers.

One of the immediate results of the strike was the formation of
the South Wales Miners' Federation, a union which would
dominate organized labour in Wales for the next half-century.
Affiliation with the Mineworkers' Federation of Great Britain
provided additional evidence of the miners' disillusionment with
the sliding scale and of a new-found belief in the value of strong
union organization. Over the ensuing decade, the attachment of
rank-and-file members to their new union was cemented. The
Irish participated equally in this development, as shown by the
evidence of Fr Dent of Rhymney. Dent had provided financial
assistance to families in his congregation during the strike and
had assisted with the distribution of food to children, but in 1908

---

[65] L. J. Williams, 'The strike of 1898', *Morgannwg*, IX (1965). The sliding scale was
finally abolished in 1903.

[66] AAC box 76, bundle of letters labelled 'Colliers strike April 1 to Aug. 1 1898'.

he wrote bitterly of the absence of miners from his church services on Good Friday, complaining that only women and children attended, 'and the resolutions of the [South Wales] Miners' Federation as to work on Good Friday carry more weight than the exhortation given on Palm Sunday'.[67] The union had clearly become an important source of authority for Irishmen in mining settlements.

Irish involvement in organized labour was demonstrated by their role in the severe industrial unrest of 1910–11. At Newport docks in particular, the Irish established a strong position. During the Houlder dispute in the port in 1910 union-breaking blackleg labour from London met with a hostile reception from the Irish. On their arrival at the port, a docker called O'Neill shouted abuse at the strike-breakers and urged the assembled crowd to attack them. 'Are we going to let them take the bread out of our mouths?', he demanded. 'Let us go for them.' It was only the intervention of two union officials, John O'Leary and John Twomey, that secured the strike-breakers' safe return to London. During the dockers' strikes of the following year, Albert Kenny and John O'Leary of the NALU and O'Shea of the Dockers' Union played a pivotal role in the Newport Joint Strike Committee. Men by the name of Lynch and McAuley were also active on this committee.[68] The NALU's annual report for 1911 provides unequivocal proof that the Irish had become entrenched in the union. By that date, Twomey occupied the position of general secretary and John Kelly that of treasurer, while John O'Leary was Newport district secretary, and a number of branch secretaries were of Irish origin.[69]

Despite these advances, stereotypes of the feckless, unruly Irish labourer persisted in some quarters. Recalling the famous riots he had witnessed in Tonypandy during the coal strike of 1910, the novelist Rhys Davies attributed them to 'a section of the industrialised race . . . composed of . . . rootless ruffians and barbarous *aliens*, particularly Irishmen who were . . . bored with the monotony of work'.[70] It was a pitiable attempt to scapegoat

---

[67] AAC box 55, Fr Frederick Dent to Bishop Hedley, 6 November 1908.

[68] Leng, *The Welsh Dockers*, pp.48–52, 57–64.

[69] NALU, *Report and . . . Balance Sheet, Year Ending January 31st, 1912* (Swansea, 1912).

[70] Quoted in David Smith (ed.), *A People and A Proletariat: Essays in the History of Wales, 1780–1880* (London, 1980), pp.231–2.

the Irish for events in which they had no part and an echo of a passing mentality. Sometimes grudgingly, fellow workers began to recognize the Irish contribution. Writing home in 1915, a former slate quarryman from north Wales who had migrated to the south complained at having to mix with 'the unprincipled Irish who are disorderly and without taste, and as with common navvies like beer for drink'. Nevertheless, he conceded that the Irish were 'of greater value in the labour market than hundreds of the enlightened quarrymen of the North and a great deal more independent'.[71] Comments like this support Stephen Fielding's comment that trade-union consciousness was not necessarily the same as class-consciousness. It took joint participation in political institutions to achieve that, a development which did not occur on a widespread basis until after the First World War.

The pattern of steady Irish immigration during the late nine-teenth century, albeit on a smaller scale than during the Famine years, changed drastically during the first decade of the twentieth century, when the numbers of the Irish-born in Wales fell by a third. The most likely explanation for this dramatic reduction is a combination of two factors: the incidence of mortality among Irish immigrants and a falling-off of Irish immigration to south Wales. This picture is confirmed by the number of Irish entering Glamorgan between 1901 and 1911, the number falling back to 3,800 after the high point of the previous decade.[72] A similar pattern was outlined for neighbouring Monmouthshire by the authors of the printed census of 1911, when they chose a sample unit for a more detailed analysis of migration than the conven-tional summary tables allowed. Compared to other immigrants

[71] Quoted in Dafydd Roberts, *Y Chwarelwyr a'r Sowth* (Gwynedd, 1982), p.13.

[72] Brinley Thomas, 'The migration of labour into the Glamorganshire coalfield, 1861–1911', in Minchinton (ed.), *Industrial South Wales*, pp.51–2. One contributory factor to the low levels of Irish immigration during these years might have been the willingness of large numbers of agricultural labourers from adjacent areas, such as the Welsh countryside and the border counties of England, to migrate to south Wales, thus meeting the requirements of the expanding coal industry without the necessity of looking further afield. The Irish-born accounted for approximately 20 per cent of the non-Welsh population of Glamorgan in 1871, but only 9 per cent in 1891. See T. M. Hodges, 'The peopling of the hinterland and the port of Cardiff, 1801–1914', in Minchinton (ed.), *Industrial South Wales*, p.12. For a more recent assessment of population movements, see Philip N. Jones, 'Population migration into Glamorgan, 1861–1911: a reassessment', in Prys Morgan (ed.), *Glamorgan County History*, vol.VI (Cardiff, 1988), pp.173–202.

from non-adjacent counties, the age structure of the Irish-born population was significantly older than the remainder of the population, a fact which lends weight to the belief that Irish immigration had been declining for a decade.[73] This reduction in immigration from Ireland cannot be attributed to a lack of opportunities in south Wales; overall immigration to the region continued at unusually high levels during the first decade of the twentieth century, as industry absorbed workers in their thousands.

With immigration declining, Irish workers (whether Irish-born or not) were able to consolidate their position in the workforce. During the mid-nineteenth century, boundaries between the Irish and other members of the workforce had been drawn by the discriminatory recruitment policies of employers and policed by periodic violent collective action by native workers. Even though this period is characterized by the complementarity of interests between capital and labour, as compared with the unrest of the earlier decades, ethnic conflict at the workplace persisted. The result was to construct definitions of skill along ethnic lines as much as in terms of an individual's ability to perform particular tasks, especially in the iron and coal industries. Both the perception and the reality of the Irish as a pool of cheap unskilled labour began to be transformed during the 1880s when a sea-change occurred in their relationship with the remainder of the workforce, even if that change occurred unevenly. To the extent that it is possible to study relationships at the workplace, it would appear that the borders between different ethnic groups were shifting. In general, it is true to say that by the mid-1880s riot had ceased to be the preferred method of excluding the Irish, while their participation in trade unions was on the increase. Nevertheless, the long-term effect of the persistence of 'collective bargaining by riot' should not be underestimated, especially as it resulted in the Irish being virtually excluded from the Rhondda Valleys, the fastest growing and most dynamic coal-mining area in the south Wales coalfield.

[73] *Census of England and Wales, 1911: General Report with Appendices* (London, 1917), pp.229–30.

VI

'THIEVING LIKE AN IRISHMAN':
THE IRISH AND CRIME

Despite the prevalence of riot and revolt during the 1830s and 1840s, Wales subsequently acquired an enviable reputation for orderliness and a comparative absence of criminality which cast the preceding years of turbulence into the shadows. The mid-Victorian decades are notable for the absence of the bitter class conflict which had so alarmed the authorities in the preceding decades and had required the frequent use of the military to quell disturbances. A picture of Wales as a peaceful, loyal and unusually religious country was now established. In fact, the carefully cultivated image of a godly, law-abiding people resistant to worldly temptations is more complex. As David Jones has shown, two concepts of order and justice – the official and the popular – competed and coexisted with varying degrees of harmony. During the mid-century decades the balance tipped inexorably towards official justice in the towns, where the effects of the new county police forces, created in 1856, were seen most clearly. The police concerned themselves not only with crime as such but also with the imposition of order on working-class districts where drunkenness and unruly behaviour were considered to have a destabilizing effect.[1] Given the part which some police officers had played in maintaining surveillance over lodging houses during the Famine years, the Irish were an obvious target for their attentions.

The way a particular society defines crime reveals a great deal about the borders between acceptable and unacceptable behaviour, about who is categorized as a full member of the group and who is considered an outsider. Outsiders (however they are defined) continually provide a challenge to the host

---

[1] David Jones, *Crime in Nineteenth Century Wales* (Cardiff, 1991); *idem* and Alan Bainbridge, 'The "conquering of China": crime in an industrial community, 1842–64', *Llafur*, 2, 4 (1979); Keith Strange, 'In search of the celestial empire: crime in Merthyr, 1830–60', *Llafur*, 3, 1 (1980). On the Irish, see Roger Swift, 'Crime and the Irish in nineteenth century Britain', in R. Swift and S. Gilley (eds.), *The Irish in Britain, 1815–1939* (London, 1989).

society. In nineteenth-century Wales, attitudes to criminal behaviour were shaped by deep-rooted preconceptions about the destabilizing effect of mobile and rootless people on a settled population. Pervasive stereotypes of the footloose Irish vagrant, based on sporadic contact with itinerants over the previous two centuries, were now combined with the anxieties engendered by rapid social and economic change to create a powerful image of a feckless, indigent and potentially criminal people. Such views permeated writings on a variety of social issues and emerged at unexpected moments, demonstrating the degree to which stereotypes were casually, almost unconsciously, deployed.

A revealing example of the tendency to categorize the Irish almost unthinkingly as criminals occurred in 1846, when the radical journalist Gwilym Hiraethog wrote a searing indictment of the social effects of illiteracy and restricted access to education. In doing so, he drove his point home by sarcastically contrasting the 'respectable' crime of defrauding banks, committed by educated forgers who possessed the wherewithal to abscond to America, with the 'low and disgusting' opportunist crime of the poor of stealing a shirt or petticoat from a hedge. 'By forging, an educated man steals like a gentleman', he commented acidly, 'but the poor illiterate man thieves like an Irishman.'[2] As a radical who drew heavily on his personal experience to convey a political message, Hiraethog couched his writings in a colloquial idiom familiar to his readers. In this context, his concluding simile – 'thieving like an Irishman' ('dwgyd fel Gwyddel') – would have struck a chord among his readers. The apparently casual use of this phrase is merely one example of how harmful stereotypes had become embedded in the language of everyday life.

Suspicion of the outsider and anxiety about the social consequences of rapid industrialization were not peculiar to Wales, as shown by the extended controversy over the 'Condition of England' question. What was distinctive, however, was that from 1847 a bitter controversy concerning the morals and character of the Welsh people transformed the debate into one about the moral worth of different nationalities. The controversy

    [2] Gwilym Hiraethog, *Llythyrau'r Hen Ffarmwr*, ed. E. Morgan Humphreys (Cardiff, 1939), p.3.

arose from the angry public response to the publication of the Reports of the Commissioners of Inquiry into the State of Education in Wales in 1847.[3] As the three commissioners were English barristers unacquainted with the country, its language, and elementary education for the working class, they relied extensively upon the clergy of the Established Church for their evidence, despite the fact that this group was an increasingly isolated and predominantly Anglicized element of Welsh society. Public outrage was directed at the reports' gratuitous comments on the alleged loose morals of the Welsh – especially Welsh women – and the connection made between the Nonconformist denominations and immorality. As attendance at places of worship was far higher in Wales than in England, and the Established Church catered for no more than a small minority of churchgoers, these accusations were interpreted as nothing less than the indictment of a nation. Nonconformists responded by vehemently rejecting the reports' conclusions, bitterly accusing Anglicans of 'treachery'. 'The Treachery of the Blue Books', as the episode came to be known, provided a potent grievance demanding redress and it exerted a powerful influence upon the formation of a politically conscious Nonconformist nation in the second half of the nineteenth century.

Nonconformist writers applied themselves energetically to the task of disproving the reports' invidious accusations. Foremost among them was the Revd Evan Jones, better known by his bardic name of Ieuan Gwynedd, a Nonconformist minister and accomplished journalist in both Welsh and English.[4] Ieuan Gwynedd was spurred by righteous indignation to counter the commissioners' claims in a series of meticulously researched pamphlets. However, his reasoned arguments based on a skilful use of official statistics were underpinned by a set of assumptions about the moral condition of society which was fully in accord with those of the writers he condemned. His views on the matter were set out most explicitly in a revealing article published in January 1852. In this article, Ieuan Gwynedd admitted the

[3] PP 1847 XXVII, Reports of the Commissioners on the State of Education in Wales. On the effects of the reports, see Ieuan Gwynedd Jones, *Mid-Victorian Wales* (Cardiff, 1992), ch.5; Prys Morgan (ed.), *Brad y Llyfrau Gleision* (Llandysul, 1991).

[4] See G. H. Jenkins, 'Ieuan Gwynedd: Eilun y Genedl', in Prys Morgan (ed.), *Brad Y Llyfrau Gleision*, pp.101–24.

difficulties involved in determining the balance between good and evil in any nation. Nevertheless, he felt it a necessary task to undertake this enterprise, insisting that nations, like individuals, had moral characters which were open to analysis and understanding through a rigorous study of their habits and mores. But despite the emphasis he placed on avoiding misrepresenting a nation's moral character, the specific examples he quoted were, in reality, nothing more than crude stereotypes. In his view the French were models of politeness, but as slippery as a sow's corkscrew tail; Arabs were noted for their moderation but thought nothing of coveting their neighbours' property; Jews were industrious, but also helpless deceivers; the English were famed for their love of freedom, but were cruel oppressors in their own colonies. At the end of this litany, the Irish won pride of place. 'Irish women', asserted Ieuan Gwynedd,

> are very chaste, but terribly lazy. The men are proverbially kind, but as false as the devil. Shoot a man! Bless you! What is shooting a man to an Irishman? He would shoot his best neighbour seven times over if ordered to by some secret terrorist society, and would laugh upon discovering that he had mistaken his prey in the end.[5]

Such negative images achieved wider currency. In the wake of anti-Irish disturbances at Ebbw Vale and Brynmawr, on the border between Monmouthshire and Breconshire, in the summer of 1853, a Welsh periodical put flesh on the bones of what was customarily, but obliquely, referred to as the 'natural antipathy' between Welsh and Irish:

> It is certain that the Irish are greatly to be blamed, for many things. They undercut wages in many areas through working below price. They can well afford that, because some dozen of them live helter-skelter in some hole of a house, and they send their wives and children about begging, and live on the worst fare. And if someone dares say a word to them, it would not be surprising if they did not stab a knife between his ribs.[6]

---

[5] 'Drwg a da cenedl y Cymry', *Y Gwron Cymreig*, 7 January 1852, reprinted in *Gweithiau Barddonol a Rhyddieithol Ieuan Gwynedd*, ed. William Williams (Dolgellau, 1876), pp.470–2.

[6] *Y Diwygiwr* (August 1853), 257.

The similarities between this passage and the sentiments expressed on a different occasion by Ieuan Gwynedd, quoted above, are striking.

These were more than isolated examples of individuals' prejudice. In the protracted debate on the Education Reports, immigrants came to represent the quintessential 'other' which, by the alleged starkness of the contrast, underlined the essential goodness of the Welsh as a people. Nonconformist writers deplored the effects of industrialization and urbanization by attributing immorality to incomers. Thus, Dr Thomas Rees believed that because of the immigration of English and Irish labourers into the north-east and south-east of Wales, 'the peculiar characteristics of the Welsh labourer are to a great extent obliterated in these counties'.[7] These sentiments were shared by Henry Richard, Member of Parliament for Merthyr Tydfil from 1868 to 1888. Richard took refuge in the notion of an idealized, and rural, 'Wales Proper' as the cradle of the true Welsh character; for him, the large towns of Merthyr, Cardiff and Swansea had 'long ceased to be distinctively Welsh'.[8] Both writers were intent on demonstrating that the Nonconformist Welsh were morally superior to their godless English neighbours, a view rooted in the slight to the Welsh people contained in the Education Reports of 1847. The connection between immigrants and immorality in the minds of Welsh commentators persisted long after the debate on the Blue Books had subsided, as shown by the views contained in a paper read at the National Eisteddfod at Merthyr Tydfil in 1881, in which it was claimed that the 'ignorant and dissipated habits' of English and Irish immigrants to the mining districts of south Wales inflated the area's crime statistics and gave a misleading impression of Welsh criminality.[9]

An amusing – yet significant – example of the influence of this ideology is provided by a historical gazetteer of Glamorgan, published in 1874, which explained the reasons behind a change in the name of a neighbourhood surrounding the ironworks near Rhymney. 'Sodom and Gomorrah' was the name generally used from the time of building, but at a later date it was changed to

[7] Thomas Rees, *Miscellaneous Papers on Subjects Relating to Wales* (London, 1867), p.14.
[8] Henry Richard, *Letters and Essays on Wales* (2nd edn, London, 1884), pp.67–8. Similar, albeit more qualified, sentiments can be found in 'Carcharau Cymru', in *Y Tyst a'r Dydd*, 30 August 1872.
[9] T. D. Jones, *Home Life of the Welsh Collier* (1881), p.3.

the more innocuous Welsh name of 'Pontlotyn'. The reason proffered for the change was as follows:

> Sodom and Gomorrah had been from the beginning the principal residence of Rhymney's Irish, and through their drunkenness and fights with the Welsh, the place acquired a bad name. For a long period around 1860, some of the Irish were taken almost every week to Merthyr's magistrates' court to be tried for drunk and disorderly behaviour. And as there was a tendency for the name Sodom and Gomorrah to convey an image of evil places, so that the country would not think them akin to Sodom and Gomorrah of the land of Canaan, it was decided to change the name to Pontlotyn instead. And by that name it is known at present.[10]

Naming is one way of appropriating. Nonconformists chose biblical names such as Soar, Siloam and Horeb for their chapels in the area as evidence of their virtuous scriptural genealogy. A popular literary culture steeped in the Bible was sensitive to an imputation that it harboured in its midst a place synonymous with immorality of the kind which could be read about in the Old Testament.

Nonconformists were not the only group loudly to proclaim their outrage at the Education Reports. A number of prominent Welsh Anglicans were equally incensed by that episode and stoutly defended their fellow countrymen and women against attack. After all, the accusations of lawlessness and licentiousness could be interpreted as an indictment of their failure to exert the measure of social control expected of them as putative exemplars for the working class. The response of Sir Thomas Phillips of Newport is indicative of this conjuncture. Phillips had been knighted following the Chartist rising of 1839 when, as Newport's mayor, his spirited defence of the town earned him nationwide fame. His substantial tome in response to the accusations of the Education Commissioners, published in 1849, was the most comprehensive rebuttal of their claims and a clear exposition of the magistracy's views on crime.[11] Phillips sought to refute the reports' accusations by comparing Welsh criminal

---

[10] Dafydd Morganwg, *Hanes Morganwg*, (Aberdare, 1874), p.450; cf. J. S. Jones, *Hanes Rhymni a Phontlottyn* (Dinbych, 1904), p.131.
[11] Thomas Phillips, *Wales: The Language, Social Condition, Moral Character, and Religious Opinions of the People Considered in their Relation to Education* (London, 1849).

statistics with those of England. He, too, felt it appropriate to exclude from his analysis Glamorgan and Monmouthshire – the two most populous Welsh counties – 'in order to bring these comparisons to bear more directly upon the Welsh population'. His justification for excluding this part of the country was the presence in it of a large immigrant population from England and Ireland, 'many amongst them driven thither by crime and want, and characterised by much that is lawless and unrestrained'.[12] By contrast, when he analysed the statistics of the Spring circuit of 1848 for the six counties of north Wales, Phillips found that in Merioneth there were no prisoners for trial, while the remaining five counties yielded only forty-three. Of this total there were twenty-six convictions: fifteen for stealing, four for misdemeanours, two for arson, one for manslaughter and three for assault. When broken down on the basis of nationality, it was discovered that the convict for manslaughter was English, one of the arsonists was a Scot, while two of the three convicted of assault were Irish. This left only one Welshman in five counties convicted of offences against the person.[13]

Thus, in the mid-nineteenth century both Anglican and Nonconformist commentators excluded the industrialized counties of south-east Wales from their analysis of crime on *a priori* grounds. By selecting an area whose criminal statistics would confirm a preconceived view of Welsh morality, they took a partial view of Welsh society and presented it in terms of its organic and authentic whole. This allowed a comparison of the incidence of recorded crime in rural Wales with that of rural and urban England combined in order to demonstrate the superior morality of the Welsh. The effect of depicting society in terms of a virtuous native community being progressively undermined by an encroaching alien population was to deflect the manifest tensions of Welsh society onto external factors.

The influence of these ideas is clearly discernible in comments made by other magistrates. In 1852 H. A Bruce, the stipendiary magistrate of Merthyr Tydfil and Aberdare, delivered a lecture to the Young Men's Mutual Improvement Society at Merthyr in which he analysed the social and political condition of the town.

---

[12] Ibid., pp.71–2.
[13] Ibid., p.76.

Like many of his contemporaries, he believed that crime was brought into the town by migrants. He asserted that the great majority of criminals were vagrants, 'above all' the Irish, although, as David Jones has pointed out, his own statistics belie this statement. Even so, there was an enormous disparity between the size of the Irish-born population and the amount of recorded criminal activity for which they were held responsible, the Irish-born accounting for only 4.8 per cent of the town's population, while Bruce maintained that natives of Ireland committed fully one-third of indictable offences in the police district.[14] On one particular day some six weeks previously, he had committed eight persons on separate charges of felony, only one of whom (a thirteen-year-old orphan) was 'in the remotest degree connected with Merthyr'. Bruce felt justified in concluding that criminal activity in the town was primarily the province of 'strangers, and the lower class of Irish, who swarm in the worst parts of the town'.[15] That the town's character was not besmirched by the behaviour of the native working class was taken as evidence of superior Welsh morality.[16]

John Coke Fowler, deputy chairman of the Glamorgan Sessions and stipendiary magistrate of Swansea, came to similar conclusions in two lectures on 'The Characteristics and Civilisation of South Wales' delivered at the Royal Institution of South Wales in 1873. Among the themes he addressed was the remarkable absence of crime in all Welsh counties, except Glamorgan. For Fowler, the 'unpleasant appearance' of Glamorgan had to be understood in terms of the varied geographical origins of the population. He found that of the 7,857 prisoners held in Swansea gaol in 1872, some 1,461 (18.6 per cent) had been born in Ireland, 1,570 (20 per cent) were English-born, while 4,471 (56.9 per cent) were natives of Wales. Thus, although the Irish-born accounted for only 3.4 per cent of the town's population in 1871, natives of Ireland provided 18.6 per cent of prisoners in Swansea gaol. Fowler believed that over and above the statistics adduced to support his argument, his

---

[14] H. A. Bruce, *Merthyr Tydfil in 1852: A Lecture Delivered to the Young Men's Mutual Improvement Society at Merthyr Tydfil* (Merthyr Tydfil, 1852), p.7. In 1851 the total population of the town was recorded as 63,080, with an Irish-born community of 3,051. Jones and Bainbridge, 'The "conquering of China"', 14.

[15] Ibid.

[16] See Charles Wilkins, *The History of Merthyr Tydfil* (Merthyr Tydfil, 1867), p.337.

audience would have a conception of the 'real character of the Welsh population' which proved beyond reasonable doubt that they were a law-abiding people.[17] That this image achieved truly national currency was demonstrated by the comments of David Williams of Castell Deudraeth, magistrate for the counties of Merioneth and Caernarfon in north Wales, who equated a lack of criminal activity in the slate-quarrying areas of those counties with the absence of Irish and English immigrants.[18] The connection between the Irish and crime in north Wales was so deeply entrenched that as late as 1892 John Denvir could comment wearily that 'As a rule it is only when Pat commits some delinquency that his nationality is prominently brought forward'.[19]

Clearly, therefore, social commentators and those responsible for administering the law shared a set of assumptions about the relationship between immigrants and criminality which served to bolster prevailing attitudes towards the Irish and might well have resulted in closer scrutiny of them by the police. These writings tell us as much about the anxieties and aspirations of the authors as they do about the purported objects of their inquiry and suggest that a more critical approach to the evidence on Irish criminality is called for.

One indicator of the incidence of crime is provided by official statistics. This source presents problems of interpretation in so far as fluctuations in officially recorded crime cannot be regarded simply as an indicator of changes in criminal behaviour, especially as variations in crime rates over time might be as much the result of the creation of new categories of crime and changing policing practices as of changes in behaviour. Nevertheless, official statistics provide the essential starting-point for any discussion of the incidence of crime and provide invaluable information on the categories of offences associated with the Irish. Official statistics of those who committed crimes serious enough for incarceration from 1856 record the birth-place of

[17] John Coke Fowler, *The Characteristics and Civilisation of South Wales. Two Lectures Delivered at the Royal Institution of South Wales, Swansea* (Neath, 1873), pp.25–6. The total population of Swansea in 1871 was 51,702, with an Irish-born contingent of 1,756.

[18] PP 1861 XXI (Part II), p.580. 'There is a large population in the quarries; they are all Welsh. There is no crime there. If an Englishman or an Irishman come among them, the Welsh make it too hot for him to remain there long.'

[19] John Denvir, *The Irish in Britain* (London, 1892), p.408.

prisoners. Samples taken at four-year intervals reveal underlying trends for this category of criminals. These figures show that the proportion of Irish-born criminals in Welsh prisons increased from 15.2 per cent (429) in 1856 to a high point of 20.2 per cent (1,023) in 1868, thereafter declining towards the end of the century. Moreover, in the 1860s – when Thomas Rees and Henry Richard penned their vigorous defences of Welsh character – there was, in fact, some basis for their contention that over half the gaoled criminals in Wales had been born outside the country, as in two of the three years of that decade sampled Welsh-born prisoners accounted for a little less than 50 per cent of the inmates of Welsh gaols. In all other years sampled, however, Welsh-born prisoners accounted for well over half the total.[20] These figures demonstrate that the rhythm of Welsh criminality was at variance with that of immigrants in general, whether they were Irish- or English-born.

These figures are consistent with Roger Swift's findings for England, namely, that the Irish-born were almost three times as likely to face prosecution as their neighbours.[21] Nevertheless, they understate the incidence of Irish crime because they refer to the Irish-born alone and because the overwhelming majority of the Irish were concentrated in a handful of towns. The proportion of Irish-born males imprisoned in Cardiff gaol, for example, was significantly higher than for Wales as a whole. In 1856 they accounted for 23.4 per cent of males incarcerated in the town, rising to 30.2 per cent in 1868 before declining to 9.3 per cent by 1893. On the other hand, the figures for Irish females reveal a salient difference. Although in absolute terms far fewer women than men were imprisoned, Irish-born women formed a much higher proportion of female criminals as a whole than the comparable figures for Irish-born men and male criminals in general. In 1856 27.3 per cent of female inmates at Cardiff were of Irish birth, rising to a staggering 46.2 per cent in 1868 before declining to 11.4 per cent by 1893.[22] What appears to be a consistent decline in Irish criminality by the 1890s can be

---

[20] In 1860 49.5 per cent (1,627) and in 1868 48.6 per cent (2,464). See Appendix III.

[21] Swift, 'Crime and the Irish in nineteenth century Britain'.

[22] In only five years of the sample between 1856 and 1893 did the proportion of Irish-born male criminals exceed that of Irish-born female criminals: 1870, 1881, 1882, 1883 and 1888. See Appendix IV.

explained by the slackening of Irish immigration after the Famine and the diminishing numbers of Irish-born in Wales due to death and possibly some re-emigration as the decades passed.

How is the over-representation of the Irish-born in criminal statistics in the mid-nineteenth century to be accounted for? This is a difficult area where the interpretation of imperfect and unreliable data poses many problems. Some contemporaries sought an explanation in terms of the 'moral character' of the Irish nation, drawing attention to the existence of fundamental flaws in the Irish character. They identified the innate propensity of the Irish man and woman to commit crime, which was compounded by an overweening affection for the bottle and the alleged deleterious effects of Catholicism upon morality.[23] However, more immediate factors propelled the Irish into closer contact with the forces of law and order. During the Famine years the police had extended the scope of their activities to include supervision of aspects of poor relief and the new public health legislation, the upshot of which was a perception of the immigrants as a public-order problem. Close police scrutiny of urban areas which contained a large proportion of Irish residents inevitably led to a higher rate of detection for petty crimes in them than elsewhere, while in other areas, less enthusiastically policed, much crime went unreported or even unnoticed.

An analysis of cases brought before the Glamorgan Quarter Sessions in two ten-year periods, 1845–55 and 1865–75, sheds light on the kind of offences for which the Irish were prosecuted.[24] These samples were taken by name-spotting the Irish in the records, in some cases cross-checking names with newspaper reports. As a result, they include both Irish-born and some of their descendants and so are not strictly comparable with the official statistics quoted above. In the first period, larceny of one form or another accounted for the overwhelming majority of Irish offences, with theft of food and clothing predominating. Life in an overcrowded urban environment

---

[23] See the correspondence between H. A. Bruce and Henry Richard in 1875, split between NLW MS 14022E and Glam. RO, D/D BR 162.

[24] Based on Glam. RO, Q/S M, Quarter Sessions Minute Books, Midsummer 1845 to Easter 1855, and Epiphany 1865 to Michaelmas 1874. Unlike the gaol statistics, which categorized prisoners by country of birth, the Quarter Sessions Minutes record offenders by name, leaving the probability that the descendants of the Irish-born are included. In this respect, the two sources are not entirely compatible.

provided unprecedented opportunities for rural incomers to indulge in petty theft, and newspaper reports emphasized the impulsive nature of many transgressions. A large proportion of these thefts undoubtedly stemmed from the poverty of a section of the population which was often undernourished and inadequately clothed.

A striking feature of the period between 1845 and 1855 is the prevalence of theft related to industrial concerns. Theft of timber, rope, iron or copper reflected the changing objects of crime for immigrants from a rural background. Yet most striking in this category is the theft of coal. Of the ninety-seven Irish people prosecuted at the Quarter Sessions for this offence, mainly between 1848 and 1855, eighty-four were women. The theft of coal from the works, particularly at Merthyr, and from the canals and railways was an issue of contentious debate at this time, with some magistrates showing a marked reluctance to convict, maintaining that it was the responsibility of the proprietors of the works to police their own domain.[25] It is safe to assume that many more examples of this crime went unrecorded. For those who did come before the courts and were convicted of stealing coal the sentence was generally fourteen days' imprisonment with hard labour, although individual cases could vary significantly. At the Epiphany Sessions in 1851, Timothy O'Brien was sentenced to fourteen days' hard labour, while Catherine Sullivan got three weeks. At the same time, Honora Long, Margaret Sullivan and Honora Sullivan were imprisoned for one month each, while Mary Shea, with a previous conviction, was sentenced to three months in prison – all for the same offence.[26]

Offences connected with industrial concerns cropped up in the second period (1865–75) also, although they were far less numerous than before. Once again, thefts of various kinds formed the vast majority of cases, and in particular theft of food and clothing. An increasing proportion of these – though still a small number – were committed by servants who had stolen from their employers. A notable feature of this second sample is the increase in crimes of personal violence such as assault,

[25] Jones and Bainbridge, 'The "conquering of China"', 17–18.
[26] Glam. RO, Q/S M (21), 214, 235 and 239.

wounding and sexual violence. In total, 108 Irish cases of this nature came before the Quarter Sessions, only fifteen of which could be attributed to women. While seven cases of rape, or assault with intent to rape, were prosecuted, a much larger proportion of violent crimes – fully one-fifth – involved assault on the police. The extent to which this is indicative of a significant rise in violence against the person in the Irish community is open to question. As early as 1852, H. A. Bruce had maintained that half the cases of assault against the police at Merthyr involved Irishmen, yet these cases did not progress as far as the Quarter Sessions in the first period, being dealt with at a lower level by magistrates.[27] H. A. Bruce's lecture itself might well have contributed to changing perceptions of the severity of punishment appropriate for the crime.

Changing perceptions of violence affected the attitudes of the police. During the 1840s anxiety about threats to the political order gradually gave way to mounting concern about assault and violence against the person. In this context, it is necessary to distinguish between instances of intercommunal violence, where the Irish and Welsh clashed, and violence between the Irish themselves. The Chief Constable of Glamorgan viewed railway navvies in general, and the Irish in particular, as a destabilizing element and potential trouble-makers, although they provided him with a useful excuse for increasing the size of his force. Four additional constables were requested in 1848 after five constables and one superintendent were dispatched to the Vale of Glamorgan to quell disturbances between Irish and Welsh navvies on the South Wales Railway. He used the same reason to secure an additional constable in the Vale in 1856.[28] The prevalence of 'faction-fights' between Welsh and Irish at Maesteg and Aberkenfig found him requesting additional constables in 1857.[29] Fights between the Irish and Welsh frequently made the headlines of local newspapers, but disturbances involving different groups of Irish people were more common. The Chief Constable of Glamorgan complained in 1857 that at Bridgend 'a

[27] Bruce, *Merthyr Tydfil*, p.7.
[28] Glam. RO, Q/S, Chief Constable's Reports, Midsummer 1848, Easter 1856.
[29] Ibid., Easter 1857. In fact, it has been argued that the Irish in Britain were 'a police problem as distinct from a crime problem'. J. M. Feheney, 'Delinquency among Irish Catholic children in Victorian London', *Irish Historical Studies*, XXIII (1983), 319.

number of Irish congregate on Sundays and often create great disorder – it often requires two or more constables to quell the disturbance'.[30] His preoccupation with disorder among the Irish was not unique. In July 1866 the head constable of Swansea Police petitioned the town council on the necessity of establishing an extra police station at Greenhill – the so-called 'Little Ireland' district of the town – owing to the 'turbulence' of the residents; the force needed to be augmented by two constables to quell the 'frequent tumults' occurring there.[31]

Much of this violence originated in the practice of faction-fighting which had been a feature of fairs in pre-Famine Ireland. Groups of men with cudgels would fight to settle a feud between hostile families or villages, or even as a simple show of bravado. During the 1830s attempts to curb this practice in Ireland achieved a measure of success, but the practice survived emigration. In Wales, faction-fights occurred between migrants with tenacious loyalties to their town or region of origin. At Swansea there were divisions between natives of Waterford and Tipperary, on the one hand, and the vast majority from Cork, on the other.[32] Rivalries stemming from such clannishness were a fruitful source of friction. Reports of a fight involving about one hundred Irish people at Cardiff's Landore Court in 1848 claimed that violence of this order had been a regular occurrence there for the previous four years. Even more local allegiances could be mobilized in a violent manner. A fight at Newport in 1857 between two Irish sea-captains – one from Dungarvan, the other from Cork – ended in an all-in fight between supporters hailing from each town.[33] A sense of ethnic solidarity with other Irish people could be slow to develop.

Close police supervision was intended to control and eventually to eradicate these practices. This would explain the disproportionate rate of arrest and conviction for Irish assaults on police officers. In addition to this, the Irish were singled out in the press as sinister knife-carriers who habitually used the

[30] Ibid.
[31] Cambrian, 13 July 1866.
[32] Gearóid Ó Tuathaigh, Ireland Before the Famine, 1798–1848 (Dublin, 1972), p.150; J. W. Richards, Reminiscences of the Early Days of the Parish Church of St Joseph's, Greenhill (Swansea, 1919).
[33] Cardiff and Merthyr Guardian, 26 August 1848; Monmouthshire Merlin, 23 February 1867.

weapon on unsuspecting victims. The riot at Cardiff in 1848 had been sparked off by a stabbing, and the press also described in gruesome terms the immigrants' fondness for the knife after disturbances in Monmouthshire in 1853. An image of the Irish as fractious knife-wielders was so strongly rooted that when a local newspaper reported the stabbing of one Irishman by another at Pontypool in 1867, it began simply with the words 'The Knife Again'.[34] Possibly a fondness for using a knife in brawls was, like faction-fighting, a reflection of the high levels of violence which had existed in pre-Famine Ireland. It is equally possible, however, that as much as the use of the knife itself, the prominence accorded instances of Irish stabbing reflected unease in Welsh society about physical attacks carried out by outsiders; the Irish were not the only group to be accused of the 'un-British' use of a weapon in street disturbances.

As the century progressed, personal violence was increasingly suppressed, controlled or redirected. At Merthyr in 1867, for example, the local press contrasted the brutal violence of the faction-fight with the 'healthful pastimes' of the sports day organized by the mainly Irish Philanthropic Society.[35] By the end of the century, the ritual violence of the faction-fight was channelled into boxing as a formal and supervised (if not yet entirely respectable) leisure activity. Boxing held a particular attraction for working-class Irishmen. Joseph Keating recalled that in his childhood 'boxing was a most admired accomplishment in our quarter', and contests were held regularly.[36] Fr O'Hare, who in 1892 succeeded Canon Richards at Greenhill, Swansea, set himself against drink and other 'physical abuses' and established a boxing school for Catholic boys in the parish hall.[37] The widespread popularity of the sport was demonstrated by the visit to Cardiff of John L. Sullivan, the renowned Irish-American boxer, in January 1888, when the Liberal establishment uneasily drew comparisons between the size of the crowds lining the streets to greet him and those which had turned out to see the Liberal prime minister William

---

[34] *Y Diwygiwr*, August 1853; *Monmouthshire Merlin*, 23 February 1867.
[35] *Cardiff and Merthyr Guardian*, 30 August 1867.
[36] Joseph Keating, *My Struggle for Life* (London, 1916), p.7.
[37] Richards, *Reminiscences*, pp.26–7.

Gladstone.[38] It is no coincidence that the most revered son of
Irish immigrants to Wales was the boxer 'Peerless' Jim Driscoll;
his nickname was bestowed on him by an uncharacteristically
appreciative American press after his unsuccessful attempt to
wrest the world boxing title from one of their own fighters.[39] By
promoting boxing and other sports among young men, the
clergy consciously strove to channel male aggression into sport
and create a leisure culture which rejected alcohol.

The majority of Irish cases brought before the lesser courts in
mid-century concerned common assault, disorder and petty
theft, a group of crimes associated with drunkenness and destitution. Contemporaries repeatedly made the connection between
drink and deviancy. This was a reputation the Irish carried with
them from Ireland where the illicit distillation of poteen
flourished. In a country with no poor law until 1838, shebeen-
keeping was a recognized resource of poverty-stricken widows
who hawked their wares from market to fair, and even to
funerals. Although illicit distillation was known among the Irish
in Britain, the practice lost much of its economic and cultural
significance outside Ireland. In its place, the profusion of Irish
beerhouses provided a convivial atmosphere for the re-creation
of elements of peasant culture and their adaptation to a new
urban society. Nevertheless, the Irish were considered to be more
partial to spirits than the Welsh.[40] Away from the overcrowded
courts and lodging houses, the labouring Irish found in the beerhouse an opportunity for story-telling, dancing and singing, as
well as drinking. Beerhouses were semi-legal in character and
provided a context for the forging of a secular ethnic consciousness unimpeded by policeman or priest. Our knowledge of what
occurred within the walls of the Irish beerhouse is sadly deficient:
which stories were told and songs sung, and whether new ones
relating to their condition as emigrants were generated. Ballad
literature bemoaning the woes of 'ould Ireland' circulated among
the Irish in Britain, most probably in the beerhouses, but firm
detailed evidence of the contexts in which they were sung and by

---

[38] *South Wales Daily News*, 4 January 1888.

[39] John O'Sullivan, 'How green was their island?', in Stewart Williams (ed.), *The
Cardiff Book*, II (Cardiff and Bridgend, 1974), pp.20–36; Dai Smith, 'Focal heroes', in *idem*,
Aneurin Bevan and the World of South Wales (Cardiff, 1993), pp.328–32.

[40] K. H. Connell, *Irish Peasant Society* (Oxford, 1968), pp.17–18, 21–2, 46; PP 1877 XI,
Select Committee on Intemperance, p.159.

whom is lacking. What is clear, however, is that this was the cultural milieu most readily associated with Irish drunkenness, violence and law-breaking.

This brief survey, together with less systematic evidence culled from newspaper reports, bears out J. A. Jackson's judgement that the Irish were noted more for crimes of disorder and degradation stemming from poverty than for acts of organized crime.[41] Two distinctive categories of deviancy often related to social distress were the subjects of special condemnation by those in authority. Both vagrancy and prostitution were considered evils inimical to the well-being of society and were therefore to be controlled or stamped out.

Vagrancy alarmed the authorities because vagrants were not amenable to discipline and demanded sustenance from the inhabitants of the areas through which they passed without working for their daily bread. The determination of local authorities to rid themselves of the problem was demonstrated at Newport in 1854, when the Superintendent of Police was appointed as receiving officer for the poor because vagrants were disinclined to attend the police station.[42] However, not all vagrants were averse to a brush with authority, and they could seem all the more threatening for their occasional rebelliousness when incarcerated in the workhouse. In May 1867 John O'Donner was charged with destroying his clothes whilst at the Swansea workhouse and was sentenced to one month's hard labour at the House of Correction. At Corwen workhouse in 1886, John Dooley and William Kerney were found naked after tearing their clothes; both were sentenced to fourteen days' imprisonment with hard labour for the offence. As David Jones has shown, this crime was both complex and common.[43] On occasion, it was an attempt to obtain a better suit of clothes, while on others the perpetrators actively wished to be incarcerated in order to obtain better medical treatment or shelter. Sometimes, it was merely the consequence of unbridled anger. In rural Wales arson was the characteristic offence of Irish and English vagrants. In January 1861, for example, an Irish boy

---

[41] J. A. Jackson, *The Irish in Britain* (London, 1963), pp.72–95.
[42] PP 1854 XVII, Select Committee on Poor Removal, p.496.
[43] *Cambrian*, 3 May 1867; D. J. V. Jones, '"A dead loss to the community": the criminal vagrant in mid-nineteenth century Wales', *Welsh History Review*, 8, 3 (1977), 334.

who had been refused lodgings for the night at Tenby set fire to a
hay rick in revenge. In December 1863 Thomas Riley and James
Foster called at a farmhouse at Leighton, near Welshpool, where
they were treated 'curtly'; they responded by setting fire to stacks
of oats and barley.[44] Retribution by cursing those who refused
hospitality was a peculiar custom of Irish vagrants. The case of
Johanna Colgan illustrates the gravity of such a curse for the
Irish. George Borrow encountered Colgan, near Merthyr Tydfil,
in the 1860s; there she related how she was 'bedevilled' after
being cursed by a mendicant on her thriving farm in Limerick.
She convinced herself that she was powerless against the curse
and gave in to lethargy and drink, persuading one of her sons to
follow her. When the parish priest failed to cast out the evil
spirits, she was driven out of the village. Becoming a mendicant
herself, she, in turn, cursed those who refused to give her alms.[45]

While Irish vagrants were often a thorn in the flesh of rural
society, prostitution was identified as primarily an urban
problem. In a report on the state of Swansea in 1845, Dr Bird
spoke of the overcrowded lodging houses and the '250 to 300
prostitutes' as kindred subjects; twelve years later, the town's
mayor forcefully reiterated the view that prostitution was one of
the more dire moral consequences of overcrowding.[46] Prostitution was identified as an undesirable consequence of urban
growth elsewhere. In an editorial on 'Vice in Newport', a local
newspaper maintained that the town suffered inordinately from
crime compared with other ports because of the combination of
drunkenness and 'the very large number of a degraded order of
females'.[47] Newport was not alone among Welsh ports in this
respect. 'It is well known', wrote one indignant commentator

---

[44] Ibid., 336–7.
[45] George Borrow, *Wild Wales: Its People, Language and Scenery* [1862] (Fontana edn,
Glasgow, 1977). At the same time, Borrow found Irish tinkers at Chester who were about
to enter Wales, while at Llangollen and Ruthin his Welsh guide informed him that the
Irish vagabonds had driven away the gypsies who formerly had resided in the area. This
was viewed as a change for the worse as the guide described the Irish as 'savage, brutish
people, sir; in general without shoes and stockings, with coarse features and heads of hair
like mops . . . the men tinker a little, sir, but more frequently plunder. The women tell
fortunes and steal whenever they can (pp.34–6, 77–9).
[46] H. T. de la Beche, *Report on the State of Bristol and Other Large Towns* (London, 1845),
p.82; W. H. Michael, 'The influence of habitation on the community: overcrowding in
dwellings', *Transactions of the National Association for the Promotion of Social Science, 1857*
(London, 1858), p.411.
[47] Editorial in *Monmouthshire Merlin*, 4 July 1857.

about the Bute Town area of Cardiff, 'that from the Hayes Bridge right down to the Pierhead, all the streets, front and back, are crowded with dancing saloons, refreshment houses, and regularly established brothels, in each and all of which intoxicating drinks are openly sold without let or hindrance.'[48] Sundays at Bute Town, according to the same source, were set apart for a special carouse in the brothels and unlicensed drinking houses; it was suggested that even the police enjoyed their hospitality.

Were the Irish a part of this subculture of vice, as some contemporaries claimed? The available evidence indicates that the number of Irish women involved was far smaller than the opprobrium accorded them would suggest. Occasionally, when studying the Irish in Britain, it has been deemed sufficient to show that prostitutes plied their trade in areas of Irish settlement to claim that Irish women were prominent in the trade.[49] Where detailed evidence exists, this assumption can be shown to be flawed. The most detailed evidence on prostitutes in a Welsh town is that from Merthyr Tydfil. In 1866 William Menelaus, the manager of the Dowlais ironworks, prepared a report on the employment of women and children in the town. He maintained that the level of prostitution there was lower than in any town of similar size in England and Wales, particularly when considering the proportion of native prostitutes. 'In Merthyr', he wrote, 'the evil is confined to one small district, inhabited principally by low Irish, of these very few if any have been work girls, they are mostly girls too lazy to work and drawn from a class below that of the lowest workman.'[50] In spite of this pious belief, detailed biographical information on thirty-five of Merthyr's forty prostitutes in 1859–60 provides a rather different picture. Twenty-three were Welsh, six were English and six Irish. In fact, it is the variety of backgrounds of prostitutes at Merthyr and the variety of reasons for becoming prostitutes which emerges most strongly from the illuminating diary of a scripture reader hired by the town's Anglican rector.[51] Some of these women were casualties

[48] *Reformer and South Wales Times*, 28 March 1862.
[49] Examples are provided in Fergus D'Arcy, 'The Irish in 19th. century Britain: reflections on their role and experience', *Irish History Workshop Journal*, I (1981), 52.
[50] Glam. RO, Dowlais Iron Company Records, D/DG Section C, box 5. 'Report on the Employment of Women and Children', 15.
[51] NLW MS 4943B; The Scripture Reader's Journal, 2 January–26 May 1860.

of the contracting female labour market which William Menelaus had found so encouraging. Others had been deserted by their husbands or were unmarried mothers with children to support; some were little more than children.

Although as many as half of these prostitutes intimated a desire to abandon their way of life, it was evident that they were enmeshed in a web of personal relationships and economic dependence that made extrication difficult. In January 1860 Margaret Flyn, aged seventeen, who had been in Merthyr as a prostitute for only two months, sought maintenance in the workhouse with eight other prostitutes after hearing a sermon by the Revd John Griffiths. By the following evening, however, she and three others had left to take up their trade once again. Before leaving, she told her landlady not to disclose her whereabouts to the scripture reader, who believed that her action was the result of a conversation with old acquaintances. Other prostitutes, such as Ann Sullivan, had paramours who lived off their earnings.[52] Such circumstances made it difficult for the women to move away and begin a new life.

By the end of March 1860, the scripture reader was able to record some success in his campaign to reclaim 'fallen women'. Of a total of sixteen women whom he had persuaded to leave Merthyr by this date, four were Irish. Realizing that the greatest obstacle in the women's path was the influence of their 'paramours', he set about trying to persuade the men to marry the women. He achieved some success with this strategy also.[53] In this work, the Anglican Church treated the women as victims of enervating conditions who needed to be extricated from the personal relationships and circumstances in which they were trapped and exposed to the beneficial effects of religion. Consequently, a plan to establish a House of Refuge for prostitutes in south Wales met with an enthusiastic response from the Church. However, it would be misleading to portray all prostitutes as victims of circumstance. For some at least, prostitution was one of the few occupations which gave working-class women a degree of financial independence unobtainable in an economy characterized by male-dominated labour. Prostitution itself was

[52] Ibid., 13–14, 26–7, 36.
[53] Ibid., 58–60.

not a crime, but moral reformers targeted prostitutes as symbols of the moral degradation which was believed to encourage criminal activity and vice. When prostitutes did appear before the courts, it was often on charges connected with their trade, such as stealing from the person. Magistrates avoided prosecuting even the most persistent offenders by requesting them to leave the town rather than convict or imprison them. When Ellen Sullivan appeared before Newport police court in 1865 on a charge of being a drunk and disorderly prostitute, the Superintendent of Police reported that she had appeared there on eleven occasions during the previous three years alone, and he had not searched the records further back. Yet the defendant was discharged on promising to leave the town for Tredegar.[54] In north Wales, young girls with Irish surnames were prominent in the ranks of prostitutes, especially in ports like Holyhead and Caernarfon. When Mary McNally, a prostitute at Caernarfon, was charged in 1878 with being drunk and disorderly, using bad language and abusing people, she was given the choice of three months' imprisonment or leaving the town immediately; McNally coolly replied that she would wait for the five o'clock steamer across the Menai Straits 'as she would not like to travel in daytime without a shawl'.[55] Ellen Hogan, also a prostitute at Caernarfon, showed an equal lack of respect for the magistracy. She informed the bench in 1872 that the 'houses where girls assembled' had been done away with and that 'prostitution must be carried on somewhere'. On being gaoled for a week, she prophesied defiantly, 'that much won't do me any good'.[56]

Court cases of all kinds were eagerly reported by the press. Journalists found in them an inexhaustible supply of morality tales and entertainment, their sensationalist reports relaying the court's proceedings to a much wider audience than those who attended in person. The court was an arena in which the distribution of power in society was most closely delineated and where those who transgressed society's rules were dealt with. To some extent the court scene represented a drama in which participants were expected to play the parts conventionally allotted to them: the penitent prisoner, the upright police

---

[54] *Monmouthshire Merlin*, 4 March 1865.
[55] *Carnarvon and Denbigh Herald*, 2 February 1878; D. J. V. Jones, *Crime in Nineteenth Century Wales*, p.196.
[56] *Carnarvon and Denbigh Herald*, 29 June 1872.

constable and the admonitory magistrate. But it was an unscripted drama, and not everyone cheerfully fulfilled the expectations of officialdom.

The vast majority of criminals appear to have passed through the courts with an implicit recognition of their vulnerable position, accepting their punishment meekly and without demur. In the lower courts a fine, or even a verbal admonition, was deemed sufficient for many transgressors. Nevertheless, some of the accused refused to be intimidated by the inbuilt deference of the court and challenged officials who gave evidence against them. For example, in August 1857 Swansea police court witnessed the rebellious behaviour of James and Patrick Murphy, who were accused of being drunk and disorderly. On hearing the evidence of a police constable against him, James retorted: 'Well, you are a liar and no mistake, if I was cross wid you, I'd knock you down like a cock.' Patrick voiced his disapproval in stronger terms: 'Why, by —, you'd swear a — coal-heaver was a canary', the blanks indicating the newspaper's unwillingness to offend the sensibilities of its readers while providing a strong hint of what had been omitted. Both men were fined 5s. and costs. James Murphy managed to win the last word: 'Well, I won't pay anything, I've done nothing to nobody, and I am not afraid of going to prison.'[57] Cultural stereotypes placed an oppressive weight on the shoulders of the Irish in the court. Some lightened that burden – consciously or otherwise – by responding to those caricatures in a way which reduced tension by provoking laughter. Stereotypes of the Irish held two conflicting elements in tension: that of the menacing, turbulent and depraved peasant, on the one hand, and that of the wide-eyed garrulous and comic countryman, on the other. Both elements could be present at the same time depending on the context. Both elements carried distinct racial overtones.

The Irish were as stupid in Welsh-language jokes of the period as they were in the English music hall.[58] In this genre of humour the 'thick Paddy' betrayed his ignorance every time he opened his mouth, to the great merriment of listeners. Irish immigrants could not have been ignorant of this facet of British working-class

[57] *Cambrian*, 28 August 1857.
[58] E.g., *Seren Gomer* (May 1846), 150.

culture and, under particular circumstances, they might turn such an offensive stereotype to their favour. With the view of the 'thick Paddy' in mind, it did not appear out of character to behave garrulously in court, gesticulating wildly at appropriate junctures of the story, in order to impress upon the magistrate that he was dealing with a misguided fool deserving of pity rather than a criminal to be severely punished for wrongdoing. With their convoluted attempts at a verbatim rendition of an Irish accent in print, newspapers diffused in the wider society an image of the hapless fool.

Drama fequently turned into farce. Observers were regularly reduced to laughter by the evidence of Irish defendants who were usually called Paddy, Mick or Bridie. At Newport police court in 1850, Michael Murphy was summoned for assaulting a fellow Irishman, the case producing an exchange which is typical of local newspaper coverage:

> Magistrate: How is it Murphy that you are so often charged with assaults?
> Murphy: Och, wisha, sir, faix it is bekase I am so quiet entirely. (Laughter).
> Magistrate: Do you call it quiet to give that man (complainant) a black eye?
> Murphy: 'Pon my sawkins, sir, he began tantalizing me, and axed me for six pence that was unlawfully due to him. (Laughter).
> Hayes: A ma bouchell, taize you, indeed, I'll tell you another version, didn't you give me this thundering black eye? (Roars of laughter).[59]

Reports of this type, which appeared in almost all local newspapers during the mid-Victorian period, provide the most consistent body of evidence in support of the belief that ethnic stereotyping of the Irish was cultivated on a low-level, day-to-day basis. Because of such reports, the faction-fight and other forms of personal violence involving the Irish alone came to be regarded as 'merely' Irish feuds. Accordingly, the protagonists often received little more than a verbal admonition and were ordered to pay the costs. While magistrates and the police disapproved of such upsets, there was a sharp contrast between the levity shown towards defendants in such cases and the attitudes to those arraigned for assaults against the police.

[59] *Cardiff and Merthyr Guardian*, 6 April 1850.

Evidence from the courts is a reminder that social attitudes towards minorities play a significant part in their contact with the legal system. The pronouncements of magistrates encouraged a belief that an individual's moral character was strengthened by contact with a stable community life and that immigrants were especially vulnerable in comparison with an allegedly law-abiding native working class. Pervasive images of the Irish as an unruly minority with a propensity for drunkenness and violent behaviour were reinforced in the minds of police officers whose role consisted as much in imposing order on working-class neighbourhoods as detecting crime, and who often became the objects of Irish resentment. A drive against public disorder, drunkenness, gambling, and petty pilfering was one of the characteristics of the new police forces after 1856. Many aspects of working-class life were considered to be socially undesirable and so their neighbourhoods were subjected to rigorous policing to eliminate nuisances. To some extent, therefore, the over-representation of the Irish in criminal statistics was a product of the fact that they were, as a group, disproportionately working-class in complexion.

The high incidence of petty crime suggests that in mid-nineteenth-century Wales a great deal of Irish criminal behaviour was a result of the social disorganization which derived from the poverty and despair afflicting Famine refugees. The prevalence of crimes such as the theft of coal during the winter months to provide warmth in the home strongly indicate that the poor were forced into breaking the law on occasion in order to secure the necessities of life. Whether these crimes of want declined in number as the economic condition of the Irish as a group improved is difficult to say with any certainty. It is possible that those labourers worst affected by the vagaries of the trade cycle resorted to stealing during an extended period of unemployment, making the encounter with the legal system a cyclical as opposed to a regular event. It would be precisely during periods like this that the non-financial benefits of peasant life were missed most keenly.

Cultural preconceptions reinforced the results of social disorganization. The debate on crime in nineteenth-century Wales was inextricably bound up with ideas of nationality and ethnicity, about the boundaries between different cultural groups and how those boundaries should be regulated. Accent and place of origin mattered. In order to strengthen its own identity after the strictures of the Education Reports of 1847, Nonconformist Wales needed to be able to point to a group which personified the opposite of everything it purported to stand for. By unhappy coincidence, the Great Famine deposited large numbers of destitute Irish men and women on Welsh shores just as the heated controversy was getting under way, and they fitted the polemicists' bill. Immigrants of all kinds were castigated for their excessive criminality, but the worst moral strictures were reserved for the Irish with their peasant background and Catholicism, which was so repugnant to Protestants. When nineteenth-century commentators drew stark lines demarcating the two groups, they were simplifying and distorting matters, reducing diversity to a monochrome picture. Irish immigrant institutions sought to reject this bleak contrast by striving to create a culture of respectability which served as a means of 'improving' the individual and raising the image of the group as a whole among the members of the host society.

VII

FRIENDLY SOCIETIES, TEMPERANCE AND RESPECTABILITY

The disproportionate criminality of the Irish in the mid-nineteenth century, described in the previous chapter, is suggestive of a community disorganized by the upheavals of emigration. In their eagerness to categorize immigrants as members of an out-group with cultural practices alien to the host society's value systems, social commentators in mid-nineteenth-century Wales equated Irishness with squalor and moral corruption. Of course, not all Irish immigrants inhabited a squalid underworld of vice and depravity – on the contrary, it was only one aspect of a multifaceted ethnic experience. Immigrant culture demonstrated a remarkable capacity for regeneration and innovation in urban Wales. Side by side with the beerhouse culture of the poorer immigrants there existed an Irish associational life wedded to the same ideals of rationality, respectability, self-reliance and self-improvement as those which defined the identity of the native 'aristocracy of labour'. Within this world, some of the Irish carved for themselves a niche for the expression of a distinctive and dynamic ethnic identity. This vigorous associational life underlines Panikos Panayi's contention that we should think in terms of a plurality of ethnicities within an immigrant group, rather than search for a single immutable identity.[1]

Irish clubs and societies were concrete expressions of a desire to establish support networks which provided safeguards against the vagaries of everyday life in an unfamiliar environment. Provident members of the workforce who enjoyed the regularity of employment and income to be able to contribute regularly to a common fund banded together in associations of subscribers. Payments from the fund were made to individual members at times of illness or unemployment. On the death of a member a sum sufficient to pay for a decent burial was paid to the family.

---

[1] P. Panayi, *Immigration, Ethnicity and Racism* (Manchester, 1994).

Women's societies also provided insurance against ill health, although they were far fewer in number than the men's societies. After the Famine influx, there is no evidence of the existence of women's societies, or branches of societies, which catered exclusively for Irish women in Wales, and it must be assumed that where they did participate in the associational life of friendly societies they did so through that of the men. Similarly, in some circumstances, Irish men and women could become members of societies established by the Welsh, although the extent to which this occurred is impossible to determine. This chapter is concerned solely with the friendly and temperance societies established by and for the Irish, and with the associational life which grew up around them. In some cases, societies and clubs were organized on a relatively informal basis, enjoying no more than a transitory existence and remaining unregistered with the legal authorities; others took root and thrived over many decades.

The provision of insurance against sickness was sufficient in itself to attract and retain members of friendly societies but, as the generic title suggests, they also provided opportunities for convivial association at the club room, which was usually to be found in a public house. Monthly meetings, an annual dinner and celebration and, in some cases, an annual trip or sports day, were the high points of the society's year. In order to organize their business efficiently, societies created structures which allotted positions of trust and responsibility to specific individuals. Chairmen, secretaries and treasurers were elected from among the membership, in the process creating independent networks of status and esteem. By providing for their own people – both materially and culturally – these associations became the instruments for cultivating in members a sense of personal independence. Self-help and thrift were their watchwords.

Some immigrant communities provided a fertile ground for the growth of friendly societies. As has been seen already,[2] a network of Irish friendly societies had been established in some Welsh towns before the Famine. Ethnic institutions were more common where 'immigration had been heaviest, although they could be found in the smaller settlements also. For example, in August 1856 the Hibernian Benefit Society of Abersychan, a

[2] Chapter II.

small industrial settlement near Pontypool in Monmouthshire, celebrated seventeen years of unbroken activity with great pomp and ceremony. According to one account, the two hundred members taking part in the procession on that occasion, led by the Newport Catholic Band, 'presented the finest appearance of any society of the kind which had been seen in the neighbourhood this season'.[3] The much larger town of Newport, on the other hand, boasted the most popular Irish friendly societies before the Famine, although there are conflicting reports on their condition by the early 1850s. Observers of a procession in 1850 consisting of members of the Hibernian Society betrayed a tangible feeling of relief after the harrowing scenes witnessed during the previous five years: 'We expected to see a ragged regiment of tatterdemalions marching along, but what was our surprise to behold a company of young and middle-aged men, who in point of dress and propriety of demeanour would bear comparison with any body of gentlemen in the country.'[4] Other evidence suggests that the town's Irish societies were only a shadow of their former selves by the mid-1850s. In 1854 it was claimed that they no longer paid benefits and, consequently, ageing members were forced to rely on the parish for assistance, thereby undermining the very *raison d'être* of the society.[5]

This exigency must have been especially galling for members who had maintained their subscriptions, because during the crisis years of the late 1840s and early 1850s the Irish were castigated for an alleged improvidence in financial matters which led to dependence upon parish relief. At a time when the cost of providing poor relief for large numbers of Famine refugees caused considerable concern, the authorities paid greater attention to the cultivation of habits of self-help and thrift among them. The prevailing view was expressed by G. T. Clark, manager of the Dowlais Ironworks, when he claimed in 1861 that the Irish were 'unthrifty, their wages low, and they live much together in the dirtiest and least healthy parts of the town'. Nevertheless, Clark did accept that they were not indifferent to

[3] *Monmouthshire Merlin*, 23 August 1856.
[4] *Cardiff and Merthyr Guardian*, 6 April 1850.
[5] Moreover, in 1854 there was not one Irish member of the town's Building Society or its Freehold Land Society, both of which functioned as benefit societies. PP 1854 XVII, Report from the Select Committee on Poor Removal, pp.504–5.

improving their lot: 'That the general character of the body is improving is shown by the improvement in their clubs and benefit societies.'[6] This was a rare recognition that the Irish were not imprisoned in the conditions of the Famine years.

Friendly societies provided opportunities for the 'respectable Irish' to assert their independence and so differentiate themselves publicly from the 'low Irish'. A controversy in Cardiff in 1861 over vindictive accusations against the Irish poor made by R. W. Lewis in his capacity as assistant overseer of the Board of Guardians revealed that a culture of thrift and self-help flourished among 'many hundreds' of the Irish. In response to Lewis's assertions, it was claimed that members of the Hibernian Club were amply provided with sickness benefit, thereby obviating the need for recourse to parish relief. The principal accusation was that in the case of a pregnant woman's confinement the Irish poor were much readier to apply for assistance than was the case with the Welsh or English, a characteristic which was explained not in terms of lower wages but rather because they allegedly lacked 'a spirit of independence'. At the same time, St Patrick's Savings Bank benefited from the savings of those who had abstained from drink, and St Patrick's United Assurance Sick and Burial Society numbered its members in thousands. A letter-writer protested: 'It takes time to recover from the wounds received from unequal legislation, landlord oppression and orange tyranny, which compelled us to leave our native soil, and to seek subsistence in a foreign land.'[7] Stripped of its indignant rhetoric, this statement contains an important kernel of truth. Under the impact of urbanization, immigrant culture was as fluid as that of the majority population, and characterizations derived from the Famine years and their immediate aftermath are an inadequate description of immigrant culture in subsequent decades.

Our knowledge of the initiation ceremonies and private rituals of friendly societies in Britain is sadly deficient, although it is possible to surmise that the induction of new members was carried out according to solemn practices designed to make a lasting impression on the newcomer. Formal acceptance of the

---

[6] PP 1861 XXI, Report from Commissioners on Popular Education in England (II), Appendix A, p.595.
[7] *Cardiff Times*, 26 July, 6 August 1861.

rules of the society under solemn oath and in the presence of the officers, and possibly other members too, was undoubtedly the minimum required. An indication of the type of ritual enacted when inducting a new member can be gleaned from a pamphlet published by the Ancient Order of Hibernians in 1912; new members were asked:

> Are you Irish or of Irish descent?
>   A Roman Catholic who has complied with your Easter Duty during the past Paschal time?
>   Do you now belong to any Society, secret or otherwise, condemned by the Catholic Church?[8]

Formal acceptance of a member in this way must have made an enormous impression upon the individual being admitted because it represented the crossing of a threshold of status and esteem within the community. For many Irish men and women, acceptance into the ranks of a Hibernian friendly society was an important rite of passage. In the absence of fuller information about private rituals, it is the public ceremonial which must receive closest attention. Observers (both Irish and non-Irish) and participants were affected by the enactment of rituals in the public domain; consequently, control of the form and tone of public expressions of Irishness acquired added significance.

Friendly societies' parades and processions were rituals of ethnic solidarity which ostentatiously proclaimed the difference between the poor Irish and those who aspired to respectability, and by extension they serve as a rough index of the ability of one section of the immigrant group to integrate into the civic culture of a town. Just as the condition of starving and diseased refugees in 1847 had challenged the descriptive powers of local journalists, so the orderly celebrations of friendly societies reassured them. Style and outward appearance were concrete manifestations of beliefs and attitudes. At Cardiff in August 1867, for example, the following scene was reported: 'On the morning of Monday last, Bute street and Adam street presented quite a gay and lively appearance. Flags and streamers were flying in profusion and some were stretched across the roadway in honour

---

[8] *Ritual of the Ancient Order of Hibernians, Board of Erin* (Dublin, 1912), p.5.

of the 22nd anniversary of the [Cardiff Hibernian Friendly] society.'[9] As the events of that day conform to a pattern observed in most Welsh towns in mid-century, they bear retelling in greater detail. The society met at the Tredegar Arms Inn at 10 a.m. and proceeded to St Peter's Catholic church, Roath, where a special service was conducted by Fr Gavalli and Fr Signini. The procession consisted of the steward with a banner proclaiming 'God Save the Queen: Success to the Port and Trade of Cardiff', followed by the Grangetown brass band and the society's members carrying banners and flags embroidered with mottoes. Among these were: 'Hibernia Rising in Prospects', 'Daniel O'Connell, the Friend of Religious Liberty', and 'Our Union Benevolence, Our Motto Charity'. If the function of these epigrams was to give succinct expression to the values of participants, then they suggested a faith in material and religious progress in common with the assumptions of the most vocal spokesmen of Protestant Welsh society. At the same time, they suggest an attempt to marry a distinctively Irish identity with loyalty to the locality: local and national patriotisms were deemed compatible. The political message conveyed by the banners was the reassuring one that honouring the memory of Daniel O'Connell and the fight for religious freedom was not inconsistent with loyalty to the throne.

After the service, the society paraded through the main streets of the town to the accompaniment of the drum and fife band of the Catholic school before returning to their club room where about 180 people sat down to lunch. The spectacle had the desired effect upon other citizens of the town, as the *Cardiff and Merthyr Guardian* made clear:

> Before we close our report, we cannot help remarking upon the respectable appearance and the good order maintained by the members during the day. It is a source of gratification to learn that the funds of this society now amount to about £1,000 and during the past six months upwards of £100 have been expended on sick relief.[10]

[9] *Cardiff and Merthyr Guardian*, 9 August 1867.
[10] Ibid.

In its determination to ascertain the precise extent of the society's funds, the newspaper betrayed a flicker of continuing anxiety about the capacity of the Irish for self-help and a lingering fear that they might become chargeable to the parish. Yet the tone of paternal approval which pervaded the report must have warmed the hearts of the society's members. In the absence of an immigrant Irish newspaper press in Wales at this time to provide its own representations and interpretations of parades and processions, the role of the local press in reporting events in a sympathetic way was of some consequence to the Irish.

Given the tendency of commentators in mid-century to identify the Irish with the most squalid housing and insanitary areas of the towns, the territorial dimension of the parades was significant. Public celebrations provided an opportunity to break free from a constricting stereotype of the 'ghetto Irish'. By parading through the main thoroughfares, they asserted the claim of their own culture to use public space in the same manner as comparable Welsh societies and thereby came to participate more fully in a wider municipal culture. If, as Peter Bailey has argued, respectability was a 'role' played by the working class when they felt it advantageous to do so, then there were some Irish immigrants who readily adopted such roles as a way of earning esteem and defusing the pervasive atmosphere of hostility which they encountered in so many aspects of their everyday lives.[11] But this role was more than a cynical strategy to achieve acceptance; for many working-class Irish men and women, 'respectability' embodied aspirations for a better and more stable life in an otherwise unpredictable world.

The attempt to foster respectability and promote rational recreations inevitably conflicted with older patterns of behaviour. In particular, St Patrick's Day celebrations were the occasion when divergent definitions of immigrant identity competed for recognition and supremacy. When Irish navvies working on the South Wales Railway celebrated their patron saint's day in Swansea in 1850, they did so by carousing and fighting. Apparently, this was the first time that the festival had been publicly celebrated in the borough, and the local newspaper

---

[11]   P. Bailey, *Leisure and Class in Victorian England* (London, 1987 edn), pp.169–82.

expressed the hope that because of the 'shameful obscenities' witnessed by onlookers, it would be the last.[12] Despite the fact that navvies were a transient group whose distinctive lifestyle, clothing and behaviour marked them off as different and unrepresentative, they were not the only immigrants to mark the day in a boisterous manner. At Cardiff in 1860 an Italian priest exclaimed melodramatically that 'St. Patrick could not be supposed to pass without Bacchus-Orgies', adding that the occasion produced 'plenty of Drunkards'.[13] It was the violence which often resulted from drunkenness that was of particular concern, as exemplified by an incident in Cardiff in 1870:

> Patrick Maloney and Joanna Maloney were charged with an assault on Ellen Marley on St Patrick's Day . . . and on that day, all being the worse for drink, the women began to row, each seizing the other by the hair of the head. The male defendant, seeing his wife in a fix, came up and beat the complainant about the head with the handle of a whip used by him to thrash his donkey, and this caused the relatives on each side to join in.[14]

While such incidents continued to punctuate the patron saint's day, they became less frequent, and by the 1870s the festival was assimilated to a more orderly and respectable working-class culture. Unflagging pressure from the Catholic clergy to celebrate St Patrick's Day in a more abstemious fashion marked out the festival as one which the church wished to appropriate and control.

For several decades, if not for a longer period of time, competing ways of celebrating St Patrick's Day coexisted uneasily. While many Irish men and women enjoyed the day's festivities in their own beerhouses, drinking and dancing in honour of the patron saint, others used the occasion to display their credentials as members of respectable society. For the latter, the standard dress of males participating in processions consisted of a black frock coat and white trousers with a top hat and white gloves; often a green scarf or sash embroidered with the Irish harp completed the ensemble. This style of clothing, so far removed

[12] *Cambrian*, 22 March 1850.
[13] Fr Joseph Costa to Fr Provincial Rinolfi, 20 March 1860, Derry's Wood Archives.
[14] *Cardiff and Merthyr Guardian*, 26 March 1870.

from everyday working attire, was at once a statement of independence from the world of work and a reproach to those who could not achieve such independence. At Merthyr Tydfil in 1858, for example, the local press observed that the St Patrick's Day turnout was 'really creditable', adding that 'The men were all neat and substantially dressed, many of them even sporting "white ducks", the procession was quite an agreeable surprise and many persons who showed their prejudice by calling them paddies added the remark that they looked exceedingly well.'[15] The purchase of clothing for special occasions was beyond the means of many labourers in mid-century and appealed primarily to a group described on one occasion as 'mainly artizans'.[16]

By celebrating their saint's day in such an organized and public manner, the Irish ran the risk of nurturing a 'triumphant tribalism' (to quote the leading historian of the American Irish) which would simply antagonize the native population; this was precisely the response encountered in the north of England, where St Patrick's Day processions were viewed as evidence of aggressive nationalism.[17] However, the Welsh evidence does not point in this direction.

The greatest threat to peaceful coexistence between Britain and Ireland during the 1860s was the activities of the Fenian Brotherhood, a revolutionary organization dedicated to the overthrow of British rule in Ireland and to the creation in its place of a sovereign republic. The Brotherhood found fertile ground for its ideas and aspirations among the expatriate Irish in both Britain and America, and its presence among the Irish in Wales was well known.[18] To parade in such circumstances with a motto declaring 'God Save the Queen' was an unambiguous political statement. Moreover, the celebration of Daniel O'Connell's constitutional campaign for Catholic emancipation in the 1820s can also be interpreted as an implicit reproach to those who favoured the use of revolutionary methods to address Irish

---

[15]   *Cardiff and Merthyr Guardian*, 20 March 1858.

[16]   *Monmouthshire Merlin*, 23 March 1850.

[17]   Kerby A. Miller, *Emigrants and Exiles: Ireland and the Irish Exodus to North America* (Oxford 1985), p.526; Steven Fielding, *Class and Ethnicity: Irish Catholics in England, 1880–1939* (Buckingham, 1993), p.73.

[18]   See ch.IX below. Denouncing the Fenian outrages at Manchester in 1867, the *Cardiff and Merthyr Guardian*, 30 August 1867, applauded the behaviour of Merthyr's Catholic Philanthropic Society which had recently held a popular sports day at Morlais Castle.

grievances. Here we see evidence of a wider process whereby, in Kenneth Moss's words, the Irish 'rhetorically and symbolically grounded their present in a remembered and constructed past'.[19] Mobilizing figures like O'Connell allowed the 'respectable' Irish to draw on a history of constitutional Irish nationalism in a way directly comparable to, but at odds with, the Fenians' claim to represent an authentic militant voice grounded in a centuries-long tradition of military resistance. From the late 1870s, however, St Patrick's Day increasingly became an occasion for reflection on Ireland's political grievances. On 17 March 1878, for example, a committee was formed at Cardiff to raise funds for former political prisoners who were experiencing hardship after their release from gaol; a staff of twenty-seven collectors was appointed and the local committee co-ordinated its activities with the central committee in London.[20] More usually in subsequent years, political allegiance at the festival was expressed through seemingly anodyne toasts to 'the Irish nation' and 'the Irish Parliamentary Party' at celebratory dinners.[21]

In general, the societies which paraded in honour of their patron saint eschewed direct involvement in political activity, unlike similar Irish societies elsewhere in Britain. According to John Denvir, an Irish Nationalist organizer among the Irish in Britain who possessed an intimate knowledge of immigrant communities in all parts of the country, the Hibernian societies of south Wales were purely benevolent fraternities and had no connection with the Ancient Order of Hibernians, an organization which, in the north of England, was linked to the secret society of Ribbonmen.[22] By the outbreak of the First World War, the Ancient Order of Hibernians had a strong presence in south Wales, though it does not appear to have been an overtly political organization in the region. Nevertheless, it would be misleading to suggest that members of Irish friendly societies in Wales were apolitical, for their celebrations were frequently

[19] Kenneth Moss, 'St Patrick's Day celebrations and the formation of Irish-American identity, 1845–1875', *Journal of Social History*, 29, 1 (1995), 130.

[20] *Cardiff Times*, 23 March 1878.

[21] See, for example, *Star of Gwent*, 17 March 1882.

[22] J. Denvir, *The Irish in Britain* (London, 1892), pp.127–36. The Ribbonmen acted as a Catholic defence organization and thrived only in those areas where Orange lodges were active; see Lynn H. Lees, *Exiles of Erin: Irish Migrants in Victorian London* (Manchester, 1979), pp.222–3. The Orange Order was conspicuous by its absence from most of Wales.

punctuated with references to Irish patriotism and toasts to those Irish Nationalist leaders who espoused constitutional action to redress their country's grievances. But the societies were not in themselves channels for political activity.

Local attitudes to exhibitions of Irish respectability can be gauged by the fact that in 1859 one newspaper even sermonized on the necessity of celebrating St Patrick's Day, it being the 'bounden duty' of every true Irishman 'to make himself as happy as a Welshman on the 1st day of March' (that is, St David's Day).[23] On the whole, public celebrations of St Patrick's Day were deemed compatible with the prevailing values and customs of the host society. At Newport, for example, respectable celebrations on 17 March afforded the Irish the means of winning public esteem, even to the extent of attracting the support of the local gentry. In 1859 a St Patrick's Day fête was held at the army barracks in the town:

A great number of invitations had been addressed to the gentry of the district and the public were admitted into the barrack yard by ticket . . . the officers and soldiers engaged in the sports . . . previous to the commencement of the sports the invited guests partook of an elegant luncheon provided for them by the officers in the mess room.[24]

Equally approving comments occurred in other towns in the region. Even the newspaper which in 1850 had expressed a fervent wish that the festival would never again be celebrated in Swansea referred on a later date to the 'exemplary propriety' of those marking the occasion.[25] A flavour of the changed character of the festivities is provided by the following report of events in the town in 1872:

ST. PATRICK'S DAY. – This event was celebrated to-day by a grand procession of the Catholic clergy and the Hibernian Club. Many of the streets were gaily decorated, and the inhabitants turned out in hundreds to witness the display. Among the most noticeable features of the procession, we may notice were Dr Corry's company of Hibernian Minstrels, 18 in number, wearing national emblems, and conveyed in well-appointed

[23] *Cardiff and Merthyr Guardian*, 12 March 1859.
[24] *Cardiff and Merthyr Guardian*, 19 March 1859.
[25] *Cambrian*, 22 March 1867.

equipages. They were well received, and some of the more popular members were frequently greeted with cheers. We may add that the day was suitably celebrated at the Music Hall by the introduction of original national songs and the display of allegorical tableaux.[26]

Rather than epitomizing alienation and estrangement, St Patrick served as a non-threatening symbol of immigrant identity which encompassed religion, respectability and peaceful Irish patriotism. This symbolic marker of respectability was well established by the 1860s, in spite of the attempts of more politicized movements to stamp their imprint on the festival. A branch of the National Brotherhood of St Patrick, a movement with strong links with Fenianism, thrived briefly in Cardiff in the 1860s, but it does not appear to have been established in other Welsh towns.[27] With this exception, St Patrick was presented as the authentic symbol of Irish nationality, transcending the centuries yet amenable to reinvention and reinterpretation in new contexts.

Other ways of marking the day were not eliminated entirely – they merely retreated to the private domain. On 18 March 1882 the head constable of Cardiff wrote to the parish priest of St Peter's in Roath informing him that there had been no prisoners for trial at the police court that morning. 'Yesterday being St Patrick's Day,' he said, 'it spoke very well for the Irish residents of Cardiff.'[28] The letter reveals as much about police expectations as it does about Irish behaviour in 1882, for had it not been for boisterous behaviour on previous occasions, the police would hardly have troubled to congratulate the priest on an absence of prosecutions. That same year, the Irish in Newport were commended for their peaceful behaviour, a comment which might have been prompted by reports of disturbances in the Irish countryside.[29] In fact, the manner in which public festivities were conducted was of crucial significance in the formation of a respectable Irish identity. It has been argued that the creation of such an identity in New York was reflected in, and perhaps

---

[26] *South Wales Daily News*, 19 March 1872.
[27] See ch.IX below for further details.
[28] AAC, box 88, W. Hemmingway to Fr Richardson, 18 March 1882.
[29] *Star of Gwent*, 24 March 1882.

shaped by, communal rituals and commemorative ceremonies;[30] on a lesser scale, the same was true of south Wales.

'Respectable' immigrants sought to convey to outsiders the nature of their political and social aspirations primarily through the medium of their banners. As none of these has survived, any attempt to analyse the iconography of respectable Irish labour is severely hampered. Nevertheless, some indication of the principal themes and symbols can be gleaned from newspaper reports which described what they had seen. An indication of the visual impact of one of these processions is provided by a report in 1861 of the participation of the Cardiff St Patrick's Total Abstinence Society in the celebrations of the third anniversary of the South Wales Total Abstinence Restrictive and Prohibitory Association. St Patrick's Society had only recently been established by Fr Joseph Costa and Fr Stephen Bruno and boasted a membership of 575 men and women. In the celebratory procession, members were 'not only well but most respectably attired', and displayed 'splendid and costly banners and flags, mounted upon the richest silk and painted by first class artists'.[31]

Religion was a prominent theme. A spectator of the same procession remarked that

> the members of this association, as would be observed by their banners, do not wish to disguise the fact that they are also members of the Roman Catholic Church, and they ask their Protestant brother and sister teetotallers to concede to them the same liberty in religious matters which they have always claimed for themselves.

The illustrations on these banners were heavily imbued with Catholic symbolism. St Cecilia, the patron saint of musicians, was depicted on a banner made by the French consul at Cardiff and presented to the drum and fife band; there were two other large silk banners among the many flags, the first sporting an image of St Patrick and the second a tableau showing the Virgin Mary trampling the 'drink demon'.[32] As these descriptions (culled from newspaper reports) suggest, these banners would have provided an invaluable source for the analysis of

---

[30] Moss, 'St Patrick's Day celebrations', 125–48.
[31] *Reformer and South Wales Times*, 27 September 1861.
[32] Ibid.

representations of masculinity and femininity in Irish immigrant culture had they survived. In their absence we can only speculate on the artistic quality of their iconography and wonder at the additional dimension they might have provided to the study of respectable immigrant culture.

The spectacle created by processions with their richly decorated and colourful silk banners and their well-dressed and orderly participants left such a deep impression on observers that on the occasions when they failed to take place, the press commented on their absence. The *Star of Gwent*, for example, drew attention to a tendency to celebrate St Patrick's Day in more subdued fashion in Newport in the early 1880s. Whereas on 17 March 1881 the band of the Catholic Association had been in evidence and 'the streets were thronged in some parts with those who determined to give more tangible proof of their endearment to the "ould counthrie" ', a year later it was the lack of excitement which drew the newspaper's attention. On that occasion, Irish men and women marked the festival by wearing shamrock and by attendance at the Gaiety Theatre, which had staged an Irish play, but the ostentation of previous years was lacking.[33] This was not the case in all towns. By the 1890s, St Patrick's Day processions in Swansea continued to be well attended and included the town's main thoroughfares. In 1894 a local newspaper reported approvingly of the celebrations:

There is one day in the year when we realise the fact that we have a very large number of Irish people resident in Swansea. To-day Irish people all over the world are doing honour to the patron saint of the 'ould counthry' – the blessed St. Patrick. Consequently, in the button-hole of the coat of every 'bhoy' in Swansea one may see the sprightly little leaves of the 'dear little Shamrock'. The celebrations really began last (Friday) evening with a grand dramatic entertainment at St. David's Schoolroom; this afternoon, however, the great event, viz.: THE CATHOLIC PROCESSION, came off under conditions that were, from an atmospheric standpoint, all that could be desired. As the dramatic entertainment is got up by the Catholics of St. David's Church, so are the St. Joseph's Church members responsible for the procession which has taken place this (Saturday) afternoon. By half-past three o'clock all the inhabitants of Greenhill were in the streets, many of them wearing across their shoulders the green band of Ireland. At the

[33] *Star of Gwent*, 18 March 1881, 24 March 1882.

junction of Llangyfelach and Cwmbwrla roads, the crowd was very dense, from thence to St. Joseph's Church the pavements were lined with men, women, and children, all waiting to see the great event of the afternoon. The processionists assembled at ST. JOSEPH'S CHURCH at four o'clock, but it was some twenty minutes later before a procession headed by Messrs. Harry Payne and Morris Welsh, on horseback, began to move. There were no less than four brass bands, the Dowlais Brass Band heading the procession, while a little further in the rear came the Swansea Town Band.

The members of the Catholic Temperance League of the Cross were present in great force, headed by their drum and fife band and Mr Griffin, the major and vice-president of the Swansea Branch. The Llansamlet Band also graced the procession with its presence. There was a splendid muster of Irishmen of the town and district, a fair number of the members from St. David's being present. Very picturesque did THE HUGE PROCESSION look, each of the individuals forming it being ornamented with his band of emerald green, and the majority carrying a liberal supply of shamrock either in their coats or hats. The weather was all that could be desired, and the banners, of which there were a very artistic selection, floating proudly in the breeze. Of course most of the banners were to the honour and glory of the good St. Patrick, and several bore the motto which is so characteristic of his life and work 'Pro Christo et patria'. There were two carriages in the procession, containing Fathers Phillipson, O'Hare, Cox, Geary, Fulton, and others. Proceeding down Llangyfelach-road, the procession came DOWN HIGH-STREET and Wind-street, thence up Rutland-street to Oxford-street, and from there, via St. Helen's and the Ffynone district, back to St. Joseph's, where a service was held.[34]

As this description demonstrates, public celebration of the festival had been appropriated by the Catholic church in Swansea by this date. Societies invariably included a religious service in their St Patrick's Day or anniversary celebrations, a practice encouraged by the clergy who otherwise harboured an ingrained suspicion of oath-bound societies. Some societies, such as the St David's Catholic Guild at Swansea and the Catholic Friendly Society at Holywell,[35] were overtly religious. Others merely used the same premises as the church for meetings. At Tredegar, the Heart and Hand Hibernian Society shared the

[34] *South Wales Daily Post*, 19 March 1894.
[35] PP 1842 XXXVI, A Return Relating to Friendly Societies Enrolled in the Several Counties of England and Wales, p.27; PP 1865 XXX, Report of the Registrar of Friendly Societies in England, p.210.

same room in the Miners' Arms as that used for celebrating Mass, while at Rhymney the Hibernian Friendly Society rented the Catholic schoolroom for meetings.[36] By lending their support to friendly societies, priests had found one way of chipping away at Protestant perceptions of Catholicism as a morally degenerate and socially outcast religion. At the same time, they used the pulpit to underline the importance of incorporating respectable values into the warp and weft of everyday life.

Given the strength of Protestant Nonconformity in urban Wales and the virulent reaction in the press to incidents such as the 'Papal Aggression' crisis of 1850, it is perhaps surprising that the parades of overtly Catholic societies were viewed with equanimity – even approval – by the local press. Elsewhere in Britain, the reaction was less encouraging. In Liverpool, for example, the identification of St Patrick's Day parades with Catholicism stung the Orange Order into action, with Orange marches being held on 12 July as a countervailing demonstration of Protestant strength.[37] There is no evidence of similar demonstrations by Protestants in south Wales, and the presence or absence of the Orange Order appears to have been a crucial factor in determining local responses to Irish parades. However, it is also worth noting that public manifestations of an Irish identity on St Patrick's Day were largely absent from many Lancashire towns. This has been interpreted by one historian as 'a sign of communal self-confidence and maturity'; he maintains that 'social life in the Irish community was becoming sufficiently mature that processions of green-sashed enthusiasts were not needed to remind the Irish of their cultural and national identity'.[38] This might have been true in the longer term, but the experience of south Wales indicates that in particular circumstances the public celebration of St Patrick's Day was a means of integration into the wider urban context without compromising an Irish identity.

[36] PP 1852 XXVIII, Return of All Friendly Societies, p.11; PP 1883 LXVII, Reports of the Chief Registrar of Friendly Societies, p.574.
[37] Frank Neal, *Sectarian Violence: The Liverpool Experience, 1819–1914* (Manchester, 1988), pp.40, 58, 117–18. Interestingly, the Catholic clergy in Liverpool were wary of – even hostile towards – St Patrick's Day parades in mid-century.
[38] W. J. Lowe, *The Irish in Mid-Victorian Lancashire: The Shaping of a Working-Class Community* (New York, 1989), pp.131–4.

On some issues, Catholics and Protestants in Wales shared fundamental values. In spite of deep and often bitter religious disagreements, the campaign against drunkenness was one area where Catholics and Protestants worked towards the same end, if through different organizations. The latter were ready to waive their deep suspicion of Catholicism – albeit grudgingly – in their zeal to promote temperance among working people. The work of Fr Theobald Matthew, the Irish temperance campaigner, inspired the following cautious comment from the foremost Welsh Nonconformist journal: 'While we view Catholicism as one of the main buttresses of the kingdom of darkness . . . we do not wish to be so narrow and prejudiced as to deny some individuals within the encampments of the Roman Church the respect and admiration they might deserve.'[39] Like religion, temperance is an indispensable key to understanding the culture of respectable labour in the nineteenth century. The quest for sobriety was considered a *sine qua non* of achieving the related ideals of thrift, self-help, and self-reliance which together constituted the hallmarks of respectability. Advocates of temperance might periodically fall prey to the attractions of alcohol, but it was the fact of continuously striving for the ideal which set them apart from the 'low Irish'.

Pursuit of the ideal of sobriety was not without its complications. Given the centrality of bread and wine in the celebration of the Mass, it is understandable that some priests were uneasy with movements which exhorted complete abstinence from alcoholic beverages. The objections to total abstinence encompassed both theological and secular considerations. 'My experience', wrote Fr Owen King of Neath in 1899, 'has been so far, that total abstinence means neglect of the sacraments, tendency to interfere with other people's business, pharisaical temperament and the substitution of "respectability" for religion – in fact "teetotalism" becomes the sole religion of many who have taken up with it.'[40] In 1853 Fr Millea of Dowlais had given a series of temperance lectures at Merthyr Tydfil,[41] but as with the establishment of friendly and benefit societies, so with temperance organisations, Newport was the pioneer among the Irish in

[39] *Y Traethodydd*, 1864, 110.
[40] AAC, box 52, Fr Owen King to Bishop Hedley, 15 September 1899.
[41] W. R. Lambert, *Drink and Sobriety in Victorian Wales* (Cardiff, 1983), p.153.

Wales. Here, as elsewhere, temperance was an entrenched feature of the celebrations of clubs and societies. When the Hibernian Club celebrated Whitsun in 1855, its members partook of 'the cup which cheers, but not inebriates'.[42] Yet, it was the implicit recognition that such sentiments appealed only to a minority of immigrants that actuated Dr Cavalli and Fr Richardson of Newport to extend the temperance mission to the 'lower orders' in 1858. Their seemingly boundless enthusiasm was converted into tangible successes. It was claimed that by issuing medals for sobriety and providing other inducements, their work 'resulted in many hundreds being reclaimed from drunkenness'.[43]

The Roman Catholic Society for the Suppression of Drunkenness was one of the first organizations of its kind among the Irish in Britain. It was formally inaugurated at Newport in December 1857 and made great strides during the first year of its existence. Meetings were held in a room lent free of charge by the Tredegar Wharf Co.; there anniversary celebrations took place in November 1858. On the first night of the festivities, a crowd of 700 was entertained by the society's own fife and drum band, while on the second night 900 people paid an entrance fee of 1d. per head as a contribution to the cost of the band's instruments, and it was reported that the floor nearly collapsed from the weight of numbers in the room. After only one year's activities, the society's membership stood at 1,200. Branches had been established at Cardiff, Treforest and Swansea also, but it was activities in Newport which drew most attention. 'Very few cases of drunkenness are now met with among the Irish', asserted the *Merlin*, 'and the police testify to the great improvement which has taken place in their homes and conduct.'[44] By April 1859 the society's swelling membership compelled it to look for a new meeting place. The fact that the Assembly Room of the Town Hall was made available to it and that the town clerk attended a meeting of one thousand members demonstrates the society's importance within the associational life of Newport at this time. New branches had been established at Merthyr and Dowlais

[42] *Monmouthshire Merlin*, 1 June 1855.
[43] Ibid., 10 April 1858.
[44] Ibid., 20, 27 November 1858.

during the year and membership continued to grow. At the April meeting the fundamental aim of the society was restated in explicit terms: 'We have an enemy – not drink, but drunkenness; and we will not rest until we conquer.'[45] Behind the auspicious statements of temperance activists lay the prosaic reality of periodical backsliding, as well-meaning teetotallers yielded to the temptations of excessive drinking. To counter this, the Newport Association divided the town into districts with twenty-three stewards charged with the duty of stiffening flagging morale, arrangements which were remarkably successful. The annual report for 1859–60 claimed that of the two thousand members only about eighty had fallen away; some seventy-five of these redoubled their efforts, 'some after falling again and again'.[46]

In effect, Irish Catholics at Newport created an alternative working-class culture based on sobriety, respectability and religion. Although not Irish himself, Fr Richardson made a clear appeal to constitutional Irish nationalism by calling for three cheers for Daniel O'Connell at every meeting. Even children were catered for from 1863 with the establishment of the Society of St Joseph.[47] Within this world nearly all status aspirations could be met by the awarding of medals and testimonials denoting an individual's length of membership and ability to withstand the temptations of drink. One of the novelties of the Newport Association was the creation of 'veteran' status for members who demonstrated a long-standing commitment to temperance; veterans were distinguished by a different insignia each year, while during the third year a bar like a military medal, inscribed with the words 'By the Help of Mary Immaculate', was awarded.[48] Public processions provided the occasions for displaying this new status, while celebrations and annual outings by train to various 'beauty spots' in the vicinity provided alternative attractions to the beer-shop. Great emphasis was laid upon individual initiative as a means to success within the group.

Women, who were actively encouraged to join the society, found created for them a role which was both sharply defined and clearly circumscribed. Thus, married women acquired the onerous responsibility of reclaiming their fathers, brothers and husbands from the pub by making the home an island of security and comfort in a sea of temptation and degradation. This was to be achieved by the assiduous cultivation of domestic skills solely intended for the succour of their menfolk. Speakers invited to address the Newport Association frequently laid down the behavioural tramlines which Irish women were expected to follow. In April 1859 Newport's town clerk, Thomas Woolett, drew attention to:

> the deficiency of Irish girls as regarded their needle, telling them that if they devoted themselves to that, and looked after the clothing of their fathers and brothers, they would not only assist in saving something for the bank, but they would make their relatives, even if poor, appear respectable. He enjoined upon the females the desirability of cleanliness and tidy habits in their households; for if men had nice and comfortable houses they would not be driven to the beerhouse (Cheers).[49]

This advice was evidently an idealization, an exhortation to strive towards perfection, rather than a description of actual behaviour, and it would be rash to assume that all members of the Association succeeded in achieving the ideal. Nevertheless, the vocal approbation which punctuated such pious statements would suggest that a majority of the audience at least shared that ideal.

Presented here is the ideal of a respectable man earning a family wage in order to maintain his wife and children without their needing to enter the job market. In return, the married woman was to strive to create the Victorian domestic ideal of a 'haven in a heartless world'. By creating a congenial home environment and cultivating domestic skills such as needlework, she could contribute indirectly to the family economy by preventing unnecessary expenditure on clothing and undesirable expenditure in the beer-shop. Implicitly, the proponents of these views recognized that although respectable married women who remained at home did not earn a wage, their contributions to the household clearly had financial implications; hence the emphasis placed on developing needlework skills. This was not merely an

[49] Ibid., 30 April 1859.

attempt to control women's lives by providing them only with the skills they might use in the domestic sphere; it was a recognition that such skills were a crucial element in sustaining a family economy where the woman was not engaged in waged labour. Moreover, self-reliance in the home, it was claimed, would also lead to freedom from the pawnshop. As insobriety usually led to debt, dependence upon the pawnshop was to be discouraged as a factor perpetuating the enervating cycle of drunkenness and poverty. 'The immense profits from those transactions', asserted Fr Richardson in a thinly veiled appeal to antisemitic prejudice, 'went into the hands of those who were strangers to their religion – strangers to Christianity.'[50]

The short-term assistance to be obtained from pawnshops was compared unfavourably with the longer-term benefits to be derived from the use of savings banks. Fr Richardson's exhortations to sobriety were underpinned by reminders of the financial gains which would accrue to those who turned their back on drunkenness and practised thrift. The success of this message can be gauged from the amounts of money passing through the accounts of Irish societies at Newport. Between 1859 and 1860 the Newport Association's funds more than doubled, from £200 to £500.[51] The Newport Guild of St Patrick had been established in 1859 as a sick-benefit society to complement the activities of the Association for the Suppression of Drunkenness. The average weekly subscription to the guild was only 4d., and yet it had begun to pay benefits only six weeks after its establishment. In January 1862 the Catholic Penny Savings Bank at Newport had above £1,000 in 260 individual accounts containing amounts varying from 2d. to £80; since its establishment in March 1858 it had handled more than £2,545. Also by 1862 the Catholic Burial Society boasted 630 members and had nearly £40 in the bank besides stock worth about £25.[52]

A comparison of the rosy picture revealed by these figures with the more modest funds of Irish friendly societies elsewhere in Wales in the 1860s demonstrates the unusual success with which a large portion of the Irish working class at Newport was brought within the ambit of 'respectability' (Table VII.1). The

[50] Ibid.
[51] Ibid., 17 March 1860.
[52] Ibid., 18 January 1862.

low membership of registered Irish friendly societies in towns such as Swansea and Merthyr Tydfil suggests that an organized culture of thrift and sobriety was less widespread elsewhere. The Newport Association for the Suppression of Drunkenness was clearly exceptional. Much of its success can be accounted for by the energetic leadership of Fr Richardson and his unrivalled skill in maintaining membership – so much so that his departure for London in the early 1870s pitched the Association into a spiral of decline.[53]

Table VII.1 Funds of some Irish friendly societies in south Wales in 1864

Society	Town	Members	Funds
Heart and Hand Hibernian Society	Tredegar	NA	£125
Hibernia Society	Aberavon	82	£127
Hibernia Liberal Benefit Society	Cardiff	289	£924
Hibernia Brothers Society	Dowlais	NA	£124
Erin go Bragh Society	Merthyr	80	£59
Hibernia Brothers Society	Merthyr	57	£48
Hibernia Friendly Society	Rhymney	83	£176
St David's Catholic Guild	Swansea	40	£10
Hibernia Liberal Benefit Society	Treforest	14	£36

Source: P.P. 1864 XXXII, Report of the Registrar of Friendly Societies in England [sic], Appendix IV, pp.125, 173, 177–8.

In contrast with Newport, Cardiff, with its rapidly increasing population throughout the century, is indicative of the failure to root the doctrine of respectability in a broader-based Irish constituency. One indicator of this is the fate of a branch of the Association for the Suppression of Drunkenness established in the town by Fr Richardson of Newport in 1859, a branch which soon lapsed into inactivity because of lack of support. This initiative appears to have caused more trouble than it was worth, as Fr Joseph Costa wearily reported:

> Day and night the drunkard's music sounds on my ears. Day and night fights and riots and quarrels and other scandals are heard and seen. The

[53] Lambert, *Drink and Sobriety in VictorianWales*, p.154.

house of the Mission is constantly visited by drunkards, even after midnight, who are dragged thither by their broken-hearted wives to take the pledge. The blessed pledge . . . they take it today and break it tomorrow.[54]

Renewed attempts were made to promote teetotalism among the Irish in Cardiff in March 1861. After only five months' activity, it was claimed that the new body 'now works wonders', yet despite its imitation of more successful 'democratic' organizations, it failed to achieve the same levels of success experienced at Newport. Supporters of temperance drives painted the effects of drunkenness on individuals in a lurid manner, often emphasizing the deleterious consequences for the family. Urging Catholics to join the Association, 'Catholicus' described the chain of events which led to despair: payment on a Saturday was followed by a drinking spree over the weekend, resulting in quarrels leading to rows and an appearance before the court and a fine. In the meantime, wives were at home without money and, without the benefit of paternal supervision, the children ran wild in the streets, devoid of religion or morality.[55] These comments provoked a heated response from T. F. Meagher, who argued that the hundreds of sober Irishmen in the town should not be tarred with the same brush as the drunkards.[56]

Nevertheless, Irish temperance organizations at Cardiff achieved limited support, as shown by the fact that when a branch of the Roman Catholic Association for the Suppression of Drunkenness was relaunched in 1867 it managed to attract no more than four hundred members, a figure which should have been closer to a thousand according to a local parish priest. Ten years later, a magistrate drew attention to the unusually high incidence of drunkenness among Irish women compared with the remainder of the town's female population.[57] By contrast, the success of the Hibernian Benefit Society, active in Cardiff since

[54] Fr Joseph Costa to Fr Provincial Rinolfi, 2 August 1859, Derry's Wood Archives.

[55] *Cardiff Times*, 28 November 1862.

[56] *Cardiff Times*, 19 December 1862. Meagher asserted that 'Catholicus' was a Catholic priest, a claim categorically denied by the newspaper's editor.

[57] Costa to Rinolfi, 7 August 1861, Derry's Wood Archives; *St Peter's Chair*, II (November 1889), 23, extracts from the Cardiff Diary of the Fathers of the Institute of Charity: entry for 29 September 1867; PP 1877 XI, Select Committee on Intemperance, p.158.

1847 and based on 'thoroughly reliable and economic principles', can be seen as a pragmatic response to the acute housing problems arising from the town's pell-mell growth, although even the membership of this society numbered fewer than three hundred in the 1860s.[58]

The failure to inculcate the habits of sobriety and thrift into a majority of the Irish in Cardiff (and in many other towns in Wales) was thrown into high relief by the evidence presented to the Royal Commission on the operation of the Welsh Sunday Closing Act in 1890. Alderman P. W. Carey assured his questioners that the Catholic clergy were 'nearly without exception strong abstainers from drink', a position that contrasted sharply with the picture of the shebeen-keeping Irish that emerged from evidence presented to the Commission by more hostile witnesses.[59] Sunday closing in Wales from 1881 was hailed as one of the crowning glories of Welsh Liberalism and the first legislative expression of Welsh nationhood to be granted by the imperial Parliament. Working people in the mining, quarrying and agricultural areas of the country enthusiastically supported the principle of the Act. In these areas the Act's provisions were enforced in the spirit as well as the letter of the law, but in the towns of the south Wales coastal belt political consensus on the efficacy of the legislation appeared forced, where it existed at all. One of the few working people to give evidence to the Royal Commission in 1890 was Henry Murphy, a Cardiff iron-moulder and chairman of the Cardiff Working Men's Liberal Club and Institute, who described himself as 'a Radical in politics'. He headed a delegation from a meeting of 2,500 working people which demanded the repeal of the Act of 1881.[60]

A growing estrangement between the political ideals of the temperance movement and the actual behaviour of the majority is discernible in the decade after the Act was passed. Shebeens (or, as they were sometimes called, in Welsh, *cwrw bachs*) thrived in the penumbra of illegality created by the legislation. They were a means of retailing liquor without a licence and Bishop

---

[58] *St Peter's Chair*, X (April 1897), 112. A detailed balance sheet for the building society is published here. On Cardiff's housing problems, see M. J. Daunton, *Coal Metropolis Cardiff, 1870–1914* (Leicester, 1977), pp.73–124.

[59] PP 1890 XL, Report of the Royal Commission Appointed to Inquire into the Operation of the Sunday Closing (Wales) Act, 1881, pp.64–6, 500–2.

[60] Ibid., pp.547–51.

Hedley denounced the illicit trade in a pastoral letter read in all churches in the diocese. Alderman P. W. Carey, an Irish wholesale wine merchant at Cardiff, believed that 'in regard to the nationality of the shebeen keepers, unfortunately there is no doubt that a great many of them, but still I would not say the majority of them, belong to my nationality'. Fr Cormack concurred with Carey's evidence, stressing that 'all the nationalities in the town are numerously represented'.[61]

Such evidence demonstrates the limitations of societies intent upon reforming their members' behaviour. Friendly societies and the temperance movement enjoyed only partial and uneven success, varying in strength and influence from place to place and over time: in 1913, for example, the membership of the Ancient Order of Hibernians in the diocese of Cardiff stood at 5,000.[62] However, in the absence of statistical evidence over time it is impossible to estimate with any accuracy the proportion of Irish immigrants who enrolled as members of friendly societies and participated in temperance associations. These organizations had a stronger appeal to the less mobile portion of the immigrant community who enjoyed enough job security to plan ahead. Membership of a burial society, for example, suggested a settled existence and a commitment to living in a particular locality not often associated with the Irish, many of whom perceived themselves as exiles and hankered after returning to their homeland later in life. In the absence of savings, the cost of burying a relative could push low-income families into destitution and consequently those who anticipated remaining in Wales tended to support immigrant friendly societies. It would also appear that as far as the Irish were concerned, men were more likely to organize friendly societies than women. The latter relied primarily upon informal networks for sociability, based upon home and neighbourhood, and where they did organize their activities they tended to do so through the sewing group and other Catholic sororities.

Despite these qualifications, care must be taken not to underestimate the influence of ideals of respectability. As such ideals were rarely translated into behavioural absolutes, it is plausible

[61] Ibid., pp.xxxiv–xxxv, and 500–2. The text of Hedley's pastoral letter is reproduced on p.501 of the report.
[62] Fr Fennel to Bishop Hedley, 24 March 1913, AAC, box marked 'Friendly societies'.

to suggest that individuals moved in and out of a culture of respectability at different stages of the life cycle and the economic cycle: a person was rarely captured once and for all. Peter Bailey overstates the argument when he writes that 'respectability was assumed or discarded, like a collar, as the situation demanded'; this underplays the significance of respectability for some individuals. Nevertheless, changing economic contexts or peer pressure could discourage or confirm particular forms of behaviour.[63] 'Backsliding' was a notoriously common phenomenon in temperance circles, as shown by the sophisticated organization put in place in Newport by the Catholic Association for the Suppression of Drunkenness to prevent it occurring. Similarly, for many working people who conformed to the public imperatives of respectability on club or festival days, older forms of recreation were not entirely supplanted by newer forms of associational life.

Because of this continuing link with a wider working-class culture, clubs and friendly societies provided the matrix within which an Irish Catholic culture could be reforged. They linked a peaceful Irish patriotism with civic identity and bound them together with the mutual pecuniary interest of members. Here, the role of the clergy in encouraging and cajoling the Irish to comply with new forms of piety and religious behaviour is significant. In 1913, a parish priest set out the clergy's view of the opportunities for gaining a foothold for religion in the friendly society movement:

> Personally, I consider the establishment of a branch [of the Ancient Order of Hibernians] in a parish as good as a mission for many of our careless and indifferent Irish people. It stimulates them to come to the sacraments, and they find in the Order that *public opinion* which at home in Ireland sweetly leads our people to mass and to the sacraments. It also affords our people a blend of religion and patriotism, which is most helpful to them.[64]

Creating this 'public opinion' – that is, a set of attitudes in the community conducive to the cultivation of respectability, religiosity and patriotism – was a major preoccupation of parish

---

[63]   Peter Bailey, *Leisure and Class*, p.184.
[64]   Fr Fennel to Bishop Hedley, 24 March 1913.

priests, who believed that combating stereotypes of the indigent Irish would reflect well upon the Catholic church. In a society in which Protestants were suspicious of Catholics, and at times openly hostile to them, emphasizing the link between respectable Irish societies and the church was a prudent act. This attitude was of a piece with reforms in popular piety within the church. From the mid-nineteenth century, it had embarked on an ambitious project to reform the behaviour and popular religious practices of the immigrant Irish in such a way that Mass and the sacraments became the focus of religiosity, in contrast with the more diffuse folk religion of pre-Famine Ireland. By securing for himself a key role in the celebrations of Irish clubs and friendly societies, the priest entrenched his position of influence in an otherwise secular associational life, thus tying the church more closely to the everyday lives of the people and providing it with a position from which it could champion orthodox piety.

Nevertheless, while recognizing the importance of religion in the celebrations of temperance organizations and friendly societies, it would be misleading to interpret their activities in terms of an agenda solely determined by the clergy. On the contrary, had the ideals of self-dependence and sobriety not been shared by the members of these societies, it is difficult to see how their loyalty could have been retained. Significant numbers of men and women in the immigrant community clearly acquiesced in the ideal of respectability and saw it as a way of defining the borders of an ethnic identity which proclaimed its compatibility with the dominant ideals of Welsh society at the same time as it asserted its difference. This duality was most visible in the concerted attempts to make St Patrick's Day celebrations orderly and respectable. Moreover, because these organizations confronted the problem of dependence on poor law relief – the central anxiety of Welsh society concerning Irish immigrants during the Famine years – they created an avenue out of the suspicious attitudes of the middle decades of the century and laid the foundations of wider social integration.

VIII

A 'DEVOTIONAL REVOLUTION'? RELIGION AND BELIEF IN IMMIGRANT CULTURE

For most historians of Irish emigrant communities, religion bulks large. In particular, the Catholic church is customarily viewed as a unifying force, defining the borders of immigrant identity and providing an institutional focus for the community which no other institution could supply. Moreover, most historians concur that assimilation was hampered by the affiliation of the majority of the Irish to a religion which was anathematized by the predominantly Protestant receiving society, with religious differences compounding occupational inequalities and alleged residential segregation. As the central and most prominent institution of immigrant life, therefore, the Roman Catholic church is seen as reinforcing a sense of separateness and alienation. This interpretation seems particularly compelling in the case of Wales where, by the mid-nineteenth century, the Protestant Nonconformist denominations had won the allegiance of an exceptionally large proportion of the rural and urban working class. Unlike Lancashire and the west of Scotland, there were few Irish Protestants among the migrants to Wales.[1] However, in spite of the manifest importance of the Catholic church in immigrant life and the thoroughly Protestant character of the Welsh, a simple equation of the Irish with Catholicism masks as much as it reveals. Migrants carried with them cultural baggage which was not readily discarded. Belief systems and cultural practices originating in the Irish countryside before the Famine often conflicted with institutional Catholicism, and for many migrants the points of contact with orthodox religion involved conflict and resistance rather than acquiescence and submission to priestly authority. Here, as in other aspects of immigrant life, it is the variety of responses which is striking.

[1] For an important study of the Protestant Irish, see Graham Walker, 'The Protestant Irish in Scotland', in T. M. Devine (ed.), *Irish Immigrants and Scottish Society in the Nineteenth and Twentieth Centuries* (Edinburgh, 1991), pp.44–66. On religion in Wales, see E. T. Davies, *Religion and Society in the Nineteenth Century* (Llandybïe, 1981); I. G. Jones, *Explanations and Explorations: Essays in the Social History of Victorian Wales* (Llandysul, 1981); and W. R. Lambert, *Drink and Sobriety in Victorian Wales, c.1820–c.1895* (Cardiff, 1983).

In the 1840s many priests and bishops in Britain remained largely unaware of the full complexity of the relationship between the church and the belief systems and practices of Irish peasants, viewing the immigrants as a contributory factor in the rejuvenation of native Catholicism. Bishop Brown, vicar apostolic for the Welsh District between 1840 and 1850 before his subsequent appointment to the new diocese of Newport and Menevia, identified the church's primary task in south Wales as bringing priests and places of worship within easy reach of the immigrants. The assumption was that access to a place of worship was sufficient to ensure Irish attendance at Mass. By the beginning of the 1850s, therefore, the Roman Catholic church faced the daunting challenge of trying to accommodate the vastly inflated numbers of potential churchgoers now resident in the towns of south Wales. The Famine influx exposed the inadequacies of existing church provision, for in 1851 over half the Catholic chapels in the region were still to be found in rural areas where few of the Irish lived, and so the church was compelled to make strenuous attempts to bring places of worship, however makeshift, within reach of the newcomers. As immigration increased and the discrepancy between the location of buildings and potential congregations widened, the church embarked on desperate remedial action to reclaim lost ground.

Bishop Brown tackled the problem in a pragmatic manner. In some towns and villages where no Catholic church or chapel had been built, services continued to be held in private houses or pubs, while the accumulation of funds for building a permanent place of worship remained a difficult task. Advising a priest in 1859, Brown set out his approach in the following terms:

> As for a chapel I greatly prefer, where funds are scarce or insufficient, to provide a Chapel and a School, one almost important as the other, to make the same building serve for both, as you may have seen at Treforest and Merthyr. Such buildings are not much less acceptable to the labouring Irish cong[regatio]n than an architectural Chapel, and infinitely cheaper, which is of importance to a needy Diocese.[2]

---

[2] Bishop Brown to Fr Gastaldi, 25 November 1849, AAC, box 65.

His policy was to suggest projects, to help initiate them where possible, but to insist on the self-sufficiency of the particular mission concerned thereafter. At that point, his contribution was restricted to offering advice on investment and improvements. Brown abhorred debt and expected the clergy to share his views and behave accordingly. This approach yielded positive results. Thirteen new Catholic chapels were built between 1840 and 1850, while a further fourteen were built in the period 1851–60, and another sixteen from 1861 to 1870. Even so, there were siren calls for additional provision. As late as 1866, the parish priest of Aberdare exclaimed: 'In God's name, let us be up and doing. We don't want grand buildings – anything, anything, anything to instruct the people – talk of Heathen Lands – it is at our door and great must be the responsibility.'[3] In spite of this insistent demand for action, building activity slowed to only eight new places of worship in each of the three decades after 1870, before increasing once again to sixteen in the years 1901–10 in response to the dramatic population growth throughout south Wales in that decade. This was a prelude to the frenetic building activity of the 1920s, when new churches, chapels and out-stations sprang up like mushrooms as a contiguous parochial system was established in the region.[4]

How many of the Irish filled the pews of these chapels? The evidence for a conclusive answer to this question is lacking, but the picture revealed by the Religious Census of 1851 provides suggestive indicators. The crude vital statistics for the Catholic church in Wales as a whole reveal a remarkable improvement on the position reported to Rome in 1839, when the total number of Catholics was enumerated as 6,269.[5] By 1851 there was an Irish-born population of 19,747 in the eight Welsh counties in which the church was active. As the vast majority of these would have been baptized Catholics, we are left with an increase in the potential bedrock Catholic constituency of some 200 per cent in

---

[3] Bishop Brown to Fr Signini, 20 December 1855; Brown to Fr Thomas McDowell, March 1860; unnamed priest at Aberdare to Brown, 26 October 1866. AAC, unnumbered box.

[4] Based on the *Catholic Directory and Annual Register* from 1838; cf. I. G. Jones, 'Ecclesiastical economy: aspects of church building in Victorian Wales', in R. R. Davies et al. (eds.), *Welsh Society and Nationhood: Historical Essays Presented to Glanmor Williams* (Cardiff, 1984), pp.216–31.

[5] W. M. Brady, *The Episcopal Succession in England, Scotland and Ireland, AD 1400–1875* (3 vols., 1876–7), 3, pp.315–16.

eleven years. This population – which continued to grow in the following decade – was served by twenty-five priests from nineteen churches and chapels. Nevertheless, the total number of Catholic attendances on census Sunday in 1851 was only 5,585.[6]

The pattern of Roman Catholic attendance differed from that of Protestants. The Protestant churches and denominations organized morning, afternoon and evening services, while the Catholic church tended to hold a number of Masses during the morning. Protestants would be expected to attend more than one service on the Sabbath, whereas one attendance at Sunday Mass was deemed sufficient for Catholics. The importance of attending services regularly for maintaining an individual's identification with, as well as membership of, a particular denomination could also vary. Protestant Nonconformity was sustained partly by its relationship of conflict with the Established Church: an individual's failure to attend any place of worship meant that the non-attender was claimed as a *de facto* member of the Church of England as the State Church. In the case of Irish immigrants – and especially in Wales, where overall attendances at places of worship were higher than in England – non-attenders were perceived as *de facto* supporters of the Catholic church. Consequently, it might not appear as quite so vitally important to attend a religious service regularly in order to preserve an identity with the church. This was the case in mid-century despite the exhortations of the clergy to their parishioners to attend Mass at least once a week on a Sunday. It was possible to be Catholic by identification in nineteenth-century Britain as well as by practice, an identification which was nourished from within the group but which was also sustained by the attitudes of outsiders.

The statistics collected on Census Sunday, 30 March 1851, provide figures for the total number of attendances at each service in a place of worship. However, the raw data need to be treated with caution, especially when attempts are made to abstract information concerning non-Protestant bodies and in specific localities. As an individual could have attended more than one service on that day, the statistics are a poor indicator of the number of individuals attending. In order to circumvent this

---

[6] Census of Religion, 1851.

problem, historians such as Ieuan Gwynedd Jones have developed a method for arriving at an index of attendance which serves as a reasonably accurate means of ascertaining differential rates of attendance.[7]

This index is arrived at by expressing the total number of attendances at all services on Census Sunday as a proportion of the total population of the district. Although failing to take account of different habits of worship among the various churches and chapels and tending to favour the Nonconformist bodies, these calculations are a reliable means of ascertaining differential rates of attendance. This method can be adapted further to arrive at an index of attendance for the Irish-born which can be compared with that for the native Welsh. By expressing the total number of attendances at all services in Catholic chapels as a proportion of the Irish-born population recorded in the Census of Population for 1851, it is possible to arrive at a rudimentary index of attendance for Irish Catholics in Wales. This can be done only for areas where it is known from other sources that both Irish-born Protestants and native Catholics are numerically insignificant. This method is of particular relevance in Wales, where the growth of Catholicism was associated almost exclusively with Irish immigration.

Table VIII.1 Index of religious attendance, 1851

District	Total no. of Irish-born	Total Catholic attendances	Irish Index of attendance	District Index of attendance
Newport	2,737	2,200	80.4	64.4
Cardiff	3,317	1,450	43.7	70.3
Merthyr	3,706	750	20.2	80.1
Swansea	1,369	500	36.5	71.1
Wrexham	711	360	50.6	74.4

[7] I. G. Jones, 'Denominationalism in Swansea and district', in *idem, Explanations and Explorations*, pp.53–80; 'Introduction' to I. G. Jones and D. Williams (eds.), *The Religious Census of 1851: A Calendar of the Returns Relating to Wales*, vol.I, *South Wales* (Cardiff, 1976), pp.xi–xxxv. Horace Mann, the civil servant responsible for conducting the census excluded Catholics from some of his calculations 'as the practice adopted by that body of having several distict congregations at the morning service would interfere with the estimate. This practice will account, in some measure for the fact that their Returns show frequently a greater number of persons than could be accommodated at one time.' Horace Mann, 'On the statistical position of religious bodies in England and Wales', *Journal of the Statistical Society of London*, XVIII (1855), 144n.

These figures suggest that the typical index of attendance for Irish Catholic communities was approximately 35–50 and that church attendance was higher among the Protestant denominations (ranging from a figure of 64.4 to 80.1 in the principal towns). It should be remembered, of course, that this index is only a crude pointer to the extent of religious practice and that it must be used with caution. Nevertheless, the figures reveal significant variations in the levels of attendance at Catholic chapels in different towns. Why was this? In his study of religion during the industrial revolution in south Wales, E. T. Davies suggested that these variations could be explained by differences in the density of Irish settlement; thus, the index of attendance was lower in the district of Merthyr Tydfil, where the Irish were more widely dispersed among a number of industrial settlements, and higher in Newport, where they were more concentrated.[8]

In so far as the concentration of Irish settlers in a locality acted as a spur to the establishment of a mission to them, the density of settlement was a contributory factor in explaining why attendance was higher in some areas than in others. However, this explanation is inadequate in itself, as it is predicated on the belief that in order to fill the pews the church had the relatively simple task of making places of worship accessible to the Irish. As has been seen, religious practice among the Irish was irregular irrespective of the density of settlement. The difference between Newport and the other Welsh towns can be accounted for by the fact that Catholicism was far more securely established there than elsewhere in Wales. An impressive Gothic church was under construction at the time of the Chartist Rising in 1839, and a poor-school was established in the 1840s on the initiative of Dr Baldacconi, the parish priest. It was reported in 1849 that there were 'flourishing schools' under the supervision of the Brothers of the Order of Charity and the Sisters of the Order of Providence. The combination of Catholic education and a succession of priests acutely aware of the evangelical nature of their mission to the poor made a decisive impact.

The exceptional circumstances of Catholicism in Newport merely underline the impression left by the census statistics that a

[8] E. T. Davies, *Religion in the Industrial Revolution in South Wales* (Cardiff, 1965), pp.187–9.

large proportion, in most places a majority, of Irish men and women – nominal Catholics who had been baptized by the church – were habitual non-attenders at Mass. Here we are not dealing with backsliders dominated by unbelief, but rather with a variant of popular religion at odds with theological and ritual orthodoxy. This fact was often obscured in the writings of Catholic commentators, who saw the Irish as the saviours of Catholicism in Britain. Their excitement at the swelling Catholic ranks as a result of the arrival of thousands of Irish men and women soon yielded to a realization of the gulf separating their own religious culture from that of the majority of the newcomers. As Hugh McLeod has pointed out in his study of New York, viewing Irish Catholicism from the standpoint of the clergy alone can obscure some of the most salient aspects of the migrant's religious life.[9]

Pre-Famine Irish peasants adhered to a spirituality structured more by the seasons and agricultural festivals than by the church and its official teachings. They inhabited a mental world populated by spirits and fairies to whom they accorded alternately fear and respect, and they espoused a religiosity derived from a belief in the efficacy of magical powers. However, in the aftermath of the Great Famine a period of radical change in religious behaviour was initiated and the content of popular Catholic piety was transformed. The so-called 'devotional revolution' ushered in a new era during which levels of church attendance in Ireland rose to 90 per cent within fifty years.[10] One historian has traced the roots of these changes to the emerging preponderance of the farmer and his way of life in Irish society resulting from the effective elimination of the cottiers and labourers as a class during the Famine.[11] In the cultural world of the latter, orthodox religion and magic overlapped, with spirits, ghosts and witchcraft coexisting with the priest in varying degrees of harmony. Frictions generated by the attempts to press such a culture into the mould of

[9] Hugh McLeod, 'Popular Catholicism in Irish New York, c.1900', in W. J. Shiels and Diana Woods (eds.), *The Churches, Ireland and the Irish* (Oxford, 1989), pp.353–73.

[10] Emmet Larkin, 'The devotional revolution in Ireland, 1850–75', *American Historical Review*, 77 (1972), 626 and 636; David W. Millar, 'Irish Catholicism and the Great Famine', *Journal of Social History*, IX (1975).

[11] Eugene Hughes, 'The Great Hunger and Irish Catholicism', *Societas*, VIII (1978). Cottiers rented cabins and small plots of land from farmers and paid for them largely in labour.

orthodoxy carried over into emigrant settlements. It follows that the majority of those who emigrated before and during the Famine years were unlikely to be regular churchgoers.

Migration to an urban and industrializing society did not automatically or immediately entail the 'disenchantment' of the peasant's world, to use Max Weber's incisive phrase. For example, oral tradition continued to emphasize the extraordinary powers of the clergy. In the pre-Famine world the priest was a figure believed to possess magical powers, and consequently an aura of mystique surrounded this celibate man at once part of, and yet set apart from, the rest of society. Among the feared and respected qualities attributed to Irish priests were those of premonition of death. This derived from a belief that each death had an allotted time and that, consequently, an accidental or unexpected death was considered both shameful and vile. Echoes of this mentality were to be found among the Irish in Wales. According to William Flynn, who was born in Merthyr Tydfil in the 1840s, Fr Carroll, an Irish priest who served Dowlais and Merthyr in the 1830s and 1840s, was credited with daunting powers. The priest would walk from Dowlais to Merthyr to say Mass and was regularly insulted by the Welsh on his return. Flynn takes up the story:

> One Monday when coming home to Glebeland Place, he [Fr Carroll] was passing through Old Arch in Castle Street when a Welshman spat upon him. He spoke to a passer-by in Irish:
> 'Are you an Irishman?'
> 'Yes, Father', was the reply, 'don't you see that man spitting upon you?'
> 'Yes', replied Father Carroll, 'but by this time tomorrow he won't do so.'
> This man then walked home with Fr Carroll for protection from the jeering man who followed him.
> The following day at about the same hour in the afternoon, a procession up Castle Street brought the dead body of the man who had spat upon Fr Carroll the day before. He had been killed in the works. Fr Carroll's remark to the Irishman was town's talk for some time afterwards.[12]

Similarly, the oral tradition concerning Fr Elias, who spent a short sojourn in Merthyr in the 1860s, provided another instructive lesson in the dangers of interfering with the clergy. Eugene

---

[12] Papers of Fr J. M. Cronin, Glam. R.O., D/Dxha 4/1.

Sullivan, who had heard the poignant tale from his mother, recounted how the priest had been the subject of gossip: 'Three families – McCarthy, Cambell and Henebury, circulated scandal about him and Bishop Brown removed him . . . he went around to say goodbye leaving little picture souvenirs and declared he was innocent.' All three families involved in the incident subsequently came to grief, suffering dire poverty and encountering serious accidents and other misfortunes.[13] The moral of these tales was clear to all who heard them.

In this context, belief that the curse of a priest carried with it very real and damaging consequences was less an irrational delusion than a means of adjustment to the strains and frustrations of everyday life, supplying both an intelligible explanation of misfortune in an unpredictable world and a means of dealing with it. Such beliefs derived from Irish peasant society, but they acquired a new relevance in the context of the insecurity which derived from emigration and the hazards attendant upon life in an urbanizing society. The clergy were acutely aware of the roots of the esteem in which they were held. In 1882 Bishop Hedley reprimanded Fr O'Haire of Rhymney, who had visited Cardiff to preach a mission, for an 'impudent act'. O'Haire had 'publicly and in the street declared the curse of God to rest on a certain house'. His action was directed against an 'openly adulterous' couple, partly as a ritual of public shaming and partly in the knowledge that a priest's curse would be the cause of great anxiety.[14]

Nevertheless, a priest's curse was not deemed to be effective in all cases, and as time passed such beliefs were either displaced altogether or assimilated into orthodox Catholicism. By the end of the century, priests could no longer rely on the intimidatory effect of the curse. This was made abundantly clear by incidents such as that which occurred at Bridgend in 1904 when Fr G. R. White threatened to put a curse on a member of his congregation. 'I find', he informed the bishop, 'that sometimes in stubborn cases the mere mention of the word curse – without

[13] Ibid.

[14] Bishop Hedley to Fr O'Haire, 22 April 1882, and O'Haire to Hedley, 23 April 1882, AAC, box 44. However, a Welshman at Rhymney defended O'Haire, maintaining that 'he is not doing superficial work, skimming over the surface, but he is diving into all the cesspools & dragging out the ugly monsters that have been buried so long in their filth & misery'. L. J. Davies to Hedley, 4 May 1882, AAC, ibid.

any wish attached to it – is more effective than a lot of less vehement language.' In this instance he had miscalculated, because an Irish woman reproached him for not knowing how to treat Irish people properly, not being Irish himself.[15] The episode illustrates how the Irish did not always accept unquestioningly the statements and behaviour of the clergy, and it is difficult to imagine how the clergy could have retained the respect of the Irish if they had shown nothing more than outright hostility to popular practices. Also, as this incident suggests, non-Irish priests had to work harder for acceptance.

In general, parish priests developed a perceptive understanding of Irish working-class culture combined with a set of proposals to reform popular practices. They placed a strong emphasis on the need to cultivate individual devotion, channelled through the church, by regular attendance at Mass and more frequent participation in the sacraments. Such innovations were broadly related to 'Romanizing' tendencies within the church and the triumph of Ultramontanism. This movement was an attempt to bring popular practice into line with the ideals of the Catholic Counter-Reformation. At the beginning of the nineteenth century, Catholic priests in Wales were still accorded the inoffensive title 'Mr', rather than the more controversial 'Father', while their congregations cultivated a subdued profile in accordance with their legal status. After 1829 there was mounting pressure for a Catholicism more in line with that of continental Europe, although the bishops appear to have been wary of moving too far too quickly after the remarkable anti-Catholic outburst which greeted the restoration of the hierarchy in England and Wales in 1850. As Monsignor George Talbot, writing from the Vatican in 1865, confided to Bishop Brown, 'I tell your Lordship in confidence that the Bishops in England are rather more backward in certain usages which many of the Continental Bishops practise.'[16] Less exalted members of the church also came in for criticism. Bishop Brown reserved particular criticism for the 'unreformed' practices of Irish Catholics. He complained to the third Marquis of Bute that those whose formative experience of Catholicism derived from pre-Famine

[15] Fr G. R. White to Bishop Hedley, 19 August 1904, AAC, box 74.
[16] Monsignor George Talbot to Brown, 10 January 1865, AAC, unnumbered box.

Ireland had received an 'imperfect early religious training' which resulted in their neglect of Sunday Mass in Wales.[17] This attitude was not shared by all his priests. Fr Bruno was positively lyrical in his praise of the immigrants he visited in the areas surrounding Cardiff. 'God bless the poor Irish', he exclaimed to the Fr Provincial of the Institute of Charity in 1855. 'Amidst their rags a good soul is often to be found, and so strong a faith that nothing can entice them to divert from the religion of their ancestry.'[18] Yet few priests endorsed his ringing praise, more typically complaining of apathy and indifference. Writing from Cardiff in 1859, Fr Joseph Costa painted a bleak picture of Irish neglect of the church, commenting that when he visited them in their houses he found them

> either out of the Church altogether or neglecting Church on Sunday constantly. If I look in the Church on weekdays, I see eight or ten worshippers, generally not one child, and some waifs . . . In the evenings during the week prayers are said three times but you count half a dozen of old women. And those who should attend to evening's prayers are in the public house.[19]

At times, the priests' determination to reform the behaviour of Irish immigrants raised a barrier between them and the very people they were trying to reach. This was the case at Pontllanfraith in 1910, when the parish priest was criticized for denouncing his congregation as 'the scum of Ireland and rotten Catholics'. A member of the congregation protested that there would be more support for a priest who 'would treat them as Irishmen and not as apostates'.[20] Attempts to reform popular practice inevitably resulted in friction between priest and congregation.

Roman Catholic missioners who came to Wales in the 1840s and 1850s possessed a heightened awareness of their pastoral duties and sacerdotal ministry. They rejected the circumspection of dress and behaviour which had characterized the 'old'

---

[17] Brown to the third marquis of Bute, undated, AAC, box 123.
[18] Fr Bruno to Fr Provincial Pagani, 18 June 1855, Derry's Wood Archives of the Head House of the Rosminians.
[19] Fr Joseph Costa to Fr Provincial Pagani, 2 August 1859, ibid.
[20] William Hill to Bishop Hedley, 12 June 1912, AAC, box 61.

Catholicism and brought with them an energetically evangelical approach to the poor. The Institute of Charity, or Rosminians, were foremost in this movement. Italian priests of the Order were active in Cardiff, Newport and Merthyr Tydfil, and were credited with introducing the Roman collar as a feature of clerical dress. The received picture of Catholic congregations being served by Irish priests alone was far from being the universal experience in the mid-nineteenth century. By 1864, for example, there were more Italian than Irish priests in Wales, while Dutch and Breton clergy supplemented the English, Irish and Welsh priests.[21] This varied cultural background channelled new influences into the parishes.

Priests such as the renowned evangelical Fr Luigi Gentili – reputedly the first priest to convert a man on a train – encouraged Marian devotions, more frequent attendance at communion and the sacraments, and greater lay participation in services by the adoption of plainsong. Although the mission he conducted at Newport was not an unqualified success, he did manage to inspire priests and laity to renewed activity.[22] Little by little, the content of popular Catholicism changed. This new form of piety was reinforced by the establishment of a network of confraternities and sodalities and a profusion of societies and guilds targeted at specific groups within the congregation. As was seen in chapter VII, many of these organizations, like the temperance societies, enjoyed a relatively short period of dynamism before lapsing into inactivity until the next mission or change of parish priest. All sections of the community were catered for by parochial activities. Children were catechized and socialized into new religious habits by a combination of attendance at Catholic elementary schools and membership of societies such as the Children of Mary for girls and altar servers' guilds for boys. In the larger parishes adults were able to join a variety of prayer societies as well as confraternities. Organiza-

---

[21] See *Catholic Directory and Annual Register* from 1845. Cf. Sheridan Gilley, 'Catholic faith in the Irish slums: London, 1840–70', in H. J. Dyos and Michael Wolff (eds.), *The Victorian City, Images and Realities*, vol.II (London, 1973); *idem*, 'Papists, Protestants and the Irish in London, 1835–1870', in G. J. Cuming and D. Baker (eds.), *Popular Belief and Practice* (Cambridge, 1972); W. J. Lowe, 'The Lancashire Irish and the Catholic church, 1846–1871', *Irish Historical Studies*, XX (1976–77).

[22] C. Leetham, *Luigi Gentili, A Sower for the Second Spring* (London, 1965), pp.3, 68, 194, 244–5.

tions like the Catholic Young Men's Society, which established a
strong presence in south Wales, were instrumental in maintaining a connection between young adult males and the church.[23]
Towards the end of the century, branches of the Society of St
Vincent de Paul, a Roman Catholic organization for charitable
and rescue purposes among the poor, helped to nurture a social
conscience among lay men.

Women were considered to have a special role and
responsibility for the transmission of Catholicism from one
generation to another. It was argued that as their proper sphere
of influence was the home, they had closer contact with children
than did men and, therefore, provided an example which would
influence impressionable minds. They were also perceived to be
the most sedulous attenders of church services and the sacraments. Older women were praised for their links with a special
spirituality derived from life in the Irish countryside. As Canon
J. W. Richards wrote of the Greenhill district of Swansea:

> I found very few old men amongst my flock . . . But women survived. I
> found an exceptional number of old grannies, and I confess to a deep
> respect for these venerable survivals of a bitter past; they were the one
> strong conservative element in this flock, the one link between the old life
> and the new. They were the depositories of the faith and piety, the folklore
> and wake ceremonial and of the poetry ingrained in the Irish nature . . . I
> have dwelt on this topic, for the race of biddies I knew have all gone to
> their long home. There are, doubtless, biddies now but not the real thing.
> They have never heard the cry of the banshee, or met real 'Little People',
> or confessed in Irish or cursed like 'Peggy Rhu'.[24]

Wonder at these women's links with a supposedly authentic,
unpolluted and quintessentially Irish spiritual experience sat
oddly with the clergy's determined attempts to reform popular
religion. Possibly it was precisely because this culture had lost its
grip on the majority of immigrants by the time Richards wrote
these words immediately after the First World War that he could

---

[23] In June 1922 the Catholic Young Men's Societies of Great Britain held their annual
conference at Cardiff, at which Hilaire Belloc spoke on 'The present position of the
church in Europe'. *Catholic Young Men's Societies of Great Britain: Guide Book and Souvenir [of
the] 47th. Annual Conference* (Cardiff, 1922).
[24] J. W. Richards, *Reminiscences of the Early Days of the Parish and Church of St. Joseph's,
Greenhill* (Swansea, 1919), p.11.

speak about it in such nostalgic terms. It is significant that he regarded confession in Irish as part of the disappearing world of pre-Famine religious culture. Specific arrangements for confession in the immigrants' native tongue had been made by one of his predecessors at Swansea, and a similar provision was available in some other industrial settlements. Fr Signini, an Italian Rosminian at Cardiff, went so far as to compile his own Irish-language vocabulary to enable him to hear confessions.[25] In general, Irish-speakers in Wales did not pass on the language to their children, and their native tongue died with them. An Irish-medium school was held at Swansea in mid-century,[26] but it was more usual for English to be the language of instruction in Catholic schools. It is in this context that Canon Richards's wistful recollections about Irish-speaking 'biddies' – the so-called depositories of folklore and wake ceremonial – must be seen. As the century progressed, the Irish woman's role in the life of the church was more likely to be expressed through the sewing group and the Union of Catholic Mothers or kindred organizations.

The nature of popular religious experience and the impact of the reformers on it are best assessed by examining the ways in which attitudes to two central rites of passage – death and marriage – underwent change. Taken together with rites surrounding birth, these define, in John Bossy's words, the 'borders of a Christian kinship',[27] and so constitute the key points in the life cycle which the church attempted to dominate and control by imposing its own rituals.

Death

In a society with high levels of infant mortality, endemic diseases such as typhoid and tuberculosis, and sporadic epidemics of virulent diseases such as cholera, death was a close companion of everyday life. For those who lost relatives – either during or after the separation of exile – the psychological pain could be intense.

---

[25] Archives of St David's Priory, University of Wales Swansea, 8(e), Diary of Notices delivered at Sunday Services, 1862–5, *sub* 'V Sunday in Lent' 1863; Leetham, *Luigi Gentili*.

[26] Gerald Spencer, *Catholic Life in Swansea, 1847–1947* (Swansea, 1947), p.20.

[27] John Bossy, 'The Counter-Reformation and the people of Catholic Ireland, 1596–1641', in T. D Williams (ed.), *Historical Studies*, VIII (Dublin 1971), 162.

This double separation of emigration and death allowed little space for emotional recovery. To one bereaved Irish woman in 1854, the threat of removal to Ireland by the Poor Law authorities following the death of her husband was intolerable. 'My husband is dead and buried here and you cannot send me to Ireland', she protested.[28] Rituals of separation surrounding death were punctiliously enacted by kin who sought to reaffirm the unity of the group in the face of the death of a relation or friend.

The church aimed to cultivate a situation in which death without Catholic faith and the ministrations of an ordained priest was, in the words of Bishop Hedley, 'a dreadful mystery, and after death a blank'.[29] While stories about ghosts and other manifestations of the spirit world were woven into the texture of pre-Famine agrarian life, apparitions and visitations were not unknown among the Irish abroad. In 1880 Hedley had to deal with a Dominican nun who tried to inform the Pope of apparitions of the Virgin Mary and various saints at Pontypridd between November 1876 and the beginning of 1880. These apparitions, which the nun erroneously interpreted as a sign of the impending conversion of Wales to Catholicism, were apparently witnessed by a dozen people of all ages.[30] In the absence of systematic testimony, changes in the way people thought about an afterlife are impossible to document. However, it would not be unreasonable to assume that the decline of the Irish language among migrants, and protracted residence in an urban context, eventually led to a distancing from thought patterns associated with the 'magical'. For the town-bred second and third generations in particular, a spiritual experience was more readily accessed through the sacraments of the church than the world-view of a rural society they had not known. Even so, folk rituals surrounding death which did not bear the imprimatur of the church did not simply lapse or die out of their own accord; like other aspects of popular culture attempts to reform them were resisted.

In Ireland, Catholicism had failed fully to establish a monopoly over rites associated with the burial of the dead, and popular practice drew on elements of pagan folk-belief as well as

---

[28] PP 1854 XVII, Report from the Select Committee on Poor Removals, p.492.
[29] *Welsh Catholic Herald*, 20 June 1902.
[30] Sister M. Iltyd Morgan to the Pope, 23 August 1880, AAC, unnumbered box.

the rites of orthodox Christianity. It was the belief of organized religion that behaviour associated with these rituals was inconsistent with a Christian burial that fired the zeal of reforming priests. Central to the Irish peasantry's accommodation with bereavement was the wake. Despite clerical disapproval since at least the seventeenth century, the wake continued to flourish in early nineteenth-century Ireland. To an outsider, the practice appeared to deny the emotions of grief and sadness. 'The wake of a corpse', wrote Thomas Crofton Croker in 1824, 'is a scene of merriment rather than of mourning.'[31] The wake consisted of a gathering in the house of the dead person where family, friends and other local people congregated to pay their respects, tell stories and play games during the long hours of the night.

When the Irish emigrated they continued to wake their dead.[32] When Joseph Keating recalled the death of his grandmother in the Welsh mining village of Mountain Ash in the 1870s, he described an event similar to that observed by Crofton Croker in the Irish countryside half a century earlier. It is the most detailed description of Irish wake ceremonial in Wales to have survived. 'At the wake', wrote Keating,

> we played games and told tales of enchantments. When an Irish Catholic died in The Barracks [the Irish locality] – either a natural death at home or a violent death in the mines – all who could attended the wake. Our kitchen was crowded with men and women, young and old, till three o'clock in the morning. Two lighted candles were at my grandmother's head and another at her feet. On a table near her were saucers of red snuff and tobacco, and a dozen short and long clay pipes. We played Cock in the Corner, Hunt the Button, and told or listened to tales of leprechauns, giants, and old hags – wonderful stories that had never been written or printed. The characters in them often arrived at lonely mountain tops, so bleak and far from anywhere else that in those places the cock never crew, the wind never blew and the 'divil' never stopped to put on his morning gown.
>
> The tales enthralled me.
>
> A few of the people on coming in would kneel beside the corpse. As soon as their prayers were finished they joined heartily in the games. We talked

---

[31] Thomas Crofton Croker, *Researches in the South of Ireland* [1824] (reprint, Shannon, 1969), p.170; S. J. Connolly, *Priests and People in Pre-Famine Ireland, 1780–1845* (Dublin, 1982), pp.100–20.

[32] J. A. Jackson, *The Irish in Britain*, pp.50–2.

of everything except the dead. Good humour, humanity and religion were mixed together and the wakes brought relief and consolation to sorrow.[33]

Pat 'Kiker' O'Leary, born in Cardiff in 1890, also emphasized the gregariousness and play element of the wake. 'There were pipes and baccy and the quarts of beer flowed all night', he recalled. 'To stop ourselves sleeping we played hunt the button.' This game entailed one of the company having to discover which of the others held a button concealed in a clenched fist. On more macabre occasions the button would be found in the hand of the corpse.[34]

The conspicuous consumption of alcohol and tobacco at the wake was an act of sociability which served to reaffirm group solidarity in the face of the death of one of the group's members. A Tonypandy publican who customarily supplied beer for Irish wakes in four-and-a-half gallon casks before the First World War recalled:

> And they used to have the lid of the coffin in the middle of the room and anybody who went there to the Irish wake, you see, would go there, have a drink of beer and they would put some money into the inside of the lid of the coffin to help to bury him. And that's true, I saw that many a time.[35]

Thus the wake had a financial as well as a social function. When a member of a poor family died, the deceased's relations frequently experienced great difficulty in meeting the costs of the funeral. Often the funeral was delayed as long as possible until money could be saved, and the provision of alcohol at the wake was a convenient way of raising funds. Such practices were necessary where the deceased's relatives did not receive payments from a friendly society to cover the costs of burial.[36]

Catholic priests viewed the boisterousness of the wake with considerable misgivings. Such rituals excluded them from, or at

---

[33] Joseph Keating, *My Struggle for Life* (London, 1916), p.59.
[34] John O'Sullivan, 'How green was their island', in Stewart Williams (ed.), *The Cardiff Book II* (Bridgend, 1974), p.22; Seán Ó Súilleabháin, *Irish Wake Amusements* (London, 1969).
[35] Transcript of an interview with Mr Bryn Lewis, 28 January 1973, South Wales Miners' Library, Swansea.
[36] Burial societies linked to Irish friendly societies existed in several Welsh towns. See *Star of Gwent*, 6 December 1873; Fr Gerald Spencer, *Catholic Life in Swansea, 1847–1947* (Swansea, 1947), p.38.

best pushed them to the margins of, one of the most important rites of passage for organized religion, that of the transfer to the 'higher state'. As a result, the practice represented an implicit threat to the authority of the church. Death was the final breach in the group's ranks, and ensuring that the church dominated the rites surrounding it meant that Catholicism would play a key element in people's lives at a crucial time of disorientating separation. The priests' anxiety about their marginalization was compounded by an abhorrence of what they deemed to be the excessive drinking and unseemly behaviour indulged in at wakes. Drunkenness was now deemed unacceptable, and the play element which accompanied the long night's vigil was considered 'disrespectful'. Speaking of his arrival in Newport in mid-century, Fr Bailey called to mind the 'painful scenes' he witnessed: 'drunkenness at the christening, drunkenness at the marriage, drunkenness in the public streets, at most of the funerals and at all the wakes'. But by 1867, he maintained, 'drunkenness at wakes is entirely suppressed'.[37] It is likely that this success was short-lived, as the fortunes and influence of the town's Roman Catholic Association for the Suppression of Drunkenness declined in the 1870s.

Where the influence of Catholic temperance movements was more circumscribed, the clergy made fewer inroads into popular practice. For example, the story of the 'Lazarus of Newtown' fuelled their determination to reform what was considered disreputable and disrespectful behaviour. On the third day of a wake in Cardiff's Newtown district, a young widow entered the room where her dead husband's body was laid out, only to see him rising up from the table. This 'miracle' was produced by three tipsy men who had tied a rope around the corpse and pulled it into a sitting position as the door opened. As a result of this incident, the parish priest attempted to prohibit drinking at local wakes, although with what degree of success is open to question.[38]

In their campaign to suppress wakes Catholic clergy found a somewhat unlikely ally in the Medical Officer of Health at Cardiff. During an outbreak of scarlatina in 1875, H. J. Paine

---

[37] *Monmouthshire Merlin*, 6 July 1867.
[38] O'Sullivan, 'How green was their island', p.23.

discovered that the difficulties experienced in isolating patients in overcrowded working-class areas were compounded by the Irish practice of holding a wake over the corpses of those who had died from the disease. Paine sought and received the assistance of the Catholic clergy vigorously to discourage the practice, but in many cases even this was insufficient to persuade families that the custom could be dangerous and should be discontinued. Recalcitrant households were threatened with removal of the diseased corpse to the public mortuary under a magistrate's order unless they co-operated; in all cases the threat itself was sufficient to achieve the desired result.[39] Critics of overcrowding in British towns noticed the tendency of the poor in general to retain the corpse longer than was strictly necessary before burial took place, thereby prolonging contact between the dead and the living.[40] Attacks on the wake provided an opportunity to reduce the time between death and the interment of the body.

In contrast with the jocularity of the wake, the corpse in Ireland would be accompanied to the grave by keening. This practice was succinctly described by Arthur Young in his tour of Ireland between 1776 and 1779: 'both men and women, particularly the latter, are hired to cry, that is to howl the corps to the grave, which they do in a most horrid manner.' By 1824 Thomas Crofton Croker found that the practice was in decline.[41] A public ritual such as keening – as ostentatious in its grief as was the wake in its merriment – was at a discount in urban Wales where the sensibilities of Welsh people might be offended by vocal demonstrations of grief in public. Some demonstrations of grief reminiscent of keening did occur. One of these took place in Cardiff in 1862, when a family of Irish immigrants were suffocated in their beds by the fumes of a charcoal fire; according to one report, the other residents of the house were roused by the 'peculiar funeral wail of the startled and affrighted relative'.[42]

---

[39] H. J. Paine, *The Officer of Health's Report on the Sanitary Condition of Cardiff During the Year 1875* (Cardiff, 1876), p.25; *idem, The Officer of Health's Report on the Sanitary Condition of Cardiff During the Year 1876* (Cardiff, 1877), pp.21–2.

[40] W. H. Michael, 'The influence of habitation on the community: overcrowding in dwellings', *Transactions of the National Association for the Promotion of the Social Sciences, 1857* (London, 1858).

[41] Arthur Young, *A Tour in Ireland . . . in the Years 1776, 1777 and 1778, and Brought Down to the End of 1779* (ed. A. W. Hutton, 1892), Part 1, p.249; T. Crofton Croker, *Researches*, pp.172–3.

[42] *Reformer and South Wales Times*, 14 February 1862.

This example does not replicate the ritual described by observers of Irish peasant life and the evidence that keening survived emigration is scarce.

Emigrants' funeral customs impinged on the public domain in other ways. The place of burial was a cause of concern to immigrants, who were as particular about their place of burial in Wales as, reportedly, they had been in Ireland. In 1850 the Anglican vicar of Wrexham found that his churchyard was 'rather crowded on the lower or eastern side, and has chiefly been appropriated for the burial of paupers and Irish residents, who would rather carry their dead to Chester, than not be allowed to bury in this old yard'. His opinion was supported by the clerk to the local registrar.[43] With the opening of municipal cemeteries, where separate sections of the burial ground were set aside for the Anglican, Catholic and Nonconformist denominations, the question of where an interment took place was assimilated to organized religion.

The Burials Beyond the Metropolis Act of 1853 provided for establishing local burial boards to allocate space in new municipal cemeteries to both the Established Church and Dissenters. In October 1853 the joint Newport and St Woolos Burial Board in Monmouthshire was the first in Britain to be set up under the Act, and its deliberations proved to be a fecund source of local disharmony. Purchasing land for the proposed cemetery was a relatively simple task. However, the division of the ground between different religious denominations was more problematic. For the purposes of burial, the board defined Roman Catholicism as a dissenting creed to be treated on the same basis as Protestant Nonconformity, thus requiring no special treatment. Spokesmen for the estimated 3,000–4,000 Catholics in Newport demurred, pointing out that their religion required the consecration of ground for burial and that this was best achieved by allocating a particular area for Catholic interments. This the Board fiercely opposed. Protestants were unwilling to cede control of municipal land to the Catholic church, a decision deeply rooted in anxieties about the encroachment of papal authority on Protestant territory which had resurfaced

---

[43] G. T. Clark, *Report to the General Board of Health on a Preliminary Inquiry into the Sanitary Condition of the Inhabitants of Wrexham* (London, 1850), pp.22–3.

during the so-called 'Papal Aggression' incident of 1850. After a protracted dispute and a petition by Catholics to the Home Secretary, Lord Palmerston, it took the threat of legal action for the Newport Burial Board to capitulate and recognize the rights of Catholics.[44]

A similar case occurred at Rhymney in 1884, when the local Board obtained permission from Whitehall to borrow £2,500 to open a public cemetery. The Marquis of Bute, a convert to Catholicism, who was to provide the land, stipulated that separate sections be allotted to the Established Church and the Catholic church. As by law this move entailed consecrating the ground and erecting a chapel, the clause caused great controversy among the majority of Nonconformists on the Board who were reluctant to deploy public funds to support either Catholicism or Anglicanism. Eventually, the motion was passed by one vote in the teeth of tenacious opposition.[45] Here again, the issue of Irish burial places was assimilated to denominational rivalry. Elsewhere the matter was resolved in more amicable ways. When the municipal cemetery at Cardiff was laid out in 1859, the Corporation not only allotted a large and well-situated section for Catholic use, but it also erected a substantial Catholic Mortuary Chapel. In 1879 additional land was set apart for Catholic use and in 1885 a bronze bell was added to the chapel at the Corporation's expense.[46]

Marriage

Marriage according to orthodox Catholic rites was considered desirable by the church for a number of reasons. Doctrinally, it considered marriage a sacrament as well as a civil contract, a position which prevented the acceptance of divorce.[47] In a society with a plurality of religions, the undermining of

[44] For the debate, see the *Star of Gwent*, 6, 20 May, 12 August 1854. Also John Wilson, *Art and Society in Newport: James Flewitt Mullock and the Victorian Achievement* (Newport, 1993), pp.18–19.

[45] Thomas Jones, *Rhymney Memories* (Newtown, 1938), pp.99–100.

[46] *St Peter's Magazine*, VIII (1927), 138; J. H. Matthews (ed.), *Cardiff Records*, vol.IV (Cardiff, 1903), p.511; *idem, Cardiff Records*, vol.V (Cardiff, 1905), pp.22–3.

[47] For a statement of this position, see the letter signed by the bishops of England and Wales, 11 April 1866, printed in the Appendix to the Report of the Royal Commission on the Laws of Marriage, PP 1867–8 XXXII, p.43.

Catholicism by intermarriage was always potentially present, even if at times this threat was greatly exaggerated. Marriage within the church strengthened the ethnic solidarity of immigrant settlements by creating a network of interlocking kinship groups. By this process the role of the church itself among the Irish would be strengthened.[48] Consequently, the church expended considerable amounts of energy on its attempts to enforce orthodox rites of marriage.

Non-Irish Catholic priests in Wales were frequently presented with the problem of unorthodox practices which the Irish claimed would have been acceptable in Ireland. In 1846 Fr Joseph Jones of Henblas, near Abergele in north Wales, sought advice from the bishop as to whether he should officiate at a private service in the bride's house without prior publicity, 'as it is customary in Ireland'.[49] Reading the banns ('publicity') was a customary way of involving kin and the wider community in marriage, and the attempt to restrict the service to a private, unannounced event clearly struck Fr Jones as being in some way improper. In 1855 Fr Lewis Havard of Brecon was presented with a thornier problem. Some years earlier, an Irish woman in his congregation had been forced to take part in a Protestant marriage ceremony in Ireland, although she had never lived with the man and never considered herself married. Now she wished to marry another man: could she do so? This was the question Havard put to the diocesan vicar-general, who inquired why the woman had gone through with the service in the first place. Havard replied:

the presumption is, I should say, that the intention requisite for the validity of marriage may not have been possessed on the part of the woman. And this becomes more explicable when it is remembered that the marriage thus contracted in Ireland would have been invalid. The woman not knowing the difference between circumstances of the two countries could

[48] Marriage vows pledged before a Catholic priest had no civil standing before 1837 and so the hierarchy instructed the laity to go through the Anglican service in addition to the Catholic rites. According to J. R. Gillis, many Irish immigrants disobeyed this injunction and satisfied their consciences by simply appearing before the Catholic priest. J. R. Gillis, *For Better, For Worse: British Marriages from 1600 to the Present* (Oxford, 1985), p.205.

[49] Fr Joseph Jones to Bishop Brown, 16 November 1846, AAC, box 110.

well be under the impression that a marriage in a Protestant Church and before a Protestant clergyman would be invalid.[50]

Vexatious problems of this kind caused the clergy headaches, but it was with the more pressing question of mixed marriages – that is, marriages between Catholics and members of other religious bodies – that a good deal of diocesan correspondence was concerned.

A number of conditions had to be met before the Catholic church would approve a mixed marriage. It sought an undertaking that the Catholic party would be allowed free exercise of his or her religion and that any children would be baptized and brought up in the Catholic faith. This verbal undertaking was given voluntarily by the non-Catholic party and the church had no means of enforcing it thereafter. Approval for mixed marriages was usually granted speedily. Nevertheless, even Bishop Brown felt he should consult Rome in 1863 on the propriety of a Jew and a Catholic marrying in church.[51] In the decades immediately following the Famine, it would appear that intermarriage between Welsh and Irish was relatively infrequent. Although there are no statistics to confirm this, qualitative evidence suggests that this was the case. After a Welshman was murdered by an Irish navvy at Swansea in 1848, an anonymous threatening letter demanding revenge was pushed under the door of a Welshman whose daughter had married an Irishman.[52] The incident demonstrates that while intermarriage took place at that time, the attempted intimidation of only one house suggests that it was not widespread. However, given the demographic imbalance between males and females in the Irish community, it is questionable whether strict endogamy was a realistic option in the long term. In all major towns of south Wales, and especially in the iron-producing town of Merthyr Tydfil, there was a predominance of Irish males over females.[53] As one social

---

[50] Correspondence between Fr Lewis Havard and the Very Revd J. Wilson, one letter undated, the other 1 March 1855, AAC, box 116.

[51] Bishop Brown to Fr Signini, 3 September 1863, AAC: 'In one case a dispensation was granted for a marriage that had been contracted with a Unitarian – but I know not whether a marriage with a Jew had been tolerated.'

[52] *Cambrian*, 19 May 1848.

[53] Colin G. Pooley, 'Segregation or integration? the residential experience of the Irish in mid-Victorian Britain', in Roger Swift and Sheridan Gilley (eds.), *The Irish in Britain, 1815–1939* (London, 1989), pp.68–9.

anthropologist has observed, 'Ethnic groups . . . nearly always have ideologies encouraging endogamy, which may nevertheless be of highly varying practical importance.'[54]

In his study of Cardiff, John Hickey identified the last quarter of the nineteenth century as the crucial period for an increase in mixed marriages. This period also coincided with the intense debate on the 'leakage' of communicants from the church, an indicator of this being Bishop Hedley's influential pastoral letter on mixed marriages which was read from the pulpit of all churches in the diocese. In this letter Hedley reiterated the church's stance and warned Catholics of the potentially dire consequences for the church of sustained intermarriage.[55] But despite an increasing awareness of the problem, few parish priests registered mixed marriages separately. A more reliable impression of the incidence of those mixed marriages approved by the church can be obtained from a parochial survey carried out in 1890 in response to a request from Rome.

Replying to a questionnaire from the Sacred Congregation for the Propagation of the Faith, parish priests in Newport, Cardiff, Merthyr and Swansea outlined trends in the fortunes of Catholicism over the previous decade and identified points of particular importance.[56] The incidence of intermarriage varied from one town to another. It was estimated that one-fifth of marriages conducted in Catholic churches at Newport were mixed, and that 'not more than three or four' couples over the decade had deliberately broken their undertaking concerning religion. At St David's, Swansea, only forty-one of 305 marriages were mixed, of which there were six cases of parents refusing to have their children baptized and ten cases where the partners were converted to Catholicism. At Merthyr there had been only twenty-three approved mixed marriages during the decade;

[54] *St Peter's Magazine*, III (1923), 52–3; Thomas Hylland Erikson, *Ethnicity and Nationalism: Anthropological Perspectives* (London, 1993), p.12.

[55] John Hickey, *Urban Catholics* (London, 1967), pp.122–4; J. Wilson, *Life of Bishop Hedley* (London, 1930), p.119. Pastoral letters were also published as pamphlets, selling between 1,000 and 1,500 copies, which rapidly sold out, sometimes leaving Hedley himself without a copy.

[56] These replies are to found in AAC, box 51: Fr Cavalli (Newport), 22 April 1890; Monsignor Williams (St David's, Cardiff), 22 April 1890; Canon Richards (St David's, Swansea), 24 April 1890; Canon Wilson (St Joseph's, Swansea), 24 April 1890; Canon Wade (Merthyr Tydfil), 24 April 1890.

according to the parish priest, 'all we know have honourably fulfilled their engagements.'

Priests were unanimous in their view of the key role of women in transmitting the faith to children of a mixed marriage. At Newport it was believed that 'matters are worse when the mother is the non-Catholic. The children being mostly with her she cannot give them any true religious training, not having it herself.' At Cardiff, Monsignor Williams was confident that a Catholic mother 'would usually procure the baptism of the child stealthily if opposition were made', while Canon Wade of Merthyr summed up the prevailing wisdom when he opined: 'it is more difficult to keep children right when the mother is a non-Catholic, she having the complete early control of the children.' The marked matrifocal orientation of immigrant Catholicism is clearly discernible in these statements. The female role model presented by the church was that of compliance with the prevailing structure of patriarchal authority, which derived its strength in part from the image of the passively suffering Virgin Mary.

In discussing intermarriage, all these commentators recognized the limitations of their personal experience, concerning as it did directly only those marriages conducted in their own churches. Mixed marriages also occurred outside the church and without clerical approval. Fr Cavalli recognized that it was difficult to provide the precise number of such marriages at Newport because 'such parties carefully conceal the fact', but his inquiries led him to believe that there were only four or five per year. Monsignor Williams was more circumspect, stating that if a couple wished to conceal their marriage then the priest rarely found out. At both Swansea parishes there was an average of about five mixed marriages without church approval annually, while the number in Merthyr was double that figure. At Cardiff, Monsignor Williams observed that few Catholics were married at the Registrar's Office because church approval was withheld so rarely, a significant point when it is remembered that civil marriages accounted for 43 per cent of all marriages in the town in 1881.[57] Each of the priests who responded to the inquiry

---

[57] Olive Anderson, 'The incidence of civil marriage in Victorian England and Wales', *Past and Present*, 69 (1975), 72.

underlined the tentative nature of his conclusions, emphasizing that the mobility of members of the congregation did not permit precise statistical returns. In addition, the survey was restricted to the larger parishes with sizeable congregations, and it is possible that the experience of smaller Irish settlements differed significantly. Nevertheless, a clear trend towards more frequent mixed marriages emerges from these responses. It is also clear that many Irish people showed less concern about the possible religious implications of their actions than did the clergy. Monsignor Williams explained why this was so:

> the Catholic party rarely gives up the faith in theory, but not infrequently does so in practice, and becomes indifferent, especially if he, or she, has a genuine love and admiration for the other party. The argument in the mind is that if Protestantism can produce a man (or a woman) as good as the party admired, it cannot be bad.[58]

This was precisely the kind of reasoning which loosened the bonds of a tenacious adherence to Catholicism in some mixed marriages. Church commentators paid relatively little attention to the examples of non-Catholic spouses converting to Catholicism, although there is a suggestion that this occurred in some cases.

One of the defects of the 1890 survey is that it gives little sense of the nature and pace of change in habits over time. There are, however, some indications of the timing of a decisive change in the incidence of intermarriage in Cardiff. In the early 1920s a Catholic magazine which carefully monitored the largest parish in the city found the birth rate of 40 per 1,000 in a congregation of between five and six thousand 'a splendid tribute to the high standard of morality of our people'. Regarding marriage patterns, however, the statistics published were less encouraging. Mixed marriages had been increasing steadily as a proportion of the whole for some years, and in 1922 they exceeded 50 per cent for the first time. The editor drew his own conclusions about what was to become a more emphatic trend in the inter-war years. 'This intermarriage', he wrote portentously, 'shows that whereas a generation ago our people did not as a whole mix with

---

[58] Return by Monsignor Williams, 22 April 1890, AAC, box 51.

the people of this country, today the blending of the Irish and the Welsh is going ahead at a great pace.'[59]

Attempts to nurture regular devotions and a more orthodox form of religious piety met with only limited success. The Irish accepted those elements of religious dogma which appeared to be meaningful to their lives and which did not appear to contradict 'traditional' values. Often innovations in religious practice did not wholly supersede pre-existing patterns of behaviour but were superimposed on them. Nonetheless, by a tortuous process of confrontation, conciliation and accommodation, the nature of religious devotion and piety among practising Catholics in Wales changed perceptibly in the seventy years after 1850. It is far more difficult to establish with any degree of certainty to what extent this development was reflected in more regular attendance at church. Official statistics throw little light on this question. The bare details supplied to the Royal Commission on the Church of England and Other Religious Bodies in Wales demonstrates the Catholic Church's scant regard for statistical knowledge.[60]

Where statistics for individual parishes exist, they appear to show that Irish Catholicism in Wales consisted of a core of regular attenders fluctuating between 25 per cent and 50 per cent of the total, with a wider circle of men and women who attended infrequently, if at all, but nevertheless identified themselves as Catholic.[61] This was the crux of the 'leakage' issue: the majority of the Irish were not so much rejecting the church outright as remaining indifferent to its demands on them. Anxiety about leakage occurred in the context of a more general debate about the utilization of working-class leisure time, meagre though that was. Sunday closing of public houses in Wales in 1881 was a notable success in attracting popular support for a

[59]   *St Peter's Magazine*, III (1923), 52–3.
[60]   PP 1910 XIV, Royal Commission on the Church of England and Other Religious Bodies in Wales, vol.I, p.42 and Appendix L. In 1905 there was one priest for every 456 parishioners in Wales as a whole, whereas the ratio in Glamorgan was 1:1,060 and in Monmouthshire 1:720.
[61]   See Appendix VI and AAC MS book, titled 'Status Animarum'. The figures quoted here are not comparable with the Index of Attendance derived from the 1851 Census of Religion, as the latter does not provide percentages.

measure openly regarded as a means of social control. Other innovations such as the provision of public libraries and museums
complemented such legislation. Concern was expressed, however, that rugby football, boxing and other sports attracted the
working class at the expense of the chapel and more spiritual
pursuits. As far as Roman Catholicism was concerned, sporting
activities were merely one more aspect of the thickening network
of parochial activities, and parish teams arranged matches
against one another in a number of sports.

For the same reasons, the church placed the establishment of
Catholic elementary schools high on its agenda for retaining
working-class allegiance. After the passage of Forster's Education
Act in 1870, denominational education occupied an increasingly
contentious position in Welsh life. The schools provided the
principal avenue for socializing the Irish into a reforged Catholic
culture, and the clergy defended them with gusto. The need to
interweave nationality and religion in Catholic education was set
out clearly in a parish magazine which asserted, in 1895, that
allowing the new local School Boards to interfere in Catholic
schools would lead to the protestantizing and 'denationalizing' of
Irish children. 'Take away our religious training', it warned, 'and
the young, under secular and Protestant influence, will not only
grow ashamed of Priest, Faith and Church, but will also learn to
hang the head at the very sound of an Irish name.'[62] The extent
to which schools were capable of fulfilling these expectations is
open to question. Outside the large towns the most important
factor militating against them preventing 'leakage' from the
church was the incidence of geographical mobility in the Irish
community. A sudden reduction in the number of pupils following the departure of their parents in search of work elsewhere
could mean the school losing its government grant, thereby
jeopardizing the school's existence. The clergy's predicament in
such cases was set out clearly by Fr Fitzgerald of Cwmbrân, in
Monmouthshire, in a letter to the Welsh Department of the
Board of Education in 1895:

> As regards the future attendance, it may increase and it may not. Should
> the works in the neighbourhood go down, then this school would go down

[62] *St Peter's Chair* (July 1895), 127.

with them; and it seems most probable at present. The precarious state of work in the neighbourhood explains the apparent discrepancy between the numbers on the books of this school and the average attendance. It is a fluctuating population and so is the attendance at school . . . [63]

Even in the larger towns, school attendance by the poorer Catholic children at the end of the century was 'very spasmodic'.[64] Nevertheless, the church continued to expand its provision and redoubled its efforts to persuade Catholics to send their children to parish schools.

At the same time, alternative spheres of influence in which the priest had no purchase existed and developed in response to new social and economic conditions. At Rhymney in 1908, Fr Dent found that the congregations at his Good Friday services were composed of women and children alone. The Irish colliers did not attend because that day was treated as a working day like any other.[65] In the face of challenges from the secular world, the church sought to appropriate any independent expression of Irishness to Catholicism itself. As early as 1863, the parish priest at Swansea demanded from the pulpit: 'Can a man be accounted a true, loyal-hearted Irishman if he refuse obedience to his spiritual superiors?'[66] Evidently, the question was meant to be rhetorical. Fifty years later, at a banquet of the Irish National League at Cardiff, Bishop Hedley identified religion as one of the essential components of Irishness and advocated St Patrick as a model for the national movement.[67]

Some priests went beyond the mere identification of Irishness with Catholicism and demanded that nationality be subordinated to religion. 'There is a class', wrote Fr J. H. Jones of Caernarfon to a Catholic newspaper in 1890,

who want to be Irishmen *first* and Catholics and Christians afterwards; but this is impossible. The result of their attempt is that they are on the direct

---

[63] Fr Fitzgerald to the Board of Education, 6 February 1895, PRO, ED 21/22930.

[64] Attracta Josephine Egan, 'The development of Catholic education in Gwent, 1840–1979', unpublished University of Wales M.Ed. thesis (1979), 168.

[65] Fr Frederick Dent to Bishop Hedley, 6 November 1908, AAC, box 55.

[66] Archives of St David's Priory, University College Swansea, (8), Diary of Church Notices. *sub* 'Sunday within the Octave', 1863.

[67] Manuscript report of a banquet of the Irish National League, 17 March 1913, AAC, box 37.

road to immorality, socialism and infidelity. The true children of St. Patrick are Catholics *first*, and Irish afterwards.[68]

As a committed Conservative who had stood in Local Board elections on the platform of denominational education, Fr Jones's analysis of the articulation of immigrant identity was unashamedly political. His letter to the press was prompted by the election of the young radical Welsh nationalist, David Lloyd George, as the Liberal Member of Parliament for Carnarvon Boroughs on a policy of Home Rule for Ireland and as a determined opponent of denominational education. 'By helping to send George to Parliament', Fr Jones declaimed melodramatically, 'Catholics . . . have sent another Herod to slaughter the innocents.'[69] Jones was exceptional among Catholic clergy only in the venom of his attack, not as regards the main thrust of his argument.

Increasingly, the church intervened in the contentious and divisive questions of local politics, notably in relation to the funding of elementary education. The Irish were constantly urged to vote for candidates sympathetic to their religion, even where a politician's views on other issues were uncongenial to the voter. In many cases, these demands clashed with allegiances to Irish nationalism. In this sense, political action demonstrated the self-conscious articulation of immigrant culture and the often conflicting values of religion and nationality. It provides further evidence of the plurality of identity to be found among those who thought of themselves as being in some way Irish, and clearly exposes the limits of the achievements of the 'devotional revolution' among emigrants. Catholicism was a major component of an ethnic identity, but despite its strenuous efforts the church could not determine how all Irish people perceived themselves and the world in which they lived.

[68] *Catholic Times*, 10 April 1890: cutting in PRO, ED 21/21571.
[69] Ibid.

IX

FROM FENIANISM TO FREE STATE: IRISH
IMMIGRANTS AND POLITICS, 1860–1922

Since the middle of the nineteenth century, Irish Nationalism has been distinguished by the way it has embraced, and found succour from, the diaspora, particularly in Britain and North America. Events in Ireland continued to shape the political priorities of many Irish emigrants and their descendants in decisive ways, despite the fact that a large proportion of the second and third generations might never have set foot on Irish soil. Movements seeking outright independence from Britain, such as the Fenians, or merely a more limited measure of self-government within the Empire, such as the Home Rulers, found support among migrants whose romantic attachment to Erin was frequently matched by a readiness to provide financial as well as moral support. Those who settled in Britain in particular came to be valued by movements in Ireland as a useful adjunct to their activities. Irish leaders threatened to mobilize emigrants to chastise Unionist candidates in British constituencies with the 'Irish vote'. Yet, in spite of the persuasive rhetoric, it is questionable whether the immigrants ever operated politically in such a disciplined and co-ordinated a manner as Irish politicians wished or their opponents feared. Ethnic politics reflected the divisions and uncertainties which existed in other aspects of immigrant life and as such illuminate the way in which awareness of a particular definition of Irish identity was both cultivated and questioned.

Recent studies have emphasized the limitations of an ethnic identity as a basis for the political mobilization of the Irish in Britain in the second half of the nineteenth century.[1] The attempt to confine political activity to questions concerning the

[1] Graham Davis, *The Irish in Britain, 1815–1939* (Dublin, 1991), ch.6; Alan O'Day, 'The political representation of the Irish in Great Britain, 1850–1940', in Geoffrey Alderman (ed.), *Governments, Ethnic Groups and Political Representation: Comparative Studies on Government and Non-Dominant Ethnic Groups in Europe, 1850–1940* (Dartmouth, NY, 1993), pp.31–83; David Fitzpatrick, 'The Irish in Britain, 1871–1921', in W. E. Vaughan (ed.), *A New History of Ireland*, vol.VI (Oxford, 1996), pp.674–87.

governance of Ireland restricted the immigrants' ability to intervene in local politics by privileging the debate on national issues. The only concerted attempt to intervene in the arena of local politics occurred on a denominational rather than an explicitly ethnic basis in elections to the local School Boards established in the wake of the Education Act of 1870. Compared with the cohesion and sense of purpose of ethnic mobilization in some American cities, the Irish in Britain lacked a broad base on which to build.

Those who entertained the thought of mobilizing Irish voters in British elections in the mid-nineteenth century were thwarted by the simple fact that the overwhelming majority of the immigrants were excluded from the franchise on grounds of social class and sex. The same constraints operated against the native population, but the disproportionately working-class profile of the Irish ensured that far fewer of their number were entitled to vote. This handicap, combined with the recent history of the Great Famine, ensured that extra-parliamentary politics offered a more direct appeal to expatriates disillusioned with the status quo. There could be no clearer illustration of the alienation of the Irish from British society than the readiness of significant numbers in their midst to indulge in violent action on some occasions to achieve political ends. For the English, Welsh and Scots, a willingness by the Irish to explore this avenue reinforced and intensified entrenched stereotypes of the wild Irishman and supplied an additional pretext for denying the Irishman's ability to govern his own affairs. In particular, the activities of the Fenian movement in the 1860s and 1870s fuelled the host society's prejudices and reinforced a belief that the newcomers had to be monitored carefully for the slightest sign of unruly behaviour and sedition.

Fenianism

In the late 1850s there emerged in Ireland and America several secret societies committed to achieving a sovereign Irish republic. On St Patrick's Day 1858, James Stephens founded the Irish Republican Brotherhood (IRB) in Dublin, while early in 1859 the Fenian Brotherhood was created as its American counterpart.[2] The latter attracted large numbers of experienced soldiers to its ranks during the 1860s, many of them Irish-Americans who had fought with the Union Army in the Civil War. This transatlantic link, together with the support of some of the Irish in Britain, makes Fenianism a quintessential product of the post-Famine diaspora, and it ensured that political developments in Ireland in the second half of the century would have important ramifications for a number of countries. The movement harnessed and fed off the grievance of alleged British negligence and misrule during the Famine, that painful cataclysm which had been responsible for propelling so many Irish people abroad. A sense of exiledom found concrete political expression in Fenianism and served to accentuate the separateness of the Irish as a group who continued to fight the battles of their homeland instead of engaging with the political life of the countries in which they now lived.

During the early 1860s the progress of republican politics among the Irish in Britain was inextricably bound up with the National Brotherhood of St Patrick. This Dublin-based organization established in March 1861 has been variously described as 'a loose collection of people with nothing in common except the vaguest attachment to the principles of nationality'[3] and 'little more than a front organisation for Fenianism'.[4] Its aim was to foster a sense of Irishness by celebrating St Patrick's Day in an overtly political way and by encouraging cultural activities, including the reading of Irish newspapers. The National Brotherhood was fiercely criticized by the Catholic Church, partly because of its anti-clericalism and partly because it was an oath-bound society. Both characteristics were anathema to the bishops, although not all of the lower clergy found its aims and ethos repugnant. At Cardiff, for example, where the movement became active in 1863, its fortunes were inextricably bound up with clerical conflict. In May 1863 Fr Duggett, a former parish priest of Treforest in south Wales, now living in Birmingham, complained to Bishop Brown about his suspension from priestly

[2] R. V. Comerford, 'Conspiring brotherhoods and contending elites, 1857–63', in Vaughan (ed.), *A New History of Ireland*, vol.V, pp.415–30; Patrick Quinlivan and Paul Rose, *The Fenians in England, 1865–1872* (London, 1982); John Newsinger, *Fenianism in Mid-Victorian Britain* (London, 1994).

[3] Comerford, 'Conspiring brotherhoods and contending elites', p.426.

[4] F. S. L. Lyons, *Ireland Since the Famine*, revd edn (London, 1971), p.131.

faculties. Earlier in the month he had addressed a Cardiff audience – claimed to number 3,000 – criticizing the use of non-Irish clergy to minister to Irish immigrants, adding that the Brotherhood had arranged for him to speak twice again at Cardiff and once at Merthyr.[5] The question of non-Irish clergy had a particular resonance in south Wales, where the largest missions at Cardiff, Merthyr Tydfil and Newport had been allotted to the care of the predominantly Italian Institute of Charity (Rosminians). In fact, by 1864 there were more Italian than Irish priests in Wales, with a smattering of Welsh, English, Dutch and Breton clergy filling the ranks.

At Cardiff, Fr Signini wrote anxiously of the excitement and the spirit of discord aroused by Duggett's lecture. Signini had believed the Brotherhood to be extinct in the town, but the priest's visit gave it a new impetus: members of the Brotherhood had worked for Duggett 'with great zeal' and his visit led to the appointment of a local committee to organize meetings. According to Signini, £50 worth of tickets ('if not more') had been sold for the controversial lecture. There was also concern about Duggett's proposed visit to Newport, as he was billed to speak with 'two red hot Irish priests'.[6] One of these, Fr Patrick Lavelle of County Mayo, was vice-president of the National Brotherhood and a redoubtable opponent of the reforming Irish prelate, Archbishop Paul Cullen. Lavelle had challenged episcopal authority by defending the right of a downtrodden people to rebel against a tyrannical government, and the two had clashed over the proper behaviour of a priest in the case of the funeral of a Young Irelander.[7] By the end of May 1863, the divisions at Cardiff were on the brink of becoming irreconcilable. J. J. Buist, one of the town's few prominent non-Irish Catholics, demanded that the bishop take immediate action 'to check the insane efforts made here to alienate the Irish population not only from their local clergy but from the Government of their lawful sovereign'.[8] The bishop made no public statement on the matter,

[5] Fr C. Duggett to Bishop Brown, 12 May 1863, AAC, box marked 'Incoming Correspondence, 1861–3'.

[6] Fr Signini to Brown, 14 May 1863, and Fr Cavalli to Brown, 27 May 1863, AAC, loc. cit.

[7] Lyons, *Ireland Since the Famine*, pp.130–1.

[8] J. J. Buist to Brown, 27 May 1863, AAC, loc. cit.

but episcopal discipline would seem to have been quickly reasserted and the Brotherhood lapsed into inactivity.

More diffuse support for republican ideals was not so easily dissipated. During the following years, England, Wales and Scotland became the centre of the Fenian conspiracy as the movement made insufficient headway in Ireland itself. In retrospect, 1865 appears to have been the most promising year for a rising in Ireland, but the moment passed without action because of the leadership's indecision. In that year, James Stephens, the movement's chief organizer, based in America, estimated that 80,000 Fenians had been enrolled in Ireland and Britain, excluding those in the armed forces.[9] At best this figure is imprecise. A more detailed picture of membership figures in Britain was passed to the British Consul in Philadelphia by an agent in the Fenian headquarters there in October 1867. He reported that there were 3,000 members in Wales, compared with 8,000 in Scotland and 7,000 in England. Of these he estimated that approximately one in ten would be prepared to undertake 'special service', the Fenian euphemism for the destruction of public buildings and other diversionary tactics to be instigated in the event of a rising.[10]

The discrepancy between the figures for 1865 and those of 1867 suggests either the unlikely explanation that membership dropped precipitously in those two years or, more probably, that no reliable membership figures exist. Even if the latter is the case, the figure of 3,000 members in Wales is not improbable and is certainly consistent with other evidence. One particular incident strongly suggests that the Fenian leadership in Ireland did not keep a close track of recruitment in south Wales. On becoming assistant medical officer at a colliery in Abertillery in Monmouthshire in the late 1860s, Dr Mark Ryan, who had first heard of Fenianism when he migrated from County Galway to Lancashire earlier in the decade, wrote to the headquarters in Dublin seeking information about local Fenian contacts. He was provided with a list of names of individuals who had been active in the IRB in Bristol, whom he met and assisted in restarting the movement in that city. Ryan was unaware of the existence of a

[9] Lyons, *Ireland Since the Famine*, p.127.
[10] Charles Cartwright, Consul, to Home Office, 23 October 1867. PRO, HO45/7799/44.

Fenian cell only a few miles away at Merthyr Tydfil, and it is possible that the movement's headquarters possessed no knowledge of it either.[11] Local evidence demonstrates that Fenianism was strongly rooted in the towns of Merthyr Tydfil and Cardiff, with smaller pockets in other settlements. When G. T. Clark, a trustee of the Dowlais Iron Works, gave evidence to the Royal Commission on Trade Unions in 1867, he was questioned particularly about the Irish. 'I believe that they are one and all Fenian sympathisers', he stated, 'and I daresay they all subscribe, but I can only say they are perfectly orderly.'[12] His impression of orderliness was soon shown to be misplaced.

Following the indecision of 1865, the Fenian leadership decided that the rising would take place in 1867. An audacious plot in February of that year to capture Chester Castle and dispatch arms and men to Ireland by railway and ship via the north Wales port of Holyhead was foiled only by treachery within the Fenian ranks. The rising, planned for 4–5 March, was a failure and relatively few men took up arms. At Manchester in September, the bloody escape of Fenian prisoners and the subsequent public executions of Irish revolutionaries supplied the movement with martyrs.[13] Events like these greatly exercised the Welsh press, which was obsessed with the 'Fenian threat' in 1867. The *Cardiff and Merthyr Guardian*, which had praised the Irish at Merthyr for their 'civilised' ways in August, damned them in September as snakes who threatened the Empire. Angrily reacting to the Manchester outrages, it stated: 'We must "kill" the snake this time, and once and forever by a vigorous policy rid the Empire of the incubus that oppresses it.'[14] It was believed that the Brotherhood held secret meetings in south Wales, and towards the end of the year rumours of disturbances and revolt circulated unrestrainedly. Government instructions to local militias to protect their arms against Fenian capture, and the widely reported fact that revolvers were being issued to police in south Wales, heightened rather than assuaged local anxiety. Gunsmiths and ironmongers took extra precautions to safeguard

[11] Mark Ryan, *Fenian Memories* (Dublin, 1945), pp.49–51.
[12] PP 1867–8 XXXIX, Fifth Report of the Royal Commission on Trade Unions, p.87.
[13] Quinlivan and Rose, *The Fenians in England*, pp.16–75.
[14] *Cardiff and Merthyr Guardian*, 30 August, 27 September 1867.

their merchandise, and the guard on the Custom House at Cardiff was increased. Commanding officers of the Volunteers at Newport, Swansea, Merthyr, Aberdare, Port Talbot, Neath, Briton Ferry and other parts of Glamorgan also implemented extraordinary measures. When, in late October 1867, a detachment of troops from Pembroke arrived at Cardiff expecting a Fenian outbreak in the Rhymney Valley, it appeared that the worst fears had been realized.[15] It was a false alarm.

By the end of the year, fear of a Fenian outbreak in south Wales had reached fever-pitch. One alarmist report spoke of the inhabitants of Ebbw Vale keeping a night watch, arming young men and defending the armoury with a troop of the Monmouthshire Volunteers.[16] A letter to the *Merthyr Telegraph* from an 'Ebbw Vale Irishman', dated 22 October 1867, had already prudently claimed that there was 'no symptom of Fenianism' among the 400 Irish labourers there. 'Old sores have been re-opened', the writer lamented, 'hatred and animosity unparalleled have been created in the breasts of the Welsh and English towards the poor Irish.'[17] At Merthyr, police constables were armed with revolvers in expectation of an attack, while at Cardiff, Superintendent Stockdale was warned that a number of American Fenians had set sail for an unknown destination in the Severn Channel, believed to be Cardiff. Stockdale promptly notified the relevant authorities and two days later a naval gunboat was observed steaming towards Lundy Island.[18] No more was heard of the matter.

Mounting anxiety about the political sympathies of the Irish in Britain found some justification when a bomb planted by Fenians exploded at Clerkenwell in London on 13 December 1867.[19] The police in south Wales responded to news of this event by taking pre-emptive action. On Christmas Day they arrested two men at Dowlais who had been under police surveillance for some time and had been observed socializing in a house where the company sang republican songs and used 'violent' and 'seditious' language. Patrick Coffee, a tinman by

[15] *Cardiff and Merthyr Guardian*, 25 October 1867.
[16] *Y Tyst Cymreig*, 16 November 1867.
[17] *Merthyr Telegraph*, 2 November 1867.
[18] *Y Tyst Cymreig*, 16 November 1867.
[19] Quinlivan and Rose, *The Fenians in England*, pp.103–32.

trade, had been seen administering the Fenian oath to William Casey, who subsequently turned Queen's evidence.[20] Another eight suspects were arrested in dawn raids at Penydarren and Dowlais as they made their way to work on 31 December, while another one hundred Irishmen reportedly fled the area because of the arrests.[21] Their anxiety appeared to be well founded, as another two suspects were brought in on 2 January 1868. All fourteen prisoners were remanded for another week, without the police producing evidence against them. Inveterate critics of Fenianism were unnerved by the suspects' treatment. Even the *Merthyr Telegraph*, which found the 'unenviable notoriety' thrust on the town a depressing omen for the new year, believed that the magistrate had exceeded his powers and was open to accusations of breaching *habeas corpus*; it felt that even Fenians had a right to be protected by proper legal procedures.[22]

This cavalier attitude taken by the authorities to the legal process was a direct consequence of their belief in the gravity of the situation. Arrangements for detaining the prisoners were of an extraordinary kind. Pending a hearing at Merthyr on 6 January, the defendants were housed in Cardiff gaol, some eighteen miles distant. Rumours that they would be sprung from captivity, as the Manchester Fenians had been audaciously freed earlier, resulted in the enrolment of special constables to place a cordon around the building, the officers maintaining constant communication between gaol, police station and barracks. Nothing was left to chance. On the day of the trial armed policemen accompanied the prisoners to Merthyr, arriving on the mail train at 5 a.m. in order to avoid the large crowds of onlookers who gathered in the town at a later hour to witness their arrival.[23]

Of the fourteen men arrested, eight were charged with treason-felony, a charge which, unlike high treason, did not carry the death penalty. The trial revealed that the Fenians were organized

---

[20] *Merthyr Telegraph*, 28 November 1867. It has been suggested that Casey was an *agent provocateur*. See Ursula Masson, 'The development of the Irish and Roman Catholic communities of Merthyr Tydfil and Dowlais in the nineteenth century', unpublished University of Keele MA thesis (1975), 98–103.

[21] *Merthyr Telegraph*, 4 January 1868. The same morning, 150 special constables were enrolled to deal with disturbances.

[22] Ibid.

[23] *Merthyr Telegraph*, 11 January 1868.

in a cell, or 'circle', and were not lacking in military experience. Their military background was put to practical use by drilling Fenian recruits on the mountains around the town, and a fund had been opened to buy arms.[24] However, police raids yielded no more than one revolver and the material for making cartridges. In their defence, the prisoners claimed that they had done nothing of a treasonable nature, pointing out that their meetings had been convened openly at a public house. The defending barrister also questioned the reliability of the prosecution's evidence, reminding the magistrates that the principal prosecution witness, Patrick Coffee, had already broken his solemn Fenian oath and so could not be considered trustworthy. This appeal was partially successful in that it secured the release of Robert Barrett.[25] By the end of their examination, the magistrates had whittled the number of defendants down to two, namely, Patrick Doran and Patrick Ryan. Both men were remanded for trial at the spring assizes in Swansea in March, where they were both found guilty of treason-felony, Doran being sentenced to seven years' penal servitude and Ryan to five.[26]

Patrick Doran was the undisputed leader (the 'Head Centre') of Fenianism at Merthyr and he remained an articulate and self-possessed spokesman in court. Writing to a friend from his prison cell in Swansea, he displayed an indomitable spirit and unshakeable faith in the Fenian cause:

> . . . if it be my fate to pine in a prison pen in Pentonville, or Portland, or to toil beneath the torrid sun of an eastern or southern sky, I'll prove by my conduct how I can cheerfully, calmly and contentedly suffer, since it is for the cause of Ireland.[27]

Such fluency and eloquence signify a good education and a strong intellect; Doran was undoubtedly exceptional in his

---

[24] Ibid.; *Bristol Daily Post,* 7 January 1868. Cutting attached to the report of Thomas H. Ensor, Crown Prosecutor, to the Home Office, PRO, HO45/7799/346. The eight charged were Patrick Doran ('A' or Head Centre); William Holland ('B' or Captain), late of the Kerry militia; Thomas Reardon ('B' or Captain), believed to be a former member of the Cork militia; Robert Barrett, formerly a member of a St Helena regiment; Mark Farley, formerly a soldier; John Mara, formerly a member of the Kilkenny militia; and Patrick Ryan and Patrick Casey, both of whom had been members of the Wexford militia.

[25] *Merthyr Telegraph,* 18 January 1868.

[26] Ibid., 14 March 1868.

[27] Ibid., 28 March 1868.

determination and commitment as well as his leadership qualities. Many others joined the movement for the opportunities afforded to socialize in a congenially militant Irish environment, rather than for ideological reasons. While copies of the *Irishman* newspaper and seditious songs were discovered in the police raids, most Fenians would have been more familiar with the latter than the former. The Fenian circle met at the Exile of Erin beerhouse in Dowlais, where republican politics merged easily with conviviality. New members, known as 'friends', were initiated by taking the following oath on a religious book:

> In the presence of the Almighty God, I do solemnly swear allegiance to the Irish Republic now virtually established, and that I will be ready at a moment's notice to take up arms in defence of its honour and integrity, and to obey the commands of my superior officers; and finally I take the oath as a soldier of liberty – so help me God.[28]

Relatively few of those who took the oath did so in the belief that they were joining a disciplined military conspiracy, still less that they might be called on to fight.

Although the Fenians posed no significant military threat in Wales, reactions to the arrests in Merthyr and Dowlais exposed deep anxieties within the host society. Fear of Fenian disturbances spreading to Swansea brought about the re-forming of the special constabulary in the town in January 1868, with local notables such as Colonel Vivian and Major Francis becoming superintendents.[29] Working-class attitudes were summed up in the pugnacious words of an adapted music-hall ballad sung by miners from Tredegar who marched to Merthyr on the first day of the trial:

> Tramp, tramp, tramp, the boys are marching,
> Who comes knocking at the door?
> 'Tis the Fenians with their flags
>   But we'll tear them all to rags
>   And they'll never come to Dowlais any more.[30]

---

[28] *Bristol Daily Post*, loc. cit. Other versions of the Fenian oath can be found in Lyons, *Ireland Since the Famine*, p.125.

[29] Walter William Hunt, *'To Guard My People': An Account of the Origin and History of the Swansea Police* (Swansea, 1957), p.66.

[30] J. Ronald Williams, 'The influence of foreign nationalities on the life of the people of Merthyr Tydfil', *Sociological Review*, XVIII (1926), 149n. Knowingly or not, the words were sung to the same tune as T. D. Sullivan's anthem, 'God save Ireland'.

Fear of Fenianism was a minor, but insistent, theme in Welsh popular culture in this decade. There was great demand for 'Cân y Ffeniaid' ('The Song of the Fenians') in Merioneth in 1868, a ballad which began by referring to the 'Swarm of accursed rebellious and traitorous agitators'. Its popularity is puzzling given the fact that fewer than a hundred Irish-born residents were enumerated in the county in 1861. In the neighbouring county of Caernarfonshire, where the Irish were scarcely more numerous, the chief constable issued a request for special constables to come forward; within a month, it was announced that more than 4,500 specials had volunteered their services in the event of a rising.[31] This was a remarkable popular mobilization in support of authority by any standards. Indeed, it is remarkable how anxieties about Fenianism penetrated rural areas where even Irish harvesters would have been a rare sight. One example of this occurred in Radnorshire, where it is believed that the movement's activities influenced the decision to reconsecrate an Anglican church dedicated to the Irish St Brigid. These examples suggest that while there was some foundation for anxieties about Fenian activities in the towns, news of the movement precipitated something verging on a moral panic elsewhere. Fenians were lampooned in song even on the stage of the National Eisteddfod itself.[32]

Fenianism provided the Catholic clergy with an opportunity to demonstrate their allegiance to the Crown, thereby assuaging Protestant fears of a conflict of loyalties between the Papacy and the government. At Gellifaelog church in Dowlais, a meeting of 600 Irish people convened by Fr Millea condemned the Fenians and supported the church's denunciation of secret and proscribed societies. Other anti-Fenian meetings organized by the church were held at Cardiff (attended by a thousand people), Brynmawr, Tredegar and Rhymney.[33] The church grasped its opportunity to lead Irish opinion while Fenianism was on its

---

[31] *Carnarvon and Denbigh Herald*, 18 January, 1 February 1868.

[32] J. H. Lloyd, 'Cân y Ffeniaid gan Griffith Roberts (Gwrtheyrn)', *Journal of the Merionethshire Historical and Record Society*, VI (1969–72), 105; T. Thornley Jones, 'The "Llannau" of Cwmdauddwr parish', *Transactions of the Radnorshire Society*, XXXVI (1966), 23; Tecwyn Jones, ' "Ufudd-dod yn Barhaus": Welsh broadside ballads and the Irish Question', *Planet*, 33 (1976), 16–19; Hywel Teifi Edwards, *Gŵyl Gwalia: Yr Eisteddfod Genedlaethol yn Oes Aur Victoria, 1858–1868* (Llandysul, 1980), p.443n.

[33] *Merthyr Telegraph*, 11, 18, 25 January 1868.

heels, but it is doubtful whether broader Fenian sympathies were jettisoned so quickly. A sign of this is that in 1867 Catholic priests at Cardiff had found it necessary to enter into negotiations with local Fenian leaders in an attempt to allay public uneasiness which, if left unchecked, might begin to reflect adversely on the church.[34] Perhaps the Fenians recognized their own vulnerability also and sought a compromise with the church.

On the whole, the Welsh evidence supports R. V. Comerford's view that for the majority of its supporters Fenianism was a voluntary social movement posing as a military organization.[35] After 1868 the pretence of an armed rising was dropped and the Fenians in Britain found a focus for their energies in the Amnesty Movement, formed to aid Fenian prisoners. A pamphlet condemning the physical and psychological maltreatment of political prisoners in English gaols was published in 1869, although the government strenuously denied the accusations. A campaign to secure their release began in the 1870s.[36] Patrick Doran and Patrick Ryan, who had been incarcerated in Portland and Woking gaols respectively, received an amnesty in 1870, benefiting from Gladstone's abortive mission to pacify Ireland.[37]

The popularity of Fenianism among emigrants – whether they perceived the movement as a social phenomenon or as a military conspiracy – signifies the alienation of a significant number of Irish immigrants from political and social life in Britain. Adherence to the movement's ideals, with its total rejection of the British state, inhibited the Irish from participating in the campaign for parliamentary reform which gained momentum in the mid-1860s. Unlike the campaigns for parliamentary reform in the first half of the nineteenth century, the social basis of the

[34] Cardiff Diary of the Institute of Charity, quoted in John Hickey, *Urban Catholics* (London, 1967), p.145n.

[35] R. V. Comerford, 'Gladstone's first Irish enterprise, 1864–70', in Vaughan (ed.), *A New History of Ireland*, vol.V, pp.435–9. Comerford points out that 'the conceit that Fenianism was essentially a secret military organisation was abandoned in Britain far more openly than in Ireland', p.435.

[36] Anon., *Things Not Generally Known Concerning England's Treatment of Political Prisoners* (Dublin, 1869); Quinlivan and Rose, *The Fenians in England*, pp.144–60; Leon Radzinowicz and Roger Hood, *A History of English Criminal Law and its Administration from 1750* (London, 1986), pp.418–39.

[37] With good behaviour Patrick Ryan would have been released in February 1872 and Patrick Doran in August 1873, but both received an amnesty on 29 December 1870. PRO, HO45/9329/19461 C (3); HO45/9329/19461 (130); P.P. 1871 LVIII, Return of the Names of the Fenian Convicts Recently Released, p.461.

agitation of the 1860s was narrower, and had the Irish wished to participate in that campaign it is unclear whether they would have been welcomed. In this respect, there is a sharp contrast between the Chartists' sympathy for the demands of Irish nationalists in the 1840s and the conflicting aspirations of British and Irish radicals in the 1860s. Following the controversy over the Education Reports of 1847, Welsh politics had been cast in the mould of religious antipathies, with Protestant Noncon-formist denominations sinking their political differences the better to attack the privileges of the Anglican establishment.

Electoral Politics, 1868–1914

With the demise of Fenianism in Wales, the Catholic clergy capitalized on their opportunity to fill the vacuum of political leadership in Irish communities. Some recently created institu-tions assisted them. In November 1867, Fr Signini had convened by private circular a meeting of Cardiff's Catholic voters, attended by approximately 150 men, at which a Catholic Electors' Association was established with an elected com-mittee.[38] The initiative was probably a response to the passing of the Reform Act of that year and provides an early example of how middle-class Catholics were beginning to organize politic-ally in order to promote their own religious interests. However, the Association could not be concerned solely, or even primarily, with Irish issues, because a number of its influential members were drawn from outside the immigrant community. Such organizations provided a political voice for the church which would often conflict with the demands of Irish Nationalism.

Unlike Fenianism, with its populist appeal, the membership of an association of electors was, by definition, circumscribed by the limitations of the franchise. In 1866 a mere 4 per cent of the population in Welsh boroughs possessed the vote, a proportion which rose to only 11.9 per cent after the Reform Act of 1867.[39]

---

[38] Extract from the diary of the Institute of Charity, St Peter's Church, Cardiff. Reproduced in *St. Peter's Chair, II* (December 1889), 289.

[39] I. G. Jones, 'Parliament and people in mid-nineteenth century Wales', in T. Herbert and Gareth Elwyn Jones (eds.), *People and Protest, 1815–1880* (Cardiff, 1988), p.58.

This meant that whereas the culture of Fenianism was socially inclusive, electoral politics excluded the vast majority of Irish men and all women. In this context a great deal depended on the ability of political leaders to convince the unenfranchised that they represented all sections of the community; that is, they had to create a sense of political community in order to represent it. That this was not a trouble-free strategy is illustrated by an incident in Merthyr Tydfil during the general election of 1868. In September of that year, Henry Richard, the Liberal candidate, met the Irish to explain his stance on Irish issues. When he had finished speaking, a member of the audience read aloud extracts from one of Richard's recent speeches in which he had fulminated against Catholicism and, without waiting for an explanation, he left the meeting followed by some of the audience. However, after hearing Richard's explanation of his remarks, several of those who remained spoke in his favour.[40] It was a sign that some of the Irish were willing to embrace constitutional action with less reticence than the recent Fenian activities might have suggested, but it also signalled the existence of political divisions which would widen and harden in later years.

Catholic voters found a pressing reason for organizing electorally in the wake of the Education Act of 1870. The Act was essentially a compromise between the existing voluntary schools, provided mainly by religious bodies, and the new schools designed to plug the gaps in that provision. Decisions about local need and funding were taken by new elected local School Boards, and electoral allegiances in School Board elections divided along denominational lines from the outset. At Swansea, the church was quick to respond to the challenge. In 1870 the parish priest of St David's emphasized the duty of each Catholic to vote 'in the interests of his Religion', while at the same time he provided detailed instructions from the pulpit on how and where to cast the vote. In 1873 the congregation was told bluntly: 'Vote for Canon Price.'[41] It was common for priests themselves to stand in School Board elections, thus emphasizing the

[40] *Y Tyst Cymreig*, 25 September 1868.
[41] Archives of St David's Priory, Swansea, University of Wales, Swansea. Diary of church notices delivered at Sunday services, vol.9, *sub* 'Second Sunday in Advent', and vol.10, *sub* 10 and 16 November 1873.

denominational character of the contests while, in the process, blurring the distinction between the secular and the sacred domains. Equally important, it legitimized the dissemination of political guidance from the unassailable position of the pulpit; few other elected representatives enjoyed the luxury of delivering a political message in the knowledge that they would not be heckled.

Securing the election of a Catholic candidate was no easy task, as was shown by the first election to the School Board at Cardiff in January 1875. As at Swansea, candidates divided on sectarian lines. Perhaps surprisingly, Fr Hayde of St Peter's topped the poll, and the other Catholic candidate, J. A. le Boulanger came third. This remarkable result was made possible by an organized and disciplined use of the voting system. As there were eleven places on the Board, each voter had eleven votes to distribute among the candidates, and as only two Catholic candidates came forward, a Catholic voter could split all eleven votes between the two. Similarly, Anglicans secured places by limiting the number of their candidates standing for election, whereas the Nonconformist vote was split between seven candidates. The results are shown in Table IX.1.[42]

Table IX.1 Results of the School Board elections at Cardiff in 1875

	Candidates elected	Votes cast	No. of voters
Nonconformists	6	20,223	1,835
Anglicans	3	8,754	796
Roman Catholics	2	6,420	584

The selection of acceptable candidates and the disciplined coordination of Irish voters to support them were crucial if Catholic representation was to be secured. This was recognized in more explicit fashion in 1877 when an unofficial Catholic school board was established in Cardiff to work in parallel with the official Board in supervising Catholic education and fund-raising.[43] This

[42] Liam Joseph Affley, 'The establishment and development of Roman Catholic education in Cardiff during the nineteenth century', unpublished University of Wales M.Ed. thesis (1970), 95.
[43] M. J. Daunton, Coal Metropolis Cardiff, 1870–1914 (Leicester, 1977), p.144.

mark of independence helped to accentuate a separate Catholic identity in local politics.

During the next half-century, the clergy would be accused of dominating Irish voters in Wales by giving priority to religious matters to the exclusion of all else. In reality, their intervention did not go unquestioned, succeeding in exerting influence but ultimately failing to exercise complete control.[44] The clergy themselves believed that their influence in politics was beneficent and sorely needed by their parishioners. According to the reminiscences of Canon J. W. Richards of Swansea, the Irish lacked

> a centre around which to rally and this a resident clergy supplied, not by way of dictation from a pulpit, but of a fellow citizen of light and learning who could guide and influence them aright, and if they chose, would become the spokesman for their rights and interests.[45]

This rosy picture of enlightened paternalism is only partially borne out by political behaviour. The clergy did not provide the only 'rallying points', as is shown by the prominent part played by members of the small Irish middle class in municipal politics. James Murphy, who became the first Roman Catholic mayor of Newport in 1868, was described in the borough records as 'an employer of labour'; he and his brother were involved in a business connected with the railways.[46] Cardiff's first Irish mayor was P. W. Carey, one-time vice-consul for the United States in the town and subsequently a wine and spirits merchant. He was elected to the corporation in 1880, became an alderman in 1886, and mayor in 1894.[47] An Irish mayor of Wrexham, John Beirne,

[44] For two opposing views see: W. M. Walker, 'Irish immigrants in Scotland: their priests, politics and parochial life', *Historical Journal*, XV (1972), 649–67; and Ian S. Wood, 'Irish Nationalism and radical politics in Scotland, 1880–1906', *Scottish Labour History Journal*, IX (1975), 21–38.

[45] J. W. Richards, *Reminiscences of the Early days of the Parish and Church of St. Joseph's, Greenhill* (Swansea, 1919), p.14.

[46] Anon., 'Two Irish Catholic mayors of Newport', *Presenting Monmouthshire*, III (1973), 5–6. The Murphy brothers owned a business described in the 1870s as a railway wagon works and as a wheel and axle works. I am indebted to Chris Williams for this information.

[47] *Contemporary Portraits: Men and Women of South Wales and Monmouthshire* (Cardiff, 1896), p.x.

was appointed in 1877.[48] Others became officers in political societies and helped to agitate about Irish and Catholic issues by organizing meetings and electoral activity.

More than any other occupational group, doctors provided a secular counterpoint to clerical influence in Irish communities. In the late nineteenth century Irish universities produced a glut of doctors, many of whom sought employment in those industrial areas of Britain undergoing rapid growth.[49] The area of greatest unmet medical need in south Wales was that containing the iron-producing and coal-mining villages, particularly in Monmouth-shire, where there were too few Welsh doctors to meet demand. Some used this experience as a stepping stone to advancement in Ireland or in other parts of Britain, while others developed careers in the region. An example of the former is Dr Mark Ryan, a prominent Fenian, who spent a number of years as an assistant medical officer at Cwmtillery colliery in Monmouth-shire in the 1860s before returning to Ireland.[50] By contrast, Dr James Mullin of Cookstown, County Tyrone, left Ireland for Wales in 1880 to become assistant to a general practitioner in the valleys before establishing his own flourishing practice at Cardiff.[51] Colliery medical schemes provided welcome employ-ment for Irish doctors such as Dr Dwyer and Dr O'Sullivan in the industrial villages of Cwm and Beaufort in Monmouthshire in the decades before the First World War, and others were employed at Llanhilleth, Crumlin and Abertillery.[52] Against this background it should not be surprising that a woman described in 1896 as 'the first and only Lady Doctor in Wales' was Dublin-born Dr Mary Hannan, who had practised in India under a scheme for supplying medical aid to Indian women.[53] A small number of entrepreneurs, including figures like T. J. Callaghan,

[48] A. H. Dodd, *A History of Wrexham, Denbighshire* (Wrexham, 1957), pp.170–1. Beirne had come to Wrexham as a boy and subsequently built up a successful chandlery and brewing business.

[49] J. J. Lee, *The Modernisation of Irish Society, 1848–1918* (Dublin, 1973), pp.17–18, 33.

[50] Mark Ryan, *Fenian Memories*, p.49.

[51] James Mullin, *The Story of a Toiler's Life* (London and Dublin, 1921), pp.143–53, 159ff.; Peter H. Thomas, 'Medical men of Glamorgan: James Mullin of Cardiff, 1846–1919', in Stewart Williams (ed.), *Glamorgan Historian*, 10, pp.94–126; John Denvir, *The Life Story of an Old Rebel* (Dublin, 1910), pp.177–8.

[52] Ray Earwicker, 'Miners' medical services before the First World War: the south Wales coalfield', *Llafur*, 3, 2 (1981), 44; Fr O'Donaghue to Bishop Hedley, 31 March 1908, AAC, box 96.

[53] *Contemporary Portraits*, p.xix.

Charles P. O'Callaghan and S. Henry Callaghan, were exporters who achieved prominence in the coal industry by the end of the nineteenth century. Competition – and sometimes open conflict – between these different groups for status and parity of esteem in the eyes of the wider Irish community and the host society surfaced regularly.

At the same time as the Catholic church was mobilizing support in defence of Catholic schools, Irish Nationalists also became aware of the benefits of organizing the emigrant vote. Home Rule Associations grew up independently in all major British towns, and through the efforts of John Barry of Manchester they were welded into a country-wide organization in 1873. Down to 1914, the organization underwent several changes in name according to the prevailing fashion in Ireland: the Home Rule Confederation of Great Britain, the Irish National Land League of Great Britain, the Irish National League of Great Britain, and the United Irish League of Great Britain.[54] In Ireland, Isaac Butt's Home Government Association was replaced by the Home Rule League in 1873, while the return of fifty-nine Home Rulers to Westminster the following year ended the Liberal–Conservative duopoly in Irish politics.

Irish issues figured prominently in Welsh politics, and particularly in those towns with sizeable Irish populations. Parliamentary candidates were pressed by Irish electors to explain their own positions on Ireland, on the understanding that the nature of their response might influence how the Irish vote was cast locally. Yet, as was to become clear, the assumption that Irish voters formed a unified, disciplined bloc, unswervingly committed to the cause of Nationalist politics, was deeply flawed. The fault line, fracturing any unity of purpose in the immigrant community, lay along the divide between an aspiration to settle the problems of their homeland and a determination to influence the society in which they now lived. At times during the following decades that divide became an unbridgeable chasm. The dilemma stemmed in part from the insistence of the clergy to give religion an unquestioned priority in politics, whereas others demanded that Irish self-government was of foremost

---

[54] Denvir, *Life Story of an Old Rebel*, pp.172–3; O'Day, 'The political representation of the Irish in Great Britain, 1850–1940'.

importance. These conflicts and contradictions were played out in immigrant politics and achieved their clearest public expression during election campaigns.

Against the background of the failure of Gladstone's portentous mission to pacify Ireland, Liberal candidates in the general election of 1874 were at pains to emphasize their party's positive contributions to Irish life. At Merthyr Tydfil, Henry Richard, the sitting Liberal MP, spoke of Gladstone's 'useful' Irish legislation, and a Liberal newspaper reminded the voters of Newport, Swansea and Cardiff that the Liberal Party had removed the Protestant supremacy in Ireland and established tenant right.[55] But the issue of denominational education reared its head once again. At Cardiff, a group of Irish electors scrutinized the Liberal candidate's views on Home Rule and found them satisfactory, although they disagreed with his views on education. A report that a local priest, Fr Lockhart, had issued a manifesto supporting the Conservative incensed the Liberal press. Lockhart's right to advise and counsel his parishioners was conceded, but by placarding the town in favour of a particular candidate Liberals claimed that he had overstepped the bounds of his legitimate jurisdiction. A meeting of only forty Catholic voters chaired by Fr Lockhart was contrasted with a 'monster demonstration' organized by the Irish Home Rule Association in favour of the Liberal candidate.[56]

That the Irish had not voted in unison was demonstrated by the election results. Of the parliamentary seats with large concentrations of Irish voters, the Liberals were safe at Merthyr Tydfil and Swansea, scraped home by a mere nine votes in Cardiff, and were defeated in Monmouth Boroughs (which included the town of Newport). It appeared that the Irish at Newport and (in spite of the hopeful boasts of the Liberal press) a large proportion of their countrymen at Cardiff, had voted for the Conservatives. The *South Wales Daily News* contemptuously rebuked them: 'They have aided to build up a strong Tory majority and now they are kicked aside like an old scaffolding which, although essential in the construction is worthless and

[55] *South Wales Daily News*, 28 January, 3 February 1874.
[56] Ibid., 29, 30 January, 4, 10, 11 February 1874.

unsightly when the building is completed.'[57] A perception of the Irish vote as large enough to influence the outcome of parliamentary elections was accepted almost unquestioningly. Nevertheless, newspaper coverage of elections in the late nineteenth century is strongly suggestive of a politically divided and even fickle section of the electorate.

The principal reason for this was that conflicting appeals to Irish loyalties by the Catholic clergy and Irish Nationalists were compounded by party political divides. As a rule of thumb, the Liberal Party was more sympathetic to Irish reform and, eventually, Home Rule than was the Conservative Party. But Liberals were distinctly cool and often antagonistic to the claims of Catholics to rate-funded denominational education. The support of Protestant Nonconformity was too valuable to the Liberal Party for it to compromise on an issue like education which stirred deep passions. On the other hand, the Conservative Party loudly proclaimed its support for Catholic education at the same time as it resisted any reforms which could be construed as weakening the unity of the British state. Irish voters in British constituencies were thus required to make difficult choices.

This dilemma was most apparent in Cardiff during the 1880s, although similar divisions were visible elsewhere in Wales. The Conservative government's Irish policy was made a prominent issue in the election of 1880 by the prime minister, Benjamin Disraeli, and it elicited a spirited response from the Irish Home Rule Confederation of Great Britain. The Confederation's advice to the Irish in Britain was simple: 'Vote against Benjamin Disraeli, as you would vote against the mortal enemy of your country and your race.'[58] In response, the Liberal candidate at Cardiff, E. J. Reed, was quick to declare his sympathy for Irish interests, although he spoiled the gesture by immediately dismissing the possibility of entering into 'any pledges that might coerce my judgement hereafter'.[59] At the same time, the Conservative *Western Mail* attempted to shift attention from national issues to local concerns, claiming that 'The Liberals had persistently

---

[57] Ibid., 20 February 1874. See also: Iwan Humphreys, 'Cardiff politics, 1850–74', in Stewart Williams (ed.), *Glamorgan Historian*, 8, pp.105–20.

[58] *South Wales Daily News*, 9, 11 March 1880.

[59] Ibid., 11 March 1880.

excluded their [the Irish] representatives from every position of honour' and that they had attempted to prevent a Catholic woman from working as a nurse in the local pauper hospital.[60]

Evidence that the Tories could command well-organized support among the Irish first became evident on 14 March 1880, when the Catholic Registration Association convened a meeting of 600 voters who pledged their votes to the Conservative candidate. Alarm at the news of this meeting prompted the Executive Committee of the Home Rule Confederation in London to send A. M. Sullivan MP to Cardiff to heal the rift between Liberals and Catholics. Claiming that the visit would be divisive, the Catholic Registration Association held an even bigger meeting.[61] This placed the Home Rule Executive Committee in a quandary. After lengthy deliberations, it was decided to cancel Sullivan's visit and to compromise by advising Irish voters in Cardiff to remain neutral in the approaching contest. This *volte-face* was an undisputed victory for the Conservatives. At a celebratory gathering of Catholic voters, Arthur E. Guest, the Conservative candidate, reassured his audience that, if elected, he would remember that 'he was not only the representative of what was called a Welsh constituency but that he was the representative of an Irish one as well'.[62] This ringing declaration made the necessary appeal to Irish sensibilities without encumbering the speaker or his party with specific promises.

The Liberal press fought back by emphasizing the class differences between Catholic spokesmen, such as the middle-class le Boulanger, and the working-class Irish. Two-thirds of the coal-trimmers and dock workers were Irish and, it was claimed, predominantly supporters of the Liberal Party, although few of them had been enfranchised by the Reform Act of 1867. All attempts to persuade the Home Rule Confederation to change its advice of neutrality failed, and A. M. Sullivan declined the invitation to endorse E. J. Reed's candidacy. In the event, the Liberals scraped home in the constituency with a majority of 348 votes (4.8 per cent), but in contrast with Monmouth Boroughs, where the Irish opted on this occasion for the Liberals, the Irish

[60] *Western Mail*, 11 March 1880.
[61] Ibid., 15 March 1880; *South Wales Daily News*, 20 March 1880.
[62] *Western Mail*, 23 March 1880.

vote in Cardiff was evidently split.[63] The dispute embittered relations between Liberals and Irish Nationalists in the town. While recognizing that some of the Irish had cast their vote in their favour, Liberals insisted that as the Irish contingent as a whole had failed to support them, the successful candidate would not feel bound to support their claims in Parliament.[64]

By this date, the Home Rule Confederation of Great Britain itself was riven with divisions, the influence of the Irish in Britain declining steeply between 1879 and 1883, when the land issue was paramount in Irish politics. Registration of voters had all but halted and the Confederation had signally failed to weld the Irish into a cohesive and unified bloc, while outrage at the assassination of the Chief Secretary and his Under-Secretary at Phoenix Park in Dublin in 1882 precipitated a violent response against Irish communities in some parts of Britain, including Tredegar in south Wales.[65] In these circumstances, it seemed prudent not to assert the claims of Irish Nationalism too loudly. However, Irish electoral strength in British constituencies was enhanced by the Reform and Redistribution Acts of 1884–5, which created what one historian has described as a 'political revolution' in Wales.[66] This 'revolution' consisted of the reorganization of constituencies, together with the enfranchisement of a large section of the male working class. On the whole, the greatest benefits were felt in the county divisions, while the more populous urban centres remained relatively disadvantaged.

The character of Irish Nationalism was changing also. By 1885 the Irish Parliamentary Party was more tightly disciplined than before, under the leadership of Charles Stewart Parnell, a shrewd politician who aimed to play off one party against the other to secure the maximum benefit for Ireland. This strategy prompted him to open informal negotiations with the caretaker Conservative government which remained in office between Gladstone's resignation in June 1885 and the general election of November that year. Parnell succeeded in winning some concessions from the Conservatives, and consequently exhorted the

[63] *South Wales Daily News*, 16, 19, 23 March, 3 April 1880.
[64] *Western Mail*, 8 April 1880.
[65] See Louise Miskell, 'Custom, conflict and community: a study of the Irish in south Wales and Cornwall, 1861–1891', unpublished University of Wales Ph.D. thesis (1996), and Jon Parry, 'The Tredegar anti-Irish riots of 1882', *Llafur*, 3, 4 (1983).
[66] K. O. Morgan, *Wales in British Politics, 1868–1922* (3rd edn, Cardiff, 1980), pp.64–6.

Irish in Britain to support them in the forthcoming election. Naturally, these machinations incensed Liberals in south Wales, who demanded that Parnell be 'crippled and outvoted by crushing majorities' in order to avoid the prospect of Ireland dictating policies to British governments. At Merthyr Tydfil both Liberal candidates in the two-member seat decried the Irish strategy, and Henry Richard went so far as to question in patronizing tone whether the Irish were capable of managing their own affairs should Home Rule be granted.[67]

Elsewhere, Liberals made determined efforts to win over the Irish vote in spite of Parnell's exhortation. At Newport, the Liberal candidate, with the backing of Alderman Murphy, reminded the Irish of his support for Irish causes. At Swansea, Lewis Llewellyn Dillwyn recalled his own contribution to the legislation disestablishing the Irish Church in the 1860s as evidence of his support for Irish aspirations, while at Cardiff E. J. Reed was characteristically cautious in expressing support for a measure of Irish local government. By contrast, the Parnellite line was forcefully put by J. O'Connor, the former MP for Tipperary, who on a visit to south Wales spoke of the need to make 'one [party] chastise the other' by voting Conservative.[68] More than in any other parliamentary election, the way the Irish voted had ramifications far beyond merely local concerns.

Overall, the results of the election were startling: the Liberal majority over the Conservatives stood at eighty-six seats, exactly the same number as that won by the Irish Parliamentary Party, thereby delivering to Parnell and his party the balance of power in parliament. As a result, extravagant claims were made about the influence wielded by Irish voters in British constituencies, Nationalists claiming that the Irish vote had been decisive in anything from twenty-five to fifty constituencies, the precise number varying according to the hubris of individual commentators. In Wales, the extent of the Liberal victory was impressive, with the Conservatives retaining only four of the thirty-four seats. Whether the Irish played a decisive role in any Welsh constituency is more questionable. In Monmouth Boroughs, for example, it was believed that the former importance of the

[67] *South Wales Daily News*, 27 August, 13 October, 11, 14 November 1885.
[68] Ibid., 4, 11, 12, 23, 25 November 1885.

Catholic vote had diminished in relative terms because of the general increase in the electorate; a similar change was reported at Cardiff. In the new constituency of West Monmouthshire, the Irish could only affect the size of the Liberal majority, not determine the outcome.[69] Other factors contributed to a weakening of the Irish vote. The rules of qualification were such that a frequent change of residence could disfranchise those who were qualified, in principle, to vote, whereas a successful challenge to an individual's right to vote in the registration courts could have the same effect. Apathy, partly a result of the legal difficulties placed in the way of working-class voters, also played its part.[70] These factors affected the Irish disproportionately because of the predominantly working-class profile of their communities, but few politicians felt sufficiently confident to eschew entirely appeals for their support.

The inability of Irish voters to turn an election result was demonstrated with great clarity in a by-election in Cardiff Boroughs in February 1886 when the sitting member, Sir E. J. Reed, was compelled to seek re-election after his appointment as a Lord of the Treasury in Gladstone's ministry. Despite Reed's heavily qualified statements on Irish matters on previous occasions, Irish support was forthcoming at an early stage of the campaign and undoubtedly contributed to his increased majority. The question was this: how many of those who voted Conservative in November 1885 had transferred their votes to Reed? Reed's majority increased from 140 to 863 and the Liberal agent calculated that only 300 Irish voters had changed sides since the general election. Moreover, Irish voters were said to be deeply divided between the imperatives of Parnell's electoral strategy and the political demands of the Catholic church. Of the 1,100 Catholic voters in Cardiff Boroughs, some 800 were Irish, and two rival organizations competed for their allegiance. Membership of the Irish National League stood at only 200, with the remaining 600 under the direction of the Catholic Registration Association, a body 'made a handle of by

[69]   Ibid., 23, 25 October, 25 November 1885.

[70]   For local studies which support this view, see: John McCaffrey, 'The Irish vote in Glasgow in the late nineteenth century: a preliminary survey', *Innes Review*, XXI (1970), 30–6, and Alan O'Day, 'Irish influence on parliamentary elections in London, 1885–1914: a simple test', in R. Swift and S. Gilley (eds.), *The Irish in the Victorian City* (London, 1985), pp.98–105.

Tory Catholics for Tory purposes', according to the Liberal *South Wales Daily News*.[71] This contest demonstrated that even in propitious circumstances the Irish vote was not decisive.

Gladstone's conversion to Irish Home Rule in December 1885 created a radically different context for Welsh–Irish political relations. Despite manifest divisions among Welsh Liberals on the issue, the singular personal affection in which Gladstone was held in Wales prevented many waverers from deserting him. This loyalty was put to the test when a Home Rule Bill was defeated and Gladstone resigned.[72] In the ensuing general election Welsh Liberal candidates placed Irish Home Rule first on their manifestos, although the innately cautious Sir E. J. Reed harboured reservations about the policy. In the months leading up to the election, clamorous support for Home Rule was to be heard on the platform and in the press. Some spoke portentously of a realignment of Irish and Welsh sympathies in order to allow both countries to obtain their different national aspirations. Tom Ellis, the young radical MP for Merioneth, personified this new spirit, and his views were nourished by the enthusiasm with which Michael Davitt's speaking tours in north Wales in February and south Wales in May, were greeted by the quarrymen and coal miners respectively. Although initially Davitt was sceptical of such an intervention, the response to his visit persuaded him of the existence of a kindred spirit among the peoples of Wales and Ireland.[73]

With Home Rule at stake, Liberals entertained the hope that the Irish in south Wales could be relied on to unite behind Gladstone. Prominent Cardiff Irishmen who had previously opposed Sir Edward Reed now stated their intention to vote Liberal. Even Councillor Carey, a staunch Conservative, was prepared to repudiate his party affiliation for this election, and the Catholic Registration Association also broke with its practice of exhorting the Irish to vote Conservative.[74] While support for

[71] *South Wales Daily News*, 1 March 1886.
[72] Morgan, *Wales in British Politics*, pp.70–4.
[73] Ibid.; Michael Davitt to W. J. Parry, 28 December 1885, 7 January 1886, NLW, W. J. Parry MSS 8823C. See also J. Graham Jones, 'Michael Davitt, David Lloyd George and T. E. Ellis: the Welsh experience', *Welsh History Review*, 18, 3 (1997), 450–82.
[74] *South Wales Daily News*, 18, 23, 28, 29 June 1886. The upsurge in ethnic harmony was temporarily marred by disturbances between the Irish and Welsh at Merthyr Tydfil on 21 June. See *South Wales Daily News*, 24 June 1886.

Gladstone united the Irish, some Catholics grew anxious at the long-term implications for Catholicism of this shift. Colonel Ivor Herbert, scion of an established Welsh Catholic family, drew Bishop Hedley's attention to the 'violent language' used by a Catholic priest in Monmouthshire which he feared would be detrimental to 'keeping the Irish within moderate bounds'.[75] Such protestations were in vain.

Any attempt to dampen political enthusiasm was hampered by the arrival in south Wales of a succession of influential Irish politicians, especially Parnell, who addressed public meetings in Cardiff and Newport in support of local Liberal candidates. At Cardiff, he was met at the station with great pomp and escorted to Dr Mullin's house in Cathays by a spectacular procession, which included the drum and fife band of the Irish National League, the Cardiff Hibernian Band and members of the Wolfe Tone branch of the Irish Land League. At the Park Hall, Parnell addressed a crowd of four thousand and an overflow meeting of one thousand people on the merits of Home Rule and the need to support Sir Edward Reed, whereas at Newport, he denounced attempts by the Tory candidate to divide the Catholic vote along religious lines and reiterated the call to vote Liberal.[76] Other leading Irish Nationalists journeyed to south Wales to bolster the Liberal cause.

In Wales, the result of the general election was a reaffirmation of widespread support for Gladstone's policies, although this was at variance with the result in England, where the Liberals suffered heavy losses.[77] The Irish in Wales rallied more solidly behind the Liberals than in any other election. Increasingly, Welsh Liberals acknowledged that settling the Irish question was a precondition for tackling their own pressing national griev-ances, such as disestablishment of the Anglican Church. On the other hand, Gladstone's forthright support for Home Rule

[75] Col. Ivor Herbert to Bishop Hedley, 19 June 1886, AAC, box 90. Herbert did not name the priest in question.
[76] *South Wales Daily News*, 29, 30 June 1886. According to Dr Mullin, Parnell habitually slept with a revolver under his pillow at this time.
[77] The results were 25 Liberals, 3 Liberal Unionists (two of whom returned to the Liberal fold), and 3 Conservatives. Morgan, *Wales in British Politics*. For a judicious discussion of the election riots at Cardiff where the crowd was described as 'a Parnellite mob' and anti-Irish prejudice surfaced, see Joanne Cayford, 'The *Western Mail*, 1869–1914: a study in the politics and management of a provincial newspaper', unpublished University of Wales Ph.D. thesis (1993), 367–84.

effectively bonded the Irish Parliamentary Party to the Liberals and restricted Parnell's room for manoeuvre. A new spirit of co-operation, known as the 'Union of Hearts', was clearly articulated by T. P. O'Connor, the Irish Nationalist MP for the Scotland Division of Liverpool:

> I need not say how delighted I am to see that Wales has remained true to the Liberal cause. The action of Wales, indeed, throughout the whole struggle has endeared her name to every Irishman. If only the rest of the country had had the quick intelligence and the quick appreciation of the facts of the case such as were displayed by Wales, peace and union of hearts between all sections of the British people would have been accomplished.[78]

Such cordial feelings persisted after the election. In April 1887 the Cardiff Working Men's Radical Association met to oppose the Irish Crimes Bill, the government's harsh response to the land agitation. Describing the measure as 'organized tyranny', they called on Welsh MPs to oppose it. Later that month, Sir E. J. Reed spoke in Cardiff on the same platform as T. D. Sullivan MP, Lord Mayor of Dublin, at a public meeting convened to denounce the measure. Other Welsh towns had already expressed their disapproval, but the Cardiff meeting was to start 'a wave of agitation to roll over the whole Principality'.[79] The government was to be left in no doubt that Wales took a unified stance on the issue.

An opportunity to reciprocate this goodwill and support was provided when the Sixth Annual Convention of the Irish National League of Great Britain met in Cardiff in October 1887. More than five hundred delegates and a number of Irish MPs attended what T. P. O'Connor described revealingly, albeit with some exaggeration, as 'the annual Parliament of the Irish race in Great Britain'. O'Connor informed delegates that the Convention had been held in Cardiff 'because we wish in this way to express our feelings of gratitude for the splendid un-animity with which the great Welsh people backed up the policy of justice to Ireland'. Implicit in his speech was a recognition that

---

[78] *Flintshire County Herald*, quoted in *South Wales Daily News*, 9 August 1886.
[79] *Western Mail*, 4 April 1887; *South Wales Daily News*, 12, 13 April 1887.

this unanimity derived from Liberal sentiment, a fact which compelled Irish people in Wales to make clear political decisions. O'Connor issued a special address calling on Irish voters to support Gladstonian Liberals in the forthcoming municipal elections, and at an evening banquet Alderman Carey of Cardiff was challenged to make his position clear after years of expressing sympathy for both the Conservative Party and Home Rule.[80] In the longer term, the conference presaged more frequent visits by Irish politicians to south Wales.

Political activity in the Irish community in south Wales received a fillip from the intense agitation of the mid-1880s. Public meetings, visits by Irish MPs, and the excitement surrounding the first county council elections of January 1889, all provided opportunities to organize Irish voters. Registration of voters was a crucially important aspect of this activity, because, despite the extension of the franchise in 1867 and 1884, there remained a number of pitfalls which could disfranchise a person who, in theory, was entitled to vote. The Cardiff Catholic Association was set up to address this problem. In 1874 there were between three and four hundred Catholic voters on the electoral register in Cardiff. By 1890 the number had increased to 1,330 on the parliamentary register and 1,361 on the register for municipal elections, 'though the Catholic population has not increased to any extent, if at all, since then'.[81] If the Catholic vote was not to be seriously depleted each year by unopposed challenges to the eligibility to vote, considerable effort and resources were required to defend cases before the Revising Barrister. Yet in June 1890, William Williams, the president of the Association, expressed the fear that both commitment and adequate finances to meet the challenge were lacking.[82] This situation is to be explained in part by divisions within the Irish Parliamentary Party, following the Parnell divorce scandal. By refusing to resign the party leadership, Parnell precipitated a damaging split, with opposing factions unreconciled even after his sudden death in October 1891.

At the parliamentary level, Irish aspirations continued to be frustrated. Gladstone formed an administration in 1892 with

[80] *South Wales Daily News*, 31 October, 1 November 1887.
[81] *Cardiff Catholic Registration Association: Report of Work for 1889* (Cardiff, 1890).
[82] Ibid.; see also Denvir, *Life Story of an Old Rebel*, pp.242–4.

Irish support, but a second Home Rule Bill was blocked once again by the House of Lords. Home Rule then faded from the parliamentary stage until the second decade of the twentieth century. These developments had consequences for the politics of the Irish in Britain. In Wales, the close ties between Irish Nationalists and Liberals held out a real prospect of the former being absorbed into Liberalism. One sign of this convergence was that the branch of the Irish National League at Merthyr Tydfil called itself the 'W. E. Gladstone' branch, and the League was consistently in favour of Gladstonian Liberals in Wales in the general election of 1892.[83] The only problem standing in the way of a complete merger was religious education, which remained a contentious issue in local politics. To some extent, local School Board politics displaced the 'national' concerns which had dominated the 1880s.

In a pastoral letter read in every church in the diocese in 1895, Bishop Hedley encouraged Catholics to mobilize for the forthcoming general election. Recognizing the fact that the majority of Irish Catholics in Wales now supported the Liberal Party, Hedley pointed out that 'a more truly liberal policy in regard to Voluntary Schools and other questions' would strengthen the chances of Liberal candidates. He drew attention to the case of one Welsh Liberal MP who had yielded to 'persuasion'. Sir Edward Reed held the marginal seat of Cardiff Boroughs and relied on an uneasy coalition of Nonconformist and Irish Catholic support to retain it – a coalition most sharply divided over education. Reed mollified Catholics by conceding the need for a 'fair distribution' of the education rate between Board and voluntary schools, while reassuring Nonconformists with the proviso that state aid should be accompanied by 'reasonable popular control of expenditure'.[84]

This weasel-worded compromise failed to convince Nonconformists. In order to extricate himself from a difficult situation, Reed sought the assistance of Dr James Mullin, a leading Irish Nationalist in south Wales. Realizing that the seat could fall to the Conservatives if either Catholics or Nonconformists were alienated, Mullin agreed to write a letter to Reed denouncing

[83] See, for example, *South Wales Daily News*, 4 April, 4, 16 June, 2, 4 July, 29 October 1889.
[84] *St Peter's Chair*, July 1895, 125.

Reed's claims to represent the interests of Catholic education and Irish Nationalism. Reed then circulated copies of this letter privately to those Nonconformists who had complained to him about his stance on education, thus avoiding the potential divisions which would inevitably arise out of a public declaration.[85] This covert stratagem is indicative of the extent to which Irish Nationalists in British constituencies were unable to adopt an entirely independent position towards the two political parties once the Liberals had declared their support for Home Rule. Even so, Mullin's complicity in Reed's machinations did not save the seat for the Liberals in Cardiff in 1895.

Other changes in the Irish community conspired to place religion at the centre of immigrant politics in Wales in the 1890s. An important means of expressing a community's identity in the late nineteenth century was the press, and until the 1890s the Irish in Wales lacked a newspaper or magazine of their own. Hitherto, they had depended on publications from Ireland circulating in Wales for an Irish perspective on political developments. This changed in 1885 when a monthly magazine, *St Peter's Chair*, began publication in St Peter's parish in Cardiff. It circulated throughout south Wales and dealt with all aspects of religious life, providing a forum for the discussion of local politics which emphasized the Catholic perspective. In 1898 it was superseded by a weekly newspaper, the *Welsh Catholic Herald*. Although the paper carried local news and a column in Welsh on its front page (by 'Gwas Teilo'), it was, in fact, published in London as one of twenty-three similar publications owned by Charles Diamond, formerly MP for Monaghan (1892–5). Diamond was the proprietor of the vast majority of Catholic newspapers in Britain. By the end of the decade, the centre of gravity of the Catholic press in Britain was firmly established in London, and it is significant that a very large percentage of the *Herald*'s content was syndicated. The newspaper's tone was set in its first issue in an article by Bishop Hedley which called for the paper to be a 'pious' publication, and by an editorial which

---

[85] Mullin, *Story of a Toiler's Life*, pp.193–6. This episode confirms K. O. Morgan's description of Cardiff Liberalism as a 'bizarre coalition', *Wales in British Politics*, pp.168, 181. On the peculiar character of Cardiff Boroughs, see Henry Pelling, *Social Geography of British Elections, 1885–1910* (London, 1967), pp.352–3.

stated that the paper would be 'thoroughly and loyally Catholic, not "Liberal-Catholic", or Catholic with any sort of qualification'.[86] Circulation figures for the *Herald* are not available, but it certainly sold considerably more than Nationalist newspapers: for example, William O'Brien's *United Ireland* sold a mere 226 copies in Wales 'in its best days'.[87]

Incipient political divisions among the Irish in Wales were soon revealed by the paper. By the 1890s opposing views on how immigrants should relate to the host society polarized around the extent to which the pursuit of Home Rule within the Empire should result in cultural integration or whether it ought to facilitate the assertion of a militantly distinctive cultural identity. Attitudes to the centenary of the rising of 1798 laid bare these divisions. Although the commemorations provided an opportunity for the reaffirmation of republican values, those values were recast and reinterpreted in the light of current preoccupations. Speakers at formal celebrations gave the impression that the United Irishmen were simply the forerunners of the Home Rulers, despite the irreconcilable differences between the aims and methods of the two movements.[88] This is demonstrated most clearly in a speech made by Dr James Mullin, JP, in March 1899 in which he explained the loyalties of a successful Irish Nationalist in south Wales when toasting 'the Queen and an Irish Parliament':

> in toasting Ireland as a nation they were not actuated by a spirit of hostility towards the British Empire. No section had done more to build up the Empire than Irishmen, and he trusted that they would always be able to take their part in the plunder.[89]

[86] There has been some confusion among historians about the date of the first issue of the *Welsh Catholic Herald*. Owen Dudley Ewards and Patricia J. Storey have suggested that the paper first appeared in 1894, although no copy for that year is extant. Edwards and Storey, 'The Irish press in Victorian Britain', in R. Swift and S. Gilley (eds.), *The Irish in the Victorian City* (London, 1985), pp.158–78. The same date is used by Beti Jones in the directory *Newsplan Cymru/Wales* (London and Aberystwyth, 1994), p.214. In his comprehensive study of the press in Wales Aled Jones suggests 1902 as the date: *Press, Politics and Society: A History of Journalism in Wales* (Cardiff, 1993), p.123. In fact, the issue which appeared on Friday, 30 September 1898 bears the imprint 'No. 1'; a copy of this issue can be found in Cardiff Central Library.

[87] Fitzpatrick, 'The Irish in Britain, 1871–1921', p.680.

[88] *Welsh Catholic Herald*, 4, 25 November 1898.

[89] Ibid., 24 March 1899.

At the same time, he expressed his outright opposition to the Gaelic League, which was then becoming active in south Wales and which clearly threatened the integrationist ethos of Home Rule politics. The affirmation of Empire and Irish Home Rule, on the one hand, and the cultural agenda of the Gaelic revival, on the other, marked out alternative visions of the future for an immigrant culture gradually finding an accommodation with the host community. The Gaelic League was established in 1893 to promote the use of the Irish language. It had no political alignment until 1915, but its ethos and activities posed problems for Home Rulers in Wales, who had discovered a bridge to the local political culture through Gladstonian Liberalism. This was particularly the case for middle-class Irish men and women.

Dr Mullin was not shadow-boxing when he denounced the League. A branch of the Gaelic League had been established in Cardiff only a month previously and classes in the Irish language were held weekly. Connections with sympathetic Welsh politicians were soon established. In March 1899 Edward Thomas ('Cochfarf'), chairman of the Free Library Committee, promised that books required by the Gaelic League would be purchased for their use.[90] In June, the same year, a deputation of the Gaelic League left Cardiff for the annual Gaelic festival, the Oireachtas, in Dublin, while in July Patrick Pearse and Dr Boyd represented the Gaelic League at the National Eisteddfod of Wales at Cardiff, where Pearse was invested as a member of the Gorsedd (or Order) of Bards under the title 'Areithiwr' (Orator). He announced that he had received the promise of support from the Welsh Parliamentary Party for proper recognition of the Irish language in schools in Ireland. Pearse, who was to be executed for his leadership of the 1916 rising, was particularly impressed by the bilingual policy adopted in schools in Glamorgan, writing about it approvingly in the League's journal, *An Claidheamh Soluis*.[91]

---

[90] Ibid., 17 March 1899.

[91] Ibid., 2 June, 21, 28 July 1899. Pearse's bardic name was particularly apposite. One historian has described him as 'a speaker of extraordinary power and magnetism', Lyons, *Ireland since the Famine*, p.333. See also: Gwyn ap Gwilym, 'Padraig Pearse a'r Eisteddfod Genedlaethol', *Taliesin*, 32 (1976), 87–93; Philip O'Leary, '"Children of the same mother": Gaelic relations with the other Celtic revival movements, 1882–1916', *Proceedings of the Harvard Celtic Colloquium*, VI (1986), 101–30.

These divergent tendencies were a portent of the reorientation of Irish politics after 1918, when the Irish Parliamentary Party was displaced by Sinn Féin, and the Irish in Britain were compelled to re-evaluate their own stance on Irish politics. In the short term, they were overshadowed by yet another educational controversy which gave religion renewed salience in political life and drove a wedge between the Irish and the Welsh. This was the notoriously bitter 'Welsh Revolt' which followed the passage of the Conservative government's Education Act in 1902. This Act invested local committees of county or county borough councils with authority over primary, secondary and technical education. Both voluntary and Board schools were to be financed from the rates, an arrangement which would provide Catholic schools with a more secure financial base. In the uproar which ensued, Welsh Nonconformists emotionally described the measure as 'Rome on the Rates', but their opposition was only given coherent shape and durability from 1903 by Lloyd George's skilful marshalling of discontent. Lloyd George succeeded in persuading twenty-nine local authorities to refuse to implement the Act in defiance of government policy.[92] This, then, was the 'Welsh Revolt'.

Catholic schools experienced severe financial problems as a result of the delay in implementing the Act in Wales.[93] The controversy turned on the question of whether finance from the public purse should allow local authorities to take direct control of a school's affairs. This claim – entirely repugnant to Catholics who feared for the dilution of the Catholic ethos of their schools – was openly stated as a precondition for the receipt of funding. At Treforest, for example, Fr McManus was informed that no money raised from the rates would be spent on voluntary schools in the district 'unless and until, the full control of such schools is handed over to the Committee'.[94] Catholics were indignant at receiving such peremptory demands. In towns such as Swansea, the bitterness of these years was slow to dissipate, and the education authority continued to display inveterate hostility to

[92] Morgan, *Wales in British Politics*, pp.181–98; G. O. Pierce, 'The "Coercion of Wales" Act, 1904', in H. Hearder and H. R. Loyn (eds.), *British Government and Administration: Studies Presented to S. B. Chrimes* (Cardiff, 1974), p.215.

[93] See, for example, Fr James Reilly to Dept of Education, 17 November 1903. PRO, ED 21/22535/03/8884Z.

[94] D. M. Jones to Fr McManus, 15 October 1903. PRO, ED 21/22661.

Catholic education for many years after the immediate problem had passed.[95] The episode demonstrates the continued potency of education in Welsh public life and the strength of mutual distrust based on sectional interests.

The issue was never properly resolved. The passage of a Default Act in 1904 intensified Nonconformist anger by depriving Nonconformists of the ability to make grants, on the grounds that Welsh local authorities had failed in their proper duties. The stand-off between local authorities and government had moved into a critical phase and it was only brought to a conclusion in December 1905 when the Conservative government fell. The deep emotions surrounding the revolt over the Education Act of 1902 undoubtedly gave a strong impetus to the Liberal campaign in the general election of 1906. But with the bitterness of the controversy still in the air, there was speculation about the allegiance of Irish voters. Only in Merthyr Tydfil were matters clear-cut. Keir Hardie had been elected there as the first socialist MP in Wales in 1900 as the junior member in a two-member seat. Although elected specifically as a representative of labour, Hardie was also sympathetic to Irish and Welsh issues, and he received the united support of Irish voters in the general election. Local branches of the United Irish League pledged him their support, and Michael Davitt visited Merthyr to speak in favour of Hardie's candidature at the request of Irish leaders in Dublin.[96]

Elsewhere in Wales, Irish intentions were by no means certain. In Swansea Town constituency the Catholic clergy urged their congregations to vote Conservative, while T. P. O'Connor MP and local nationalists advised support for the Liberal candidate. The majority of the Irish in the constituency voted Liberal, although it was said that 'they could not be depended on at the critical moment'.[97] At Cardiff, the disaffection of Irish voters over the Education Act cost the Liberals control over Cardiff Council in 1904 and led to uncertainty about Irish intentions in the general election.[98] In contrast with the perceived fickleness of the Irish vote, Welsh support for the Liberal Party was even

[95] See correspondence in PRO, ED 21/22737/8.
[96] *South Wales Daily News*, 12, 15 January 1906; *Merthyr Express*, 13 January 1906.
[97] *Western Mail*, 17 January 1906.
[98] Morgan, *Wales in British Politics*, p.219n.

more resounding than usual, not a single Conservative gaining election for a Welsh constituency in 1906. However, the Liberals' landslide majority at Westminster in that year served to marginalize Irish and Welsh issues as the government no longer depended on support from Ireland and Wales to remain in office. Moreover, Liberal MPs preoccupied with social and economic reform showed little interest in the old Gladstonian programme.

Paradoxically, it was the stubbornness of the House of Lords in frustrating reform which gave the Irish their next chance. Conflict between the government and the Lords came to a head in November 1909, when Lloyd George's 'People's Budget' was rejected, precipitating a general election in January 1910. By this time the split in the Irish Parliamentary Party had been healed under John Redmond's astute leadership, and the price of support for the Liberal government was an unequivocal commitment to a measure of Home Rule in an attempt to reassert the old agenda. In an article in the *South Wales Daily News*, Matthew Keating, the newly elected MP for South Kilkenny who had been born and raised in Mountain Ash in south Wales, demanded that Ireland be given a free hand to deal with her own affairs 'in the statesmanlike spirit of Mr Gladstone'.[99] Such an appeal had more resonance in Wales where Gladstone's stock remained high.

When Asquith announced his support for Irish self-government in a speech at the Albert Hall, the United Irish League of Great Britain promptly issued a manifesto stating that acceptance of this speech would be a condition of their support for Liberal or Labour candidates in British constituencies.[100] The United Irish League in south Wales endorsed this decision, although some Welsh Liberals publicly chided the League for sounding the first sectional note of the campaign.[101] Despite several losses in Wales, the Liberals continued to dominate the political landscape, but substantial Liberal losses in England meant that Irish Nationalists once more held the balance of power at Westminster. Home Rule

---

[99] *South Wales Daily News*, 8 December 1909.
[100] Ibid., 11 December 1909; United Irish League of Great Britain, *To the Irish Electors of Great Britain*, 16 December 1909 (copy in D. A. Thomas Papers, Cardiff Central Library).
[101] *South Wales Daily News*, 11, 28 December 1909.

was back on the agenda for the first time since 1892. Irish Nationalist organization in south Wales was reinvigorated by these events and the influence accorded the Irish vote grew as the constitutional crisis deepened over the summer. In September 1910, for example, the Cardiff branches of the United Irish League recorded a net increase of 211 in the Irish electorate as a result of their work in the Revision Court. Their confident progress was in sharp contrast to the declining fortunes of the town's Catholic Association, whose problems stemmed in part from the receding relevance of denominational education in parliamentary politics in the face of constitutional debates. The Association also suffered from acute internal frictions. Tensions between Bishop Hedley and lay members of the Association led to the bishop threatening to dissolve the body altogether.[102]

The strength of the Irish Parliamentary Party in Parliament during the run-up to the second general election of 1910 once again encouraged an overestimation of Irish strength in British constituencies, as had happened before in the 1880s. This was certainly the case with Francis Johnson of the Independent Labour Party. Writing to John Redmond in March 1910 about the constituency of Mid Glamorgan, Johnson averred that although the Irish vote was not proportionately as large as in other constituencies, it was 'still a factor of sufficient importance as to have a great influence on the final result'.[103] In reality, there was no basis for such an exaggerated claim, and Johnson may have been simply telling Redmond what he wished to hear. Elsewhere in south Wales the Irish were organized and enthusiastic, but once again were unable to prevent Cardiff Boroughs from falling to the Conservatives. Irish electoral influence appears to have lain more in a general feeling that they were an unknown quantity requiring appeasement than in the number of votes they were able to command.

---

[102] Thomas Jeremy to Bishop Hedley, 28 September 1910, AAC, box 70; J. J. Buist to Hedley, 29 April 1910, ibid.; J. F. Burke to Hedley, 2 May 1910, ibid.

[103] Francis Johnson to John Redmond, 23 March 1910, Francis Johnson Collection 1910/115. Microfilm copy in NLW. Before 1914 Irish support for the Labour Party in Wales was limited because of the fear that the party would split the progressive vote, thereby allowing the Conservatives to win. Merthyr Tydfil was exceptional because it was a two-member constituency, electing a Liberal and the socialist Keir Hardie in tandem from 1900. Labour had established a heartland in the south Wales coalfield by 1914, but Irish voters were relatively few in number in the area. On the rise of Labour in Wales, see Deian Hopkin, 'The rise of Labour in Wales, 1890–1914', *Llafur*, 6, 3 (1994), 120–41.

At Westminster, the results of the general election of 1910 presaged what appeared to be a final settlement of the Irish question. Reform of the House of Lords now proceeded apace with Irish support, on the implicit understanding that Home Rule would soon become a reality. The constitutional crisis was resolved by the Parliament Act of 1911, which reduced the Lords' veto to an ability to delay legislation for only two years; now, any measure passed in the Commons in three successive years automatically became law. A Home Rule Bill began this new legislative process in 1912 against a background of ugly disaffection in Ulster. The Government of Ireland Act, which reached the statute book in September 1914, contained two provisos: that it should not be implemented until the end of the war with Germany which had just broken out, and that it should not come into operation until there had been amending legislation to deal with Ulster. This delay proved to be fatal to the Act, because it was overtaken by political circumstances following the Easter Rising of 1916 and the opposition to Irish conscription in 1917.

On the eve of war, it seemed that the Irish were poised to become fully integrated into Welsh political culture, controversies over education notwithstanding. Integration was a gradual process, occurring over a period of thirty years, during which time Catholic education and Home Rule were the issues by which Irish participation in local and parliamentary politics was gauged, and on the basis of which party allegiance was defined. But the Irish clearly did not operate as a single, unified, electoral bloc, primarily because of the existence of class divisions and competing status aspirations among those who saw themselves as the natural political leaders in immigrant life. Conflicts between the clergy and a small, articulate Irish middle class for leadership of immigrant politics produced tensions which ensured that party allegiance was no simple matter. The enfranchisement of large sections of the male working class in 1884 was an additional factor underlining the social and economic plurality of what was described in misleadingly monolithic terms as 'the Irish vote'.

From World War to Free State, 1914–1922

With the prospect of Ireland finally achieving Home Rule, John Redmond pledged the support of the Irish Volunteers to the defence of the Empire in its hour of need. At a time of international crisis, he assured Parliament, the British people could count on the loyalty of Ireland. Even though Redmond's enthusiasm for the war effort was conspicuously in advance of that of his colleagues and of the movement in Ireland, it nevertheless found a rapturous response among the Irish in Britain. Irish brigades were formed voluntarily in London, Liverpool and Tyneside, while in south Wales popular figures such as the boxer 'Peerless' Jim Driscoll, who would become the Army boxing team's trainer before the war ended, gave a lead for the Irish to join Welsh regiments. Irish institutions occasionally formed a conduit for recruitment. A conspicuous example of this phenomenon was the voluntary enlistment by two hundred members of the Merthyr branch of the Ancient Order of Hibernians.[104]

Given these circumstances, the Easter Rising of 1916 came as a great shock to the Irish in Britain. It has been claimed that the event largely bypassed the Irish in Liverpool because of the efficacy of British war propaganda.[105] Initially, there was a hostile reaction. The Liberal press in Wales roundly deplored the events in Dublin and pointed out that members of Sinn Féin, who were perceived to be the major culprits, represented only a small minority of the nationalist movement. 'There is no branch of the Sinn Feiners in South Wales', the *South Wales Daily News* quickly reassured its readers.[106] The Irish Parliamentary Party also denounced the leaders of the rising, Redmond speaking of his 'detestation and horror' at the events.

Similar feelings were expressed by Irish Nationalists in south Wales. A meeting of the five branches of the United Irish League at Cardiff endorsed Redmond's statement, as did meetings at Aberdare and Merthyr Tydfil.[107] Particularly vitriolic in his attack on developments in Ireland was Dr James Mullin, the

[104] Joseph Keating, 'History of the Tyneside Irish Brigade', in F. Lavery (ed.), *Irish Heroes in the Great War* (London, 1917); John O'Sullivan, 'How green was their island?', in Stewart Williams (ed.), *The Cardiff Book*, II (Cardiff and Bridgend, 1974), pp.24–5; *Merthyr Pioneer*, 30 November 1918.

[105] See Bernard O'Connell, 'Irish Nationalism in Liverpool, 1873–1923', *Eire-Ireland*, X (1975), 24–37.

[106] *South Wales Daily News*, 26 April 1916. However, the trade unionist, Arthur Horner, recalled: 'We heard those details [of the executions in Dublin] in Wales and anger rose, even among those who supported the war.' Arthur Horner, *Incorrigible Rebel* (London, 1960), p.27.

[107] *South Wales Daily News*, 22 April, 1 May 1916.

senior Irish Nationalist in the region. Recalling his meeting with Patrick Pearse, one of the leaders of the rising, in Cardiff in 1899, Mullin dismissed him as 'a man of very mediocre intelligence. Argumentative and of a very aggressive disposition, he was commonplace both in character and appearance . . .'[108] Mullin explained his own philosophy in typical Gladstonian fashion: he was an Irishman when Ireland was in difficulties and a 'Britisher' when Britain was in difficulties. He added that he did not know a single person who sympathized with Sinn Féin. In spite of Mullin's jaundiced view of Pearse's character, there is no reason to doubt his belief that Sinn Féin lacked sympathizers among the Irish in Wales at this time. The seeds planted in Dublin in 1916 were not immediately transplanted to emigrant communities. Faith in the leaders of the Irish Parliamentary Party remained undimmed. However, the execution of the leaders of the Rising and the imposition of conscription on Ireland in February 1917 undermined the authority of the Irish Parliamentary Party and called into question the link with Liberalism. The upshot of these events was that in the post-war period the Irish in Wales would increasingly gravitate towards the Labour Party or the Independent Labour Party (ILP).

A protracted discussion about Irish relationships with British political parties took place at the annual convention of the United Irish League of Great Britain at Manchester in October 1918 in anticipation of the general election of that year. Eventually, a motion urging the severance of links with the Liberal Party was withdrawn and delegates reiterated their faith in the actions of the Irish Parliamentary Party.[109] It is clear, however, that in the localities the Irish had begun to form political alliances on an *ad hoc* basis in order to maximize their influence among the anti-Coalition candidates of different parties. In some places, Irish Nationalists had already established a durable relationship with the labour movement. At Merthyr Tydfil, for example, the United Irish League and the ILP co-operated on amicable terms. At the end of November 1918, the Labour press in Merthyr exhorted the Irish to vote for James Winstone, the ILP candidate and vice-president of the South Wales Miners' Federation,

---

[108] *South Wales Daily News*, 2 May 1916. For a hostile description of Pearse's visit to Cardiff, see Mullin, *The Story of a Toiler's Life*, pp.202–5.
[109] *South Wales Daily News*, 28 October 1918.

because the sitting Liberal MP had voted against John Dillon's motion to exclude the Irish from the National Service Bill in February 1917. At a pre-election meeting of the town's Robert Emmet branch of the United Irish League, one speaker had remarked that 'there was an inseparable link between the Home Ruler and the Labour Party', and subsequently it was claimed that Labour had taken 98 per cent of the town's Irish vote.[110] Winstone failed to capture the seat, but the ties between Labour and the Irish were cemented during the campaign.

Elsewhere, the picture was less clear-cut. The inability of the United Irish League centrally to take a decision about party allegiance created conflicts with the local branch at Cardiff. Cardiff differed from Merthyr electorally by 1918 in that it now contained three parliamentary constituencies in which the Irish vote was unevenly spread. It was estimated that the Irish could muster 4,000 votes in the East Division, a figure which accounted for approximately half the Irish vote in the city. Controversy centred on the constituency of Cardiff South, where the National Executive of the United Irish League advised Irish voters to support the candidature of Sir Edward Curran, a Liberal supporter of the Coalition. An Irishman and a Gladstonian Liberal, Curran was on record as supporting Home Rule, yet he remained unacceptable to Nationalists in Cardiff, who protested that they had already decided to back the Labour candidate.[111] In the event, neither candidate won.

In 1918 the Labour Party won ten parliamentary seats in Wales and polled an unprecedented 163,000 votes (30.8 per cent of the total).[112] Yet in the seven seats where the Irish were heavily concentrated, not one Labour candidate was returned. The so-called 'khaki' election had been called under the extraordinary conditions of wartime and was held shortly after the end of hostilities, when Lloyd George appealed for continuing support for the Coalition government. Those candidates of all parties who refused to accept the prime minister's official endorsement by accepting his 'coupon' were frequently punished by the electorate. Nevertheless, that same election provided the first

[110] *Merthyr Pioneer*, 30 November, 7 December 1918.
[111] *South Wales Daily News*, 3, 7, 9 December 1918.
[112] K. O. Morgan, *Rebirth of a Nation: Wales, 1880-1980* (Oxford, 1981), p.181.

incontrovertible evidence that the pre-war consensus on Home Rule had disappeared, never to return.

The Irish in Britain emerged from the election divided among themselves and uncertain of which direction to take. Whereas at the outbreak of war Home Rule offered the prospect of an acceptable and soon-to-be realized answer to their demands, by the end of the conflict Irish politics had taken a turn which forced a reassessment of the emigrants' approach. In 1918 Sinn Féin succeeded in shattering the hegemony of the Irish Parliamentary Party, winning seventy-three seats to the latter's six, while the Unionists won twenty-six seats. This was no mere substitution of one political party for another, but rather augured an appreciable escalation in the tension between Britain and Ireland. In January 1919 Sinn Féin unilaterally established a parliament, Dáil Éireann, in Dublin, attended by the twenty-seven Sinn Féin MPs who remained at liberty. They adopted a provisional constitution, unilaterally declared independence and issued a Democratic Programme. In support of this action, the Irish Volunteers pledged their support to the Republic and adopted the new name of the Irish Republican Army; in September, Sinn Féin, the Gaelic League and the Dáil itself were suppressed. The year ended with Lloyd George announcing his Government of Ireland Bill which contained provisions for establishing two Home Rule parliaments, one in the north and one in the south.[113]

In Britain, the Home Rule societies which had grown and matured before the war were now left stranded as the political waters ebbed inexorably away from them. The first fresh response to the changed circumstances came in March 1919, when the Irish Self-Determination League (ISDL) was established with its headquarters in London. The League was intended as a propaganda organization conducting its affairs openly and operating within the law, aiming to 'band together the Irish residents of Great Britain, in order that they shall as a body support their compatriots in Ireland, and use every means in their power to secure the application of the principle of

---

[113] Lyons, *Ireland since the Famine* (revised edn, 1973), pp.398–9, 400–14. On Lloyd George's changing attitudes to Ireland, see John Davies, 'Wales, Ireland and Lloyd George', *Planet*, 67 (1988), 20–8.

self-determination in Ireland'.[114] The name and rhetoric of the ISDL reflected the historical circumstances of its conception, the 'self-determination' of small nations becoming a commonplace term in political debate during the post-war settlement of Europe. Military violence against civilians in Ireland was denounced as 'Prussianism', behaviour which Britain had fought a war to eradicate. As army violence increased during the early 1920s, the rhetoric gained wider currency. For example, Vernon Hartshorn, Labour MP for the Ogmore constituency, would criticize the 'Hunnish ruthlessness' of government policy in Ireland in 1921, a characteristic which had previously been 'the peculiar vice of the Germans in Belgium'.[115]

Serial membership figures for the ISDL do not exist, but membership in Great Britain as a whole never exceeded 38,726. Most localities with a significant Irish community capable of sustaining other ethnic institutions boasted an ISDL presence, the number of branches rising steadily from fifty-four in November 1919 to 214 in November 1920, reaching 300 by December 1921.[116] In south Wales, the organization was active in all the major urban centres, and in many of the lesser industrial settlements also. Along the coastal belt, branches appeared at Cardiff, Newport, Barry, Bridgend, Aberavon, Swansea and Llanelli, while in the coalfield there were branches at Aberdare, Hirwaun, Dowlais, Merthyr Tydfil, Merthyr Vale, Ebbw Vale, Bargoed, Ystradgynlais, Neath, Maesteg, Tonypandy, Pontypridd and Mountain Ash.[117]

The relatively low level of membership was a cause of concern to the League. In February 1921 the ISDL in Cardiff deplored the fact that it could claim only one thousand members from an

[114] Irish Self-Determination League, *Constitution and Rules* (n.d.). This accorded closely with plans developed by De Valera during his imprisonment in Lincoln gaol. See Dorothy Macardle, *The Irish Republic* (London, 1937), p.297. There is no adequate account of the ISDL, but see David Fitzpatrick, 'The Irish in Britain, 1871–1921', in Vaughan (ed.), *A New History of Ireland*, vol.VI, pp.684–7; and Keiko Inoue, 'Dáil propaganda and the Irish Self-Determination League of Great Britain during the Anglo-Irish War', *Irish Studies Review*, 6, 1 (1998).

[115] *South Wales Daily News*, 19 February 1921.

[116] D. G. Boyce, *Englishmen and Irish Troubles: British Public Opinion and the Making of Irish Policy, 1918–1922* (London, 1972), p.86; Keith Harding, 'The Irish issue in the British labour movement, 1900–1922', unpublished University of Sussex D.Phil. thesis (1983), 238. David Fitzpatrick quotes the lower figure of 20,000 for the ISDL's membership in the year of its most intense activity, 'The Irish in Britain, 1871–1921', p.686.

[117] Based on information culled from many issues of the *Welsh Catholic Herald* and *Irish Exile* newspapers.

Irish population of thirty thousand, 'and this at the most serious crisis in the history of Ireland'.[118] Recruitment to the League was clearly responsive to escalating levels of repression in Ireland, dipping somewhat when Irish grievances moved away from the centre stage of public debate. But this weakness should not be allowed to mask the fact that the organization also reached sections of the Irish community which had remained unorganized by the Home Rulers, most notably women, some of whom became prominent in the League's affairs. To some extent this was no more than a reflection of wider patterns of social change, such as the experience of women workers during the war and the continuing agitation for full electoral rights following the enfranchisement of some women in 1918. These developments meant that the press carried regular reports and items of comment on the status of women in society and the implications of their participation in organized political activity. Against this background, attempts were made to redefine the role of women in the struggle for Irish self-determination, and reports of the League's activities made a point of boasting the successful recruitment of women members.[119]

There is some evidence of Irish women gaining positions of influence in both the trade-union and republican movements in Wales at this time. At Pontypridd, Myra O'Brien was president of the Trades and Labour Council, a body which expressed its support for the republican cause on a number of occasions. Her help was enlisted to secure Irish speakers for rallies to ensure that authentic accounts of Irish affairs could be heard locally.[120] At Merthyr Tydfil, Kitty Evans was active in the ISDL as branch secretary and local delegate to the first annual conference at Manchester in November 1920; she was arrested at Merthyr *en route* to Ireland in October 1921 carrying an attaché case of explosives destined for use by republican forces.[121] Both women were evidently exceptional in the extent of their activism, and the vast majority of Irish women in Wales did not share this experience. Nevertheless, despite its limitations, the ISDL provided an

---

[118] *Welsh Catholic Herald*, 26 February 1921.
[119] *Merthyr Pioneer*, 17 May 1919; *Welsh Catholic Herald*, 19 March 1921.
[120] Minutes of the Pontypridd Trades and Labour Council, 12 March 1920. Microfilm copy at NLW.
[121] *Merthyr Pioneer*, 4 December 1920, 22, 29 October 1921.

unprecedented opportunity for women to participate in political activity.

Prominent women from the Republican movement in Ireland were invited to speak at public meetings in Wales. The most popular of these was Hannah Sheehy Skeffington, who told packed public meetings early in 1921 that national liberation was the precondition of social progress in Ireland. At Merthyr she spoke on the same platform as Noah Ablett, the veteran syndicalist of pre-war agitation in the coalfield and miners' agent for Merthyr Tydfil. Ablett maintained that as a socialist and an internationalist the cause of Russia – the first workers' state – took precedence for him over that of Ireland. Skeffington, herself a socialist, dissented from this view, arguing instead that it was 'the duty of the Irish worker to look at the question nearest his own door'.[122] Her passion and the force of her argument carried the meeting, a remarkable achievement given the warm reception accorded news of the Russian revolution of 1917 in south Wales.

Women undoubtedly achieved a prominence in the ranks of the ISDL denied them in earlier Nationalist organizations. As has been suggested, to some extent this may be ascribed to the wider agitation concerning the role of women in society rather than to the philosophy of the ISDL itself. When the South Wales District Committee submitted a motion to the League's second annual conference on the qualifications for membership, it was phrased in an overtly prejudicial way: 'that membership of the League is confined to those of Irish birth or descent and the wives of Irishmen resident in Great Britain who shall undertake to support the objects of the League'.[123] The husbands of Irish women who had married outside the community were specifically excluded from the motion, the inference being that a husband's political beliefs determined those of his wife. The prevalence of such patriarchal attitudes inevitably meant that while opportunities for participation undoubtedly existed, women required considerable grit and determination to succeed.

In practice, the ISDL's activities consisted of organizing social events where rebel songs were sung and topical Irish affairs

---

[122] *Merthyr Pioneer*, 29 January 1921.
[123] *Agenda of the Second Annual Conference to be Held at London on Saturday, June 25, 1921* (1921), p.5.

discussed. In addition, money was collected for the assistance of Irish political prisoners, although the financial contributions of the Irish in Britain to the movement in Ireland pale into insignificance when compared with the very large sums contributed by the Irish in America. Local branch meetings provided an opportunity for passing resolutions critical of government policy which were then circulated to the press for publication, the aim being to keep public attention constantly focused on Irish affairs. A typically mundane account of a branch meeting appeared in the *Irish Exile*, the League's monthly organ, in December 1921:

> *Merthyr Vale*: The usual fortnightly meeting of the branch was held at Harvard's Restaurant, Mr James Twomey in the chair. Owing to the uncertain industrial situation our collectors are confronted with numerous difficulties; but a sense of duty to our oppressed fatherland inspires us with that determination which alone overcomes all obstacles, however mighty. The sum of £2 was sent to the Terence McSwiney Memorial Fund; and affiliation fees for twenty members to National Executive and to the Pontypridd District Committee respectively. The branch decided to give all possible support to the official organ.[124]

A modest £1,000 was contributed by the Irish in Wales to political and relief funds in Ireland during 1921.[125] The League also participated enthusiastically in the Gaelic revival by promoting classes in the Irish language. At Aberavon, for example, the Gaelic League boasted 240 eager students by March 1922, a strength of commitment mirrored in many towns throughout south Wales.[126]

Aside from its propaganda role, the ISDL confronted the question of the alignment of Irish voters in elections for British constituencies, an issue which crystallized around its relationship with the Labour Party. The ISDL's constitution was unequivocal on this point: members were prohibited from participating in 'English' politics without prior consultation with the Central Executive Council, which in turn would consult the movement in Ireland.[127] This rule was particularly problematical in south

---

[124] *Irish Exile*, December 1921.
[125] Fitzpatrick, 'The Irish in Britain, 1871–1921', p.687.
[126] *Welsh Catholic Herald*, 11 March 1922.
[127] ISDL, *Constitution and Rules*.

Wales, where members of the ISDL tended to be trade unionists, and activists were often already members of the Labour Party. Increasingly, the south Wales branches simply ignored the rule. If, as has been claimed, the ISDL was tightly controlled by its executive in London, preventing attempts to broaden the membership and widening the scope of its branches' activities,[128] then it is not an accurate description of the situation in south Wales where contacts with the labour movement were more intimate and extensive.

The prospect of an alignment of republicans with the Labour Party caused acute anxieties in government circles. In May 1919, the British Director of Intelligence submitted a report to the Cabinet stating that 'the most sinister feature at the moment is the liaison of Sinn Féin with Labour organisations which are tending towards Bolshevism', while in December of that year he remarked on the 'increasing cohesion between the Irish Sinn Feinners in England and the more advanced British Labour elements'.[129] That this convergence was not merely the fruit of an overheated imagination was illustrated most clearly in Merthyr Tydfil where, in April 1919, the Irish Liberty League re-formed as the Sinn Féin Club, claiming that the town contained 'some of the most progressive Irish self-determinists in Wales'. The new club agreed to support the ILP's local newspaper, the *Merthyr Pioneer*, and from then on the newspaper advertised and reported on ISDL meetings regularly.[130] As a mark of its new orientation, the ISDL in south Wales frequently held its meetings in trade union, ILP and Labour Party premises.

A consequence of this new kinship was that involvement in Irish politics could lead to Nationalists being introduced to socialism. A graphic example of this process is provided by Max Goldberg of Aberdare, son of an Austrian father and an Irish mother, who recalled:

> Well, I was for Ireland. My mother was Irish, and in the [Catholic] church I got linked up with Irish chaps, so I thought Irish. I didn't have any real

---

[128] Fitzpatrick, 'The Irish in Britain, 1871–1921', p.687.
[129] Cabinet Minutes, 28 May, PRO, CAB 24/80, and 23 December 1919, PRO, CAB 24/95.
[130] *Merthyr Pioneer*, 5 April 1919.

political understanding but I thought Ireland was being badly done by and therefore I lent my support to this.[131]

As a result of his involvement in the ISDL Goldberg began to study socialist analyses of the Irish question and soon became convinced that socialism was the only way of resolving the contradictions of British capitalism and its imperialist exploitation of Ireland. Experiences such as this were reinforced by speaking tours in south Wales by republicans, many of whom presented a socialist critique of Irish conditions. Among the speakers in a special series of lectures on Ireland organized by the Pontypridd Trades and Labour Council was Tom Johnson of the Irish Labour Party. In March 1921 he was followed by J. M. M. MacDonnell of the Connolly Labour College, Dublin, who analysed the subject of 'Irish Labour under the Republic'.[132] Whereas Patrick Pearse and the Gaelic revival had influenced some Irish radicals in Wales at the turn of the century, the ideas of socialist James Connolly were more actively debated in the early 1920s. Like Pearse, Connolly had been executed for his part in the Easter Rising of 1916, but it was Connolly's class analysis of Irish oppression and his demands for a socialist restructuring of society that appealed to Irish workers in Wales.

Increasingly, south Wales adopted an advanced position within the ISDL on the issue of links with the labour movement. At the annual conference in June 1921, the south Wales No. 12 branch proposed that 'closer co-operation with the Labour party is desirable'. This was a faint echo of the resounding decision of ISDL branches in the region to participate in labour politics without central authorization. In January 1921 a conference at Pontypridd on regional activity advised branches unequivocally to ally with, and affiliate to, the Labour Party in their localities. The Pontypridd branch took a lead in this respect, having affiliated to the local Trades and Labour Council in October 1919.[133] Similarly, the United Irish League was invited to send delegates to the inaugural meeting of the Mountain Ash Trades

[131] Transcript of an interview with Max Goldberg, 6 September 1972, South Wales Miners' Library, Swansea.
[132] *Welsh Catholic Herald*, 26 February, 5, 19 March 1921. At Swansea he spoke on 'The Life and Teachings of James Connolly'.
[133] Keith Harding, 'The Irish issue in the British labour movement', 242; *Merthyr Pioneer*, 8 January 1921 and 4 October 1919.

and Labour Council in December 1919, when Joseph Keating described the branch of the United Irish League as a 'self-governed and independent wing of the Labour Party'.[134]

Keating provides a fascinating case study of the process by which Irish Nationalists in south Wales gravitated towards Labour politics. The son of Irish immigrants, he left the mines at Mountain Ash to fulfil his ambition of becoming a full-time writer and novelist. Before 1914 his commitment to the Liberal consensus on Home Rule was immeasurably strengthened by the fact that his brother Matthew, who had also worked in the coal mines at Mountain Ash, entered parliament in a by-election for the seat of South Kilkenny as an Irish Nationalist in 1909. However, like many others, Joseph Keating was radicalized by the experience of war, returning to Mountain Ash in 1919 to seek the Labour nomination for the parliamentary seat of Aberdare, where he toured the constituency to argue forcefully for national-ization of the mines. His sophisticated analysis of the post-war crisis emphasized that Ireland was an integral part of the economic and general political problem, not an extraneous factor which needed to be removed before true social progress could be achieved. He skilfully linked the issue of shortages of food in the area with restrictions on the export of Irish produce to Britain. The only solution to the general crisis in the United Kingdom, he maintained, was to put workers in control of the wealth they produced. In his opinion, only a Labour government could achieve this.[135]

Keating campaigned vigorously in the constituency. He secured the backing of the *Merthyr Pioneer* and he was formally recommended for the Labour nomination by a number of lodges of the South Wales Miners' Federation. In the event, George Hall, a local miner and councillor, won the nomination, despite

---

[134] *Merthyr Pioneer*, 13 December 1919. Before the war Irish socialists in Wales had been more circumspect in their political allegiances. When Dan O'Driscoll of Aberfan invited James Connolly to lecture at Merthyr Tydfil in 1911 he wrote: 'I happen to be secretary of the Irish League and the chairman of the SDP club. Don't get frightened: there is no other way of getting at the boyhos only through the UIL. I can assure you we take Socialism to them . . .' National Library of Ireland, William O'Brien Papers, MS 13,939 (1).

[135] *Merthyr Pioneer*, 11 October 1919. Keating's autobiography, *My Struggle for Life* (London, 1916), describes his life before the war. See also J. H. Keri Edwards, 'The life and works of three Anglo-Welsh writers of East Glamorgan', unpublished University of Wales MA thesis (1962), 83–183.

– or, perhaps, because of – Keating's integrated class analysis of the political situation. George Hall held key posts in the party locally, but he tended to portray himself as a representative of community rather than of class, whereas Keating explicitly advocated class politics.[136] Parliamentary representation was the only level of Welsh politics which the Irish failed to penetrate before 1922.

At the British level, Labour perceived the governance of Ireland as a problem which could be properly addressed only when the battle for social equality had been won. This stance relegated Britain's relationship with Ireland, whether intentionally or not, to a diversion from the party's central social and economic objectives. Before the war, Labour had supported Home Rule, partly from expediency because Labour candidates tended to appeal to those working-class constituencies which contained concentrations of Irish voters.[137] By the early 1920s this policy was no longer acceptable to Ireland. In parliament, Labour equivocated on the issue until the treaty of 1922, which it welcomed with undisguised relief. Some unspecified form of Dominion Home Rule remained its meagre offer to a people who now demanded unfettered control over their own affairs. An analysis of Labour policy concerning Ireland at this time confirms a view that the party adhered to an ideology of gradualism which accepted the Empire as a vehicle for the implementation of its programme. Labour's most significant intervention in Irish affairs consisted of a series of public meetings throughout Britain in January and February 1921 to protest at the atrocities perpetrated by Crown forces in Ireland. These events, such as the one held at Cardiff addressed by Brigadier General Thompson and the railwaymen's leader, J. H. Thomas, received great support.[138] But the meetings were confined to a narrow brief of moral indignation and steered clear of endorsing direct action on the part of republicans.

In the two years leading up to the treaty, Sinn Féin carried out guerrilla attacks on Crown forces which had been sent to Ireland

---

[136] *Merthyr Pioneer*, 29 May 1920; S. V. Bracher, *The Herald Book of Labour Members* (London, 1923), p.6. Hall was unique in being an Anglican miners' MP.

[137] Dan McDermott, 'Labour and Ireland', in Kenneth D. Brown (ed.), *The First Labour Party, 1906–1914* (London, 1985).

[138] *Merthyr Pioneer*, 22 January 1921.

to suppress the republic. On the face of it, there was no reason why the Labour Party's denunciation of the hated Black and Tans should identify it with the armed conflict, yet in its quest for political respectability it clearly felt nervous about appearing too close to that struggle. Moreover, Labour's Irish support in Britain came from the ISDL which, as Dorothy Macardle wrote in her authoritative account of the Irish republic published in 1937,

> had no military side and gave no assistance to the Republican Army's activities in Great Britain. It was not an illegal organisation and had not been proscribed; its meetings, nevertheless, were banned or held under police supervision; its books and papers were frequently seized; its secretary, Sean McGrath, its treasurer and their successors in office, with other members were arrested and interviewed. These police operations served, however, only to point the lesson which it was a function of the League to teach.[139]

This description appears to be a faithful representation of the situation in south Wales, at least until the beginning of 1921. It is known that some individual miners, such as Max Goldberg and some members of the Irish community at Maesteg, stole industrial explosives to send to Republican forces in Ireland,[140] but there is no evidence of a widespread military conspiracy in the region. This judgement is supported by an incident in Dublin in February 1921, when the authorities seized an IRA document entitled 'Operations Abroad'. This document contained references to Liverpool, London, Newcastle-on-Tyne, Manchester and Glasgow, but did not mention south Wales.[141] However, by the autumn of that year the situation had changed dramatically.

As a result of the attention given to its activities in Britain after the seizure of the document in February, the IRA began to focus its attention on south Wales. The region's proximity to Ireland made it an ideal place from which to send arms and explosives to republican forces, and J. P. Connolly, an ISDL organizer, was

---

[139] Macardle, *The Irish Republic*, p.462.
[140] Interview with Max Goldberg; Hywel Francis and David Smith, *The Fed: A History of the South Wales Miners in the Twentieth Century* (London, 1980), p.23.
[141] *Hansard's Parliamentary Debates*, 5th series, vol.138, cols.632–4; *South Wales Daily News*, 22, 23 February 1921.

transferred from Tyneside to oversee the operation. Connolly's correspondence was intercepted by the authorities and this resulted in his arrest, together with that of five others in dawn raids across south Wales. There can be little doubt about the significance of this operation. 'It has been known for some time', the Director of Intelligence reported to the British Cabinet in October 1921, 'that the principal collecting point for munitions for the Irish Republican Army is South Wales, to which point munitions purchased and stolen from all parts of Great Britain were being conveyed.'[142] At Cardiff, Neath and Merthyr Tydfil arrests of individuals implicated in the conspiracy revealed the existence of a depot containing what was described as 'arms, bombs and high explosives'. The Director of Intelligence believed that 'the ramifications of the conspiracy are extensive' and exposed a network of arms collection which stretched from south Wales to Liverpool and Tyneside.[143] According to the recollections of one member of the ISDL in Liverpool who had been trained as a gunman, the 'conspiracy' went further than collecting arms. He asserted that there was 'a small section of Irishmen [in Britain] who were doing intensive military training, and making preparations for the opening of hostile military operations against Britain, and if necessary waging war against her people in England and Scotland'.[144] That 'hostile military operations' were not undertaken was partly due to the arrest of key activists and partly because the negotiations for the Anglo-Irish Treaty weakened the will to continue an armed struggle.

The role of the ISDL in all this is open to question. Some branches in the region responded to news of the arrests with horror and disbelief, evidently knowing nothing of a secret network sending arms to the IRA. The Barry Dock branch, for example, expressed anxiety that the League was being identified with the collection of arms and illegal activities. Others were more concerned with the welfare of the prisoners, with the Maesteg branch, members of which had been active in smuggling explosives to Ireland, passing a resolution condemning the

---

[142] Confidential Report on Revolutionary Organisations in the United Kingdom, 14 October 1921, Cabinet Paper 3408, PRO, CAB 24/129.

[143] Ibid., and reports dated 20 October 1921 (Cabinet Paper 3436) and 27 October 1921.

[144] Edward Brady, *Ireland's Secret Service in England* (Dublin and Cork, ?1928), p.22.

'savage sentences' passed on Irish activists in the Welsh courts.[145] It is probable that only a small circle of highly motivated men and women was involved in this activity in south Wales, but it is unquestionably the case that the ISDL provided a structure within which they could operate.

How did the Irish in Wales react to the establishment of the Free State? One indicator is that members of the ISDL began to question their role in these changing political circumstances. In January 1922 the National Executive considered its aims and future in the light of a declining membership, a development which also prompted soul-searching at branch level. In February the Director of Intelligence reported to the Cabinet that ISDL meetings were 'becoming irregular, the attendance sparse, and many of the branches are showing signs of collapse'. Agitation on the Irish question continued in south Wales, with P. J. Kelly and Sean McGrath addressing meetings throughout the region in protest at the continued imprisonment of political prisoners in Britain, but the institutional framework which sustained these activities was rapidly disintegrating.[146] From the summer of 1922, the League's affairs in south Wales began to be wound up. In July, a discussion by the militant Pontypridd District Committee on the necessity of continuing with its work resulted in a unanimous decision to dissolve the ISDL in the area on the grounds that although it had rendered valuable assistance to the cause of Irish freedom its usefulness was now at an end.[147] In August, the branches at Cardiff and Newport followed suit, and the closure of the Swansea branch occurred in November, accompanied by the revealing recommendation that a social club

---

[145] *Welsh Catholic Herald*, 5 November 1921; Confidential Report on Revolutionary Organisations in the United Kingdom, 14 October 1921, Cabinet Paper 3436, PRO, CAB 24/129. Joseph Connolly was sentenced to fourteen years in prison; Thomas Tierny, David Evans and Kate Evans were sentenced to seven years each; and Michael Donoghue to four years. All were released on 8 April 1922. When Kate Evans was interviewed on her release, she expressed her gratitude to Mrs Sheehy Skeffington and Maude Gonne for their efforts on her behalf, *Merthyr Pioneer*, 15 April 1922.

[146] *Welsh Catholic Herald*, 21 January 1922; Confidential Report on Revolutionary Organisations in the United Kingdom, 9 February 1922, Cabinet Paper 3725, PRO, CAB 24/133. J. G. Clifford, secretary of the Merthyr Tydfil branch of the ISDL, argued that as the Treaty denied Ireland full independence there remained a need for the Irish in Britain to organize politically, *Merthyr Pioneer*, 11 February 1922.

[147] *Welsh Catholic Herald*, 22 July 1922.

be opened to fill the hiatus in community life which now existed.[148]

An editorial in the *Welsh Catholic Herald* in October 1922 sounded the League's death-knell. It argued that the Irish in Wales should accept the full implications of the recent political settlement. The Free State, it pointed out, was now in a position to settle its own affairs, and consequently, agitation on Irish issues in Britain was unnecessary; indeed, it was potentially counter-productive. Moreover, there were more pressing social issues to be addressed. Continuing to concentrate on Ireland would divert the attentions of citizens of the country who were of Irish blood or sympathies from their own needs – social, economic, political and moral – and keep them in the old groove as strangers and pariahs. Irish slums needed removal, the editorial continued, and the poor, ignorant and helpless required succour, sympathy and encouragement. Irish people should be led to 'higher things and given a chance in life'. The editorial's tone suggested that allegiance to the 'ould country' after 1922 would be synonymous with remaining in the 'old groove'.[149] Such sentiments would have brought down a storm of protest in previous years.

This decisive change in political attitudes had taken place gradually, its origins lying in the rejection of militant republicanism during the 1870s and a determination in subsequent decades to embrace electoral politics at the local and national levels. A key stage in political integration was inaugurated by Gladstone's conversion to Irish Home Rule, a development which was much less disruptive of the Liberal Party in Wales than in England, allowing Home Rulers in Welsh constituencies to enter into a lasting alliance with Liberals. Only the politics of education threatened to undermine this unity of purpose, as Protestant Nonconformity vehemently opposed the funding of denominational schools. Even so, the tendency for Liberals to champion Home Rule while Conservatives lent their support to denominational education meant that political divisions among the Irish were increasingly assimilated to the principal party

---

[148] *Welsh Catholic Herald*, 19 August, 25 November 1922. Membership at Swansea had declined from 1,151 to 824 during the ten months leading up to January 1922: ibid., 21 January 1922.

[149] *Welsh Catholic Herald*, 7 October 1922.

divisions in British politics. However, the decisive transitional period for the political integration of the Irish was that between 1918 and 1922. During these years, the mobilization of the Irish through the ISDL succeeded in drawing many of them into a closer relationship with the Labour Party in a more committed and socially inclusive way than had been the case with the various electoral pacts between Home Rulers and Liberals before 1914. In the case of the Irish, ethnic networks, more than trade-union solidarity or class-consciousness, provided the matrix within which support for Labour was fostered. An involvement in Labour politics at a time when the Liberal Party's domination of Welsh politics was coming to an end meant that when the Free State was established in 1922 members of the Irish community in Wales were well prepared for a situation in which the imperatives of Irish Nationalism no longer qualified their allegiance to a British political party.

X

CONCLUSION

By the mid-1920s – some three-quarters of a century after the end of the Great Famine – there was a consensus among commentators that the Irish had successfully integrated into Welsh society. A flurry of publications, both academic and popular, proclaimed with unchallenged confidence that the Irish had become an established and accepted minority, no longer vilified for their alleged immorality or denigrated for their religion and politics. In 1926, a year after the remarkable public funeral of the boxer, 'Peerless' Jim Driscoll, in Cardiff had attracted large and respectful crowds onto the city's streets, an article entitled 'The Influence of Foreign Nationalities on the Life of the People of Merthyr Tydfil' appeared in the *Sociological Review*. It claimed that the Irish were well integrated into the town's life, asserting that they were 'now able to enter into all local activities in industry, business and social life'.[1] The author maintained that involvement with trade unionism, participation in the education system and the increased incidence of intermarriage between the Irish and Welsh were responsible for this change, adding the caveat that adherence to Roman Catholicism continued to mark out the Irish and their descendants as a group with a distinctive identity. More evidence of a rooted Irish presence at this time can be found in the first attempts to place Irish immigration in a longer historical time-span which gave due weight to the particularities of the Welsh context.[2]

Looking back through the filter of these developments, some historians have been rather too profligate in their claims for the speed of integration and the ease with which it supposedly took place. Kevin O'Connor, for example, boldly claimed a special place for Wales in the general picture of the relationship between

---

[1] J. Ronald Williams, 'The influence of foreign nationalities on the life of the people of Merthyr Tydfil', *Sociological Review*, XVIII (1926), 149.

[2] Cecille O'Rahilly, *Ireland and Wales: Their Historical and Literary Relations* (London, 1924), and *eadem*, 'The antipathy of Irish and Welsh', *Welsh Outlook*, VII (September 1920); Fr James Cronin, *Ireland and Wales: Bonds of Kinship* (Cardiff, 1925); miscellaneous articles in *St Peter's Magazine* and *Newport Catholic Magazine*.

Irish immigrants and British society when he wrote, in 1971, 'Indeed, of the three countries which make up Britain, Wales appears to offer the most relaxed and encouraging process of absorption.'[3] It was a claim based on assumptions untested by a careful evaluation of historical evidence, but O'Connor was correct in identifying integration as a process which occurred over time and, it could be added, an uneven process which proceeded at a different pace in places of varying size and social structure and within different domains of economic and social life.

As earlier chapters have demonstrated, a comforting picture of amicable coexistence is in complete contrast with the decades of social and economic upheaval following the mid-1840s, when the volume of Irish immigration increased as a result of the Great Famine and the newcomers were considered to be the key to a series of interrelated social problems bedevilling urban life.[4] Those who arrived during the mid-nineteenth century were frequently stigmatized and anathematized as unwanted interlopers, partly because of ingrained stereotypes in Welsh culture and partly because of the fortuitous circumstances which obtained in Welsh society at the time of their arrival. Rapid urban growth, the spread of disease, pressure on the Poor Law, and the determination of reformers to uncover social evils and remove them, led to the creation of a powerful image of the outcast Irish as pariahs confined to ghettos of inadequate housing and poor sanitation. Such pervasive views failed to take account of diversity among the Irish and the potential for change which existed; images generated during mid-century were deeply entrenched in public debate and are remarkable for remaining static over a long period of time. It is hardly surprising, therefore, that when Irish friendly and temperance societies paraded through the main thoroughfares of the towns, their respectable appearance excited pleasantly surprised comment in the press. In

---

[3] Kevin O'Connor, *The Irish in Britain* (Dublin, 1974), p.121. For a cautionary note on claims about integration, see Roger Swift, 'The historiography of the Irish in nineteenth-century Britain: some perspectives', in Patrick Buckland and John Belchem (eds.), *The Irish in British Labour History* (Liverpool, 1992), p.16.

[4] Nevertheless, W. R. Lambert overstates the matter when he claims that 'drink and religion formed the opium of these socially unassimilable communities of *émigré* Catholics in nineteenth century Wales': *Drink and Sobriety in Victorian Wales, c.1820–1895* (Cardiff, 1983), p.153.

fact, evidence of the existence of respectable Irish immigrants merely served to emphasize the gulf between the dominant values of Victorian society and the 'low Irish', thereby making the latter appear even more alien.

Class distinctions created one axis of division among the Irish. Middle-class individuals like Edward Dowling, the proprietor of the *Monmouthshire Merlin* in the 1830s and 1840s, or Irish doctors and businessmen, inhabited different social worlds from the majority of working-class Irish men and women; social gradations between skilled, semi-skilled and unskilled workers added more nuanced evidence of social differentiation. The salience of such social distinctions varied between towns and villages with different industrial and occupational structures, tending to be greater in places like Cardiff, Newport and Swansea, where the Irish entered a wider spread of occupations as the century progressed and a more coherent Irish middle class emerged around the Catholic Church and Nationalist politics. Religion and politics were the twin areas which brought this social élite into contact with the working-class Irish as the extension of the franchise forced members of the middle class to defend their interests. That they did so by attempting to mobilize ethnic solidarity is indicative of a willingness to forge a common cause with other Irish people above their class interests. By providing an alternative source of social and political leadership to the Catholic clergy, they also opened up a space in which the church's authority in secular matters could be contested.

In a society which attempted to prescribe separate spheres for men and women, it is also worth inquiring whether Irish women were slower to integrate than their male counterparts. In comparison with social class, this question is more difficult to answer. In an economy overwhelmingly dominated by heavy industry, with little opportunity of regular paid employment for women outside the home, Irish women had fewer avenues of contact with other members of society than did Irish men. While they had some presence (albeit a minor one) in the friendly society movement, women were visibly under-represented in the institutions which assisted Irish men in achieving social integration in the public sphere. The 'New Unions' succeeded in netting Irish dock labourers, but women working in general employment around the docks remained unorganized by the trade unions. Mass spectator sport was a product of a male culture which offered little space for women's active involvement. The women's suffrage movement appears to have made few converts among the Irish, while women were excluded from parliamentary politics until after the First World War. From 1919, the Irish Self-Determination League was one of the few organizations which offered a small number of women an active role in political life.

However, the single institution in which Irish women appear to have participated more heavily than Irish men is the Catholic Church. In the religious sphere, social networks were developed which drew women ever more closely into contact with other Irish women and possibly hampered interaction with those who were neither Catholic nor Irish. In this context, the role of women as 'cultural carriers'[5] who socialize the second- and third-generations into an awareness of group membership is an important dimension to the persistence of an ethnic identity from one generation to the next. Nevertheless, it would be a mistake to portray Irish women as being totally segregated from the host society on the basis of their sex. As the Catholic Church's concern in the 1890s about the effects of intermarriage indicates, some Catholic women did marry outside their religion, bringing them into closer contact with members of other religious groups, or of none at all; this development presupposes some social contact with non-Catholics in the first instance.

As well as disparities arising from social class and gender, it is also necessary to recognize the existence of generational differences within immigrant groups. As Roger Swift has pointed out, discussions of Irish integration frequently come up against the brick wall of a lack of systematic evidence about second- and third-generation immigrants. Only rarely was this section of the community identified specifically by commentators, as opposed to being subsumed under the catch-all category of 'the Irish', a term which conflated the Irish-born with their descendants born in Wales or elsewhere. In the mid-nineteenth century those who had not been born in Ireland comprised only a small section of the Irish 'community', but as time went by and the numbers of

[5] Ann Rossiter, 'Bringing the margins into the centre: a review of aspects of Irish women's emigration', in Sean Hutton and Paul Stewart (eds.), *Ireland's Histories: Aspects of State, Society and Ideology* (London, 1991), pp.234–5.

the Irish-born were depleted and the inflow of new immigrants slackened, the sons and daughters of immigrants increased in number and as a proportion of the 'Irish community'. Some commentators did take note of this change. A stipendiary magistrate at Cardiff made the following comments about the Irish in 1877: 'They live pretty much to themselves, and do not interfere with the Welsh population; the second or third generation of Irish are not at all bad fellows, but they have all the peculiarities of their forefathers who came over from Ireland . . .'[6] This was a common refrain among those who troubled to make the distinction. Following the vicious anti-Irish riots at the iron-manufacturing town of Tredegar in south Wales in 1882, John Denvir, an Irish Nationalist organizer in Great Britain, visited the locality to assess the condition of those who had suffered at the hands of the rioters. Ten years later, the impressions of that visit were included in his monumental study – part history, part contemporary observation, part political tract – of the Irish in Britain:

> Two generations of our people have been born and have grown up in these Welsh hill-towns. You will hear the racy Munster tongue of the original immigrant, while the accent of his children and grandchildren is indistinguishable from that of their Welsh neighbours, whose vernacular they speak; indeed, you will find some who can converse in all three tongues Irish, Welsh, and English. It is no uncommon thing to find a man of Irish extraction born in Rhymney or Tredegar, while his wife may have been born in Merthyr, and his children at Dowlais or elsewhere; yet they are all regarded by the natives, and by themselves, as being as much Irish as the original settlers who came in the famine years or still earlier . . . they are, indeed, as a rule, as Irish in heart as though born in Cork, or Waterford, or Tipperary.[7]

Denvir's acute observations shed valuable light on the Irish immigrants and their descendants who settled in this part of industrial south Wales. He suggests that not only did immigrants retain a strong consciousness of an Irish identity, but that their offspring born in Wales developed their own Irish identity. For the latter, 'Irishness' was a category which made reference back

[6] Evidence of Robert Oliver Jones, stipendiary magistrate at Cardiff, P.P. 1877 XI, Report of the Select Committee on Intemperance, p.159.
[7] John Denvir, *The Irish in Britain* (London, 1892), p.306.

to the land of their fathers and mothers, but it was articulated in terms of their own position in urban society in Wales. On the whole, it is much easier to find in the historical record evidence of those sons and daughters of immigrants who identified with Ireland than of those who remained indifferent to ethnic institutions and consequently are indistinguishable historically from other members of the population.

One rough-and-ready indicator of integration is the change in levels of ethnic hostility at the workplace and in wider society. Responses to the Irish differed from those encountered by other immigrant and minority ethnic groups in Wales because of the volume of Irish immigration and the group's occupational profile. A hostile reaction was by no means always a straightforward response to the influx of large numbers of outsiders, but at times like the end of the 1840s it was certainly a factor of some importance: the Irish migrated to Wales in larger numbers than the Italians or the Russian and Polish Jews, who arrived at the end of the nineteenth and the beginning of the twentieth centuries, although they were fewer in number than the English. In fact, the English constituted the largest immigrant group in Welsh society, but they displayed few signs of a coherent 'ethnic' identity. Secondly, the Irish competed for a wider range of jobs than did the smaller immigrant groups. Whereas the Irish could be found in a variety of occupations and industries, the Italians were concentrated in the café trade, while the Jews were also to be found overwhelmingly in small businesses, notably the pawnshop business which they dominated.[8] Consequently, the Irish were initially perceived as more of a threat to the employment of native workers.

During the half-century before the First World War, there was plentiful evidence to demonstrate that the Irish were regarded as a less alien minority in Welsh society than had been the case hitherto. Hostile relationships between ethnic groups at the workplace lost their asperity during these years, and where discord persisted it no longer escalated into large-scale violence. Even so, the decline of riot as a method of excluding the Irish cannot be taken in itself as an entirely satisfactory index of integration; after all, riots had not occurred in every town where

---

[8] Colin Hughes, *Lime, Lemon and Sarsaparilla: The Italian Community in South Wales, 1881–1945* (Bridgend, 1991); Ursula R. Q. Henriques (ed.), *The Jews of South Wales: Historical Studies* (Cardiff, 1993).

the Irish settled and lower levels of communal friction, in the form of drunken brawls on pay-day, persisted. It was the increasing participation of Irish workers in the trade-union movement which transformed a mere reluctance to exclude immigrants into a greater willingness to accept them. Thus, the decline of riot as a means of exclusion must be considered in the context of concerted attempts to organize the unskilled and the semi-skilled in the workplace from the late 1880s, and the success in organizing casual workers, especially at the docks. Although participation in trade unions did not necessarily mean that Irish workers developed a sense of common class interests with their neighbours, it did create the institutional context within which a sense of common allegiance could be forged.

Evidence of the changing position of the Irish is suggested by two incidents involving other ethnic groups in south Wales at the turn of the century. In 1903 an influx of about 200 Russian and eastern European Jews in Dowlais provoked a violent response from local labourers in an industrial settlement with substantial minorities of Irish and Spanish workers. On one occasion, the Irish were specifically singled out as being responsible for assaulting Jewish labourers, an act which nearly escalated into a riot.[9] The disturbance appears to have derived from the general air of jingoism prevalent in the town during the Boer War (1899–1902) and the grievance felt by returning reservists that their jobs had been stolen by outsiders. A comparable incident occurred in Cardiff in 1919, when race riots erupted because soldiers returning from the First World War felt aggrieved at what they saw as black men stealing both their jobs and white women. Significantly, the disturbances occurred in an area previously associated with Irish settlement and about a third of those arrested for participating in the riots had Irish surnames.[10] Taken together, these incidents suggest that by the twentieth century the Irish benefited from being able to look down on more recent immigrant groups and were willing to resort to the same tactics of exclusion as had been used against them in the mid-nineteenth century.

---

[9] *The Times*, 3 September 1903; *Western Mail*, 3 September 1903; *Merthyr Express*, 12 September 1903. I am indebted to David Morris for drawing this incident to my attention.
[10] Neil Evans, 'The south Wales race riots of 1919', *Llafur*, 3, 1 (1980), 25.

Communal violence is only one indicator of the extent of hostility to a minority group. More diffuse hostile attitudes to the Irish which had been formed and become embedded in the language and culture of Wales over many centuries, and which had intensified under the pressures of large-scale immigration during the nineteenth century, were not erased overnight. (It is worth noting the characterization of 'the Irishman' in the popular Welsh-language novel *Rhys Lewis* (1885) by Daniel Owen, which recycles the tired stereotype of the feckless and indigent immigrant. A dissolute and dishevelled figure is instantly recognizable by his wayward appearance as an Irishman to the young Rhys Lewis; he does not need to speak for his origins to be identified by the child.) Changes in attitudes of this kind are geological rather than immediate. While it is difficult for the historian to tap into the substratum of residual prejudice towards a minority group, anecdotal evidence suggests that in some quarters negative stereotypes persisted for many decades.

A factor which might contribute towards an explanation of the absence of a focus for anti-Irish feeling in the emerging mass culture of the late nineteenth century is the relative importance of rugby football rather than soccer in working-class culture in industrial south Wales when compared to other parts of Britain. Whereas in the other countries of the United Kingdom rugby was associated with the middle classes, in Wales it achieved support among all sections of society and acted as a force for integrating different cultural and linguistic groups. By contrast, the rivalry in Glasgow between Celtic and Rangers – Catholic and Protestant soccer teams respectively – is well known, with teams in other Scottish urban centres also mobilizing religious loyalties in a less confrontational manner. Similarly, loyalties to soccer teams in some towns and cities in the north-west of England reflected religious allegiances. It is true that some rugby teams in Wales boasted their Irishness – such as the Newport Hibernians and the Aberavon Green Stars – but in general rugby football acted as an agent of social integration in Welsh life, and none of the major teams were sectarian in composition or support.[11] One aspect of the sport which had the potential to

[11] David Smith and Gareth Williams, *Fields of Praise: The Official History of the Welsh Rugby Union, 1881–1981* (Cardiff, 1980), especially ch.2.

divide was the onset of international contests between Ireland and Wales from the season of 1881–2. Initially, these events were ill-starred, with fixtures cancelled on a number of occasions during the 1880s when relationships between the governing bodies of the sport in the two countries became strained.[12] Yet these were minor hiccups which failed to inflame wider passions, as was demonstrated when Wales played Ireland at Llanelli on 7 March 1891 after a series of disputed games, and the Irish team was greeted by the crowd with cries of 'Home Rule for Ireland'.[13] Moreover, additional evidence of rugby's integrative qualities can be found in the case of a player like William O'Neil, the son of immigrants from County Cork, who represented Wales at international level.[14] In a somewhat different way, the more individualist sport of boxing allowed an Irishman like Jim Driscoll to achieve both personal success and the approbation of the wider community.

In any discussion of the process of Irish integration in Wales, one area which requires consideration is that of language. One of the obstacles facing the historian in analysing changing linguistic patterns in Britain in the nineteenth century is the lack of systematic evidence about the languages spoken by the Irish, a deficiency which has not prevented some writers from making sweeping generalizations about the salience of language as an indicator of separateness. Writing in 1924 about the consequences of the industrial revolution in south Wales, Ness Edwards stated baldly that 'The Welsh natives could not understand the foreigners with their strange language and customs, and looked upon them all as enemies. The Irish, forced into a foreign land through English oppression, clung to each other with an intense clannish spirit.'[15] Unlike their compatriots in England and parts of Scotland, the Irish in Wales in the mid-nineteenth century faced a context in which a language other than English was often the language of the workplace. This meant that even those who were bilingual in Irish and English before leaving Ireland were often confronted with the challenge

---

[12] Ibid., p.63.
[13] John Billot, *History of Welsh International Rugby* (Ferndale, 1970), p.34.
[14] O'Neil won eleven international caps for Wales between 1904 and 1908, during the first 'golden era' of Welsh international rugby.
[15] Ness Edwards, *The Industrial Revolution in South Wales* (London, 1924), p.29.

of acquiring a third tongue upon arriving in Wales, particularly in the upland iron-producing towns and villages of Glamorgan and Monmouthshire where the language of the workplace and the language of social life in the mid-nineteenth century was predominantly Welsh. Many of the immigrants at that time spoke Irish, an indeterminate number being monoglot, and despite the lack of statistical information, fragmentary evidence suggests that they adapted quickly to their new linguistic environment. In those places where it was necessary to speak Welsh in order to co-operate in the workplace, the Irish, like the early English incomers, soon acquired a functional understanding of the language.

For many migrants who settled in industrial Wales in the mid-nineteenth century, language was not necessarily an insurmountable or impenetrable barrier imprisoning the members of either group within their own culture; rather, it was one of the boundaries many of them crossed in time through their interaction with the host society.[16] When Patrick Leary appeared at Glamorgan Assizes in July 1848, he maintained that he was not always able to distinguish between his countrymen and the Welsh, 'for many Irishmen can speak Welsh as well as Welshmen'.[17] A familiarity with Welsh was a feature of the Irish who settled in Rhymney, an industrial village with a long tradition of anti-Irish violence.[18] That this occurred should not be surprising, for language – whether English or Welsh – was one of the skills migrants were compelled to acquire in order to obtain employment and to perform satisfactorily the duties expected of them in the workplace. In some of the coastal towns and villages linguistic patterns were more heterogeneous. By mid-century Welsh had already lost its position of dominance in ports like Cardiff and Newport, and, consequently, in those

---

[16] According to John Hickey, 'The language of the Irish immigrant does not seem to have been of major importance as a barrier to assimilation'; Hickey adds that social status was of greater significance. John Hickey, 'The origin and growth of the Irish community in Cardiff', unpublished University of Wales MA thesis (1959), p16.

[17] *Cambrian*, 7 July 1848.

[18] For a detailed study of the Welsh language in this area, see Siân Rhiannon Williams, *Oes y Byd i'r Iaith Gymraeg* (Cardiff, 1992). For an incisive discussion of language and industrialization, see Ieuan Gwynedd Jones, *Towards a Social History of the Welsh Language* (Aberystwyth, 1994), pp.12–14. See also John Davies, *A History of Wales* (London, 1993), pp.385–6, 418–22. The first official census of the Welsh language, held in 1891, reveals little about the linguistic abilities of Irish people in Wales.

places the imperative to acquire a knowledge of Welsh was absent.

A similar pattern is discernible in the case of the second- and third-generation Irish. Even in some cases where the children of immigrants were familiar with the Welsh language, antagonism towards them was undiminished. At a court case following an attack on Irish houses at Llantrisant near Cardiff in 1848, one young boy was able to give evidence in either Irish or Welsh, but not in English.[19] Later in the century, John Denvir observed that the violent outbreak at Tredegar was not unexpected by the Irish because 'Many of them, particularly the younger generation, knew sufficient of the Welsh tongue to catch the muttered threats of vengeance let fall in public-houses and elsewhere by the native population, when none but themselves were supposed to be near . . .' Indeed, Denvir claimed, there were those who were tri-lingual, being able to converse in Irish, Welsh and English.[20] While it would be unwise to place too much importance on the views of one visitor, the timing of his comments is relevant, as the domains where Welsh was spoken in these upland industrial areas were progressively eroded from the 1880s onwards and it could be that his observations are an accurate view of circum-stances up to that time.[21]

With the onset of state education from 1870, some attempts were made to ensure that Welsh was taught in schools, a development which often elicited a lukewarm response from the governors of Catholic schools. In areas undergoing massive demographic upheaval and major linguistic change at the begin-ning of the twentieth century, a resistance to the teaching of Welsh in these schools was justified on the grounds of the ethnic background of the children catered for. The debate on this matter was articulated most clearly at Pontypridd, where the symbolic importance of language to both the managers of

[19] *Cardiff and Merthyr Guardian*, 24 June 1848.

[20] John Denvir, *The Irish in Britain* (London, 1892), pp.305–6. The oral tradition in the present author's own family is that his forebears in Merthyr Tydfil were fluent in all three languages, but that both Welsh and Irish were lost in the generation which moved to the coal-mining village of Mountain Ash at the end of the nineteenth century; at the end of the twentieth century, some members of the family are bilingual in Welsh and English.

[21] See, for example, W. T. R. Pryce, 'Language shift in Gwent, *c.*1770–1981', in Nikolas Coupland (ed.), *English in Wales: Diversity, Conflict and Change* (Clevedon, 1990), pp.48–83, and *idem*, 'Language areas and changes, *c.*1750–1981', in Prys Morgan (ed.), *Glamorgan County History*, vol.VI (Cardiff, 1988), pp.265–313.

Catholic schools and the local education administrators was clear. By the beginning of the twentieth century, this town at the hub of the central valleys of the coalfield was increasingly cosmopolitan in character with a large immigrant population. In 1914 the clerk to the local Education Committee agreed with the managers of the local Catholic school that it would not be feasible to teach Welsh there as the school 'was of a specific character and the children were brought from a certain country [i.e. Ireland]'. The local newspaper dissented from this view, believing it to be absurd to regard those of Irish stock born locally as 'Irish', claiming that Irish Catholics were no more foreign than the many English immigrants to the area who were not exempt from the requirement to learn Welsh.[22] The two parties clearly understood the symbolic significance of language in different and contradictory ways. Whereas for the managers of the Catholic school, teaching the Welsh language was perceived as an erosion of their identity, enthusiasts for the scheme saw it as a way of preventing the erosion of their language at a time when rapid social change threatened its future. The institutionalization of language teaching in the schools provided the occasion for opposition to the policy, whereas previously language appears not to have been a significant cause of conflict between the Irish and Welsh. Whereas in England Catholic schools attempted to strengthen a child's Catholic identity at the expense of its ethnic identity,[23] it is possible that in those areas of Wales where church schools opposed the teaching of Welsh an ethnic identity was reinforced by denominational schooling. However, there is no systematic evidence to show that all Catholic schools were unsympathetic to the teaching of Welsh.

An examination of the social history of language highlights the complexity of cultural interaction and should serve as a warning against deceptively easy generalizations about ethnic groups, even in the same region. We should also beware of interpreting integration solely in terms of an ethnic group becoming more and

[22] *Pontypridd Observer*, 20 June 1914, quoted in Timothy Ifor Williams, 'Patriots and citizens – language, identity and education in a liberal state: the Anglicisation of Pontypridd, 1818–1920', unpublished University of Wales Ph.D. thesis (1989), vol.2, 545–6.

[23] Mary J. Hickman, 'Incorporating and denationalising the Irish in England: the role of the Catholic church', in Patrick O'Sullivan (ed.), *Religion and Identity: The Irish World Wide*, vol.5 (London and New York, 1996), pp.196–216.

more indistinguishable from the majority culture. In the mid-nineteenth century, Hibernian friendly societies in south Wales succeeded in expressing a robust Irish identity in the same idiom of respectability, self-help and temperance as that used by comparable Welsh societies. In this instance, a particular definition of Irishness and the imperatives of the wider respectable working class were not construed by observers as incompatible. Or to put it another way, ethnicity could be mobilized to achieve accommodation with the host society at the same time as being a signifier of difference.

By the end of the period under consideration in this study, the Catholic church was the most obvious symbol of continuing difference. By establishing a network of parochial institutions, it endeavoured to envelop parishioners in a total religious culture which, it was hoped, would safeguard them from the pernicious influences – both Protestant and secular – which were held responsible for 'leakage' from the church. As has been seen, success in staving off such influences involved more than simply providing priests and buildings. It also entailed a cultural transformation, reforging popular Catholicism in such a way as to promote more disciplined forms of piety and regular observance of the sacraments which placed the Mass – and thus the priest – at the centre of religious life. Formidable progress in creating Catholic institutions was undoubtedly made, especially in the field of education, where denominational schools endeavoured to socialize children into the culture of Catholicism. In fact, even when all other manifestations of a distinctive identity are taken into account, Catholic schools were the most important abiding institutional expression of difference by the beginning of the twentieth century. Moreover, religion was not a category separate from other domains of social life. With the inception of state education, Catholic schools became a focus for controversies in local politics which could flare up into wider political conflagrations, as occurred at the time of the Welsh Revolt in 1904.[24] Nevertheless, even in the case of education there existed official channels for resolving disagreements, the Board of Education being the final arbiter of troublesome disputes.

[24] Despite such controversies, one historian of Catholic education in Cardiff has argued that 'By the year 1902 it is evident that the Cardiff Roman Catholic community had achieved a limited social integration into the everyday life of the town'. Liam Joseph Affley, 'The establishment and development of Roman Catholic education in Cardiff during the nineteenth century', unpublished University of Wales M.Ed. thesis (1970), 74.

Mobilizing Irish support in the political domain always had the potential for alienating members of the host society and causing an unwelcome and counter-productive backlash. Had there existed a determination to remain aloof from Welsh public life, as occurred briefly in the 1860s when Fenianism attracted the support of a sizeable minority of the Irish, then integration would have been doomed from the outset. While Fenianism was the dominant expression of Irish nationalism, any sympathy between the Irish and Welsh was impossible because of the ideological gulf between the dominant political movements in the two countries. That this did not happen was primarily a consequence of the inability of Nationalists to make Irish issues the only political concerns of relevance to migrants. From the mid-1880s there was a degree of convergence between immigrants and the host society as the majority of Irish Nationalists pursued the more limited aim of Home Rule within the Empire, largely by constitutional methods, and Welsh Liberals sought a resolution of the interests of Wales within the same framework. As increasing numbers of Irish men were enfranchised from the mid-1880s, Irish Nationalists sought to marshal the immigrant vote in order to pressurise both Liberal and Conservative parties to meet their demands.

Thus, changes in the character and content of Irish Nationalism meant that whereas support for Fenianism in the 1860s was an expression of the immigrants' alienation, a willingness to endorse the methods of constitutional Nationalism by the mid-1880s entailed an engagement with existing political institutions and represented a more integrative approach to public life. It is one of the paradoxes of late nineteenth-century British politics that, unlike Liverpool and Glasgow, which experienced bitter sectarian divisions in political life, the 'Orange card' was so rarely and ineffectually played in Wales, in spite of the fact that Welsh political identity was mobilized largely in terms of an assertive Protestant Nonconformity.

The Irish were not the only ethnic group preoccupied with their own political agenda. Many Jews in south Wales involved themselves in Zionist politics from the turn of the century;[25] but

[25] Ursula Henriques states that, at the beginning of the twentieth century, 'the prevailing feeling [among Jews] in Cardiff and south Wales was strongly Zionist', *The Jews of South Wales*, pp.36–8; on Zionism in the region, see also ibid., pp.63–4, 118–25.

there is no direct parallel with the Irish experience, whereby nationalism entailed a questioning of the right of Britain to govern Ireland and posed an explicit challenge to the existing political structures of the United Kingdom. However, the Irish in Wales benefited from the Liberal hegemony in Welsh politics and the unswerving devotion of Welsh Liberals to Gladstone; thus, when the Liberal Party split in two in England over the issue of Home Rule, in Wales it remained united and committed to dealing with Irish grievances. It was this conjunction of interests which prevented Liberal Unionists from exploiting anti-Catholic sentiments in the political arena.

In a small number of cases, an awareness of Welsh Liberalism's commitment to Irish Home Rule had influenced an emigrant's choice of destination. As a teenager in Ireland, Dan O'Driscoll, who migrated to Merthyr Tydfil and who would later became mayor of his adopted town, followed politics avidly:

> The chief topic in the house and the fields was Home Rule, and as I listened to the talk I realised that our only true support outside Ireland came from Wales. I read of Welsh Members of Parliament speaking and fighting in the House of Commons on behalf of Ireland, and there grew in me a bond of sympathy with these Welsh people who were ready to recognise the claims of my country.[26]

It is noteworthy that O'Driscoll made the transition to Labour politics, like the majority of the remainder of the Irish in Wales. By making this shift, they found an avenue into what would become the dominant political culture of Wales from the 1920s. The removal of the Irish Question from practical politics after 1922, and the onset of a civil war which underlined the necessity for Ireland to solve its own problems, undoubtedly helped to engender a climate which enabled the Irish in Wales to direct their energies wholeheartedly towards Welsh and British considerations.

Whether the history of the Irish in Wales during the century after the Great Famine is seen as an encouraging example of integration or as a depressing case study of the immigrants' social

---

[26] Dan O'Driscoll, 'A barren land (1938)', in Patrick Hannan (ed.), *Wales on the Wireless: A Broadcasting Anthology* (Llandysul, 1988), p.44.

dislocation and the collision of two conflicting cultural groups, depends to a large extent on the chronological perspective adopted. By focusing on the crisis years of the mid-nineteenth century to the exclusion of longer-term developments, there is a danger that the picture painted will be excessively sombre. While the tribulations of those years cannot and must not be underestimated, there is little room for doubt that when looked at in the longer term the picture, if not exactly rosy, can at least be picked out in more optimistic hues. Despite the creation of distinctive ethnic institutions, the Irish were not consigned to a ghetto and, over time, intermarriage between Catholics and non-Catholics provided evidence of closer contact at the domestic level. In the public sphere developments can be charted with greater confidence. Following the demise of Fenianism, an assertion of Irish Nationalism was integrated into the ideology and agenda of Liberal Nonconformist Wales from the mid-1880s, providing a space for the Irish in the emerging mass politics of the period. At the same time, the trade-union movement created avenues of contact between members of the two groups in the work place, thereby defusing the principal source of violent dispute which had bedevilled ethnic relations during much of the century. In addition, entrenched antipathies to the Irish, which had been renewed in the face of a large influx during the mid-nineteenth century, were slowly but steadily set aside as the century drew to a close.

By the mid-1920s, 'ethnic fade' was well advanced. Institutions which had articulated and shaped a sense of Irishness among the immigrants, and provided an arena for contesting the content and expression of that identity, were in decline or had disappeared altogether. Even though St Patrick's Day continued to be commemorated, events on that day were no more than a faint echo of the vibrant celebrations of earlier decades, and the festival was no longer the symbolic marker of a distinctive ethnic identity.

This book began with a funeral, that of the boxer Jim Driscoll at Cardiff in 1925. It has been argued that the circumstances surrounding that event are symbolic of a wider process of Irish integration which had been under way in different domains of social life for some decades beforehand. As the ultimate ritual of separation in human culture, a funeral is also an apt coda to this study, for 1925 was the first year of the long depression which devastated Welsh economic and social life between the wars, resulting in an enormous outflow of people from a country which hitherto had experienced exceptionally high levels of immigration. The slow pace of economic recovery after 1945 meant that for much of the remainder of the twentieth century there was little to attract substantial numbers of new immigrants who might have rejuvenated old ethnic institutions or created new ones.

Significantly, the most high-profile Irish institution to be created in Wales since 1945 has been concerned with history. The Wales Famine Forum was established in the 1990s to promote a keener awareness of the history of the Great Famine in general and of its impact on Wales in particular through a series of educational events and public commemorations marking the one hundred and fiftieth anniversary of the Famine. It has disseminated its message in the broadcast media where possible and through the medium of the Forum's publications, *The Green Dragon* and *Y Ddraig Werdd*. Unlike the large cities of England and Scotland, with their thriving Irish immigrant communities, the Forum has no constituency of recent immigrants of comparable size to whom it can appeal. Yet the support for its activities among the descendants of the Irish suggests that even among those people separated from their immigrant forebears by numerous generations, an awareness of a distinctive cultural heritage has not been entirely extinguished by successful integration.

APPENDICES

Appendix I
Numbers of Irish-born in England, Scotland and Wales, 1841–1921 *

Year	ENGLAND Irish-born	%	SCOTLAND Irish-born	%	WALES Irish-born	%
1841	281,236	1.89	126,321	4.8	8,168	0.78
1851	499,229	2.98	207,367	7.2	20,730	1.78
1861	573,545	3.06	204,083	6.7	28,089	2.18
1871	544,533	2.56	207,770	6.2	22,007	1.56
1881	539,502	2.21	218,745	5.9	22,872	1.46
1891	438,702	1.61	194,807	4.8	19,613	1.11
1901	407,604	1.34	205,064	4.6	18,961	0.94
1911	362,500	1.08	174,715	3.7	12,825	0.53
1921	343,174	0.92	159,020	3.3	21,573	0.81

Source: Decennial *Census of England and Wales*, 1841–1921.

* The summary tables of the Census frequently included Monmouthshire in the totals for England, despite grouping the county with Wales for most other purposes. Here, Monmouthshire is included in the totals for Wales.

These figures do not include the British-born offspring of Irish immigrants, although many would have thought of themselves as ethnically Irish. From 1871, as the effects of the Famine inundation began to fade, the figures for the Irish-born seriously underestimate the size of a more loosely defined 'Irish community'. In 1915 Elliot O'Donnell estimated that there were 100,000 'Irish' people in south Wales alone, although the basis for this estimate is not clear: Elliot O'Donnell, *The Irish Abroad* (London, 1915), p.161.

Appendix II
Numbers and cost of Irish paupers in Cardiff, 1846–1850

	No. of paupers	Cost £	s.	d.
Sept. 1846–March 1847	1804	302	1s.	0½d.
to Sept. 1847	1751	527	0s.	1½d.
to March 1848	1220	420	8s.	10¾d.
to Sept. 1848	947	329	4s.	0d.
to March 1849	1272	387	7s.	2¾d.
to March 1850	1702	342	7s.	4d.
to Sept. 1850	1308	265	19s.	2½d.
Subtotal	11454	3043	13s.	0½d.
Funerals of Irish paupers, 1846–50	493	448	0s.	8d.
Midwifery cases of Irish paupers, 1846–50	183	130	0s.	0d.
Removals to Ireland, 1847–50	326	223	17s.	5d.
Subtotal		801	18s.	1d.
Expenses paid by the Cardiff Poor Law Union on account of the Irish Famine fever		160	3s.	4d.
Total amount paid for Irish paupers		4005	14s.	5½d.

Source: 'Summary of Irish Paupers Relieved in the Town of Cardiff, and the Cost Thereof, from September 1846 to September 1850, paid by the Cardiff Poor Law Union', PP 1854 XVII, Report from the Select Committee on Poor Removals, Appendix 14, p.612.

Appendix III
Expenses incurred by the Cardiff Union on account of cholera in 1849*

	£	s.	d.
Medical expenses	770	16s.	5d.
Cost of erection of House of Refuge and expenses	442	15s.	11d.
Expenses paid for sanitary purposes	456	10s.	8d.
Total	1670	3s.	0d.

*These cases are described as being 'chiefly Irish'.

Source: 'Summary of Irish Paupers Relieved in the Town of Cardiff, and the Cost Thereof, from September 1846 to September 1850, paid by the Cardiff Poor Law Union', PP 1854 XVII, Report from the Select Committee on Poor Removals, Appendix 14, p.612.

Appendix IV
Birthplace of persons committed to Welsh prisons, 1856–1892

Year	England	Wales	Scotland	Ireland	Total*	
					M	F
1856	628 (22.19)	1643 (58.06)	23	429 (15.16)	2061	769
1860	791 (24.06)	1627 (49.50)	61	613 (18.65)	2290	997
1864	1006 (22.78)	2278 (51.57)	78	846 (19.15)	3405	1012
1868	1350 (26.62)	2464 (48.59)	78	1023 (20.17)	3891	1180
1872	947 (21.20)	2567 (57.48)	51	722 (16.17)	3185	1281
1876	1304 (24.48)	2949 (55.36)	77	821 (15.41)	3844	1483
1880	1101 (20.92)	3234 (61.46)	64	654 (12.43)	3902	1360
1884	1348 (26.68)	2903 (57.45)	75	602 (11.91)	3559	1494
1888	1378 (26.97)	3031 (59.33)	63	478 (9.36)	3846	1263
1892	1602 (30.16)	2986 (56.21)	64	526 (9.90)	3964	1348

*Includes those born in the colonies and other foreign countries.

Statistics are for the year ending 31 March and exclude debtors and military prisoners.

Figures in brackets indicate percentages of the total.

Source: Based on David Jones and Alan Bainbridge, 'Crime in nineteenth-century Wales', Social Science Research Council Report (Swansea, 1975), Table XXIX, p.112.

Appendix V

Birthplace of persons committed to Cardiff County Gaol and House of Correction, 1856–1893[1]

Year	Total[2]		England		Wales		Scotland		Ireland	
	M	F	M	F	M	F	M	F	M	F
1856	564	301	183	70	195	148	6	1	132	82
1857	754	351	254	89	233	140	8	2	196	118
1858	847	372	284	106	273	136	9	4	203	125
1859	815	398	258	103	283	129	7	2	206	160
1860	768	462	232	127	229	155	7	1	193	157
1861	865	442	194	77	372	186	3	-	199	171
1862	832	371	170	70	414	163	10	-	167	137
1863	892	371	210	72	323	175	21	-	235	132
1864	939	417	181	57	402	198	17	3	233	154
1865	759	382	134	47	343	189	18	8	201	138
1866	853	441	232	88	318	186	10	4	203	156
1867	1186	490	326	89	466	227	20	1	234	164
1868	1231	463	362	119	392	125	28	2	372	214
1869	1204	452	338	110	478	130	30	3	240	206
1870	1272	634	336	133	538	321	30	1	261	178
1871	1019	441	282	103	419	204	19	3	186	129
1872	1015	539	245	105	457	270	20	3	199	156
1873	1116	484	348	122	431	227	16	5	199	127
1874	1141	474	344	109	481	219	15	3	201	139
1975	1053	478	315	117	486	236	19	6	176	116
1876	1163	563	322	137	532	274	22	8	208	143
1877	1282	644	339	166	648	337	19	5	187	133
1878	610	338	147	59	335	207	11	3	75	66
1879	1331	634	297	144	688	348	26	1	213	140
1880	1506	619	306	120	861	396	32	2	205	99
1881	1410	660	305	132	807	428	22	1	229	98
1882	1491	711	305	143	894	478	19	1	210	83
1883	1358	667	377	198	672	361	15	3	219	102
1884	1620	831	501	249	777	453	38	2	321	124
1885	1442	684	512	203	661	389	17	3	171	83
1886	1318	610	465	166	612	345	17	3	171	91
1887	1467	665	472	169	763	379	14	8	148	100
1888	1657	563	507	140	902	357	21	7	159	49
1889	1642	521	575	134	804	300	20	5	180	76
1890	1482	550	523	139	717	327	18	4	154	75
1891	1698	530	610	134	829	307	17	1	171	81
1892	2056	698	757	219	1026	386	25	6	179	84
1893	2173	941	812	276	1055	542	25	11	202	107

[1] The County Prison from 1867.

[2] Statistics are for the years ending 30 September 1856–77 and 31 March 1878–93. They include those born in the colonies and other foreign countries and exclude debtors and military prisoners.

Source: David Jones and Alan Bainbridge, 'Crime in nineteenth-century Wales', Social Science Research Council Report (Swansea, 1975), Table XXXVII, p.120.

Appendix VI

Statistics of Roman Catholics in Wales and Monmouthshire in 1839

Mission	Baptisms	Marriages	Funerals[1]	Easter[2]	Conversions	Census[3]
Abergavenny	38	5	3	136	3	300
Bangor	4	0	1	55	0	100
Brecon	1	0	0	25	0	65
Cardiff	60	30	2	150	0	900
Chepstow	7	0	3	38	1	118
Holywell	19	3	2	140	3	300
Llanarth	12	0	4	130	4	210
Merthyr Tydfil	72	13	8	104	3	940
Monmouth	6	1	4	130	4	210
Newport	117	17	34	332	2	1800
Pontypool	40	20	15	60	0	600
Swansea	50	12	6	140	1	400
Talacre	5	2	2	0	44	150
Usk	20	1	9	33	1	76
Wrexham	33	1	2	50	14	76
Total	484	105	95	153	80	6245

[1]I.e. funerals conducted by a Roman Catholic priest.

[2]Easter communicants (obligatory only for those over thirteen years of age).

[3]I.e. the pastoral census conducted by each parish priest, including children.

Source: Mgr Baines, 'Numerus Baptizatorum, Matrimonio conjunctorum, Mortuorum, Communicantium in Paschate, Conversorum ad Fidem nec non Census totius Catholici gregis in singulis Missionibus Districtus Occidentalis Angliae, a 1a die Januarii 1839, ad 1m. diem Januarii 1840', in W. Mazière Brady, *The Episcopal Succession in England, Scotland and Ireland, A.D. 1400–1875* (London, n.d.), vol.III, pp.315–16.

Appendix VII
Religious practice among the Irish in Cardiff, 1841–1861

Year	Catholic population	Easter duties[1]	Percentage of total
1841	1200	114	9.5
1842	1100	NA	NA
1843	800	NA	NA
1844	1000	382	38.2
1845	1100	270	24.5
1846	900	422	46.8
1847	1000	500	50.0
1848	2300	500	21.7
1849	2600	530	20.4
1850	3700	720	19.5
1851	4000	960	24.0
1852	4700	850	18.1
1853	6000	950	15.8
1854	5600	1300	23.2
1855	6600	1300	19.7
1856	8900	2050	23.0
1857	8900	2100	23.6
1858	8900	2100	23.6
1859	NA	NA	NA
1860	9500	2200	23.2
1861	9800	2500	25.5

[1]Easter duties were obligatory only for those over the age of thirteen. The possibility of counting a person twice over the Easter period was obviated by counting those who attended the confessional; supplicants were required to state the period of time since their last confession.

Source: John Hickey, *Urban Catholics* (London, 1967), p.91.

BIBLIOGRAPHY

A MANUSCRIPTS
B OFFICIAL PUBLICATIONS
C NEWSPAPERS AND PERIODICALS
D WORKS OF REFERENCE
E CONTEMPORARY WORKS
F SECONDARY WORKS
G THESES AND UNPUBLISHED RESEARCH REPORTS

A MANUSCRIPTS

Cardiff Central Library
Bute Papers
D. A. Thomas Papers

Derry's Wood Archives of the Institute of Charity

Glamorgan County Record Office
Fr J. M. Cronin Papers
Dowlais Iron Company Records
Notes from Cardiff Police Journal (D/Dx Ha 5/8)
Poor Law Records
Quarter Sessions Records

Gwent County Record Office
Chartist Depositions
Friendly Societies
Poor Law Records
Quarter Sessions Records

National Library of Ireland
William O'Brien Papers, MS 13, 939(1).

National Library of Wales
Archdiocese of Cardiff Archives
Bute Collection
Calendar of the Diary of Lewis Weston Dillwyn
G. T. Clark Papers
D. R. Daniel Papers
Francis Johnson Collection (microfilm copy)
D. T. M. Jones Collection
W. J. Parry MSS
Pontypridd Trades and Labour Council Records (microfilm copy)
NLW MS 4378E, An Essay on the 'History of the Development of the Coal Industry of
the Rhondda Valleys for the last 50 years', Treorchy Eisteddfod [?1895]
NLW MS 4943B, The Scripture Reader's Journal
NLW MS 12350A, Diary of John Davies, Ystrad

NLW MS 19451D, Stuart Rendel Correspondence
Census Enumerators' Books, 1841, 1851, 1871 (microfilm copies)

Newport Public Library
Records of Chartist Trials and Examinations

Public Record Office, Kew
Board of Health Records (MH 13)
Cabinet Papers (CAB 24)
Education Department Records (ED 21)
Home Office Records (HO 40, HO 45, HO 52, HO 100, HO 144)

South Wales Miners' Library, Swansea
Transcripts of interviews with:
Tom Gale
Max Goldberg
Bryn Lewis
Oliver Powell

University of Wales, Swansea
Archives of St David's Priory, Swansea.

B OFFICIAL PUBLICATIONS

Census of England and Wales, 1841–1921.
Census of Religion, 1851.
Hansard's Parliamentary Debates.
Journal of the House of Commons, 1823.

Parliamentary Papers
PP 1824 XIX, An Account of the Sums paid by the Several Treasurers of Counties in
England and Wales for the Apprehension and Conveyance of Irish and Scotch
Vagrants Removed by Pass to Ireland and Scotland during the Year 1823.
PP 1830 VIII, Report from the Select Committee on the State of the Coal Trade.
PP 1833 V, Report from the Select Committee on Agriculture.
PP 1834 XXIX, Report from Her Majesty's Commissioners for Enquiring into the
Administration and Practical Application of the Poor Laws.
PP 1836 VIII, Report from the Select Committee on the State of Agriculture.
PP 1836 XXIX, Report of the Poor Law Commissioners.
PP 1836 XXXIV, Report on the State of the Irish Poor in Great Britain.
PP 1842 XV, First Report from the Commission of Inquiry into the Employment and
Condition of Children in Mines and Manufactories.
PP 1842 XXXVI, A Return Relating to Friendly Societies Enrolled in the Several
Counties of England and Wales.
PP 1846 XXXVI, Report from the Select Committee on Railway Labourers.
PP 1847 XXVII, Reports from the Commissioners on the State of Education in Wales.
PP 1847 LII, Correspondence Relating to the Measures Adopted for the Relief of
Distress in Ireland (Commissariat Series), Second Part.
PP 1847–8 LIII, Reports and Communications on Vagrancy.
PP 1849 XLVII, The Number of Irish Poor Relieved during 1848.
PP 1850 L, Orders of Removal.
PP 1852 XXVIII, Return of All Friendly Societies . . . Registered Under the Provisions of
the Act Relating to Friendly Societies of Last Session.

PP 1854 XVII, Report from the Select Committee on Poor Removal.
PP 1854 LV, The Number of Passengers Landed at this Port from the Coast of Ireland.
PP 1860 XVII, Report from the Select Committee on the Irremoveable Poor.
PP 1861 XXI, Report from the Commissioners on Popular Education in England.
PP 1864 XXXII, Report of the Registrar of Friendly Societies.
PP 1865 XXX, Report of the Registrar of Friendly Societies in England.
PP 1867–8 XXXII, Report of the Royal Commission on the Laws of Marriage.
PP 1867–8 XXXIX, Fifth Report of the Royal Commission on Trade Unions.
PP 1871 XXXVI, Report of the Commissioners Appointed to Inquire into the Truck System.
PP 1871 LVIII, Return of the Names of the Fenian Convicts Recently Released.
PP 1873 X, Report from the Select Committee on the Dearness of Coal.
PP 1877 XI, Report of the Select Committee on Intemperance.
PP 1883 LXVII, Reports of the Chief Registrar of Friendly Societies.
PP 1890 XL, Report of the Royal Commission Appointed to Inquire into the Operation of the Sunday Closing (Wales) Act, 1881.
PP 1893–4 XXXVII, Royal Commission on Labour, the Employment of Women.
PP 1900 LXXXII, Report by Mr Wilson Fox on the Wages and Earnings of Agricultural Labourers in the United Kingdom.
PP 1900 CI, Report on Migratory Agricultural Labourers.
PP 1910 XIV, Royal Commission on the Church of England and Other Religious Bodies in Wales and Monmouthshire.

C Newspapers and Periodicals

The Bee-Hive
The Cambrian
Cardiff and Merthyr Guardian
Cardiff Times
Carnarvon and Denbigh Herald
Catholic Opinion
Cyfaill o'r Hen Wlad
Cymru
Cymru Fydd
Y Diwygiwr
Irish Exile
Liverpool Mercury
Manchester Guardian
Merthyr Express
Merthyr Pioneer
Merthyr Telegraph
Monmouthshire Merlin
Morning Chronicle
Newport Catholic Magazine

Red Dragon
Reformer and South Wales Times
St Peter's Chair
St Peter's Magazine
Seren Gomer
South Wales Daily News (from 1919, *South Wales News*)
South Wales Daily Post
South Wales Echo
Star of Gwent
The Tablet
Tarian y Gweithiwr
The Times
Y Traethodydd
Y Tyst a'r Dydd
Y Tyst Cymreig
Welsh Catholic Herald
Western Mail

D Works of Reference

Brady, W. Mazière, *The Episcopal Succession in England, Scotland and Ireland, A.D. 1400–1875* (London, n.d.), 3 volumes.
Catholic Directory and Annual Register
Dictionary of Welsh Biography down to 1940 (London, 1959).
Geiriadur Prifysgol Cymru, vol.2 (Cardiff, 1987).

Hartigan, Maureen (comp.), *A History of the Irish in Britain: A Bibliography* (London, 1986).
Jenkins, R. T., and Rees, William, *A Bibliography of the History of Wales* (2nd edn, Cardiff, 1962).
Jones, Beti, *Newsplan Cymru / Wales* (London and Aberystwyth, 1994).
Jones, I. G. (ed.), *The Religious Census of 1851: A Calendar of the Returns Relating to Wales*, vol. II, *North Wales* (Cardiff, 1981).
Jones, I. G., and Williams, David (eds.), *The Religious Census of 1851: A Calendar of the Returns Relating to Wales*, vol.I, *South Wales* (Cardiff, 1976).
Saothar, the Journal of the Irish Labour History Society, publishes an annual bibliography of new works which includes a section on the Irish abroad.
University of Bradford, http://www.brad.ac.uk/acad/diaspora/
University of Huddersfield, http://www.hud.ac.uk/hip/
Who was Who, 1929–1941 (London, 1941).

E CONTEMPORARY WORKS

Anon., *Franciscan Missions among the Colliers and Ironworkers of Monmouthshire* (London, 1876).
Anon., 'The Gwyddyl in Cardiganshire', *Archaeologia Cambrensis*, 3rd series, V (1859).
Anon., 'The history of the rise and fall of Chartism in Monmouthshire', *Dublin Review*, VIII (1840).
Anon., *Things Not Generally Known Concerning England's Treatment of Political Prisoners* (Dublin, 1869).
Alexander, D. T., *Glamorgan Reminiscences* (Carmarthen, 1915).
Bruce, H. A., *Merthyr Tydfil in 1852: A Lecture Delivered to the Young Men's Mutual Improvement Society at Merthyr Tydfil, February 3rd., 1852* (Merthyr Tydfil, 1852).
Cardiff Catholic Registration Association: Report of Work for 1889 (Cardiff, 1890).
Catholic Young Men's Societies of Great Britain: Guide Book and Souvenir [of the] 47th. Annual Conference (Cardiff, 1922).
Clark, G. T., *Report to the General Board of Health on a Preliminary Inquiry into . . . the Sanitary Condition of the Town and Borough of Swansea* (London, 1849).
Idem, Report to the General Board of Health on a Preliminary Inquiry into the Sanitary Condition of the Inhabitants of Wrexham (London, 1850).
Contemporary Portraits: Men and Women of South Wales and Monmouthshire (Cardiff, 1896).
Croker, T. C., *Researches in the South of Ireland* [1924], ed. by Kevin Danaher (Shannon, 1969).
de la Beche, H. T., *Report on the State of Bristol and Other Large Towns* (London, 1845).
Denvir, John, *The Irish in Britain* (London, 1892).
Idem, The Life Story of an Old Rebel (Dublin, 1910).
Edmunds, William, *Traethawd ar Hanes Plwyf Merthyr* (Aberdare, 1864).
Edwards, Ness, *The Industrial Revolution in South Wales* (London, 1924).
Evans, Revd J., *Letters Written during a Tour through North Wales in the Year 1798, and at Other Times* (London, 3rd edn, 1804).
Fowler, John Coke, *The Characteristics and Civilizations of South Wales. Two Lectures Delivered at the Royal Institution of South Wales, Swansea* (Neath, 1873).
Howells, John, 'Reminiscences of Cardiff, 1838–40', *The Red Dragon*, V (1884).
Irish Self-Determination League (ISDL), *Agenda of the Second Annual Delegate Conference to be held at London on Saturday, June 25, 1921* (1921) .
Idem, Constitution and Rules (n.d.).
Jones, J. S., *Hanes Rhymni a Phontlottyn* (Denbigh, 1904).
Jones, T. D., *Home Life of the Welsh Collier* (1881).
Kane, Robert, *The Industrial Resources of Ireland* (Dublin, 1844).
Keating, Joseph, *My Struggle for Life* (London, 1916).

Idem, 'History of the Tyneside Irish Brigade', in F. Lavery (ed.), *Irish Heroes in the Great War* (London, 1917).

Kenrick, G. S., 'On the parish of Trevethin', *Journal of the Statistical Society of London*, IX (1846).

Idem, 'Statistics of Merthyr Tydvil', *Journal of the Statistical Society of London*, IX (1846).

Lavery, F. (ed.), *Irish Heroes in the Great War* (London, 1917).

Mann, Horace, 'On the statistical position of religious bodies in England and Wales', *Journal of the Statistical Society of London*, XVIII (1855).

Massey, Tuthill, 'Letter on fever in South Wales', *Dublin Quarterly Journal of Medical Science*, VIII (1849).

Matthews, J. H. (ed.), *Cardiff Records*, vols.IV–V (Cardiff, 1903–5).

Michael, W. H., 'The influence of habitation on the community: overcrowding in dwellings', *Transactions of the National Association for the Promotion of Social Science, 1857* (London, 1858).

Morganwg, Dafydd, *Hanes Morgannwg* (Aberdare, 1874).

Mullin, James, *The Story of a Toiler's Life* (London and Dublin, 1921).

National Amalgamated Labourers' Union, *Report of Branches and General Statement and Summary of Accounts from Opening of the Union, June 6th. 1889, to December 27th. 1890* (Cardiff, 1891).

Idem, Report and . . . Balance Sheet, year ending January 31st., 1912 (Swansea, 1912).

O'Donnell, Elliot, *The Irish Abroad* (London, 1915).

Official Guidebook of the 16th. Annual Conference of the Catholic Truth Society (Newport, 1902).

O'Keefe, T. J., *Rise and Progress of the National Amalgamated Labourers' Union of Great Britain and Ireland* (Cardiff, 1891).

Paine, H. J., *Annual Report of the Officer of Health to the Cardiff Local Board of Health* [for 1853] (Cardiff, 1854).

Idem, The Officer of Health's Report on the Sanitary Condition of Cardiff during the Year 1875 (Cardiff, 1876).

Idem, The Officer of Health's Report on the Sanitary Condition of Cardiff during the Year 1876 (Cardiff, 1877).

Idem, Report on the Sanitary Condition of Cardiff during the Last Forty Years (Cardiff, 1886).

Phillips, Sir Thomas, *Wales: The Language, Social Condition, Moral Character and Religious Opinions of the People Considered in their Relation to Education* (London, 1849).

Powell, David, and Powell, Evan, *History of Tredegar* (Newport, 1902).

Pratt, J. T., *A List of the Friendly Societies in the County of Monmouth* (London, 1856).

Rammell, T. W., *Report to the General Board of Health on a Preliminary Inquiry into the Sewerage, Drainage and Supply of Water, and the Sanitary Condition of the Inhabitants of Cardiff* (London, 1850).

Ravenstein, E. G., 'The laws of migration', *Journal of the Statistical Society*, XLVIII (1885).

Rees, Thomas, *Miscellaneous Papers on Subjects Relating to Wales* (London, 1867).

Report to General Board of Health, on a Preliminary Inquiry into the Sewerage, Drainage, and Supply of Water, and the Sanitary Condition of the Inhabitants of the Borough of Bangor (London, 1849).

Ribton-Turner, C. J., *A History of Vagrants and Vagrancy and Beggars and Begging* (London, 1887).

Richard, Henry, *Letters and Essays on Wales* (London, 1884).

Richards, J. W., *Reminiscences of the Early Days of the Parish and Church of St. Joseph's, Greenhill* (Swansea, 1919).

Ritual of the Ancient Order of Hibernians, Board of Erin (Dublin, 1912).

Rowe, Richard, *How Our Working People Live* (London, ?1868).

Wilkins, Charles, *The History of Merthyr Tydfil* (Merthyr Tydfil, 1867).

Idem, The History of the Iron, Steel, Tinplate and Other Trades of Wales (Merthyr Tydfil, 1903).

Williams, William (ed.), *Gweithiau Barddonol a Rhyddieithol Ieuan Gwynedd* (Dolgellau, 1874).

Woolett, Robert F., *First Report of the Officer of Health* (Newport, 1853).

Young, Arthur, *A Tour in Ireland . . . in the Years 1776, 1777, and 1778, and Brought Down to the End of 1779* (ed. A. W. Hutton, 1892), Part 1.

F SECONDARY WORKS

Books
Attwater, Donald, *The Catholic Church in Modern Wales* (London, 1935).
Bailey, Peter, *Leisure and Class in Victorian England* (London, 1987 edn).
Baughan, Peter E., *The Chester and Holyhead Railway*, vol.I (Newton Abbot, 1972).
Bessborough, Earl of, *Lady Charlotte Guest: Extracts from Her Journal, 1833–52* (London, 1950).
Billot, John, *History of Welsh International Rugby* (Ferndale, 1970).
Borrow, George, *Wild Wales*, Fontana edn (Glasgow, 1977).
Boyce, D. G., *Englishmen and Irish Troubles: British Public Opinion and the Making of Irish Policy, 1918–1922* (London, 1972).
Bracher, S. V., *The Herald Book of Labour Members* (London, 1923).
Brady, Edward M., *Ireland's Secret Service in England* (Dublin and Cork, ?1928).
Brown, Roger Lee, *Irish Scorn, English Pride and the Welsh Tongue* (Tongwynlais, 1987).
Carter, H. and Wheatley, S., *Merthyr Tydfil in 1851: A Study of the Spatial Structure of a Welsh Industrial Town* (Cardiff, 1982).
Cohen, Abner (ed.), *Urban Ethnicity* (London, 1974).
Connell, K. H., *Irish Peasant Society* (Oxford, 1968).
Idem, The Population of Ireland, 1750–1845 (Oxford, 1950).
Connolly, S. J., *Priests, and People in Pre-Famine Ireland, 1780–1845* (Dublin, 1982).
Crawford, E. Margaret (ed.), *The Hungry Stream: Essays on Emigration and Famine* (Belfast, 1997).
Cronin, J. M., *Ireland and Wales: Bonds of Kinship* (Cardiff, 1925).
Davies, E. T., *Religion and Society in the Nineteenth Century* (Llandybïe, 1981).
Idem, Religion in the Industrial Revolution in South Wales (Cardiff, 1965).
Davies, John, *A History of Wales* (London, 1993).
Idem, Cardiff and the Marquesses of Bute (Cardiff, 1981).
Davies, W. H., *The Right Place, the Right Time* (Llandybïe, 1972).
Davis, Graham, *The Irish in Britain, 1815–1914* (Dublin, 1991).
Daunton, M. J., *Coal Metropolis Cardiff, 1870–1914* (Leicester, 1977).
Dawson, James W., *Commerce and Customs: A History of the Ports of Newport and Caerleon* (Newport, 1932).
Devine, T. M. (ed.), *Irish Immigrants and Scottish Society in the Nineteenth and Twentieth Centuries* (Edinburgh, 1991).
Dockery, J. B., *Collingridge: A Franciscan Contribution to Catholic Emancipation* (Newport, 1934).
Dodd, A. H., *A History of Wrexham, Denbighshire* (Wrexham, 1957).
Donnelly, James S., *The Land and the People of Nineteenth-Century Cork: The Rural Economy and the Land Question* (London, 1975).
Edwards, Hywel Teifi, *Gŵyl Gwalia: Yr Eisteddfod Genedlaethol yn Oes Aur Victoria, 1858–1868* (Llandysul, 1980).
Edwards, R. Dudley and Williams, T. Desmond (eds.), *The Great Famine: Studies in Irish History, 1845–52* (Dublin, 1956).
Erikson, Thomas Hylland, *Ethnicity and Nationalism: Anthropological Perspectives* (London, 1993).
Evans, D. Gareth, *A History of Wales, 1815–1906* (Cardiff, 1989).
Evans, E. W., *The Miners of South Wales* (Cardiff, 1961).
Fielding, Steven, *Class and Ethnicity: Irish Catholics in England, 1880–1939* (Buckingham, 1993).
Finnegan, F., *Poverty and Prejudice: A Study of Irish Immigrants in York, 1840–75* (Cork, 1982).
Fitzpatrick, David, *Irish Emigration, 1801–1921* (Dundalgan, 1984).
Francis, Hywel and Smith, David, *The Fed: A History of the South Wales Miners in the Twentieth Century* (London, 1980).

Gillis, J. R., *For Better, for Worse: British Marriages from 1600 to the Present* (Oxford, 1985).
Ginswick, J., *Labour and the Poor in England and Wales, 1849–1851* (London, 1983).
Gwilym Hiraethog, *Llythyrau'r Hen Ffarmwr*, ed. E. Morgan Humphreys (Cardiff, 1939).
Handley, James E., *The Irish in Scotland* (Glasgow, 1964).
Harris, Ruth-Ann M., *The Nearest Place That Wasn't Ireland: Early Nineteenth-Century Irish Labor Migration* (Ames, Iowa, 1994).
Henriques, Ursula (ed.), *The Jews of South Wales: Historical Studies* (Cardiff, 1993).
Hickey, John V., *Urban Catholics* (London, 1967).
Hobsbawm, E. J., *Labouring Men: Studies in the History of Labour* (London, 1968 edn.).
Idem, Primitive Rebels (Manchester, 1959).
Horner, Arthur, *Incorrigible Rebel* (London, 1960).
Hughes, Colin, *Lime, Lemon and Sarsaparilla: The Italian Community in South Wales, 1881–1945* (Bridgend, 1991).
Hunt, Walter William, *'To Guard My People': An Account of the Origin and History of the Swansea Police* (Swansea, 1957).
Jackson, J. A., *The Irish in Britain* (London, 1963).
Idem (ed.) *Migration*, Sociological Studies No. 2 (Cambridge, 1969).
Jenkins, J. Geraint, *Dre Fach Felindre and the Woollen Industry* (Llandysul, 1976).
John, Angela V., *Our Mothers' Land: Chapters in Welsh Women's History, 1830–1939* (Cardiff, 1991).
John, A. H., *The Industrial Development of South Wales, 1750–1850* (Cardiff, 1950).
Jones, Aled Gruffydd, *Press, Politics and Society: A History of Journalism in Wales* (Cardiff, 1993).
Jones, Brynmor P., *From Elizabeth I to Victoria: The Government of Newport (Mon.), 1555–1850* (Newport, 1957).
Jones, D. J. V., *Before Rebecca: Popular Protest in Wales, 1793–1834* (London, 1973).
Idem, The Last Rising: The Newport Insurrection of 1839 (Oxford, 1985).
Idem, Crime in Nineteenth Century Wales (Cardiff, 1992).
Jones, I. G., *Explorations and Explanations: Essays in the Social History of Victorian Wales* (Llandysul, 1981).
Idem, Communities: Essays in the Social History of Victorian Wales (Llandysul, 1987).
Idem, Mid-Victorian Wales (Cardiff, 1992).
Idem, Towards a Social History of the Welsh Language (Aberystwyth, 1994).
Jones, J. Owain, *The History of the Carnarvonshire Constabulary, 1856–1950* (Caernarfon, 1963).
Jones, Thomas, *Rhymney Memories* (Newtown, 1938).
Jones, William D., *Wales in America: Scranton and the Welsh, 1830–1920* (Cardiff, 1993).
Jordan, Heather, *The 1842 General Strike in South Wales* (London, n.d.).
Kinealy, Christine, *This Great Calamity: The Irish Famine, 1845–52* (Dublin, 1994).
Lambert, W. R., *Drink and Sobriety in Victorian Wales, c.1820–1895* (Cardiff, 1983).
Lee, J. J., *The Modernisation of Irish Society, 1848–1918* (Dublin, 1973).
Lees, Lynn H., *Exiles of Erin: Irish Migrants in Victorian London* (Manchester, 1979).
Leetham, C., *Luigi Gentili: A Sower for the Second Spring* (London, 1965).
Leng, P. J., *The Welsh Dockers* (Ormskirk, 1981).
Lewis, E. D., *The Rhondda Valleys* (Cardiff, 1959).
Lowe, W. J., *The Irish in Mid-Victorian Lancashire: The Shaping of a Working-Class Community* (New York, 1989).
Lyons, F. S. L, *Ireland Since the Famine* (London, 1971 edn).
Macardle, Dorothy, *The Irish Republic* (London, 1937).
MacRaild, Donald M., *Culture, Conflict and Migration: The Irish in Victorian Cumbria* (Liverpool, 1998).
Marx, Karl, *Capital: A Critique of Political Economy*, vol.I (Harmondsworth, 1976 edn).
Mathew, D. et al., *Catholicisme anglais* (Paris, 1958).

Miller, Kerby A., *Emigrants and Exiles: Ireland and the Irish Exodus to North America* (Oxford, 1985).

Minchinton, W. E. (ed.), *Industrial South Wales, 1750–1914: Essays in Welsh Economic History* (London, 1969).

Mokyr, Joel, *Why Ireland Starved* (London, 1983).

Morgan, K. O., *Wales in British Politics, 1868–1922* (3rd edn, Cardiff, 1980).

Idem, Rebirth of a Nation: Wales, 1880–1980 (Oxford, 1981).

Morgan, Prys (ed.), *Brad y Llyfrau Gleision* (Llandysul, 1991).

Morris, J. H. and Williams L. J., *The South Wales Coal Industry, 1841–1875* (Cardiff, 1958).

Neal, Frank, *Sectarian Violence: The Liverpool Experience, 1819–1914* (Manchester, 1988).

Idem, Black '47: Britain and the Famine Irish (London, 1998).

Newsinger, John, *Fenianism in Mid-Victorian Britain* (London, 1994).

O'Brien, George, *The Economic History of Ireland from the Union to the Famine* (London, 1921).

O'Brien, James, *Old Afan and Margam* (Aberavon, 1926).

O'Connell, Maurice R. (ed.), *The Correspondence of Daniel O'Connell*, vol.VI, *1837–40* (Dublin, 1982).

O'Connor, Kevin, *The Irish in Britain* (Dublin, 1974).

O'Day, Alan, *The English Face of Irish Nationalism: Parnellite Involvement in British Politics, 1880–1886* (Dublin, 1977).

Ó Gráda, Cormac, *The Great Irish Famine* (Dublin, 1989).

O'Rahilly, Cecile, *Ireland and Wales: Their Historical and Literary Relations* (London, 1924).

Ó Súilleabháin, Seán, *Irish Wake Amusements* (London, 1969).

O'Sullivan, Patrick (ed.), *The Irish in the New Communities: The Irish World Wide*, vol.2 (Leicester and London, 1992).

Idem (ed.), *Religion and Identity: The Irish World Wide*, vol.5 (Leicester and New York, 1996).

Idem (ed.), *The Meaning of the Famine: The Irish World Wide*, vol.6 (London, 1996).

Ó Tuathaigh, Gearóid, *Ireland before the Famine, 1798–1848* (Dublin, 1972).

Owen, Hugh, *The History of the Anglesey Constabulary* (Llangefni, 1952).

Panayi, Panikos, *Immigration, Ethnicity and Racism in Britain, 1815–1945* (Manchester, 1994).

Pelling, Henry, *Social Geography of British Elections, 1885–1910* (London, 1967).

Publications of the Catholic Record Society, XXVII, *Miscellanea* (London, 1927).

Price, R. T., *Little Ireland: Aspects of the Irish and Greenhill, Swansea* (Swansea, 1992).

Quinlivan, Patrick and Paul Rose, *The Fenians in England, 1865–1872* (London, 1982).

Radzinowicz, Leon and Roger Hood, *A History of English Criminal Law and its Administration from 1750*, V (London, 1986).

Redford, Arthur, *Labour Migration in England, 1800–1850* (3rd edn, Manchester, 1976).

Rees, David James, *Pontypridd South, Past and Present* (Risca, 1983).

Roberts, Dafydd, *Y Chwarelwyr a'r Sowth* (Gwynedd, 1982).

Ryan, Mark, *Fenian Memories* (Dublin, 1946).

Smith, David (ed.), *A People and a Proletariat: Essays in the Social History of Wales, 1780–1980* (London, 1980).

Smith, David and Williams, Gareth, *Fields of Praise: The Official History of the Welsh Rugby Union, 1881–1981* (Cardiff, 1980).

Spencer, Gerald, *Catholic Life in Swansea, 1874–1947* (Swansea, 1947).

Swift, R. and Gilley, S. (eds.), *The Irish in the Victorian City* (London, 1985).

Idem, The Irish in Britain, 1815–1939 (London, 1989).

Idem, (eds.) *The Irish in Victorian Britain: The Local Dimension* (Dublin, 1999).

Symons, M. V., *Coal Mining in the Llanelli Area*, vol. I, *The Sixteenth Century to 1829* (Llanelli, 1979).

Taylor, Arthur J. (ed.), *The Standard of Living in the Industrial Revolution* (London, 1975).

Thomas, Tydfil, *Poor Relief in Merthyr Tydfil Union in Victorian Times* (Bridgend, 1992).

Thompson, E. P., *The Making of the English Working Class* (Harmondsworth, 1968 edn).

Wallace, Ryland, *'Organise! Organise! Organise!': A Study of Reform Agitations in Wales, 1840–1886* (Cardiff, 1991).

Wilks, Ivor G., *South Wales and the Rising of 1839* (London, 1984).

Williams, D. Trevor, *The Economic Development of Swansea and of the Swansea District to 1921* (Swansea, 1940).

Williams, David, *John Frost: A Study in Chartism* (Cardiff, 1939).

Idem, *A History of Modern Wales* (London, 1950).

Williams, E. A., *Hanes Môn yn y Bedwaredd Ganrif ar Bymtheg* (Anglesey, 1927).

Williams, Gwyn A., *The Merthyr Rising* (London, 1978).

Idem, *The Welsh in Their History* (London, 1982).

Idem, *When Was Wales?* (London, 1985).

Williams, Raymond, *Keywords* (2nd edn, London, 1984).

Williams, Siân Rhiannon, *Oes y Byd i'r Iaith Gymraeg* (Cardiff, 1992).

Wilson, J. A., *The Life of Bishop Hedley* (London, 1930).

Wilson, John, *Art and Society in Newport: James Flewitt Mullock and the Victorian Achievement* (Newport, 1993).

Woodham-Smith, Cecil, *The Great Hunger: Ireland, 1845–49* (London, 1962).

Articles

Anderson, Olive, 'The incidence of civil marriage in Victorian England and Wales', *Past and Present*, 69 (1975).

Anon., 'Two Irish Catholic mayors of Newport', *Presenting Monmouthshire*, III (1973).

Ap Gwilym, Gwyn, 'Padraig Pearse a'r Eisteddfod Genedlaethol', *Taliesin*, 32 (1976).

Armstrong, W. A., 'The use of information about occupation', in E. A. Wrigley (ed.), *Nineteenth Century Society: Essays in the Use of Quantitative Methods for the Study of Social Data* (Cambridge, 1972).

Aspinwall, Bernard, 'A long journey: the Irish in Scotland', in Patrick O'Sullivan (ed.), *Religion and Identity: The Irish Worldwide*, vol.5 (London and New York, 1996).

Beck, N. C., 'A brief account of the copper mines in Cwm Dyli, Snowdonia', *Transactions of the Caernarvonshire Historical Society*, 31 (1970).

Behagg, Clive, 'Secrecy, ritual and folk violence: the opacity of the workplace in the first half of the nineteenth century', in R. D. Storch (ed.), *Popular Culture and Custom in Nineteenth Century England* (London, 1982).

Belchem, John, 'The Irish in Britain, the United States and Australia: some comparative reflections on labour history', in Patrick Buckland and John Belchem (eds.), *The Irish in British Labour History* (Liverpool, 1992).

Boyns, T. and Baber, C. 'The supply of labour, 1750–1914', in A. H. John and Glanmor Williams (eds.), *Glamorgan County History*, V (Cardiff, 1980).

Bossy, John, 'The Counter-Reformation and the people of Catholic Ireland, 1596–1641', in T. D. Williams (ed.), *Historical Studies*, VIII (Dublin, 1971).

Burge, Alun, 'The Mold riots of 1869', *Llafur* 3, 3 (1982).

Busteed, M. A., Hodgson, R. I. and Kennedy, T. F., 'The myth and reality of Irish migrants in mid-nineteenth century Manchester: a preliminary study', in Patrick O'Sullivan (ed.), *The Irish in the New Communities, The Irish World Wide*, vol.II (London, 1992).

Carter, Harold, 'The structure of Glamorgan towns in the nineteenth century', in Prys Morgan (ed.), *Glamorgan County History*, vol.VI (Cardiff, 1988).

Chase, Malcolm, 'The Teesside Irish in the nineteenth century', in Patrick Buckland and John Belchem (eds.), *The Irish in British Labour History*, Conference Proceedings in Irish Studies, No.1 (Liverpool, 1993).

Clapham, J. H., 'Irish immigration into Great Britain in the nineteenth century', *Bulletin of the International Committee of Historical Sciences*, V (1933).

Collins, Brenda, 'The Irish in Britain, 1780–1921', in B. J. Graham and L. J. Proudfoot (eds.), *An Historical Geography of Ireland* (London, 1993).

Comerford, R. V., 'Conspiring brotherhoods and contending elites, 1857–63' in W. E. Vaughan (ed.), *A New History of Ireland*, vol.5 (Oxford, 1989).

Idem, 'Gladstone's first Irish enterprise, 1864–70', in W. E. Vaughan (ed.), *A New History of Ireland*, vol.5 (Oxford, 1989).

Connolly, Gerard, 'Irish and Catholic: myth or reality?', in R. Swift and S. Gilley (eds.), *The Irish in the Victorian City* (London, 1985).

Cousens, S. H., 'The regional variation in emigration from Ireland between 1821 and 1841', *Transactions of the Institute of British Geographers*, 37 (1965).

Crawford, E. Margaret, 'Migrant maladies: unseen lethal baggage', in *eadem* (ed.), *The Hungry Stream: Essays on Emigration and Famine* (Belfast, 1997).

D'Arcy, Fergus, 'The Irish in 19th. century Britain: reflections on their role and experience', *Irish History Workshop Journal*, I (1981).

Davies, Brian, 'Empire and identity: the "case" of Dr William Price', in David Smith (ed.), *A People and A Proletariat: Essays in the Social History of Wales* (London, 1980).

Davies, John, 'Wales, Ireland and Lloyd George', *Planet*, 67 (1988).

Idem, 'Wales and Ireland: parallels and differences in the nineteenth century', *Planet*, 95 (1992).

Earwicker, Ray, 'Miners' medical services before the First World War: the south Wales coalfield', *Llafur*, 3, 2 (1981).

Edwards, Owen Dudley, and Storey, Patricia J., 'The Irish press in Victorian Britain', in R. Swift and S. Gilley (eds.), *The Irish in the Victorian City* (London, 1985).

Evans, Neil, 'The urbanization of Welsh society', in T. Herbert and G. E. Jones (eds.), *People and Protest: Wales, 1815–1880* (Cardiff, 1988).

Idem, 'Immigrants and minorities in Wales, 1840–1990: a comparative perspective', *Llafur*, 5, 4 (1991).

Idem, 'The south Wales race riots of 1919', *Llafur*, 3, 1 (1980).

Feheney, J. M., 'Delinquency among Irish Catholic children in Victorian London', *Irish Historical Studies*, XXIII (1983).

Fitzpatrick, David, '"A peculiar tramping people": the Irish in Britain, 1801–1870', in W. E. Vaughan (ed.), *A New History of Ireland*, vol.V (Oxford, 1989).

Idem, 'The Irish in Britain, 1871–1921', in W. E. Vaughan (ed.), *A New History of Ireland*, vol.VI (Oxford, 1996).

Fraser, Angus M., 'George Borrow's *Wild Wales*: fact and fabrication', *Transactions of the Honourable Society of Cymmrodorion* (1980).

Gilley, Sheridan, 'The Roman Catholic mission to the Irish in London', *Recusant History*, X (1969).

Idem, 'Papists, Protestants and the Irish in London, 1835–70', in G. J. Cuming and D. Baker (eds.), *Popular Belief and Practice* (Cambridge, 1972).

Idem, 'Catholic faith in the Irish slums: London 1840–1870', in H. J. Dyos and Michael Wolff (eds.), *The Victorian City: Images and Realities*, II (London, 1973).

Hall, Stuart, 'Our mongrel selves', *New Statesman and Society*, (19 June 1992).

Haslett, J., and Lowe, W. J., 'Household structure and overcrowding among the Lancashire Irish, 1851–1871', *Histoire Sociale/Social History*, V (1977).

Havill, Elizabeth, 'William Taitt, 1748–1815', *Transactions of the Honourable Society of Cymmrodorion* (1983).

Hemphill, B., 'Bishop Joseph Brown, O.S.B., the modern apostle of Wales', *Studies*, XXXIX (1950).

Hickman, Mary, 'Incorporating and denationalising the Irish in England: the role of the Catholic church', in Patrick O'Sullivan (ed.), *Religion and Identity: The Irish Worldwide*, vol.5 (Leicester and New York, 1996).

Hodges, T. M., 'The peopling of the hinterland of the port of Cardiff, 1801–1914', in W. E. Minchinton (ed.), *Industrial South Wales, 1750–1914: Essays in Welsh Economic History* (London, 1969).

Holt, T. G., 'The Glamorgan mission after the Oates plot', *Journal of Welsh Ecclesiastical History*, I (1984).

Hopkin, Deian, 'The rise of Labour in Wales, 1890–1914', *Llafur*, 6, 3 (1994).

Hopkin, D., and Williams, L. J., 'New light on the New Unionism in Wales, 1889–1912', *Llafur*, 4, 3 (1986).

Howell, David, 'Farming in south-east Wales, *c*.1840–80', in C. Baber and J. Williams (eds.), *Modern South Wales: Essays in Economic History* (Cardiff, 1986).

Hughes, Eugene, 'The Great Hunger and Irish Catholicism', *Societas*, VIII (1978).

Humphreys, Iwan, 'Cardiff politics, 1850–74', in Stewart Williams (ed.), *Glamorgan Historian*, 8 (n.d.).

Inoue, Keiko, 'Dáil propaganda and the Irish Self-Determination League of Great Britain during the Anglo-Irish War', *Irish Studies Review*, 6, 1 (1998).

Jenkins, G. H., 'Ieuan Gwynedd: Eilun y Genedl', in Prys Morgan (ed.), *Brad Y Llyfrau Gleision* (Llandysul, 1991).

Jenkins, Philip, 'Connections between the landed communities of Munster and south Wales, *c*.1660–1780', *Journal of the Cork Historical and Archaeological Society*, LXXXIV, 240 (1979).

John, Angela V., 'The Chartist endurance: industrial south Wales, 1840–1868', *Morgannwg*, XV (1971).

Johnson, J. H., 'Harvest migration from nineteenth century Ireland', *Transactions of the Institute of British Geographers*, 41 (1967).

Jones, D. J. V., ' "A dead loss to the community": the criminal vagrant in mid-nineteenth century Wales', *Welsh History Review*, 8, 3 (1977).

Idem and Bainbridge, Alan, 'The "conquering of China": crime in an industrial community, 1842–64', *Llafur*, 2, 4 (1979).

Jones, Dot, 'Self-Help in nineteenth century Wales: the rise and fall of the female friendly society', *Llafur*, 6, 1 (1984).

Eadem, 'Did friendly societies matter? A study of friendly societies in Glamorgan, 1794–1910', *Welsh History Review*, 12, 3 (1985).

Jones, G. Penrhyn, 'Cholera in Wales', *National Library of Wales Journal*, X (1957–8).

Jones, I. G., 'Ecclesiastical economy: aspects of church building in Victorian Wales', in R. R. Davies et al. (eds.), *Welsh Society and Nationhood: Historical Essays Presented to Glanmor Williams* (Cardiff, 1984).

Idem, 'Parliament and people in mid-nineteenth century Wales', in T. Herbert and Gareth Elwyn Jones (eds.), *People and Protest, 1815–1880* (Cardiff, 1988).

Idem, 'The city and its villages', in Ralph A. Griffiths (ed.), *The City of Swansea: Challenges and Change* (Stroud, 1990).

Jones, J. Graham, 'Michael Davitt, David Lloyd George and T. E. Ellis: the Welsh experience', *Welsh History Review*, 18, 3 (1997).

Jones, Philip N., 'Population migration into Glamorgan, 1861–1911', in Prys Morgan (ed.), *Glamorgan County History*, vol.VI, *Glamorgan Society, 1780–1980* (Cardiff, 1988).

Jones, R. A. N., 'Women, community and collective action: the *Ceffyl Pren* tradition', in Angela V. John (ed.), *Our Mothers' Land: Chapters in Welsh Women's History, 1830–1939* (Cardiff, 1991).

Jones, Tecwyn, ' "Ufudd-dod yn Barhaus": Welsh broadside ballads and the Irish Question', *Planet*, 33 (1976).

Jones, T. Thornley, 'The "Llannau" of Cwmdauddwr parish', *Transactions of the Radnorshire Society*, XXXVI (1966).

Kerr, B. M., 'Irish seasonal migration to Great Britain, 1800–1838', *Irish Historical Studies*, III (1942–3).

Larkin, Emmet, 'The devotional revolution in Ireland, 1850–75', *American Historical Review*, 77 (1972).

Lewis, C. R., 'The Irish in Cardiff in the mid-nineteenth century', *Cambria*, VII (1980).

Idem, 'A stage in the development of the industrial town: a case study of Cardiff, 1845–1875', *Transactions of the Institute of British Geographers*, 4, 2 (1979).

Idem, 'Housing areas in the industrial town: a case study of Newport, Gwent, 1850–1880', *National Library of Wales Journal*, XXIV (1985–6).

Lewis, J. Parry, 'The Anglicisation of Glamorgan', *Morgannwg*, IV (1960).

Lloyd, J. H., 'Cân y Ffeiniaid gan Griffith Roberts (Gwrtheyrn)', *Journal of the Merioneth Historical and Record Society*, VI (1969–72).

Lovell, John, 'The Irish and the London dockers', *Bulletin of the Society for the Study of Labour History*, 35 (1977).

Lowe, W. J., 'The Lancashire Irish and the Catholic Church, 1846–1871', *Irish Historical Studies*, XX (1976–7).

Idem, 'Social agencies among the Irish in Lancashire during the mid-nineteenth century', *Saothar*, III (1977).

McCaffrey, John, 'The Irish vote in Glasgow in the late nineteenth century: a preliminary survey', *Innes Review*, XXI (1970).

McDermott, Dan, 'Labour and Ireland', in Kenneth D. Brown (ed.), *The First Labour Party, 1906–1914* (London, 1985).

McGrath, Thomas, 'The Tridentine evolution of modern Irish Catholicism, 1563–1962: a re-examination of the "devotional revolution" thesis', *Recusant History*, 20, 4 (1991).

McLeod, Hugh, 'Popular Catholicism in Irish New York, *c.*1900', in W. J. Shiels and Diana Woods (eds.), *The Churches, Ireland and the Irish* (Oxford, 1989).

Millar, David W., 'Irish Catholicism and the Great Famine', *Journal of Social History*, IX (1975).

Moss, Kenneth, 'St. Patrick's Day celebrations and the formation of Irish-American identity, 1845–1875', *Journal of Social History*, 29, 1 (1995).

Neal, Frank, 'The Famine Irish in England and Wales', in Patrick O'Sullivan (ed.), *The Meaning of the Famine*, vol.6 (Leicester and New York, 1996).

Idem, 'Black '47: Liverpool and the Irish Famine', in E. Margaret Crawford (ed.), *The Hungry Stream: Essays on Emigration and Famine* (Belfast, 1997).

O'Connell, Bernard, 'Irish Nationalism in Liverpool, 1873–1923', *Éire-Ireland*, X (1975).

O'Day, Alan, 'Irish influence in parliamentary elections in London, 1885–1914: a simple test', in R. Swift and S. Gilley (eds.), *The Irish in the Victorian City* (London, 1985).

Idem, 'The political representation of the Irish in Great Britain, 1850–1940', in Geoffrey Alderman (ed.), *Governments, Ethnic Groups and Political Representation* (Dartmouth, NY, 1993).

Idem, 'Varieties of anti-Irish behaviour in Britain, 1846–1922', in Panikos Panayi (ed.), *Racial Violence in Britain, 1840–1950* (Leicester, 1993).

O'Donnell, Ruan, 'The rebellion of 1798 in County Wicklow', in Ken Hannigan and William Nolan (eds.), *Wicklow History and Society: Interdisciplinary Essays on the History of an Irish County* (Dublin, 1994).

O'Driscoll, Dan, 'A barren land (1938)', in Patrick Hannan (ed.), *Wales on the Wireless: A Broadcasting Anthology* (Llandysul, 1988).

Ó Gráda, Cormac, 'Industry and communications, 1801–45', in W. E. Vaughan (ed.), *A New History of Ireland*, vol.5 (Oxford, 1989).

Idem, 'Poverty, population and agriculture, 1801–45', in W. E. Vaughan (ed.), *A New History of Ireland*, vol.5 (Oxford, 1989).

O'Higgins, R., 'The Irish influence on the Chartist movement', *Past and Present*, 20 (1961).

O'Leary, Paul, 'Irish immigration and the Catholic "Welsh District", 1840–1850', in G. H. Jenkins and J. B. Smith (eds.), *Politics and Society in Wales, 1840–1922: Essays in Honour of Ieuan Gwynedd Jones* (Cardiff, 1988).

Idem, 'Anti-Irish riots in Wales, 1826–1882', *Llafur*, 5, 4 (1991).

Idem, '"Trais a Thwyll a Cherddi": Y Gwyddelod yng Nghymru, 1798–1882', in G. H. Jenkins (ed.), *Cof Cenedl*, IX (1994).

Idem, 'From the cradle to the grave: popular Catholicism among the Irish in Wales', in Patrick O'Sullivan (ed.), *Religion and Identity: The Irish Worldwide*, vol.5 (Leicester and New York, 1996).

Idem, 'A regional perspective: the Famine Irish in south Wales', in R. Swift and S. Gilley (eds.), *The Irish in Victorian Britain: The Local Dimension* (Dublin, 1999).

O'Leary, Philip, ' "Children of the same mother": Gaelic relations with the other Celtic revival movements, 1882–1916', *Proceedings of the Harvard Celtic Colloquium*, VI (1986).

O'Rahilly, Cecile, 'The antipathy of Irish and Welsh', *Welsh Outlook*, VII (September 1920).

O'Sullivan, John, 'How green was their island?', in Stewart Williams (ed.), *The Cardiff Book*, II (Cardiff and Bridgend, 1974).

Idem, 'The Stanley Street murder', in Stewart Williams (ed.), *The Cardiff Book*, III (Cardiff and Bridgend, 1977).

O'Sullivan, Patrick, 'Introduction', in *idem* (ed.), *The Irish in the New Communities, The Irish World Wide*, vol II (London, 1992).

Parry, Jon, 'The Tredegar anti-Irish riots of 1882', *Llafur*, 3, 4 (1983).

Pierce, G. O, 'The "Coercion of Wales" Act, 1904', in H. Hearder and H. R. Loyn (eds.), *British Government and Administration: Studies Presented to S. B. Chrimes* (Cardiff, 1974).

Pooley, C. G., 'Segregation or integration? The residential experience of the Irish in mid-Victorian Britain', in R. Swift and S. Gilley (eds.), *The Irish in Britain, 1815–1939* (London, 1989).

Pryce, W. T. R, 'Language areas and changes, *c*.1750–1981', in Prys Morgan (ed.), *Glamorgan County History*, vol.VI, *Glamorgan Society, 1780–1980* (Cardiff, 1988).

Idem, 'Language shift in Gwent, *c*.1770–1981', in Nikolas Coupland (ed.), *English in Wales: Diversity, Conflict and Change* (Clevedon, 1990).

Richardson, C., 'Irish settlement in mid-nineteenth century Bradford', *Yorkshire Bulletin of Economic and Social Research*, XX (1968).

Rose, Michael E., 'Settlement, removal and the new Poor Law', in Derek Fraser (ed.), *The New Poor Law in the Nineteenth-Century* (London, 1976).

Rossiter, Ann, 'Bringing the margins into the centre: a review of aspects of Irish women's emigration', in Sean Hutton and Paul Stewart (eds.), *Ireland's Histories: Aspects of State, Society and Ideology* (London, 1991).

Samuel, R., 'Workshop of the world: steam power and hand technology in mid-Victorian Britain', *History Workshop Journal*, 3 (1977).

Scourfield, Elfyn, 'Rural society in the Vale of Glamorgan', in Prys Morgan (ed.), *Glamorgan County History*, vol.VI, *Glamorgan Society, 1780–1980* (Cardiff, 1988).

Smith, A. W., 'Irish rebels and English radicals, 1798–1820', *Past and Present*, 7 (1955).

Smith, David, 'Focal heroes', in *idem, Aneurin Bevan and the World of South Wales* (Cardiff, 1993).

Sollors, Werner, 'The invention of ethnicity', in *idem* (ed.), *The Invention of Ethnicity* (Oxford, 1989).

Stead, Peter, 'Working class leadership in south Wales, 1900–1920', *Welsh History Review*, VI (1973).

Strange, Keith, 'In search of the celestial empire: crime in Merthyr, 1830–60', *Llafur*, 3, 1 (1980).

Swift, Roger, 'Crime and the Irish in nineteenth century Britain', in *idem* and S. Gilley (eds.), *The Irish in Britain, 1815–1939* (London, 1989).

Idem, 'The historiography of the Irish in nineteenth-century Britain: some perspectives', in Patrick Buckland and John Belchem (eds.), *The Irish in British Labour History* (Liverpool, 1992).

'The Catholic registers of Abergavenny, Mon., 1740–1838', *Publications of the Catholic Record Society*, XXVII, *Miscellanea* (London, 1927).

'The diary of Lewis Weston Dillwyn', in *South Wales Record Society Publications* No. 5 (Newport, 1963).

Thomas, Brinley, 'The migration of labour into the Glamorganshire coalfield, 1861–1911', in W. E. Minchinton (ed.), *Industrial South Wales, 1750–1914: Essays in Welsh Economic History* (London, 1969).

Thomas, Peter H., 'Medical men of Glamorgan: James Mullin of Cardiff, 1846–1919', in Stewart Williams (ed.), *Glamorgan Historian*, 10 (1974).

Thompson, D., 'Ireland and the Irish in English radicalism before 1850', in J. Epstein and D. Thompson (eds.), *The Chartist Experience: Studies in Working Class Radicalism and Culture, 1830–1860* (London, 1982).

Thorne, Roland and Robert Howell, 'Pembrokeshire in wartime, 1793–1815', in Brian Howells (ed.), *Pembrokeshire County History*, vol.III, *Early Modern Pembrokeshire, 1536–1815* (Haverfordwest, 1987).

Treble, J. H., 'Irish navvies in the north of England, 1830–50', *Transport History*, VI (1973).

Idem, 'O'Connor, O'Connell and the attitudes of Irish immigrants towards Chartism in the north of England, 1838–48', in J. Butt and I. F. Clarke (eds.), *The Victorians and Social Protest* (Newton Abbot, 1973).

Walker, Graham, 'The protestant Irish in Scotland', in T. M. Devine (ed.), *Irish Immigrants and Scottish Society in the Nineteenth and Twentieth Centuries* (Edinburgh, 1991).

Walker, W. M., 'Irish immigrants in Scotland: their priests, politics and parochial life', *Historical Journal*, XV (1972).

Way, Peter, 'Labour's love lost: observations on the historiography of class and ethnicity in the nineteenth century', *Journal of American Studies*, 28, No.1 (1994).

Williams, Allan M., 'Migration and residential patterns in mid-nineteenth century Cardiff', *Cambria*, IV (1979).

Williams, Gwyn A., 'Locating a Welsh working class: the frontier years', in David Smith (ed.), *A People and A Proletariat: Essays in the Social History of Wales* (London, 1980).

Williams, J. Ronald, 'The influence of foreign nationalities on the life of the people of Merthyr Tydfil', *Sociological Review*, XVIII (1926).

Williams, L. J., 'The New Unionism in south Wales, 1889–92', *Welsh History Review*, I (1960–3).

Idem, 'The strike of 1898', *Morgannwg*, IX (1965).

Wills, Wilton D., 'The Established Church in the diocese of Llandaff, 1850–1870: a study of the Evangelical movement in the south Wales coalfield', *Welsh History Review*, IV (1969).

Wood, Ian S., 'Irish Nationalism and radical politics in Scotland, 1880–1906', *Scottish Labour History Journal*, IX (1975).

G Theses and Unpublished Research Reports

Theses

Affley, Liam Joseph, 'The establishment and development of Roman Catholic education in Cardiff during the nineteenth century', University of Wales M.Ed. (1970).

Cayford, Joanne, 'The *Western Mail*, 1869–1914: a study in the politics and management of a provincial newspaper', University of Wales Ph.D. (1993).

Davies, J. Gwyn, 'Industrial society in north-west Monmouthshire, 1750–1851', unpublished University of Wales Ph.D. thesis (1980).

Donovan, P. W., 'Unskilled labour unions in south Wales, 1889–1914', University of London M. Phil. (1969).

Edwards, J. H. Keri, 'The life and works of three Anglo-Welsh writers of East Glamorgan', University of Wales MA (1962).

Egan, Attracta Josephine, 'The development of Catholic education in Gwent, 1840–1979', University of Wales M.Ed. (1979).

Harding, Keith, 'The Irish issue in the British labour movement, 1900–1922', University of Sussex D.Phil. (1983).

Hickey, J. V., 'The origin and growth of the Irish community in Cardiff', University of Wales MA (1959).

Irish, Sandra, 'Spatial patterns in the small town in the nineteenth century: a case study of Wrexham', University of Wales Ph.D. (1987).

Jones, Rosemary A., 'A study of the 1852 general election in the Cardiff Boroughs', University of Wales MA (1982).

Lynch, G. J. J., 'The revival of Roman Catholicism in south Wales in the late eighteenth and early nineteenth centuries', University of Wales MA (1941).

Masson, Ursula, 'The development of the Irish and Roman Catholic communities of Merthyr Tydfil and Dowlais in the nineteenth century', University of Keele MA (1975).

Miskell, Louise, 'Custom, conflict and community: a study of the Irish in south Wales and Cornwall, 1861–1891', University of Wales Ph.D. (1996).

Eadem, 'The Irish in mid-nineteenth century Wales: a village perspective', University of Wales BA (1992).

Rees, J. C. M., 'Evolving patterns of residence in a nineteenth century city: Swansea, 1851–1871', University of Wales Ph.D. (1983).

Smith, G. P., 'Social control and industrial relations at the Dowlais Iron Company *c*.1850–1890', University of Wales M.Sc. (Econ.) (1981).

Thomas, Roger R., 'The influence of the Irish Question in Welsh politics, 1880–1895', University of Wales MA (1973).

Wheatley, S. E., 'The social and residential areas of Merthyr Tydfil in the mid-nineteenth Century', University of Wales Ph.D. (1983).

Williams, Allan M., 'Social change and residential differentiation: a case study of nineteenth century Cardiff', University of London Ph.D. (1976).

Williams, J. S., 'The origins and subsequent development of Roman Catholic education in the "Heads of the Valleys" region', University of Wales M.Ed. (1974).

Williams, Timothy Ifor, 'Patriots and citizens – language, identity and education in a liberal state: the Anglicisation of Pontypridd, 1818–1920', University of Wales Ph.D. (1989).

Research Report

Jones, D. J. V. and Bainbridge, A., 'Crime in nineteenth century Wales', Social Science Research Council Report (Swansea, 1975).

INDEX